Reinhard Ibler (Hg.)

Unter der Mitarbeit von Friedrich von Petersdorff

Der Holocaust in den mitteleuropäischen Literaturen und Kulturen: Probleme der Politisierung und Ästhetisierung

Materialien des Internationalen Workshop,
Gießen 18.-19. Juni 2015

Reinhard Ibler (ed.)

Assisted by Friedrich von Petersdorff

The Holocaust in the Central European Literatures and Cultures: Problems of Poetization and Aestheticization

Proceedings of the International Workshop,
Gießen 18-19 June 2015

Literatur und Kultur im mittleren und östlichen Europa

herausgegeben von Reinhard Ibler

ISSN 2195-1497

9 *Olena Sivuda*
"Aber plötzlich war mir, als drohe das Haus über mir zusammenzubrechen."
Komparative Analyse des Heimkehrermotivs in der deutschen und russischen Prosa nach dem Zweiten Weltkrieg
ISBN 978-3-8382-0779-7

10 *Victoria Oldenburger*
Keine Menschen, sondern ganz besondere Wesen ...
Die Frau als Objekt unkonventioneller Faszination in Ivan A. Bunins Erzählband *Temnye allei* (1937–1949)
ISBN 978-3-8382-0777-3

11 *Andrea Meyer-Fraatz, Thomas Schmidt (Hg.)*
„Ich kann es nicht fassen, dass dies Menschen möglich ist"
Zur Rolle des Emotionalen in der polnischen Literatur über den Holocaust
ISBN 978-3-8382-0859-6

12 *Julia Friedmann*
Von der Gorbimanie zur Putinphobie?
Ursachen und Folgen medialer Politisierung
ISBN 978-3-8382-0936-4

13 *Reinhard Ibler (Hg.)*
Der Holocaust in den mitteleuropäischen Literaturen und Kulturen:
Probleme der Politisierung und Ästhetisierung
The Holocaust in the Central European Literatures and Cultures:
Problems of Poetization and Aestheticization
ISBN 978-3-8382-0952-4

Reinhard Ibler (Hg.)

DER HOLOCAUST IN DEN MITTELEUROPÄISCHEN LITERATUREN UND KULTUREN: PROBLEME DER POETISIERUNG UND ÄSTHETISIERUNG

The Holocaust in the Central European Literatures and Cultures: Problems of Poetization and Aestheticization

ibidem-Verlag
Stuttgart

Bibliografische Information der Deutschen Nationalbibliothek
Die Deutsche Nationalbibliothek verzeichnet diese Publikation in der Deutschen Nationalbibliografie; detaillierte bibliografische Daten sind im Internet über http://dnb.d-nb.de abrufbar.

Bibliographic information published by the Deutsche Nationalbibliothek
Die Deutsche Nationalbibliothek lists this publication in the Deutsche Nationalbibliografie; detailed bibliographic data are available in the Internet at http://dnb.d-nb.de.

∞

Gedruckt auf alterungsbeständigem, säurefreien Papier
Printed on acid-free paper

ISSN: 2195-1497

ISBN-13: 978-3-8382-0952-4

© *ibidem*-Verlag
Stuttgart 2016

Alle Rechte vorbehalten

Das Werk einschließlich aller seiner Teile ist urheberrechtlich geschützt. Jede Verwertung außerhalb der engen Grenzen des Urheberrechtsgesetzes ist ohne Zustimmung des Verlages unzulässig und strafbar. Dies gilt insbesondere für Vervielfältigungen, Übersetzungen, Mikroverfilmungen und elektronische Speicherformen sowie die Einspeicherung und Verarbeitung in elektronischen Systemen.

All rights reserved. No part of this publication may be reproduced, stored in or introduced into a retrieval system, or transmitted, in any form, or by any means (electronical, mechanical, photocopying, recording or otherwise) without the prior written permission of the publisher. Any person who does any unauthorized act in relation to this publication may be liable to criminal prosecution and civil claims for damages.

Printed in the EU

Inhalt / Contents

REINHARD IBLER:
Introduction   7

Die Ästhetisierung des Holocaust: Diskussionen und Strategien /
Aestheticizing the Holocaust: Discussions and Strategies   11

ANJA GOLEBIOWSKI:
Schreiben nach Auschwitz? Reaktionen der polnischen Literatur
auf den Holocaust   13

KATARZYNA ADAMCZAK:
Ästhetik des (sekundären) Bildes in neuesten polnischen Dramen:
Zyta Rudzkas *Fastryga* und Artur Pałygas *Żyd*   23

URSZULA KOWALSKA:
Between the *Post-* and *Popmemory*. Holocaust Narrative in
Contemporary Culture – an Attempt of Exemplification   43

ANDREAS OHME:
Die Transzendierung der Geschichte durch die Poetisierung
der Darstellung in Jiří Weils Prosazyklus *Barvy* (*Farben*)   57

HANA HŘÍBKOVÁ:
Jiří Weil: *Žalozpěv za 77 297 obětí*   79

CHARLOTTE KITZINGER:
„Und, da das Schweigen Gift mir wird im Munde, / Gebe ich
weinend von der Schande Kunde". Karl Schnogs (1897 – 1967)
satirische Holocaustdichtung   89

AGATA FIRLEJ:
Humour and Irony as Forms of Aestheticization of Shoah Narrations:
the Play *Doma u Hitlerů* by Arnošt Goldflam   103

Holocaustdichtung zwischen Poetizität und Prosaisierung /
Holocaust Poetry between Poeticity and Prosaization   115

CHRISTIANE CHARLOTTE WEBER:
Lyrische Grüße an Deutschland – Manfred Herzfeld und andere
'ungeübte' Verfasser von Holocaustgedichten 1945 bis 1949   117

ŠTĚPÁN BALÍK:
Czech Bystanders Writing Poetry about the Shoah. Different Ways
of Poetic Languages in the First Post-War Literary Reactions 129

ARKADIUSZ MORAWIEC:
Tadeusz Różewicz's Poetics of Testimony 145

SASCHA FEUCHERT:
Heimrad Bäckers *Nachschrift* und/als Zeugnisliteratur 161

ANNA MARIA SKIBSKA:
Towards the Unavoidable Silence: on the Shoah Context
in Andrzej Sosnowski's Poetry 171

**Das Erzählen des Holocaust zwischen Authentizität und Fiktionalität /
Holocaust Narration between Authenticity and Fictionality** 201

REINHARD IBLER:
Zwischen Dokument und Kunst: Josef Bors Werke über den Holocaust 203

HANS-CHRISTIAN TREPTE:
Jerzy Kosinskis „Autofiction" – eine mögliche Strategie,
über den Holocaust zu schreiben? 217

JIŘÍ HOLÝ:
Arnošt Lustig's *Colette, dívka z Antverp* –
Between Historical Facts and Fiction 231

ŠÁRKA SLADOVNÍKOVÁ:
The Film *Colette* – Risks of a ‚Modern' Approach
to the Depiction of the Holocaust 243

ANNA ARTWIŃSKA:
Zeitbrücken. Erinnerungen an den Holocaust
in Ivan Klímas Erzählband *Moje nebezpečné výlety* 255

MARTA ŠKUBALOVÁ:
Zum Motiv des Holocaust in der Vertreibungsliteratur 271

Personenverzeichnis / Index of Names 283

Introduction

The problems discussed in the following contributions touch a very sensitive subject. Not only since Adorno has it been questioned whether it is legitimate at all to relate the Holocaust to poetic and aesthetic phenomena, as only authentic testimonies, documents, or at least ‚unliterary', prosaic approaches were considered to be appropriate in dealing with the Nazi genocide. From the very beginning of the literary-cultural engagement with the Holocaust there were, however, also clear tendencies towards a literarization, poetization, ornamentalization etc., i.e. towards artistic means running contrary to this demand. Nowadays, as the generation of the victims and eye-witnesses is dying out and the generation of the grandchildren and even great-grandchildren has taken over the responsibility for keeping the cataclysm of the Holocaust in the collective memory, new approaches primarily affecting a work's aesthetic and artistic sphere (also in the form of provocative, taboo-breaking devices) are more and more regarded as necessary instruments to evoke the attention required for this meaningful task.

The present volume contains the proceedings of an international workshop held at Justus Liebig University Giessen on 18 and 19 June 2015. This workshop was the seventh meeting of the Czech-Polish-German project group cooperating in the field of a comparative study of Holocaust literature, theatre and film. The project, which started with a first meeting in 2010 in Giessen, had its first research cycle in 2011 and 2012 with four workshops held in Łódź, Prague (twice) and Giessen – dealing with the different periods in the engagement of the Central European literatures and cultures with the Holocaust topic.[1] The focus of attention of the project's second research cycle (2014/15) centred upon the role of special literary and artistic criteria in Holocaust literature, theatre and film. The Prague workshop on 8 and 9 May 2014 was dedicated to the problems of genres.[2] In 2015 the Giessen workshop followed and, finally, a third one was

---

[1] For further information see: Reinhard Ibler: Vorwort. In: Der Holocaust in den mitteleuropäischen Literaturen und Kulturen seit 1989. The Holocaust in the Central European Literatures and Cultures since 1989. Ed. by Reinhard Ibler. Stuttgart 2014, pp. 9-13.

[2] See the volume with the proceedings of this workshop: The Aspects of Genres in the Holocaust Literatures in Central Europe. Ed. by Jiří Holý. Praha 2015.

held in Poznań on 17 and 18 December with the title *The Reception of Literary and Artistic Works about the Holocaust*.[3]

The vast majority of the articles of the present volume is about literary problems, often exemplifying their subject using specific works mainly from Czech, Polish and German literature. But there are also texts regarding film and other media (see Šárka Sladovníková's and Urszula Kowalska's contributions). With respect to the subject of the volume, i.e. problems of poetization and aestheticization in Holocaust literature and culture, we can identify three central fields of interest.

A first group of contributions is concerned with the question whether an aesthetic approach to the Holocaust is possible and by what means such an approach can be realized. This question already played an important role in postwar literature, as Anja Golebiowski demonstrates by reference to the discussions in Poland in the 1940s and 1950s. In the works created after 2000 by representatives of the latest generation the search for strategies of aestheticization became, however, as mentioned above, a vital factor in the efforts of literature and culture to contribute to the prevention of collective amnesia (see the articles by Katarzyna Adamczak on recent Polish drama and by Urszula Kowalska showing how the Holocaust can be narrated in various – Polish and Czech – cultural media). The use of an ‚ornamentalized' language also belongs to this area, a phenomenon for example typical of some works by the Czech author Jiří Weil (who is in the focus of Andreas Ohme's and Hana Hříbková's contributions). Another issue referring to the question of aestheticization is the connection of Holocaust works with satire, humour, irony and the grotesque. This topic is taken up by Charlotte Kitzinger in her article about the satirical poetry of the lesser known German author Karl Schnog, a representative of the victims' generation, and by Agata Firlej who introduces a Hitler drama full of humour and grotesque by the contemporary Czech author Arnošt Goldflam.

A second key subject of our volume is Holocaust poetry between the poles of ‚poeticity' and ‚prosaization'. Whereas a conventional poetic expression can often be met in the sphere of occasional verse (see Christiane Charlotte Weber's article on the Holocaust poetry of German ‚untrained' authors in the post-war

---

[3] Proceedings forthcoming in 2016.

years), the representatives of ‚high' poetry often tended to use new, sometimes experimental poetic forms or even a rough, deliberately ‚unpoetic' style, as illustrated in the contributions by Štěpán Balík about the poetry of Czech ‚bystanders' and by Arkadiusz Morawiec about Tadeusz Różewicz's poetics of „stuck in a lumpy throat". Sascha Feuchert presents a work by the Viennese poet Heimrad Bäcker who by de- and reconstructing Holocaust texts written by victims, perpetrators and scholars constructs a special form of „meta-poetry". And Anna Maria Skibska reads selected texts of Andrzej Sosnowski's exceptional, enigmatic poetry – being open to a great variety of interpretations – for the first time against the backdrop of the Holocaust.

The third field of topics in the volume is formed by contributions dealing with narrative works about the Holocaust which are situated between the poles of authenticity and fiction resp. between document and art. In earlier works, especially if written by victims, literary critics often viewed with suspicion the purpose and legitimacy of mixing memories of authentic experience with clearly fictional elements. So, the works of the Czech-Jewish author and Holocaust victim Josef Bor aroused among the critics approval as well as scepticism (see Reinhard Ibler's article), and the American author of Polish origin Jerzy Kosinski even created a scandal – treated in Hans-Christian Trepte's contribution – with his famous novel *The Painted Bird* using authentic material as well as fiction. Whereas in these works the mere fact of partial fictionalization was seen as a dubious dealing with historical truth, in the novels and stories by Arnošt Lustig, one of the major Czech writers in the field of Holocaust literature, the attempt of creating an impression of authenticity by integrating often very direct and explicit naturalistic scenes dominated by brutality and cruelty, was repeatedly criticized as a tendency towards superficiality and triviality. This problem is discussed in the two texts about Lustig's novel *Colette* (Jiří Holý) and its film version (Šárka Sladovníková). The function of narrator and narration is focussed upon in two contributions. Anna Artwińska, using the example of a late short story collection by the Czech author Ivan Klíma, demonstrates the phenomenon of a „multi-layered temporality" by which a complex interaction of past and present time levels is evoked, and Marta Škubalová treats the problem of ideological manipulation in Czech and German works relating the motifs of Holocaust and expulsion to one another.

I want to thankfully mention that the workshop, the proceedings of which can be found in the present volume, would not have been possible without the financial support by the German Academic Exchange Service (Deutscher Akademischer Austauschdienst, DAAD), namely its Czech-German and Polish-German funding programmes for research cooperation within the „Projektbezogener Personenaustausch" (PPP), as well as by the Giessen Centre for Eastern European Studies (Gießener Zentrum Östliches Europa, GiZo). I also want to give my cordial thanks to Katharina Bauer, Elisa-Maria Hiemer and Magdalena Szych, the members of my chair's staff, for their organisational support of the workshop. With respect to the present publication I want to point out the very constructive cooperation with Valerie Lange of the publishing house *ibidem*. This cooperation made it possible to develop within only a few years the book series *Literatur und Kultur im mittleren und östlichen Europa* (*Literature and Culture in Central and Eastern Europe*) which soon met broad approval. I am glad and thankful that we now have the opportunity to enrich this series with a further volume. Last but not least, I am deeply indebted to Friedrich von Petersdorff who not only helped by proof-reading the English texts of this volume, but who also – for the benefit of the entire book – provided numerous suggestions and critical comments.

Giessen, July 2016

Reinhard Ibler

Die Ästhetisierung des Holocaust:
Diskussionen und Strategien

Aestheticizing the Holocaust:
Discussions and Strategies

Schreiben nach Auschwitz?
Reaktionen der polnischen Literatur auf den Holocaust

Anja Golebiowski, Gießen

Witold Gombrowicz fällte im argentinischen Exil ein hartes Urteil über den Zustand der polnischen Nachkriegsliteratur. In seinem literarischen Tagebuch sprach er 1956 von einer „künstlerischen Impotenz" („impotencja artystyczna"; Gombrowicz 1986, 326) der polnischen Schriftsteller und bemängelte die aus seiner Sicht nichtigen Konsequenzen, die sie aus der Erfahrung des Holocaust gezogen hätten:

> Ci pisarze, między innymi i przede wszystkim Rudnicki, zabrali się do ciał torturowanych sądząc, że niebotyczność cierpienia dostarczy im jakiejś prawdy, moralności, przynajmniej nowej wiedzy o naszych granicach. Niewiele znaleźli, co by okazało się płodne i twórcze. Odkryli, jak Borowski, że jesteśmy bezdennie nikczemni. [...] Odkryli, że kultura, ta pięknoduchowska estetów i intelektualistów, jest tylko pianką – to mi przedpotopowa rewelacja i dosyć dziecinna! (Gombrowicz 1986, 325f.)

> Diese Autoren, darunter auch und vor allem Rudnicki, nahmen sich die gequälten Leiber vor in der Meinung, das himmelschreiende Leiden müsste ihnen irgendeine Wahrheit, eine Moral, wenigstens etwas Neues über unsere Grenzen zeigen können. Viel Fruchtbares und Schöpferisches fanden sie nicht. Sie entdeckten, wie Borowski, dass wir bodenlos niederträchtig sind. [...] Sie fanden heraus, dass die Kultur, dies schöngeistige Produkt der Ästhetik und Intellektuellen, nur Schaum ist – meine Hochachtung, eine vorsintflutliche Enthüllung, und ziemlich kindisch dazu. (Gombrowicz 1998, 348)

Gombrowicz war ein Querdenker, ein Provokateur, der seine Aufgabe als Autor und Intellektueller darin verstand, die polnische nationale Kultur zu hinterfragen und zu entlarven. Es stellt sich jedoch die Frage, inwieweit diese Kritik gerechtfertigt war und nicht das überspitzte und subjektive Urteil einer zudem aus der Ferne erstellten Analyse? Hat die polnische Literatur in der Tat lediglich mit Banalitäten auf den Holocaust reagiert oder hat nicht doch eine intensivere Auseinandersetzung der Literaturschaffenden mit dem Holocaust stattgefunden? Der vorliegende Beitrag versucht dieser Problemstellung nachzugehen, wobei aufgezeigt werden soll, welche Wege polnische Autoren beschritten haben, um den Holocaust in Worte zu fassen, und welchen Einfluss die Erfahrung des unbegreiflichen Terrors auf die polnische Literatur gehabt hat.

Die nationalsozialistische Repressions- und Vernichtungspolitik, die wir mit dem Begriff Holocaust erfassen, hatte die westliche Gesellschaft in ihren Grundfesten erschüttert und ihre kulturellen Errungenschaften in Frage gestellt. Insbesondere das Schreiben als kulturelle Praxis rief nach dem Krieg ein starkes Misstrauen hervor. Die wohl bekannteste Reaktion, die durch dieses Unbehagen hervorgerufen worden war, ist Adornos provokante Äußerung, dass Gedichte nach Auschwitz zu schreiben barbarisch sei, was zum Dreh- und Angelpunkt für den teils bis heute andauernden Diskurs über die Grenzen der Repräsentation des Holocaust wurde. Die Skepsis beschränkte sich jedoch nicht allein auf die Textsorte Holocaustliteratur, sondern sie bezog sich ebenfalls auf die Literatur und das Schreiben im Allgemeinen. Insbesondere die jungen Autoren hegten nach dem Krieg einen tiefen Argwohn gegenüber der Sprache und den literarischen Konventionen, weshalb sie die unkritische Rückkehr zu traditionellen Schreibmodi ablehnten. Nach und nach kristallisierte sich der Holocaust als bedeutender Referenzpunkt der Nachkriegsliteratur heraus. Als eine der Reaktionen bildete sich in Deutschland in den frühen 1950er Jahren die sogenannte *Trümmerliteratur* und die *Poetik des Kahlschlags* heraus, eine Richtung, die nach radikal neuen Ausdrucksformen suchte (vgl. Lampart 2013, 102ff.). Doch noch bevor in Deutschland die miteinander verbundenen Debatten über die Darstellung des Holocaust und die neue Gestalt der Literatur überhaupt erst in Gang kamen, hatten polnische Schriftsteller bereits begonnen, sich mit den aus dem Holocaust resultierenden poetologischen und ethischen Problemen zu beschäftigen.

Unmittelbar nach Kriegsende hatten im Zuge des Wiederaufbaus des zivilen Lebens und der Wiederherstellung einer gewissen Alltagsnormalität polnische Schriftsteller die Diskussion über die künftige Richtung der polnischen Literatur eröffnet.[1] Die Frage der Literatur war nicht nur von großer Bedeutung für die Verarbeitung persönlicher Kriegstraumata durch den Akt des Schreibens, sondern ebenfalls für die nationale Identität. Die auf polnischem Boden verübten

---

[1] Zwischen 1945 und 1948 entbrannten in den Literaturzeitschriften programmatische Debatten und Streitigkeiten über den weiteren Weg der polnischen Literatur (vgl. hierzu Jarosiński 1978). Kennzeichnend für die Grundsatzdiskussionen der Zeit waren Schriften wie etwa Roman Bratnys Artikel *W poszukiwaniu nowego stylu* (*Auf der Suche nach einem neuen Stil*) von 1948, der eine neue realistische Schreibweise forderte.

nationalsozialistischen Verbrechen sind von der polnischen Nation als tiefe Schmach empfunden worden, da sie ihr Selbstverständnis auf den messianistischen Traditionen und heroischen Werten aufbaute. Für eine Vielzahl von Menschen, und insbesondere für zahlreiche Angehörige der Intelligenz, war es daher ein großer Schock, dass sie nicht imstande gewesen waren, ihre jüdischen Mitbürger vor den Nationalsozialisten zu schützen.[2] Ein weiteres tragendes Moment war, dass die Polen selber zu Opfern geworden und von den Nationalsozialisten zu ‚Untermenschen' erklärt worden waren, die lediglich als Arbeitskräfte dienen sollten. Die Nationalsozialisten hatten gezielt versucht, die polnische Intelligenz auszulöschen und das kulturelle Leben zu zerstören, was die polnische Gesellschaft bis in ihre Grundfesten erschütterte. Schließlich rechtfertigte die polnische Nation ihre Existenzberechtigung mit der nationalen Kultur und – vor allem – mit dem geschriebenen Wort. So verwundert es nicht, dass polnische Autoren das literarische Leben so schnell wie möglich wieder aufleben lassen wollten[3], woraus nach 1944 eine lebendige Literaturszene mit einer umfangreichen, wenn auch nicht immer qualitativ herausragenden Literaturproduktion erwuchs. Insbesondere in den ersten Nachkriegsjahren von 1944 bis 1948/49 konnte im Unterschied zur Sowjetunion der Holocaust in den öffentlichen Diskurs einfließen. Obwohl der Machteinfluss der kommunistischen Partei und der innenpolitische Wandel mit der Zeit unverkennbar waren, gelang es den Kommunisten nicht, die Literaturszene in ihrer Gänze zu kontrollieren, weshalb sich diese auch nach 1948 eine gewisse Diversität bewahrte.

Eine der frühesten und lautesten Kontroversen über die polnische Holocaustliteratur wurde von Tadeusz Borowski ausgelöst, der nach Kriegsende zu den jungen vielversprechenden Schriftstellertalenten zählte und mit seinen Auschwitz-Erzählungen paradigmatische Texte der Holocaustliteratur vorlegte. 1947 hatte er die Autorin Zofia Kossak-Szczucka in seiner Rezension *Alicja w krainie czarów* (*Alice im Wunderland*) aufs schärfste für ihr 1946 veröffentlichtes Buch

---

[2] Über den massiven polnischen Antisemitismus wird viel gesprochen und geschrieben. Das Verhältnis der Polen zu den Juden kann jedoch nicht einzig auf den Antisemitismus reduziert werden, worauf Krystyna Duniec und Joanna Krakowska (2014, 80) hingewiesen haben.
[3] Bereits 1944 erschien in Lublin ein erstes Kulturblatt, die Wochenzeitung *Odrodzenie* (*Wiedergeburt* oder *Erneuerung*), deren Name bezeichnend für die herrschende Aufbruchsstimmung war.

Z otchłani. Wspomnienia z lagru (*Aus dem Abgrund. Erinnerungen aus dem Lager*) kritisiert. Zum einen äußerte er Zweifel an ihrem schriftstellerischen Talent und zum anderen machte er ihr den sehr viel schwerwiegenderen Vorwurf, in ihrem vermeintlichen Erlebnisbericht ein verfälschtes Bild der Verhältnisse im Konzentrationslager Auschwitz gezeichnet zu haben:

> Jeszcze gorzej, gdy autorka próbuje kreślić sylwetki uwięzionych kobiet i wyjaśnić strukturę obozu. Oczywiście, spośród wszystkich – Polki były najlepsze, z Polek naturalnie – katoliczki, a z katoliczek – koleżanki autorki, przy czym autorka nie zastanawia się, o ile ta relacja pokrywa się z prawdą i o ile nie czyni krzywdy innym ludziom i innym narodowościom. [...] Dlaczego kobiety-Polki były najszlachetniejsze i najlepiej zachowywały się w obozie? Były häftling z Birkenau, który zetknął się z wieloma narodami raczej sceptycznie zapatrywałby się na swoisty mesjanizm czy raczej rasizm, czy inną teorię wyższości lub zasadniczej odrębności narodowej[...] (Borowski 2005, 78ff.)

> Noch viel schlimmer wird es, wenn die Autorin versucht, ein Porträt der gefangenen Frauen zu zeichnen und das Lagersystem zu erklären. Natürlich waren unter allen Frauen die Polinnen die besten, unter den Polinnen selbstverständlich die katholischen Frauen und unter den katholischen Frauen die Freundinnen der Autorin, wobei die Autorin nicht darüber nachdenkt, inwiefern dieser Zusammenhang mit der Wahrheit übereinstimmt und anderen Menschen und Nationalitäten Unrecht zufügt. [...] Warum waren die polnischen Frauen die edelsten und verhielten sich im Lager am besten? Ein ehemaliger Häftling aus Birkenau, der mit vielen Nationen zusammengetroffen ist, würde seinem eigenen Messianismus oder besser gesagt Rassismus wie auch jeglicher anderen Theorie einer Überlegenheit oder einer prinzipiellen nationalen Andersartigkeit eher mit Skepsis begegnen [...].[4]

Borowski hatte die Schriftstellerin harsch vorgeführt, die sich im Krieg als Widerstandskämpferin und Mitbegründerin der projüdischen, unter dem Decknamen *Żegota* agierenden Hilfsorganisation *Rada Pomocy Żydom* (*Rat für die Unterstützung der Juden*) einen Namen gemacht hatte. Dabei handelte es sich jedoch nicht um eine gewöhnliche literaturkritische Bewertung, sondern um das Aufeinanderprallen zweier divergierender Literaturkonzepte, was ein starkes Echo unter den Literaturkritikern hervorrief und zu einer Grundsatzdiskussion über die Richtung der polnischen Literatur führte. Teils zu Recht betrachtet Dariusz Kulesza die „Affäre" Borowski versus Kossak-Szczucka als Beginn eines Umbruchs in der polnischen Literatur (vgl. Kulesza 2006, 22).

---

[4] Übersetzungen aus dem Polnischen, wo nicht anders vermerkt, A.G.

In Borowskis Kritik schwangen die Frage nach dem *Wie-Schreiben-nach-Auschwitz* sowie die Forderung nach einer neuen ethischen Verantwortung der polnischen Literatur mit. Mit den ihr zur Verfügung stehenden ästhetischen und stilistischen Mitteln sollte die Literatur die Strukturen und Mechanismen des Bösen aufdecken. Um dies leisten zu können, bedurfte es Borowski zufolge jedoch der Abkehr von der romantischen Schreibtradition in Polen (vgl. Borowski 2005, 65). Die bisherigen Kulturmodelle und insbesondere die Selbstfiguration mussten überdacht werden. Die Literatur konnte demnach keine Schwarzweiß-Malerei mehr gebrauchen, die, wie bei Kossak-Szczucka, positive, vorwiegend polnisch-katholische Heldenfiguren und sich selbststilisierende Erzähler konstruierte. Borowski selber zeigte mit der Ästhetik seiner Auschwitz-Texte und insbesondere mit seinem, für die polnische Literatur neuartigen, Erzählertypus alternative Wege des Schreibens auf, was die Literaturkritik in zwei Lager spaltete. Vor allem die katholisch orientierten Traditionalisten warfen ihm wegen seiner wertungsfreien, distanzierten, an den *Behaviorismus* in der amerikanischen Literatur erinnernden Erzählweise Zynismus und eine nihilistische Haltung vor, wohingegen das progressive Lager, das sich insbesondere im Umfeld der Literaturzeitung *Kuźnica* bewegte, seine innovativen Erzählansätze schätzte, wie dies etwa aus der folgenden Einschätzung Zbigniew Żabickis sichtbar wird:

Narracja Borowskiego – wyjaśniał [Jan Kott] – prowadzona jest w pierwszej osobie. Ale „jest to środek stylistyczny. Nie wolno z tego powodu utożsamiać autora z bohaterem". Co więcej, jest to środek stylistyczny wysoce funkcjonalny: „Proza Borowskiego jest nie tylko wspaniałą zapowiedzią wielkiego talentu literackiego, ale również trafną i odkrywczą analizą systemu obozów koncentracyjnych, opartego na zróżniczkowanym i stopniowym udziale więźniów w zbrodni, moderstwie i gławcie. Pierwsze Borowski pokazał to, co było najstraszliwszego w obozach koncentracyjnych – nie grozę śmierci, ale udział w podłości i zbrodni". (Żabicki 1966, 161f.)

Borowskis Narration – erklärte [Jan Kott] – bedient sich der ersten Person. Doch „dies ist ein stilistisches Mittel. Aus diesem Grund darf der Autor nicht mit seinem Helden gleichgesetzt werden". Mehr noch, es handelt sich hierbei um ein höchst funktionales Stilmittel: „Borowskis Prosa kündet nicht nur ein großes literarisches Talent an, sondern sie ist gleichfalls eine treffende und innovative Analyse des Systems der Konzentrationslager, die auf der differenten und allmählichen Beteiligung der Gefangenen an den Verbrechen, Morden und an der Gewalt gründet. Borowski hat als erster das gezeigt, was in den Konzentrationslagern am schrecklichsten war – nicht die Furcht vor dem Tod, sondern die Teilhabe an der Niederträchtigkeit und den Verbrechen".

Doch nicht nur Borowski hatte Wegmarken in der Prosa gesetzt. Einen vergleichbar nüchternen, wenn auch nicht ganz so radikalen Erzählton hatte Zofia Nałkowska in ihrem 1946 erschienenen Erzählzyklus *Medaliony* (*Medaillons*) angeschlagen, der dem Genre der literarischen Reportage nahestand. Nałkowska bediente sich eines gezielt schlichten, sachlichen Stils sowie einer Ästhetik des Schweigens. Wie bei Borowski stachen insbesondere ihre Erzählerinstanzen hervor, die auf jegliche für die polnische Literatur charakteristische moralisierend-didaktische Kommentare verzichteten. Die zentrale Aussage der Texte hatte sie stattdessen auf eine leise, unaufdringliche Weise dem Zyklus als Motto vorangestellt: „Ludzie ludziom zgotowali ten los". Diese Aussage, dass es Menschen waren, die anderen Menschen dieses Schicksal bereitet haben, dem eine prägende kollektive Erfahrung zugrunde lag, ist in Polen zu einem geflügelten Wort geworden, das eine bittere Wahrheit über das Böse in der Welt zu transportieren versucht. Wie später Hannah Arendt in ihrem *Bericht von der Banalität des Bösen* (1963) zeigten auch Nałkowska und Borowski, dass es sich beim Bösen um keine transzendentale Macht, sondern um die auf freiwillig getroffenen Entscheidungen basierenden Taten gewöhnlicher Menschen handle, ganz gleich welcher Nations- oder Religionszugehörigkeit. Diese Kulturkritik negierte die unterschiedliche Wertigkeit von Menschen: Opfer und Täter waren beides schlichtweg Menschen, egal ob Deutscher, Pole oder Jude. Zu den heute bekanntesten Autoren, die das Narrativ der Selbstkritik in den ersten Nachkriegsjahren entfalteten, zählten auch Czesław Miłosz und Jerzy Andrzejewski. Ein weiteres markantes Beispiel stellt der Schriftsteller und Kritiker Artur Sandauer dar, der seinem eigenen Erzählband *Śmierć liberała* 1947; (*Der Tod des Liberalen*) einen „demaskierenden und antiheroischen Programmcharakter" („charakter programowo demaskatorski i antyheroiczny"; Sandauer 1985, 26) zusprach. Sandauer führte den „Kampf gegen die Theatralisierung der Literatur und der Heroisierung" („Walkę z teatralizmem nnaszej literatury i z heroizacją"; ebd.) jedoch nicht nur mittels seiner literarischen Arbeiten, sondern ebenso in seinen literaturkritischen Schriften.

Ein gemeinsames Bedürfnis dieser Nachkriegsautoren bestand in der Darstellung der Wahrheit, wozu Sandauer bereits 1945 aufrief:

Żądać od pisarzy, aby tworzył bohaterów, aby „wyolbrzymiał i upraszczał" – to wymagać od architekta, aby zbudował kościół od razu z wiekową patyną. Nie stylizujmy ruin, nie wyolbrzymiajmy i nie upraszczajmy (jak również nie pomniejszajmy i nie komplikujmy) – mówmy prawdę. (Sandauer 1985, 32)

Vom Schriftsteller zu fordern, Helden zu kreieren, zu überzeichnen und zu vereinfachen, wäre so, als würde man vom Architekten verlangen, Kirchen direkt mit einer jahrhundertealten Patina zu bauen. Stilisieren wir nicht die Ruinen, überzeichnen wir nicht und vereinfachen wir nicht (ebenso: schmälern wir nicht und verkomplizieren wir nicht) – sagen wir die Wahrheit.

Dieses vereinende Anliegen der Nachkriegsliteratur löste eine Debatte über den Realismus als richtungsweisende Stilformation aus. Kossak-Szczuckas Text diente dabei vielfach als Negativbeispiel eines verfälschten Realismus. Als Vorbilder für eine angemessene Schreibweise, die das Erlebte während der Okkupation in aller Gänze widerzuspiegeln bzw. das Wesen der Welt zu vermitteln vermochte, fungierten hingegen die großen Realisten des 19. Jahrhunderts. Denn wie Stanisław Burkot anmerkt, wurde ein puristischer Realismus in der Gestalt von Reportagen oder Erlebnisberichten als unzureichend empfunden, um das Erlebte darzustellen (vgl. Burkot 2002, 95f.). Um sich adäquat ausdrücken zu können, bedurfte es literarisierender Mittel, was Sandauer 1985 im Rückblick beschreibt:

Po wydaniu *Śmierci liberała* znalazłem się wówczas na rozdrożu między beletrystyką a esejem. Zdawałem sobie sprawę, że nie wszystko, co mnie niepokoi, da się wypowiedzieć w czysto pojęciowym języku krytyki; nie mogłem w nim zwłaszcza wyrazić wpełni swych okupacyjnych doświadczeń. (Sandauer 1985, 13)

Ich habe mich damals, nach der Veröffentlichung des *Todes des Liberalen*, auf dem Scheideweg zwischen Belletristik und Essay befunden. Ich war mir dessen bewusst, dass sich nicht alles, was mir Sorgen macht, mit der rein sachlichen Sprache der Kritik ausdrücken lässt; vor allem konnte ich mit dieser meine Erlebnisse aus der Zeit der Okkupation nicht vollständig zum Ausdruck bringen.

Die Bedeutung der Literatur ist in Polen im Unterschied zum westeuropäischen Diskurs, der auf Adornos Äußerung folgte, in keinem Moment in Frage gestellt worden. Ganz im Gegenteil: Die Literatur wurde sofort als Instrument angesehen, mit deren Hilfe auf die erlebten Verbrechen angemessen reagiert werden konnte. In seiner Erzählung *Piękna sztuka pisania* (*Die schöne Kunst des Schreibens*) aus dem Jahr 1948 illustrierte Adolf Rudnicki die ethische Verantwortung der polnischen Literatur, die ihm zufolge im Sprechen und Erinnern bestand:

> Ludzie – pisał – umierali w katowniach, konali w tysiączny sposób. Ich niemym testamentem, ich ostatnią nadzieją była ta, że słowo będzie im poświęcone. [...] Wierzyli w nie zarówno ci którzy szli z granatem na ulicę, by mścić się, jak i ci, którzy w obozach dogorywali z głodu trzeźwo i długo. W dniach najcięższej klęski narodowej i osobistej człowiek jasno pojmował sens sumienia, sumienia pisarza. (Rudnicki 1956, 628)

> Menschen – schrieb er – starben in den Folterkammern, sie starben auf tausend verschiedene Arten. Ihr stilles Testament, ihre letzte Hoffnung war, dass ihnen das Wort gewidmet werden würde. [...] Sowohl diejenigen glaubten daran, die um Rache zu nehmen, mit der Granate auf die Straße gingen, als auch diejenigen, die in den Lagern langsam bei vollem Verstand verhungerten. In den Tagen der schwersten nationalen und persönlichen Niederlage verstand der Mensch ganz deutlich die Bedeutung des Gewissens, des Gewissens des Schriftstellers.

Die Kriegserlebnisse bzw. die Holocausterfahrung sind eine zentrale Dominante der polnischen Nachkriegsliteratur. Entgegen Gombrowicz' polemischer Behauptung fand eine weitreichende Auseinandersetzung mit dem Holocaust in der Literatur statt, die keineswegs banalisiert werden darf. Der Holocaust hat in der polnischen Literatur deutliche Spuren auch im ästhetischen Bereich hinterlassen, was Czesław Miłosz eingehend in seinen Vorlesungen als Gastprofessor in Harvard thematisiert hat:

> Skutki tego, co się stało w Polsce, a co wyrażało się śmiercią około sześciu milionów ludzkich istnień, w poezji pojawiły się nie od razu. [...] Dopiero później, już po wojnie, polska zaczyna oddać się od sposobów stylistycznych wspólnych przedwojennej poezji wielu krajów, a robi to niewątpliwie pod naciskiem silnie odczuwanej potrzeby, chcąc znaleźć wyraz dla wyjątkowo ciężkiego zbiorowego doświadczenia. (Miłosz 2004, 81)

> Die Auswirkungen des in Polen Geschehenen, das im Tod von etwa sechs Millionen menschlicher Existenzen seinen Ausdruck fand, zeigten sich nicht sofort in der Poesie. [...] Erst später, unmittelbar nach dem Krieg, beginnt die polnische Poesie sich von den Stilverfahren zu entfernen, die der Vorkriegspoesie vieler Länder gemeinsam war, und sie tut dies zweifellos unter dem Druck des starken Bedürfnisses, einen adäquaten Ausdruck zu finden für die außerordentlich schwere kollektive Erfahrung. (Miłosz 1984, 94f.)

In den ersten Nachkriegsjahren hatte die literarische Auseinandersetzung mit dem Holocaust zu einer neuen Art der Narration sowie zu neuen Narrativen geführt, die die polnische Literatur geprägt haben. Kaum einer der führenden polnischen Autoren hat sich nicht mit dem Holocaust auseinandergesetzt. Und bis heute wird die Entwicklung der polnischen Literatur durch den Holocaust nachhaltig beeinflusst. In den letzten zehn Jahren ist ein regelrechter Boom an polnischen Holocausttexten zu beobachten, was der junge polnische Schriftsteller Jacek Dehnel (Jg. 1980) wiederum zum Anlass für eine kritische Reflexion nimmt:

> Za każdym razem, w każdym konkursie natrafiam na ileś tekstów poświęconych Holokaustowi; getta, komory gazowe, obozy koncentracyjne są ważną częścią naszej zbiorowej wyobraźni – ale, jak to często bywa, masowe wyobrażenia są odległe od prawdy historycznej. Co więcej, płaskie, sztampowe, skrzywione widzenie tamtych wydarzeń pojawia się nie tylko w tekstach amatorskich, ale też w publikowanych w głównym obiegu książkach, w filmach, w artykułach prasowych. (Dehnel 2013, 36)
>
> Jedes Mal, bei jedem Wettbewerb finde ich eine bestimmte Anzahl an Texten über den Holocaust; die Ghettos, Gaskammern, Konzentrationslager sind ein wichtiger Bestandteil unserer kollektiven Vorstellung – doch wie es so oft ist, sind die massenhaft verbreiteten Ideen weit von der Wahrheit entfernt. Mehr noch, die seichten, klischeehaften Visionen der damaligen Ereignisse finden sich nicht nur in Texten von Amateuren, sondern ebenfalls auf dem offiziellen Buchmarkt, in Filmen, Zeitungsartikeln.

Quantität geht in der Tat häufig nicht mit Qualität einher. Unter den Werken polnischer Autoren findet sich jedoch eine Vielzahl an einflussreichen Texten, die – wie schon in der zweiten Hälfte der 1940er Jahre – durch ihre Thematik und Ästhetik zu wichtigen Auseinandersetzungen mit nationalen Kulturmodellen und Werten anregen. Kurz nach dem Krieg waren es u.a. die Gedichte *Biedny Chrzescijanin patrzy na getto* (1945; *Der arme Christ schaut auf das Ghetto*) und *Campo di Fiori* (1943) von Czesław Miłosz oder eben Borowskis Prosa, welche die gängigen polnischen Literatur- und Kulturmodelle in Frage stellten. In den 1980er und frühen 1990er Jahren löste etwa Andrzej Szczypiorskis Roman *Początek* (1986; *Der Anfang*; dt. veröffentlicht unter dem Titel *Die schöne Frau Seidenmann*) große gesellschaftliche Kontroversen in Polen aus, da durch den Roman nun öffentlich über den polnischen Antisemitismus gesprochen wurde. Und auch in der jüngsten Zeit haben Texte wie z.B. die Romane *Noc żywych Żydów* (2012; *Die Nacht der lebenden Juden*) von Igor Ostachowicz oder *Więcej gazu, Kameraden!* (2012; *Mehr Gas, Kameraden!*) von Krystian Piwowarski für Aufsehen gesorgt, die sich mit dem Holocaust auseinandersetzen, um polnische Kulturmodelle zu hinterfragen und die polnische Literatur mit neuen Erzählweisen zu bereichern.

Literaturverzeichnis

Borowski, Tadeusz 1991: Alicja w krainie czarów. In: ders.: Utwory wybrane. Wrocław – Warszawa – Kraków, S. 487-497.
Bratny, Roman 1948: W poszukiwaniu nowego stylu. In: Twórczość 4,3, S. 121-125.
Burkot, Stanisław 2002: Literatura polska w latach 1939 – 1999. Warszawa.
Dehnel, Jacek 2013: Czarny Disneyland. In: ders.: Młodszy księgowy. O książkach, czytaniu i pisaniu. Warszawa, S. 36-42.
Duniec, Krystyna – *Krakowska*, Joanna 2014: Nie opłakali ich? In: dies.: Soc, sex i historia. Warszawa, S. 79-102.
Gombrowicz, Witold 1986: Dziennik 1953 – 1956. Kraków.
ders. 1998: Tagebuch 1953 – 1969. Aus d. Poln. v. Olaf Kühl. Frankfurt am Main.
Jarosiński, Zbigniew 1978: Przemiany polskiej myśli literackiej lat 1945 – 1948. In: Pamiętnik Literacki 69,2, S. 69-86.
Kulesza, Dariusz 2006: Dwie prawdy. Zofia Kossak i Tadeusz Borowski wobec obrazu wojny w polskiej prozie lat 1944 – 1948. Białystok.
Lampart, Fabian 2013: Nachkriegsmoderne. Transformationen der deutschsprachigen Lyrik 1945 – 1960. Berlin – New York.
Miłosz, Czesław 1984: Trümmer und Poesie. In: ders.: Das Zeugnis der Poesie. Aus d. Poln. v. Peter Lachmann. München – Wien, S. 93-117.
ders. 2004: Ruiny i poezja. In: ders.: Świadectwo poezji. Sześć wykładów o dotkliwościach naszego wieku. Kraków, S. 80-100.
Rudnicki, Adolf 1956: Piękna sztuka pisania. In: ders.: Żywe i martwe morze. Wyd. 3. Warszawa, S. 623-630.
Sandauer, Artur 1985: Pisma zebrane. T. 3: Publicystyka. Warszawa.
Żabicki, Zbigniew 1966: *Kuźnica* i jej program literacki. Kraków.

Writing after Auschwitz? Reactions of Polish Literature to the Holocaust

The Holocaust shook Western society deeply in its foundations and put its cultural achievements into question. Especially, the cultural technique of writing encountered strong feelings of reservations after the war. The most influential expression of this skepticism was Adorno's statement that to write poetry after Auschwitz is barbaric, this statement becoming a point of reference for the still ongoing debate on the Holocaust and the limits of its literary representation. However, the distrust wasn't limited to the genre of Holocaust literature, but it referred also to literature and writing in general. After the war many young writers distrusted the language and the literary conventions, rejecting an uncritical return to traditional modes of writing, so that the Holocaust became a common reference point for contemporary literature. In Germany, as a result, the so-called *Trümmerliteratur* emerged during the early 1950s, a literature that was seeking radically new forms of expression. Polish authors, however, had already begun to consider the poetological and ethical issues quite a while before the discussion on the representation of the Holocaust and new directions of literature intensified in Germany. The paper, therefore, outlines this Polish discourse, having become of a lasting influence on Polish literature, and explores the relationship between the Holocaust and Polish literature.

Ästhetik des (sekundären) Bildes in neuesten polnischen Dramen: Zyta Rudzkas *Fastryga* und Artur Pałygas *Żyd*

Katarzyna Adamczak, Hamburg

Semprún zur Einführung – zwischen Fakten und Affekten

Betrachtet man die Holocaustliteratur und die sich mit ihr beschäftigende Forschung, so kann die Auseinandersetzung mit der literarischen Ästhetisierung der Vernichtung von etwa sechs Millionen Juden als eines der diskussionsmächtigsten Felder bezeichnet werden (vgl. z.B. Rosenfeld 1980; Young 1992; Langer 1995; White 1999). Literarische Texte zeugen davon, dass die Shoah-Überlebenden noch während ihrer Gefangenschaft im Konzentrationslager das Problem „wie man davon erzählen sollte" erkannten. Dies lässt sich etwa dem autobiographischen Roman *Schreiben oder Leben* des spanischen Schriftstellers Jorge Semprún entnehmen, der selbst mehr als ein Jahr im KZ Buchenwald gefangen war. Am 12. April 1945, einen Tag nach der Befreiung Buchenwalds, dachte das autobiographische Ich über die Möglichkeit des Erzählens nach. Das, was ihn zweifeln ließ, war weder die Unsagbarkeit des Erlebten noch die „Form" bzw. die „Gliederung" des Berichts, sondern dessen „Substanz", dessen „Dichte":

> Zu dieser Substanz, dieser transparenten Dichte werden nur diejenigen vordringen, die es verstehen, ihr Zeugnis in ein Kunstwerk, einen Raum der Schöpfung zu verwandeln. Oder der Neuschöpfung. Nur die Kunstfertigkeit eines gebändigten Berichts vermag die Wahrheit des Zeugnisses teilweise zu übermitteln. (Semprún 1995, 23)

Das Problem der Vermittlung des Erlebten tauchte nach der Befreiung von Buchenwald erneut auf, als unter den ehemaligen KZ-Insassen die Frage gestellt wurde, ob man ihren „Geschichten zuhören [wird], auch wenn sie gut erzählt sind?" (ebd., 150). Die von dem autobiographischen Erzähler formulierte Antwort präzisiert den zuvor aufgegriffenen Aspekt der Kunstfertigkeit:

> Gut erzählt heißt: daß man gehört wird. Das gelingt nicht ohne ein paar Kunstgriffe. Genügend, daß es Kunst wird. [...] Die Wahrheit, die wir zu sagen haben, [...] ist nicht sehr glaubwürdig... Sie ist sogar unvorstellbar... [...] Wie soll man eine so wenig glaubwürdige Wahrheit erzählen, wie eine Vorstellung von dem Unvorstellbaren wecken, wenn nicht dadurch, daß man an der Wirklichkeit arbeitet, ihr eine Perspektive gibt? Also mit ein paar Kunstgriffen. (ebd., 150 f.)

„Die andere Art des Verstehens, die grundlegende Wahrheit der Erfahrung" (ebd.) lässt sich Semprún zufolge nur mit den Mitteln des literarischen Schreibens näherbringen, das durch Fiktion und ästhetische Kunstgriffe den affektiven Bezug und stellvertretenden indirekten Blick auf eine unvorstellbare Lagererfahrung ermöglicht. Denn das allein auf Daten und Fakten aufbauende Gedenken, das sich auf eine kognitive Vermittlung des Zugetragenen beschränkt, genügt nicht (vgl. Carroll 1999, 69 u. 73 f.).

Mit dem sich vergrößernden zeitlichen Abstand zur Shoah und dem Verlust auch der letzten direkten Zeugen wird die Frage nach dem ‚wie' (wie man davon erzählt) statt nach dem ‚was' (was passiert ist) immer wichtiger. Hayden White greift in diesem Zusammenhang das von dem englischen Philosophen Michael Oakeshott geprägte Konzept der ‚praktischen Vergangenheit' auf. In der praktischen Vergangenheit geht es nicht um die Erweiterung der „Wissensbank zum Holocaust", sondern vielmehr um eine Erforschung dessen, was einen ethischen Charakter hat und sich darauf bezieht, was nach dem Sammeln und der Auswertung des faktografischen Materials bleibt, dies im Hinblick auf die Frage: „Wie sollen wir – die zweite und dritte Generation – handeln?" (White 2013, 51f.; vgl. White 2010). Denn mit White sind heute die Bedeutungen, die wir zu den „modernistischen Ereignissen", zu denen auch der Holocaust zählt, zuordnen können, wichtiger als deren faktualer Inhalt (vgl. White 1999, 70). So entsteht eine beachtliche Differenz zwischen der Überlebenden-Generation und der zweiten Generation, in der „mimetisch erzeugtes Pathos des Primären [...] durch ein Ethos des Sekundären abgelöst [wird]" (Scherpe 1996, 269). Der einzige Weg für die nachgeborenen Generationen, sich einen gewissen Grad an Authentizität zu verschaffen, sieht Klaus Scherpe in dem von Jacques Derrida vorgeschlagenen Konzept der „sériature". Dabei handelt es sich um eine

> Aneinanderreihung von Sätzen, die die Erfahrung des Holocaust, ob gewollte oder nicht, *studiert*, also ihre Bedingung des *Sekundären*, der Pluralität, der künstlerischen Konstruktion und der medialen Vermittlung selber zum Thema macht. (ebd., 266)

Dies resultiere, so White, aus der Einzigartigkeit der Erfahrungen des 20. Jahrhunderts, die mit den Begriffen „holocaustal events" bzw. „modernist events" (White 1999, 70) umschrieben werden können und die sich der Darstellung mithilfe der traditionellen Techniken des „storytelling" entziehen (ebd., 74). Das

Fehlen der Erfahrung der Shoah bei den nachgeborenen Generationen gehe mit deren Unglaubwürdigkeit einher, der das Instrumentarium der modernistischen und vormodernistischen Kunsttechniken entgegenwirken könne. White schlägt in diesem Zusammenhang die Anwendung von „psychopathological techniques" vor, die er mit Fredric Jameson wie folgt beschreibt: „artificial closures, the blockage of narrative, [their] deformation and formal compensations, the dissociation or splitting of narrative functions, including the repression of certain of them" (ebd., 82). Nur sie ermöglichen es, eine zum Fetischismus und mithin zum Kitsch neigende traditionelle Narration in eine Gegennarration der Nichterzählung umzuwandeln, die in der Lage ist, solche traumatischen Erfahrungen wie den Nationalsozialismus und den Holocaust adäquat darzustellen. Somit ebnen modernistische Repräsentationstechniken den Weg für den Trauerprozess, der sich von der Last der Geschichte löst und teilweise einen realistischen Blick auf *gegenwärtige Probleme* ermöglicht (vgl. ebd.).

Die hier stichwortartig behandelten literarischen Konzepte der ‚sériature' und der ‚psychopathological techniques' als Formen einer überlieferten Erfahrung des Holocaust finden ihre Entsprechung im postdramatischen Theater, das als „Theater der Wahrnehmbarkeit" (Lehmann 2005, 169) sich durch eine bedingungslose ästhetische Formalisierung gegen die Regeln der Mimesis durchsetzt: „Soll Theater Wahrheit bieten, so muß es sich nunmehr als Fiktion und in seinem Herstellungsprozeß von Fiktionen zu erkennen geben und ausstellen, statt darüber zu betrügen. Sonst kann es keinen Ernst gewinnen" (ebd., 186). Dies geschieht mit Hans-Thies Lehmann durch folgende Merkmale „des postdramatisches Zeichengebrauchs" (ebd., 185): Zunächst ist auf das Fehlen von *Synthesis* zu verweisen, was das Chaos des alltäglichen Lebens (ebd., 140) nachahmen soll. An ihre Stelle treten stattdessen Teilstrukturen, die von dem Zuschauer im Zuge einer ihm immanenten Assoziationstätigkeit zu einer Ganzheit zusammengeführt werden *können*. Sodann sind *Traumbilder* zu nennen, aus denen Traumstrukturen folgen, die sich in Collage-Technik, Montage und Fragmentierung äußern (ebd., 142). Dem Entzug von Synthesis und den Traumbildern folgt schließlich *Synästhesie*, die sich als „disparate Heterogenität" (ebd., 143) von Theaterzeichen, die unabhängig voneinander existieren und dennoch bzw. gerade deshalb miteinander korrespondieren können, beschreiben lässt.

Diese Eigenschaften des postdramatischen Theaters, die mit den ‚storytelling'-Techniken brechen, prädestinieren es geradezu zur Auseinandersetzung mit dem Holocaust, in der das *Wie* der Darstellung fokussiert wird. Als Paradebeispiel einer solchen Inszenierung der Shoah auf der Theaterbühne in Polen gilt die künstlerische Tätigkeit von Jerzy Grotowski und Tadeusz Kantor, und deren Stücke *Akropolis* (entwickelt zwischen 1962 und 1967) und *Umarła klasa* (1975; dt. u.d.T. *Die tote Klasse*). Beide Regisseure verwiesen auf die Shoah nicht referenziell, durch Zitieren von historischen Bildern, sondern affektiv (vgl. Niziołek 2013, 105). Dabei nutzten sie eine für das Theater charakteristische Wiederholungsstrategie, die sich in diesem Fall darin äußerte, dass sie den polnischen Zuschauer in die „Situation eines gleichgültigen bzw. verächtlichen Zeugen" (ebd., 86 f.) versetzten – dies etwa in Bezug auf Czesław Miłosz' Gedicht *Biedny chrześcijanin patrzy na getto* (1945; dt. u.d.T. *Armer Christ blickt aufs Getto*) –, um durch die Konfrontation mit der Gleichgültigkeit einen nachträglichen Schock bei ihm auszulösen. Solch ein Verfahren beruhte auf den im kollektiven Gedächtnis sowie in persönlichen Erinnerungen gespeicherten Wissen und Emotionen, welche durch „verformte, stark mediatisierte oder verschlüsselte" Sprach- und Theaterbilder, die „mit Verschiebungen, Verdichtungen und *Déjà-vu*-Mechanismen" (ebd., 59) arbeiteten, schlagartig zur Sprache kamen. Es gelang dadurch eine moralisierende Aussage zu vermeiden und stattdessen eine emphatische Haltung seitens der Rezipienten ins Leben zu rufen.[1]

Geschichte in Bildern

Obgleich Grotowski und Kantor den Weg für eine neuartige Auseinandersetzung mit der Shoah ebneten, setzt das zeitgenössische polnische Drama auf eher konventionelle Repräsentationstechniken. Diese sind jedoch insofern interessant, weil sie einen wichtigen Aspekt aus den Überlegungen von White aufgreifen, nämlich eine auf die Gegenwart ausgerichtete Reflexion über die Vergangenheit.

Es ist kein Zufall, dass eine auf die Gegenwart bezogene Betrachtung der Geschichte durch White Rückschlüsse auf Walter Benjamins grundlegende Überle-

---

[1] Eine grundlegende Analyse von Grotowskis *Akropolis* und Kantors *Umarła klasa* im Kontext einer posttraumatischen Auseinandersetzung mit dem Holocaust bietet die polnisch-amerikanische Theaterwissenschaftlerin Magda Romanska (siehe Romanska 2014).

gungen zum Geschichtsbegriff ziehen lässt, zumal die von White als Motto verwendeten Worte Benjamins „Geschichte zerfällt in Bilder, nicht in Geschichten" (Benjamin 1982, 596) in den bereits angeführten Essay von White *The Modernist Event* (1999) einführen. Dieses Zitat kann als Sprungbrett für weitere Überlegungen bezüglich der Re-Konstruktion von Geschichte mithilfe der ver- und zusammengesetzten Bilder dienen, die Benjamin als dialektische Bilder bezeichnet hat. Aus seinen Ausführungen lassen sich diese als Konstellationen verstehen, deren Essenz nicht in einer starren Betrachtung der zum Stillstand gekommenen Vergangenheit liegt, sondern in einer blitzhaften Erkennung der aufgerissenen Vergangenheit im vergegenwärtigenden Prozess (vgl. Hillach 2000, 186 u. 225):

> [...] Bild ist dasjenige, worin das Gewesene mit dem Jetzt blitzhaft zu einer Konstellation zusammentritt. Mit anderen Worten: Bild ist die Dialektik im Stillstand. Denn während die Beziehung der Gegenwart zur Vergangenheit eine rein zeitliche, kontinuierliche ist, ist die des Gewesenen zum Jetzt dialektisch: ist nicht Verlauf sondern Bild, sprunghaft. – Nur dialektische Bilder sind echte (d. h. nicht archaische) Bilder; und der Ort, an dem man sie antrifft, ist die *Sprache* [...]. (Benjamin 1982, 576 f.; Hervorhebung K.A.)

Die Sprache fungiert hier als der Ort, an dem die Vergangenheit und die Gegenwart aufeinander treffen. In fragmentarische Bilder der ersteren fließen zwei kollektive Kontexte, die zum einen durch das historische Wissen, erarbeitet durch die Geschichtswissenschaften, zum anderen durch mediale Überlieferungen geprägt sind, ein, um anschließend neu kontextualisiert zu werden. Denn die Vergangenheit lässt sich Benjamin zufolge nur mit den in Gefahr aufblitzenden Bildern festhalten, in denen sich die Gegenwart und mithin das bedrohte Subjekt wiedererkennen. Dementsprechend ist nicht mehr die Vergangenheit zu ermitteln, sondern

> die zu verändernde Gegenwart, von der aus die Bilder auftauchen und sich zusammenfügen, aber nicht in einer ruhigen linear-chronologischen Abfolge, sondern in einem diskontinuierlichen Bilderwirbel, der plötzlich stillsteht und eine neue Bedeutung erhält. (Gagnebin 2006, 291)

Auch das neueste polnische Drama, das die Shoah thematisiert, operiert mit einer Bildersprache, die in der Vergangenheit angesiedelt ist und sich an der Gegenwart/Jetztzeit orientiert. Wegen ihrer komprimierten und im Vergleich zu Prosatexten geradezu asketischen Darstellungsform eignet sich die Gattung

Drama zum einen für die Erläuterung der Prozesse der Selektion, Fragmentierung, (De-)Konstruktion und Montage – nicht nur des Erzählten, sondern auch der Geschichte. Zum anderen ermöglicht das Drama durch die in seiner Performativität verankerte Vergegenwärtigung und seine dialogisch-agierende Form[2] die Analogien zum Benjaminschen dialektischen Bild aufzuzeigen. Denn das Theater und mithin das Drama – die literarische Vorlage einer Inszenierung –, das historische Ereignisse zum Thema macht,

> can become such an image, connecting the past with the present through the creativity of the theatre, constantly ‚quoting' from the past, but erasing the exact traces in order to gain full meaning in the present. (Rokem 2000, xiii)

Wiederverwendung

Auch die für meine Analyse ausgewählten Theaterstücke „zitieren aus der Vergangenheit". In *Fastryga* (*Die Heftnaht*) von Zyta Rudzka und in *Żyd* (*Der Jude*) von Artur Pałyga werden sprachliche und historisch-situative Bilder bedient, die im kulturellen Gedächtnis gespeichert sind. Sie werden von den Dramatiker(inne)n verarbeitet bzw. „recycelt" (Czapliński 2009, 91), um anschließend von dem Rezipienten für eine ganz bestimmte und in einer ganz bestimmten „Jetztzeit" (Benjamin 2007, 137) aktualisiert zu werden.

Rudzkas Drama entstand im Rahmen eines Wettbewerbs, der von der Redaktion *Notatnik Teatralny* und dem Teatr Polski in Wrocław für ein Theaterstück ausgeschrieben wurde, das auf die Ereignisse vom März 1968 zurückgreifen sollte. Die Veranstalter wollten damit einerseits das im Theaterdiskurs bis dahin aus verschiedenen Gr. nden selten behandelte Thema des polnischen Antisemitismus aufgreifen, andererseits war es ihnen wichtig, in Erfahrung zu bringen, welche Konnotationen der März 1968 bei polnischen Dramenautor(inn)en auslöste (vgl. Rudnicki 2009, 111). Den Veranstaltern ging es somit nicht um die Rezeption der Shoah. Die enge Verknüpfung der Shoah und der März-Unruhen von 1968 in diesem Drama zeigt jedoch – dies sei hier vorweggenommen –, dass sie aus dem zeitlichen Abstand durch die jüngste Generation der Dramati-

---

[2] Zur Rolle des politisch-gesellschaftlich engagierten Dramas und Theaters in Polen nach 1989 siehe Ruta-Rutkowska 2010; Kwaśniewska/Niziołek 2012.

ker(innen) im Prozess der Anamnese zwar nicht gleichgesetzt, aber zusammen gedacht werden.[3]

In *Fastryga* wird die Shoah durch eine zeitliche, räumliche, sprachliche sowie figurale Parallelität erzählt, indem die Ereignisse von 1968, die eigentlich das Hauptthema des Stückes bilden sollen, mit Mitteln dargestellt werden, welche die Literatur vor 1989 für die literarische Vermittlung der Shoah konstituiert hat. Im Handlungszentrum des Dramas stehen die Vorbereitungen von sieben jüdischen Protagonist(inn)en auf ihre Ausreise aus Polen. Der Leser ist Zeuge von Gesprächen, die sie miteinander und ihren polnischen Nachbarn – Frau Pola und ihrem pubertären Sohn Kazik – führen. Während der Lektüre wird er jedoch mit Motiven und sprachlichen Ausdrücken konfrontiert, die ihn in die Zeit des Zweiten Weltkriegs versetzen. So erfährt er vom Einnähen wertvoller Gegenstände in Kleidungsstücke vor der Abreise sowie von einem polnischen Erpresser/Denunzianten (pl. szmalcownik), der einer der Protagonistinnen verspricht, sich gegen Bezahlung um sie zu kümmern, und ihr ein ruhiges, ungestörtes Leben in Aussicht stellt. Die jüdischen Einwohner packen ihre Habseligkeiten, und man erfährt, dass sie nur zwei Federkopfkissen, eine Bettdecke sowie einen Bettbezug mitnehmen dürfen. Sie wissen nicht, wohin sie fahren, daher schlägt Czechna – eine der Protagonistinnen – vor, sich warm anzuziehen. Ebenfalls berichtet sie darüber, dass von den mitgenommenen Bratpfannen die Grenz- bzw. Zollbeamten die Emaille abkratzen, weil sie darunter Gold vermuten – eine abgewandelte Form des Motivs des ‚jüdischen Goldes'. Die jüdischen Mieter verlassen nach und nach die Wohnung, bis am Ende nur Frau Pola und ihr Sohn bleiben. Während sie mit dem Blick der Hausfrau die menschenleere, aber immer noch möblierte Wohnung mustert, informiert sie darüber, dass sie ihren jüdischen Nachbarn Brote für unterwegs geschmiert und sie sogar zum Bahnhof gebracht hat, wo sie schöne Züge – diesmal – mit Gardinen bewundern konnte. Das Stück endet mit der Beschreibung der zufriedenen Frau Pola, welche die

---

[3] Zur Verknüpfung der Shoah mit dem März 1968 siehe Artwińska 2015. An dieser Stelle ist darauf zu verweisen, dass die Betrachtung der Märzunruhen in einer semantischen Nähe zur Shoah im polnischen Theater bereits in Kantors *Umarła klasa* zur Sprache kam (vgl. Romanska 2014, 27). Romanska suggeriert zudem – ähnlich wie ihr polnischer Kollege Grzegorz Niziołek –, dass die steigende antisemitische Stimmung in Polen der 1960er Jahre zur Entstehung von Grotowskis *Akropolis* beigetragen habe (vgl. ebd., 39).

Wohnung der Nachbarn übernimmt und sie nach ihrem eigenen Geschmack einrichtet.

Rudzkas Narration beruht zunächst auf ausgewählten Primärbildern, aus denen sich die Handlung des Stückes zusammensetzt. Während der Lektüre wird die selbst erfahrene oder übermittelte Erinnerung des Rezipienten in Bewegung gesetzt, was ihm ermöglicht, sich eine eigene Vorstellung von dem zu machen, was die Textebene verschweigt. Somit hängt es einzig vom Leser und seinem Vorwissen ab, ob er sich auf diese Camouflage einlässt, sie dekodiert und anschließend zu einem sekundären Bild zusammenfügt. Dieses vermittelt dann bekannte Motive, die bereits in die Literatur des Sozialistischen Realismus eingeflossen sind (vgl. Buryła 2012, 471ff.). Davon, dass dies ein gewollter und von Rudzka auch so gewünschter Prozess ist, zeugt ihre Aussage: „Pomyślałam, że Marzec to nie tylko Exodus polskich Żydów, ale również czas wojny" (Piejko 2009, 247).[4] Die Entstehung des sekundären Bildes legt zugleich Mechanismen offen, die für das menschliche Gedächtnis charakteristisch sind. Hierbei handelt es sich mit Micha Brumlik um Narrativität, Selektivität, Affektivität, Konstruktion, Holismus und Normativität (vgl. Brumlik 1996, 35ff.).[5] Als Werkzeuge jeder individuellen Erinnerungsarbeit sind sie mithin von Bedeutung für Vergangenheitskonstruktion innerhalb einer Gesellschaft. Sie sind auch Rudzkas Werkzeuge, mit deren Hilfe sie ihre Wahrnehmung der Geschichte festhält und

---

[4] „Ich habe gedacht, dass der März nicht nur den Exodus polnischer Juden, sondern auch die Kriegszeit bedeutet." Alle Übersetzungen stammen, wenn nicht anders gekennzeichnet, von der Verfasserin dieses Beitrags.

[5] In Brumliks Ausführungen über sozialwissenschaftliche Untersuchungen zur Zuverlässigkeit des menschlichen Gedächtnisses werden die sechs maßgeblichen Eigenschaften so beschrieben: Das individuelle Gedächtnis sei narrativ strukturiert, weil die Ereignisse, die wahrgenommen oder erlebt werden, in einen größeren Kontext eingebettet und aus einem „narrativen Deutungsmuster" (37) heraus interpretiert werden; es verfährt selektiv, weil die Wahrnehmungsfähigkeit begrenzt sei; es sei affektiv, weil Erinnerungen durch Emotionen und Stimmungen beeinflusst werden; es funktioniere konstruktiv, weil die „»Tätigkeit« des Erinnerns [...] der Logik eines komplexen Erfassungssystems" (39) folge, in dem einzelne Erfahrungen unter Berücksichtigung des Kurz- und Langzeitgedächtnisses mit diversen Symbolen kodiert, bewertet und anschließend nach „vertikal und hierarchisch gegliederten Themenbereichen [...] abgelegt" (ebd.) würden; es sei holistisch, weil jede Erinnerung in Bezug auf ein komplexes Weltbild erfasst wird; es sei letztlich normativ, weil es in einem „intersubjektiven, d. h. sozialisatorisch und medial vermittelten Erwerb des Erinnerungsvermögens" (42) geprägt wurde.

sie mit den Lesern teilt. Sowohl die offenen als auch die (sichtbar) geschlossenen Lücken in ihrem Drama laden zur Reflexion über den Gestus der Dramatikerin/des Dramatikers, die/der die Fakten re-konstruiert, wie auch über das subjektive Auswahlverfahren der Geschehensmomente und tradierten Motive ein. So gelingt es Rudzka, ein Bild vom Holocaust zu vermitteln, indem sie eine „Abwesenheitsfigur" (Czapliński 2010, 373) konstruiert, die ihr Vorbild auch in polnischen Prosatexten hat. Gemeint sind hier Paweł Huelles *Weiser Dawidek* (1987), Piotr Szewcs *Zagłada* (1987; dt. u.d.T. *Vernichtung*) sowie Marek Bieńczyks *Tworki* (1999), in denen das Verschwinden der Juden und damit auch des jüdischen Lebens aus dem polnischen Kulturraum thematisiert wird. Waren die Gründe dieses Verschwindens rätselhaft (wie in *Weiser Dawidek*), mediumistisch rekonstruiert (wie in *Zagłada*) oder nur angedeutet, ohne genannt zu werden (wie in *Tworki*), so erhalten sie bei Rudzka eine neue Konnotierung, denn die textimmanenten Leerstellen in ihrem Drama sind auf die Wirklichkeit bezogener Ausdruck des nicht nur durch die Nationalsozialisten, sondern auch durch die Polen verschuldeten Fehlens der einstmals hier lebenden Juden.

Die Abwesenheit der ermordeten bzw. vertriebenen Juden und ihrer Nachkommen wird auch zur zentralen Aussage des Stücks von Pałyga. Sein Drama *Żyd* entstand zwar nicht im Rahmen des erwähnten Wrocławer Wettbewerbs, da es jedoch mit den Intentionen der Veranstalter übereinstimmte, wurde es zusammen mit Rudzkas Drama in *Notatnik Teatralny* publiziert (vgl. Rudnicki 2009, 111).

Die Handlung des Stücks spielt in unserer Gegenwart in einer vor massiven finanziellen Problemen stehenden Schule einer Kleinstadt, der unerwartet Unterstützung angeboten wird. Es treten jedoch zwei Probleme auf: Erstens, der Geldgeber ist ein Jude aus Israel, und zweitens, das Geld spendet er nur unter der Bedingung, dass die Schule nach seinem Vater, Mosze Wassersztajn, benannt wird. Der Vater lebte bis in die 1960er Jahre in der kleinen Stadt und wurde nach seiner Auswanderung nach Israel ein berühmter Dichter, der immer wieder über seine alte Heimat schrieb. Die Lehrer betonen anfangs einstimmig, dass sie keine Antisemiten seien. Nach diesem Eingeständnis zeigt sich aber, wie schwer sie sich mit der jüngeren polnisch-jüdischen Geschichte tun und wie tief der Antisemitismus in der polnischen Gesellschaft – hier in der geistigen und kulturellen Elite (vgl. Pałyga 2009, 205) – verwurzelt ist. Im Drama beginnt es bereits damit, dass der Schulleiter sich nicht traut, das Wort „Żyd" (Jude) laut auszusprechen. Er sucht vergeblich nach einem politisch korrekten Begriff für den Gast aus Israel, um nach zwei Versuchen, „osoba judaistycznego pochodzenia" (Person judaistischer Herkunft) und „Judejczyk" (Judäer), feststellen zu müssen, dass das lange aus seinem Wortschatz verbannte Wort „Żyd" – das im Polnischen immer noch eine pejorative Bedeutung besitzt (vgl. Keff 2013, 208) – die korrekte Bezeichnung ist (Pałyga 2009, 201). Doch wer ist dieser Jude und wie sollte man ihn empfangen? Der Versuch, ein Begrüßungsrepertoire und ein koscheres Menü zusammenzustellen, wird aus ängstlichem Bemühen um political correctness ad absurdum geführt:

> ANGLISTKA: Hej, słuchajcie, a może orkiestra by grała, co? Coś mi się marasi, że oni lubią orkiestry, ci Żydzi [...]
> WUEFISTA: No ja mogę zrobić bieg jakiś... Może do tej muzyki... Przy tej orkiestrze niech [uczniowie; K. A.] biegają, nie? [...]
> ANGLISTKA: Ja widziałam raz w Szwajcarii taką sztafetę, że z pochodniami biegli przez góry!
> DYREKTOR [...]: Z pochodniami. To ładne będzie. I niech harcerze ubiorą mundurki. (do Polonistki) No a pani co proponuje?
> POLONISTKA: Może Tuwima?
> DYREKTOR: No? A czemu Tuwima?
>
> Chwila krępującej ciszy.
>
> DYREKTOR: Tak? Że on tego był? Serio? [...] Dobrze. A co? Jaki utwór? [...] Żeby to proste było. I wie pani... reprezentatywne. Znane znaczy.
> ANGLISTKA: Ja wiem! Lokomotywę?
> DYREKTOR: „A tych wagonów jest ze czterdzieści...".
> WSZYSCY: „...Sam nie wiem, co się w nich jeszcze mieści".
> DYREKTOR: To mamy orkiestrę, sztafetę, pochodnie, wagony... (Pałyga 2009, 203 f.)[6]

---

[6] „ENGLISCHLEHRERIN: Hey, hört mal, vielleicht könnte ein Orchester spielen? Mir scheint, dass sie Orchester mögen, diese Juden [...]
SPORTLEHRER: Ich könnte einen Lauf veranstalten... Vielleicht zu dieser Musik... Vielleicht sollen sie [die Schüler; K.A.] zu der Orchestermusik laufen...
ENGLISCHLEHRERIN: Ich habe einmal in der Schweiz solch einen Staffellauf gesehen, wo sie mit Fackeln durch die Berge gelaufen sind!
SCHULLEITER [...]: Mit Fackeln. Das wird schön sein. Die Pfadfinder sollen aber ihre Uniformen tragen. (Er wendet sich der Polnischlehrerin zu.) Und Sie, was schlagen Sie vor?
POLNISCHLEHRERIN: Vielleicht Tuwim?
SCHULLEITER: Warum denn Tuwim?
Verlegenes Schweigen.

Die (un)bewusste Erinnerung an die Shoah wird hier an ein Schulorchester, Uniformen, einen Fackel-Staffellauf und einen Eisenbahnwaggon aus dem Kindergedicht von Julian Tuwim gekoppelt. Diese holzschnittartig konzipierte Szene lässt sich als eine bewusste Parodie auf die Ikonografie der Shoah deuten, und sie zeugt – in Bezug auf das Benjaminsche dialektische Bild – davon, wie eng Bild und Begriff in- und miteinander verflochten sind. Die Sprache wird so einerseits zu einer Triebkraft der Erinnerungsarbeit, die sich aus dem Bildhaushalt einer kulturellen Gemeinschaft speist. Erst Begriffe und die durch sie konstruierten Bedeutungen ermöglichen uns den Zugang zur Welt, deren „Gemeinsinn" (Assmann 1992, 141) wir, als Mitglieder einer kulturellen Gemeinschaft, teilen. Die auf diese Weise erzeugte „Ökonomisierung" bzw. „Umschrift" der Erinnerung an die Shoah (Eke 2014, 32), die durch zeitliche und semantische Verrückung im Verfremdungsverfahren dekodiert wird, basiert auf tradierten Bildern, deren Abrufung und Verknüpfung gleichermaßen gegen und für die Eindimensionalität der Bilder spricht. So wird das Wissen um die Shoah in Erinnerung gehalten, zugleich aber auch der undarstellbaren und pathetischen Kraft des direkt an die Shoah anknüpfenden Bildes entzogen. Hierbei spielen die Groteske und Elemente des absurden Theaters eine entscheidende Rolle. Ihre Akkumulation – die im Fall von Pałygas Drama zusammen mit den durch die versammelten Lehrer(innen) gegen Juden verübten Taten, zu denen sie sich im Handlungsverlauf bekennen, geradezu eine Ästhetik der Anhäufung bildet – legt offen, was das kommunistische Regime zu verstecken versuchte, was über Jahrzehnte hinweg in einer vom Staat gesteuerten Erinnerungspolitik verschwiegen[7]

SCHULLEITER: Ja? War er? Wirklich? [...] Na gut. Und was? Was für ein Gedicht? [...] Es soll einfach sein. Und Sie wissen schon... repräsentativ. Ich meine bekannt.
ENGLISCHLEHRERIN: Ich weiß! Die Lokomotive?
SCHULLEITER: ‚Und solche Waggons gibt es wohl Stücker vierzig...'
ALLE: ‚...Wer die alle kennt, ich glaube, der irrt sich.'
SCHULLEITER: Dann haben wir ein Orchester, einen Staffellauf, Fackeln, Waggons..."
[Das Fragment aus der *Lokomotive* von Julian Tuwim wurde von Wolfgang von Polentz übersetzt (Tuwim 2014, 35)].

[7] In Bezug auf das Polen in der kommunistischen Zeit wird immer wieder behauptet, seine Bürger hätten nichts vom Ausmaß des Holocaust und der zwiespältigen Rolle der damaligen polnischen Bevölkerung gewusst, was u.a. der Tatsache zuzuschreiben sei, dass es in der polnischen Literatur bis 1989 vergleichsweise wenige Texte gegeben hätte, die das Verhältnis der polnischen Gesellschaft zur Judenvernichtung während des Zweiten Weltkriegs themati-

oder verfälscht wurde. Doch auch in diesem Fall scheint es, dass die Groteske als Kategorie verstanden werden soll, über deren Wirkung der Rezipient entscheidet. Denn es ist schließlich der Leser, der groteske Elemente als solche dekodiert. Die Verfremdung der Welt, die auf diese Weise erzielt wird, schafft einerseits eine Distanz, die nötig ist, um die Rezeptionsblockaden zunächst zu erkennen und dann im Idealfall zu überwinden. Andererseits verweist sie auf den mit der Shoah einhergehenden Aspekt des Unvorstellbaren, des ihr Zugeschriebenen und des mit ihr Verwachsenen. Dies ist von Vertreter(inne)n der zweiten und dritten Generation in einem Verzerrungsprozess zu entsichern. So lässt sich *teilweise* gegen die Schematisierung angehen und die Erinnerung an die Shoah wachhalten. Eine Relativierung scheint jedoch hierbei mehr als nötig zu sein. Denn, wie der Literaturwissenschaftler Przemysław Czapliński konstatiert: Die Demontage der großen, für die Literatur vor 1989 charakteristischen Narration, welche sich durch Stereotypisierung und Automatisierung der Rezeptionsprozesse auszeichnete, ist nie abgeschlossen. Die Metanarration existiere in jedem Menschen und sei möglicherweise auch notwendig für eine Verständigung innerhalb einer Gemeinschaft (vgl. Czapliński 2009, 86). Dies resultiert daraus, dass einer Gruppe, welche dieselbe kollektive Identität teilt, die sich wiederum über ein gemeinsames Gedächtnis und ein gemeinsames Wissen definiert, ihre Zugehörigkeit durch „die Verwendung eines gemeinsamen Symbolsystems" (Assmann 1992, 139) im Zuge eines Sozialisationsprozesses vermittelt wird.[8] Es

---

sierten (vgl. Błoński 1994, 28; Krawczyńska/Wołowiec 2000). Stützt man sich auf die Arbeiten von Henryk Grynberg (2002) und Sławomir Buryła (2012, 480ff.) und berücksichtigt man die Tatsache, dass Texte von Seweryna Szmaglewska, Zofia Nałkowska, Tadeusz Borowski u.a. jahrelang fester Bestandteil der Schullektüre waren, so ist diese Auffassung zu korrigieren.

[8] Ähnlich argumentiert die Literaturwissenschaftlerin Ewa Wiegandt, wenn sie den autobiographischen Roman *Włoskie szpilki* (2011; *Italienische Stöckelschuhe*) von Magdalena Tulli – einer Vertreterin der zweiten Generation – bespricht. Ihrer Meinung nach lässt sich im Fall der Literatur über den Zweiten Weltkrieg und mithin über den Holocaust auf eine stereotypische Darstellung nicht verzichten, denn die Nachgeborenen seien gezwungen, auf das Wissen aus zweiter Hand zurückzugreifen (vgl. Wiegandt 2013, 153). Diesen Umstand wiederum erfasst treffend der polnische Holocaustforscher Jacek Leociak, wenn er bezüglich der Berichterstattung zum Aufstand im Warschauer Ghetto in der polnische Presse zwischen 1944 und 1989 schreibt, dass die von ihm untersuchten Texte nicht nur verraten, wie unterschiedlich – je nach politischer Lage – das Thema behandelt wurde, sondern auch viel über die Autor(inn)en selbst sagen (vgl. Leociak 2000, 49).

stellt sich daher die Frage, ob es überhaupt möglich ist, im Fall des Holocaust – der für die nachgeborenen Generationen ein vermitteltes Ereignis ist – auf die tradierte symbolische Sinnwelt zu verzichten bzw. „Worte zu entsichern" (Krysiak 2009), um so nicht nur dem „Holocaust-Reflex" (Kertész 2003, 149), sondern auch der „Abhärtung des Geistes" (Weiler 1998, 383)[9] zu entkommen. Die Dramen von Rudzka und Pałyga zeigen, dass ein Versuch lohnenswert ist. Denn auch wenn ihre Texte die Shoah-Motive in einer überzeichneten Weise bedienen, so sind sie auch einerseits Zeugnis dessen, wie der zweiten Generation die Geschichte vermittelt bzw. was während dieser Vermittlung seitens der Machthaber verschwiegen wurde – worauf unten noch einzugehen ist. Andererseits berücksichtigen sie die Kompetenzen des heutigen Lesers bzw. „aktualisieren den heutigen Leser", indem sie nicht nur „seinen Wissenszustand updaten", sondern auch versuchen, *neue* Darstellungsformen- und Mittel einzuführen, um so die Kommunikationswege aufzufrischen (Czapliński 2010, 370). Schließlich sind die hier analysierten Dramen Beispiele für einen jeweils unterschiedlichen Gestus: Rudzkas Gestus des Mitgefühls und Pałygas Gestus des Ausschlusses des Anderen. Mit anderen Worten: Rudzka verzichtet in *Fastryga* auf das eigene Ich. Eine Konsequenz hieraus ist, dass damit die Perspektive der verfolgten Minderheit gezeigt wird, wodurch diese zum Subjekt der Handlung wird. Beide Aspekte fehlen dem zweiten, in *Żyd* vertretenen Gestus, in dem die Perspektive der polnischen Mehrheit dominiert und die jüdische Minderheit zum Objekt der Handlung reduziert wird. Davon zeugt nicht nur folgendes Zitat, das die selbstbemitleidende polnische ‚Wir'-Gemeinschaft in den Vordergrund rückt:

Nie wiemy, czy [Żydzi; K.A.] piją kawę, czy jedzą bigos, czy biegają w sztafecie, czy chodzą w dresach czy w czym. Nie wiemy, jak się z nimi witać, co mówić, czego nie mówić, gdzie patrzeć, co robić, co można, czego nie można. Jedyne, co wiemy, to to, że mają brody i pejsy (Pałyga 2009, 215).[10]

---

[9] So weist Christel Weiler auf eine distanzierte Haltung der jüngeren Generationen hin, denen das wiederholte Zurückgreifen auf tradierte Schemata einen Schutzraum bietet, denn „[d]urch vieles Wiederholen verlieren die Wörter allmählich ihre Bedeutung, und der Schmerz, den sie in sich tragen, lässt nach" (Weiler 1998, 383).

[10] „Wir wissen nicht, ob sie [die Juden; K.A.] Kaffee trinken, ob sie Bigos essen, ob sie an einem Staffellauf teilnehmen, ob sie einen Trainingsanzug tragen oder etwas anderes. Wir wissen nicht, wie wir sie begrüßen sollen, was wir sagen und was wir nicht sagen dürfen, wo-

Auch der titelhafte Jude bleibt nur ein Gesprächsobjekt, das genutzt wird, um der polnischen katholischen Mehrheitsgesellschaft zu helfen, ihre Sünden zu beichten.[11] Das Drama endet mit der Begrüßung des Gastes aus Israel durch die versammelten Lehrerinnen und Lehrer, er selbst kommt aber gar nicht zur Sprache (taucht auch nicht im Personenverzeichnis auf, woraus sich schließen lässt, dass er auch während der Inszenierung nicht berücksichtigt wird). Die dialogisch-agierende Funktion des Dramas scheitert hier an der monologartigen polenzentrierten Perspektive, die für Anderes geschlossen bleibt.[12]

Einer Erklärung bedarf hierzu das Thema der unbewussten oder bewussten bzw. der ungewollten oder gewollten Erinnerung. Benjamin versteht Erinnerung – im Gegensatz zu der von Marcel Proust eingeführten und propagierten Kategorie der unwillkürlichen Erinnerung (*mémoire involontaire*) – als einen Willensakt. Der Holocaust hat sich jedoch solchermaßen in das Bewusstsein der von ihm betroffenen Nationen eingeschrieben, dass allein die Thematisierung von Juden oder von Judentum besondere Konnotationen weckt. Auf die polnische Erinnerungsarbeit treffen m.E. deshalb beide Erinnerungsarten zu. Dies ist mit dem „Schauplatz und Gedächtnisraum Polen" (Breysach 2005) zu begründen, den die sog. Jedwabne-Debatte maßgeblich geprägt hat, die nach dem Erschei-

---

hin wir schauen sollen, was wir machen sollen, was wir machen dürfen und was wir nicht machen dürfen. Das Einzige, was wir wissen, ist, dass sie Bärte und Peies haben."

[11] Niziołek spricht im Zusammenhang mit Tadeusz Słobodzianeks Drama *Nasza klasa* (2009; *Unsere Klasse*), in dem eine ähnliche Perspektive dominiert, über polnisches „Ergötzen an den eigenen Sünden" (Niziołek 2013, 550).

[12] In seinem berühmten Essay *Biedni Polacy patrzą na getto* (1987; dt. u.d.T. *Arme Polen blicken aufs Getto*) schreibt Jan Błoński, dass ein Schuldbekenntnis und die Bitte um Vergebung die polnische Gesellschaft heilen könnten. Die Schuld läge in der christlichen Sünde der Unterlassung und der kollektiven Mitschuld an der nationalsozialistischen Judenvernichtung. Sein Text lässt sich somit als ein Aufruf zur Bildung einer neuen Gesellschaft interpretieren. Eine Voraussetzung dafür wäre der Verzicht auf die eigene Unschuld, was damit zusammenhängt, dass man zusammen mit Juden und auch um die ermordeten Juden trauern würde und bereit wäre, das mythische Bild einer gutmütigen polnischen Gemeinschaft um konkrete Geschichtsbilder zu erweitern (vgl. Czapliński 2010, 344). Die historische Aufarbeitung der polnischen Mittäterschaft und deren literarische Umsetzung haben jedoch gezeigt, dass allein ein Schuldbekenntnis nicht reicht, um eine gegenüber den jüdischen Opfern angemessene Vergangenheitsbewältigung zu bewerkstelligen. Niziołek hat in seiner bahnbrechenden Monografie zum Holocaust im polnischen Theater deutlich darauf hingewiesen, dass nur – die immer noch fehlende – Empathie in der Lage wäre, der ermordeten und vertriebenen Juden zu gedenken.

nen des Buches *Sąsiedzi. Historia zagłady żydowskiego miasteczka* (*Nachbarn. Der Mord an den Juden von Jedwabne*) von Jan Tomasz Gross im Jahr 2000 entflammte und zwischen 2000 und 2003 medial ausgetragen wurde. Diese Debatte intensivierte die ohnehin bereits große Aufmerksamkeit bei der Betrachtung der auf die polnisch-jüdischen Verhältnisse bezogenen Vergangenheit und Gegenwart. Man kann daher in diesem Kontext einerseits von einer *Sensibilisierung* des kollektiven Gedächtnisses der Polen sprechen, andererseits trug diese auch zur extremen gesellschaftlichen Polarisierung bis hin zur *Kontaminierung* des Gedächtnisses bei. Denn Jedwabne steht mittlerweile stellvertretend für den polnischen Beitrag zur Judenvernichtung – wenn auch nicht im Sinne der rassenideologisch begründeten Naziverbrechen. In Bezug auf die hier analysierten Dramen und die vom Rezipienten zu leistende Erinnerungsarbeit ist folglich festzustellen, dass der Leser zwar durch den jeweiligen Kontext (im Fall von Pałygas Drama reicht bereits der Titel, bei Rudzka – der März 1968) vorbereitet bzw. *vorgewarnt* sein mag, sich somit auf eine bewusste Erinnerung einlässt. Er muss aber die durch die Sprache hervorgerufenen Konnotationen selbst in eine Bildkonstellation verwandeln und sie dann idealer Weise aktualisieren, d.h. sie im Kontext der akuten gesellschaftlichen Debatten und Probleme betrachten.[13]

Zusammenfassung

Die hier analysierten Texte der nach dem Zweiten Weltkrieg geborenen Dramatiker(innen) betrachten die Shoah aus einer vergegenwärtigenden Perspektive. Sie bauen auf einer Spannung zwischen dem primären und dem sekundären Bild auf. Lässt sich das primäre Bild problemlos deuten, so verlangt das sekundäre Bild die Aufmerksamkeit und die Mitarbeit eines Rezipienten, der entweder über einen angemessenen Wissens- bzw. Erfahrungshorizont verfügt oder mit Dan Diner einer „konstituierenden Gedächtnisgemeinschaft" angehört, deren Mitglieder sich über das Verhalten während des Zweiten Weltkriegs definieren

---

[13] Der zweite Fall lässt sich mit dem Begriff „Umspringbilder" bezeichnen. Hierbei handelt es sich um plötzlich auftauchende Elemente der Gegenwart, die als Ausgangspunkt der Narration über die Vergangenheit dienen bzw. die „Nah und Fern so verschmolzen, dass das (ferne) Grauen in die Gegenwart und den vertrauten Raum hineingeholt wird" (Asholt 2014, 90). Den Begriff führte Peter Handke in Bezug auf den charakteristischen Stil von Georges-Arthur Goldschmidt ein.

(Diner 2007, 39) – eine in der Tat wichtige Voraussetzung, um ebenfalls der Pluralität möglicher Deutungen vorzubeugen.[14] In der Entzifferungsarbeit, zu der der Leser durch eine blitzhaft auftauchende tradierte Erinnerung geradezu gezwungen wird, kontextualisiert er die Metaphern, entdeckt die Doppelschichtigkeit der Narration und macht sich deren Bezug auf die Shoah bewusst. Dieser Prozess ist als Antwort auf die von Joachim Kaiser postulierte „Mitdenk-Freiheit" (Kaiser 1965) und die von Scherpe thematisierte „Erinnerungsdiktatur"[15] der Holocaust-Überlebenden zu werten. Von dem Vergangenen wird stets erzählt, die Sprechakte selbst bauen jedoch auf den überlieferten Bildern auf. Diese dem Ökonomie-Prinzip folgende Verbildlichung resultiert einerseits aus der Unmöglichkeit der Sprache, Schmerz zu erzählen, ohne dabei unglaubwürdig zu wirken. Andererseits – durch die Überlappung von Ereignissen – werden deren gemeinsame, weil häufig voneinander abhängige oder aber aus sich heraus erschließbare Bedeutungen gewonnen, die an gegenwärtige politische und ideologische Diskussionen anknüpfen. Im Fall der Dramen von Rudzka und Pałyga wären dies zum einen der Täterdiskurs, der einen Bogen über das weit verbreitete Bild des unschuldigen Kollektivs und der schuldigen Einzeltäter schlägt, das für die Auseinandersetzung sowohl mit der Shoah als auch mit der Zeit der Volksrepublik für die polnischen Narrative charakteristisch ist; zum anderen der Antisemitismus, den Bożena Keff als eine „nicht abgeschlossene Geschichte" bezeichnet (vgl. Keff 2013). Schließlich lässt sich die Überlappungsstrategie in Rudzkas Text mit dem offiziellen Schweigen erklären, in das die beiden Ereignisse Jahrzehnte lang gehüllt waren.

Leider muss auch hier betont werden, dass der kompulsive, geradezu revisionistische Drang nach Richtigstellung der Geschichte, der in den neuesten polni-

---

[14] Ein krasses Beispiel einer Missinterpretation in den USA von Grotowskis *Akropolis* und Kantors *Die tote Klasse* liefert Romanska. Die Gründe dafür sieht die Forscherin zum einen in der Dekontextualisierung, die wiederum aus der postdramatischen Entfernung vom Text resultiere. Zum anderen aber weist sie auf das Fehlen entsprechender kultureller Kompetenz von US-Amerikanern hin, die ihnen das Entziffern der Bilder ermöglichen würden (Romanska 2014, 3f. u. 26f.).

[15] Bei Scherpe heißt es: „Nicht das Vergessen wird bekämpft wie in der Erinnerungspolitik der ersten Generation der Überlebenden, sondern die Erinnerungsdiktatur, die von den Berufsüberlebenden errichtet wurde und nur mehr als emotionale Sperre funktioniert" (Scherpe 1996, 274).

schen Dramen dominiert und anhand Pałygas Drama gezeigt werden konnte, in das Zentrum der Diskussion nicht diejenigen rückt, an die erinnert werden sollte, sondern den Erinnernden.

Literaturverzeichnis

Artwińska, Anna 2015: „Odrodziły się traumy z czasów Zagłady". Marzec 1968 jako narracja postkatastroficzna. In: Poznańskie Studia Polonistyczne. Seria Literacka 25,45, S. 187-208.

Asholt, Wolfgang 2014: Eine „écriture du désastre"? Katastrophenszenarien im Werk von Georges-Arthur Goldschmidt. In: Unfälle der Sprache. Literarische und philologische Erkundungen der Katastrophe. Hrsg. v. Ottmar Ette u. Judith Kasper. Wien, S. 77-92.

Assmann, Jan 1992: Das kulturelle Gedächtnis. Schrift, Erinnerung und politische Identität in frühen Hochkulturen. München.

Benjamin, Walter 1982: Das Passagen-Werk. Frankfurt am Main (= Gesammelte Schriften. V.1.).

ders. 2007: Über den Begriff der Geschichte. In: ders.: Erzählen. Schriften zur Theorie der Narration und zur literarischen Prosa. Frankfurt am Main, S. 129-140.

Błoński, Jan 1994: Biedni Polacy patrzą na getto. Kraków.

Breysach, Barbara 2005: Schauplatz und Gedächtnisraum Polen. Die Vernichtung der Juden in der deutschen und polnischen Literatur. Göttingen.

Brumlik, Micha 1996: Individuelle Erinnerung – kollektive Erinnerung. Psychosoziale Konstitutionsbedingungen des erinnernden Subjekts. In: Erlebnis – Gedächtnis – Sinn. Authentische und konstruierte Erinnerung. Hrsg. v. Hanno Loewy u. Bernhard Moltmann. Frankfurt am Main – New York, S. 31-45.

Buryła, Sławomir 2012: Zagłada Żydów w prozie socrealistycznej. In: Literatura polska wobec Zagłady (1939-1968). Red. Sławomir Buryła, Dorota Krawczyńska, Jacek Leociak. Warszawa, S. 465-486.

Carroll, David 1999: The Limits of Representation and the Right to Fiction: Shame, Literature, and the Memory of the Shoah. In: L'Esprit Créateur 39,4, S. 68-79.

Czapliński, Przemysław 2009: Polska do wymiany. Późna nowoczesność i nasze wielkie narracje. Warszawa.

ders. 2010: Zagłada – niedokończona narracja polskiej rzeczywistości. In: Ślady obecności. Red. Sławomir Buryła, Alina Molisak. Kraków, S. 337-381.

Diner, Dan 2007: Gegenläufige Gedächtnisse. Über Geltung und Wirkung des Holocaust. Göttingen.

Eke, Norbert Otto 2014: „Was ist wahr? Woher haben Sie denn Ihre Bilder?" Shoah-Erinnerungen in neueren Theater-Texten (Robert Menasse, Werner Fritsch, Robert Schindel, Mieczysław Weinberg). In: Der Nationalsozialismus und die Shoah in der deutschsprachigen Gegenwartsliteratur. Hrsg. v. Torben Fischer, Philip Hammermeister u. Sven Kramer. Amsterdam – New York, S. 27-49.

Gagnebin, Jeanne Marie 2006: Über den Begriff der Geschichte. In: Benjamin-Handbuch. Leben – Werk – Wirkung. Hrsg. v. Burkhardt Lindner. Stuttgart, S. 284-300.

Gross, Jan Tomasz 2000: Sąsiedzi. Historia zagłady żydowskiego miasteczka. Sejny.

Grynberg, Henryk 2002: Holocaust w literaturze polskiej. In: ders.: Prawda nieartystyczna. Wołowiec, S. 141-181.

Hillach, Ansgar 2000: Dialektisches Bild. In: Benjamins Begriffe. Bd. 1. Hrsg. v. Michael Opitz u. Erdmut Wizisla. Frankfurt am Main, S. 186-229.

Kaiser, Joachim 1965: Plädoyer gegen das Theater-Auschwitz. In: Süddeutsche Zeitung v. 4./5.9.1965.

Keff, Bożena 2013: Antysemityzm. Niezamknięta historia. Warszawa.

Kertész, Imre 2003: Wem gehört Auschwitz? Zu Roberto Benignis Film *Das Leben ist schön*. In: ders.: Die exilierte Sprache. Essays und Reden. Frankfurt am Main, S. 147-155.

Krawczyńska, Dorota – Wołowiec, Grzegorz 2000: Fazy i sposoby pisania o Zagładzie w literaturze polskiej. In: Literatura polska wobec Zagłady. Red. Alina Brodzka-Wald, Dorota Krawczyńska, Jacek Leociak. Warszawa, S. 11-28.

Krysiak, Sebastian 2009: Odbezpieczyć słowa. Rozmowa z Arturem Pałygą. In: Notatnik Teatralny 56/57, S. 189-193.

Kwaśniewska, Monika – Niziołek, Grzegorz: Wstęp. In: Zła pamięć. Przeciw-historia w polskim teatrze i dramacie. Red. Monika Kwaśniewska, Grzegorz Niziołek. Wrocław, S. 9-17.

Langer, Lawrence L. 1995: Admitting the Holocaust. Collected Essays. New York.

Lehmann, Hans-Thies 2005: Postdramatisches Theater. 3. Aufl. (1. Aufl. 1999). Frankfurt am Main.

Leociak, Jacek 2000: Rocznice powstania w getcie warszawskim w prasie polskiej: 1944-1989. In: Literatura polska wobec Zagłady. Red. Alina Brodzka-Wald, Dorota Krawczyńska, Jacek Leociak. Warszawa, S. 29-49.

Niziołek, Grzegorz 2013: Polski teatr Zagłady. Warszawa.

Pałyga, Artur 2009: Żyd. In: Notatnik Teatralny 56/57, S. 196-243.

Piejko, Magdalena 2009: Niewidzialny terror. Rozmowa z Zytą Rudzką. In: Notatnik Teatralny 56/57, S.245-248.

Rokem, Freddie 2000: Performing History. Theatrical Representations of the Past in Contemporary Theatre. Iowa.

Romanska, Magda 2014: The Post-Traumatic Theatre of Grotowski and Kantor. History and Holocaust in *Akropolis* and *The Dead Class*. London – New York – Delhi.

Rosenfeld, Alvin H. 1980: A Double Dying. Reflections on Holocaust Literature. Bloomington.

Rudnicki, Piotr 2009: Od redakcji. In: Notatnik Teatralny 56/57, S. 111.

Rudzka, Zyta 2009: Fastryga. In: Notatnik Teatralny 56/57, S. 250-282.

Ruta-Rutkowska, Krystyna 2010: Reinterpretacje przeszłości w dramacie najnowszym. In: Zapisywanie historii. Literaturoznawstwo i historiografia. Red. Włodzimierz Bolecki, Jerzy Madejski. Warszawa, S. 322-340.

Scherpe, Klaus R. 1996: Von Bildnissen zu Erlebnissen: Wandlungen der Kultur ‚nach Auschwitz'. In: Literatur und Kulturwissenschaften. Positionen, Theorien, Modelle. Hrsg. v. Hartmut Böhme u. Klaus R. Scherpe. Reinbek b. Hamburg, S. 254-282.

Semprún, Jorge 1995: Schreiben oder Leben. Aus dem Franz. übers. v. Eva Moldenhauer. Frankfurt am Main.

Tuwim, Julian 2014: Firlefanz. Ein halbes Hundert Gedichte für Kinder. Polnisch und deutsch. Norderstedt.

Weiler, Christel 1998: „Verzeihung, sind Sie Jude?" Über einen möglichen Umgang des Theaters mit Geschichte. In: Theater seit den 60er Jahren. Grenzgänge der Neo-Avantgarde. Hrsg. v. Erika Fischer-Lichte, Friedemann Kreuder u. Isabel Pflug. Tübingen – Basel, S. 375-387.

White, Hayden 1999: The Modernist Event. In: ders.: Figural Realism. Studies in the Mimesis Effect. Baltimore – London, S. 66-86.

ders. 2010: The Practical Past. In: Historein 10, S. 10-19.

ders. 2013: Historical Discourse and Literary Theory. On Saul Friedländer's *Years of Extermination*. In: Den Holocaust erzählen. Historiographie zwischen wissenschaftlicher Empirie und narrativer Kreativität. Hrsg. v. Norbert Frei u. Wulf Kansteiner. Göttingen, S. 51-78.

Wiegandt, Ewa 2013: „To" Magdaleny Tulli. In: Poznańskie Studia Polonistyczne. Seria Literacka 22,42, S. 143-156.

Young, James E. 1992: Beschreiben des Holocaust. Darstellung und Folgen der Interpretation. Aus dem Amerik. v. Christa Schuenke. Frankfurt am Main.

Aesthetics of the (Subsidiary) Image in the Latest Polish Drama: Zyta Rudzka's *Fastryga* and Artur Pałyga's *Żyd*

The constantly growing distance in time from the Shoah as well as the decease of the last contemporary witnesses go in parallel with a decrease of the individual, in the past located aesthetic approach of the holocaust survivors' generation, as opposed to perspectives of the later born generations. This is expressed by retelling the past, thereby using speech acts referring to re-constructed images. A result of this is a fragmentariness and overlap of events. They are on the one hand to be regarded as a reply to the „liberty to think for oneself", as postulated by Joachim Kaiser. On the other hand they put the object of remembrance at risk of being misunderstood by the addressees. However, only by means of specific procedures the authors of dramas can create authenticity, can escape the „dictatorship of memory" (Klaus Scherpe), and open up new spaces of memory and remembrance. The article shows how these problems are dealt with in the two Polish dramas: *Fastryga* by Zyta Rudzka, and *Żyd* by Artur Pałyga.

Between the *Post-* and *Popmemory*.
Holocaust Narrative in Contemporary Culture –
an Attempt of Exemplification

Urszula Kowalska, Poznań

> You cannot get out of history, history cannot be cancelled,
> and you cannot live outside history –
> these are desires or visions more fantastic than the time machine. […]
> History did not pass and history will not come.
> We are living in the middle of history, thousands years behind us,
> and thousands years before us. We are sticking in history up to the ears.
> Nowhere to escape, nobody to rescue us… (Hejl 1990, 237)[1]

European historians, writers, artists and museum's experts are facing nowadays the question of how to adjust memory about the Shoah to the potential of modern recipients. The phenomenon of the well-known *postmemory* is now complementary to the new phenomenon of *popmemory*. This triggers the need to reflect upon the ways in which the Holocaust functions in modern memory and if its literary or artistic recollection still remains an interpretation, defaulted to a continuous defeat when facing attempts to understand, or forewarn against threats in the 21st century.[2]

The necessity (or maybe: danger?) of accepting somebody else's experience is now affecting the third generation – grandchildren (also in a metaphoric way) of the survivors. They are also the recipients of other projects, causing different reactions: texts, movies, comic books, museum exhibitions, games, or so called ‚educational programmes'.

---

[1] „Z historie nelze vystoupit, historii nelze zrušit a nelze žít mimo historii – to jsou tužby nebo fikce fantastičtější než stroj času. […] Historie neminula a historie teprve nepřijde; žijeme uprostřed historie, tisíc let za námi a tisíc let před námi, stojíme v historii oběma nohama a vězíme v ní až po krk, nikam z ní neunikneme a nikdo nás jí nezprostí" (all translations from Czech and Polish – U.K.).

[2] Small parts of this article were presented during the international conference in Prague (V. kongres světové literárněvědné bohemistiky, Prague, 29th June – 4th July 2015) and will be published in Czech in the volume entitled *Paměť válek a konfliktů*, eds. Alexander Kratochvil a Jiří Soukup (autumn 2016).

There are some shocking changes in the artistic methods of depicting the experience of the Shoah and thereby shifting the ‚Holocaust's decorum' in contemporary literature, art and movies. There is a temporal, a technological and, most probably, a mental gap between *Schindler's list* by Steven Spielberg and *Inglourious Basterds* by Quentin Tarantino or *Shielding the Flame* by Hanna Krall and *The Night of the Living Jews* by Igor Ostachowicz.

An inspiration for writing this article was in some way the novel written by Jáchym Topol *Chladnou zemí* (2009)[3], the text in which one of the main characters belongs to the so called „bunk seekers" („hledače pryčen"). They are grandsons of the witnesses, victims of the Holocaust, representatives of so called ‚third generation'. They are upholding the common, inherited memory (or maybe the lack of memory?) and carrying – according to the motto borrowed from the Polish writer Dorota Masłowska – „someone else's scars". Nowadays they become the participants of the memory relay, their generation subsequently becomes a projected recipient of new texts of culture, of new ways of dealing with the untransferable trauma.

Modern dispute about literary, artistic and media representations of the Holocaust and the Second World War is focusing on: witnesses of the 20th century, people inheriting memory and trauma, the second and the third generation, as well as the postmodern generation that is getting to know the past only thanks to modern mass media.

> The guardianship of the Holocaust is being passed on to us. The second generation is the hinge generation in which received, transferred knowledge of events is being transmuted into history, or into myth. It is also the generation in which we can think about certain question arising from the Shoah with a sense of living connection. (Eva Hoffmann *After such knowledge*, quoted from Hirsch 2012, 1)

Mikołaj Grynberg, a photographer, psychologist and grandson of survivors of the Holocaust, is the author of two volumes of interviews with representatives of different generations, affected by the same (although not identical) trauma (Grynberg 2012; Grynberg 2014). He is also the creator of an artistic and educational project *Auschwitz – co ja tu robię* (*Auschwitz – what am I doing here?*).[4] He places himself in a position of a representative of the second generation

---

[3] The English translation, *Devil's workshop*, prepared by Aleš Zucker, was published in 2013.
[4] See http://www.auschwitz.grynberg.pal/ (15.2.2016).

which is differently described as: „generation of postmemory", „hinge generation", „guardianship of the Holocaust"... The subtitle of the volume gathering Grynberg's conversations with survivors is: *There will be no one to tell this after us, at best somebody will read this*. In the introduction, the author writes:

> I was in a hurry and I made it, but I know very well that memory, that has been guarded by them so far, is coming under our supervision. I am aware that time doesn't heal any wounds. It just blurs the past. (Grynberg 2012, 9)[5]

In his newest publication under the title *Oskarżam Auschwitz. Opowieści rodzinne* (*I Accuse Auschwitz. Family Stories*) Grynberg speaks with his „brothers and sisters after the Shoah" (Grupińska 2014, 8). The reasons why he wants to speak with them are obvious for him: „I am searching for ways to tell about things happening in our heads" (Grynberg 2014, 185); „We feel that we have a second chance, although, we have never lost the first one" (ibid., 17); „I am conscious of the fact that the temperature of this message is going to decrease soon" (ibid., 263).[6]

Grynberg's interlocutors react differently to his questions, although, independently from the generation represented by them, there is one common doubt that the majority of them shares: „What do you need this for? Don't you want to write more cheerful books?". The classical form of the above mentioned interviews fits within the traditional school of Polish reportage. The conversations with representatives of different generations of Holocaust victims are presented independently from fashions and pop-cultural trends. Nowadays, it turns usually into a meeting of three generations („owners' or rather „users' of different types of memory: in the classical version and the one enriched with prefixes *post-* or *pop-*).

Not only literature is confronted with the conflict between maintaining historical memory in an attractive form and its authenticity, between the necessity of triggering shock (one of foundations of memorizing) and the danger of drastic,

---

[5] „Spieszyłem się i zdążyłem, ale bardzo dobrze wiem, że pamięć, której dotąd strzegli oni, przechodzi pod naszą opiekę. Zdaję sobie sprawę, że czas nie leczy ran, tylko zamazuje przeszłość".

[6] „Szukam sposobu, żeby opowiedzieć innym o tym, co się dzieje w naszych głowach"; „Czuję, że mam drugą szansę, mimo, że sam nigdy nie straciłem pierwszej"; „Mam świadomość tego, że temperatura tego przekazu niedługo zacznie spadać".

unexplainable, traumatic emotions, amongst the representatives of the generation that, according to one of Grynberg's speakers „should simply carry on living" (cf. Grynberg 2012, 176).[7] Andrzej Szpociński claims that the last few years brought a significant transformation of „social memory": „*privatization* (understood as an exposition of the human dimension of historic events)" and a „*new type of historical sensitivity*, the need for authentic experiencing the past" (Szpociński 2007, 32). These transformations result in increasing historical empathy and equally in the danger of „empathic kitsch" that is near to the dangerous „ game of surviving ". One of the most important problems of modern times and historical education is the quite frequently crossed borderline of uncrossability of experience. Too detailed simulation and overflowing illusion may trigger a sort of „usurpation of suffering". Reinhart Koselleck wrote:

> Together with the generational change also the object of observation is changing. From the ‚present past' saturated with experience arises a ‚pure past', which slipped experience. [...] When memory dies, not only the distance is growing, but also the quality changes. Soon only files, enriched with images, videos and notes will be telling something. (quoted from Assmann 2009, 105)

Aleida Assmann, while talking about the retrospective character of memory and the crisis of experience, underlines the difficult passage from the living (individual) memory to an artificial (cultural) one (ibid., 109). This passage is difficult, as frequently it is combined with ‚deformation', ‚reduction' and ‚instrumentalization' of memorized content. In the times of the dusk of witnesses a race against time is going on, together with a fight for preserving the common memory of experience and certain common knowledge that might come into play only as a result of dialogue between generations.

The novel *Devil's workshop* mentioned before might be an important voice in the disputes about modern transformations of historical memory as well as about thoughtless promotions of the phenomenon, that throughout the world has gained multiple supporters (not to say: believers) – so called *edutainment*. It is worth mentioning what Vít Šisler, coordinator of the multimedia project

---

[7] The author has heard for example: „You should write about funny things, Mr Grynberg. You are going to cry for all your life. What for?" (Grynberg 2012, 175; „Niech pan pisze o wesołych rzeczach książki. Panie Grynberg, będzie pan potem płakał całe życie. Po co tak ma być?"); „What do you need this for? [...] Your life won't be better because of listening to this" (ibid., 312 et seq.; „Po co to panu? [...] Pana życie nie będzie lepsze od słuchania tego").

Československo 38-89, points out: in contemporary education there is no space for *edutainment*. 'Covering' educationally difficult content with games and plays, assuming that each attempt at enhancing attractiveness brings good results – is a mistake. There is even a term for such a simplified didactic thinking – *sugar-coated learning* (cf. Dobrovský 2014, 35).

The fundamental question to ask is: where are the limits of *popmemory* (understood as trendy and attractive 'mass-focused' method for strengthening and providing next generations with experiences from the past)? Where is the borderline between pop-cultural behavioural model of preserving memory, which could be another shocking stage of dramatizing, or maybe reconstructing memory, and popular kitsch? What happens to memory during the times of being generally fed up with the topic of war and Shoah, during the times of expending (both: the content and the form), during the times of domination of pictorial culture? Isn't it true, that purely pictorial memory is a kind of 'Biblia pauperum' – it offends lack of knowledge, influences emotions, it does not follow the classical rules of decorum? As Lisa Saltzman claims:

> In conjunction with the presentation of the history [kitsch – U.K.] transforms traumatic experience into fictional melodramas, adds a cathartic dimension to the disaster. Kitsch avoids reflection and painful confrontation required by the avantgarde culture and replaces it with pleasure of continues satisfaction. Kitsch, in conjunction with the presentation of history, the history of fascism, the Holocaust, genocide, makes this story too understandable, digestible, easy to consume. (Saltzman 2004, 204)

These are of course not really new problems. Adorno already wrote about the debt that imagination owes to history and the necessity of seeking for a form that would enable uncovering the suffering. In the outstanding monograph *Obrazy i klisze. Między biegunami wizualnej pamięci Zagłady* (*Pictures and Clichés. Between the Poles of the Visual Memory of the Shoah*) Bartosz Kwieciński writes: „Memory asks for responsibility, not solely for the comfort of participation" (Kwieciński 2012, 11).

What is this „comfort of participation" about? In my opinion, this is well explained even by the first film adaptations, for example the TV series *Holocaust* from the late 70s, or the movie that has shaped the western perception of the Shoah (and, at the same time, 'americanized' it) – *Schindler's List*. They perfectly confirm Kwieciński's conclusion: that myths and symbols constructed by mass culture are creating undoubtedly common, global, historical consciousness. In the book *Auschwitz w Internecie. Przedstawienia Holokaustu w kulturze popularnej* (*Auschwitz on the Internet – The Presentations of the Holocaust in Popular Culture*) published in 2012, Marek Kaźmierczak points out additionally that the process of trivialization of the evil in mass culture is goes along with lack of competence, sensitiveness and critical consciousness.

I am of the opinion that the examples of the Holocaust's representation and of wartime stories that are present in Polish and Czech media are showing a (not always valuable) pop-vision of memory. Though the „virus of pophistory" – a term used by Iwona Kokoszka (2010, 4) – doesn't have to rely on simplification and trivialization, it can be used in a meaningful way. Searching for new methods of expression, focused not only on feelings but also on knowledge, is still continuing.

I am going to present a selected number of happenings that raised some interest in Polish and Czech media. In my opinion they are representing a modern approach to the topics related to war and the Holocaust, above all because of the dialogue between generations that is embedded in them. As every choice this list of happenings is very limited and subjective. It should be treated only as an attempt of an exemplification of cultural and artistic phenomena popular nowadays in Poland and the Czech Republic.

Comic books

For a number of years comic books have been an artistic space where difficult topics were raised. Surely it ceased to be linked purely with entertainment, although one of the foundations of existence for this form of expression is the knowledge sharing aspect. Nowadays, quite a few inheritors of Art Spiegelman can be named and most of their attempts at intersemiotic translations could be described as quite successful ones. But how to interpret Chmielewski's *Tytus, Romek i A'Tomek jako warszawscy powstańcy 1944* (*Tytus, Romek & A'Tomek as Participants of the Warsaw Uprising 1944*)[8] in which the popular monkey

---

[8] The publisher notes: „Papcio Chmiel's work includes 36 charts presenting the adventures of Titus, Romek and A'Tomek during the Warsaw Uprising. Each board is a separate story, a little anecdote telling with the typical Papcio Chmiel sense of humor".

becomes one of the main actors of the most tragic event in modern history of Poland? Quite an opposite example is *Anne Frank's Diary* translated into the language of a comic book (Jacobson/Colón 2013).[9] It met in the Czech Republic with great enthusiasm but also with a wave of criticism because of the overwhelming numbers, facts and figures that prevent it from getting through to any recipient. These are only two extreme examples of some perils following attempts of trying to adjust difficult content to a lighter (at least by definition) form. On the first pole we have an infantilization of experience (with Titus the Monkey in a leading role), on the opposite one, the loss of a light-hearted narration for the sake of facts and figures. Both of these narrations are not convincing to the modern recipient.

But there is light in the tunnel – works such as a volume of comic stories published in 2011 *Ještě jsme ve válce. Příběhy 20. století* (*We Are Still in War. Stories of the 20th Century*). In my opinion it is worth mentioning, as the book is some sort of creative comeback to well proven methods connected to documentary literature. And at the same time the border of artistic fantasy, fiction that remains just a bonus to authentic memories, was clearly marked. The editors point out that each of the comics has been influenced by a personal experience, a story, a conversation with a witness. These conversations serve only as an inspiration. The statement from the epilogue, „We are also learning how to pass on the stories we have learnt" (Fantová/Polouček 2011, 179), should be a hint for the possessors of ultimate truths in the times of a growing commercialization of memory.

Games

On the European market new board games or role playing games appear frequently. They seem to be bored with worlds full of fairies and trolls and they reach to a less distant past as a source of inspiration. In a sense *The Charnel Houses of Europe – Shoah* from 1997 paved the way in the historical games business. More than ten years later, thanks to the application *Auschwitz Liberation Defeat* it has been already possible ‚to become' a Soviet soldier, who is lib-

---

[9] The original edition was prepared by Sid Jacobson and Ernie Colón in 2005: Anne Frank. The Anne Frank House Authorized Graphic Biography. New York.

erating a concentration camp. A few years ago a big controversy emerged because of the simulation game *Imagination is the Only Escape* created by the British Luc Bernard, who prepared the project of the game that was supposed to introduce young western recipients with the issue of the Holocaust in Europe.

But there is also a project that seems quite new (at least in the Czech Republic), being a combination of interactive game, comic book and even (as it is underlined by the coordinator Vít Šisler) a virtual museum. It fits not only into the sphere of entertainment, but is a sort of interdisciplinary project of an educationally-artistic nature. Serious game on contemporary history: *Československo 38-89*.

> Czechoslovakia 38-89 is a complex educational simulation for high school students. Its educational objective is to present key events from Czechoslovakia's contemporary history and to enable students to ‚experience' these events from the perspectives of the different actors. In doing so, the simulation aims to develop a deeper understanding of the multifaceted political, social and cultural aspects of this historical period. The simulation has been developed at the Faculty of Arts and the Faculty of Mathematics and Physics of the Charles University in Prague and the Institute of Contemporary History of the Academy of Sciences of the Czech Republic. The development of the simulation was supported by the Czech Ministry of Culture in 2011-2014. (see http://cs3889.com/ [15.2.2016])

It's worth paying some attention to an important aspect of the subjectivity of the speech, the attitude towards the experiences of and the conversations with the witnesses. Especially the role that is being entered by the potential recipient is important. His task is not coming down to for example assassinating Reinhard Heydrich or surviving the interrogation. The aim is to gain information, to familiarize oneself with the authentic documentation, to seek for messages that, according to the fictional plot of the game, would let us find out about our grandfather who was taken by Gestapo in 1942. It is here, in the participation of the ‚player', where the thin line between ethical and unethical emerges.

Film

One of film scientists from Poznań, Wojciech Otto, attempted to differentiate the Holocaust in Internet video portals, by characterizing the respective sources as „telling the truth", „propagandistic" or „provocative" (cf. Otto 2011). A work by the Jewish artist Jane Korman can be regarded as belonging to the latter category. In a short documentary *Dancing In Auschwitz* she presents the story of her father.[10] Quite possibly, the idea itself is not that bad. The actual realization is something different though cheerful dancing to the evergreen *I will survive* (in front of for example the main gate of Auschwitz-Birkenau concentration camp) in reality looks rather weird and artificial. Dressing up the participants of this dance in T-shirts with the words *survivor* and *3rd generation* creates the impression that the meeting of different generations and the dance of grandpa the survivor together with his grandchildren is fake and superficial (despite the presence of both: the witness and the testimony).

Completely different is the relationship between the survivor and his descendants in a documentary film from 2008, under the controversial title *Pizza in Auschwitz* (directed by Moshe Zimmerman). The eccentric main character of this road movie, a former prisoner, decided to return to the past and is taking his adult children on this traumatic journey. The grotesque image including spending a night, drinking cola, eating pizza and smoking cigarettes on the bunks in Auschwitz-Birkenau concentration camp was quite well received among young recipients in Poland, despite underlining „being bored with the subject" and „being used to more controversial visions" (Aksamit 2014). They are treating the main protagonist as a person not quite sane and accountable, but at the same time, they are also identifying (despite the age difference) themselves with the emotional and moving words of the daughter: „it's over, you can't recreate it!"; „we want to take you from here"; „we've got enough Holocaust"; „be happy, that we don't understand you".

New Czech docu-reality show

The time has come for a total novelty. The Czech public TV broadcaster has recently presented a show that was based on a global scale popular genre of *Living History*. The production, under the not so tasteful title *Holidays in the Protec-*

---

[10] Detailed information about the project could be found on the official artist's website: http://www.janekormanart.com/janekormanart.com/16.Dancing_Auschwitz/16.Dancing_Ausc hwitz.html (15.2.2016).

torate[11] (*Dovolená v Protektorátu*) takes a selected Czech family directly into the times of the Second World War. A three generation family is competing in this ‚game' for millions of Czech crowns. They will get them, if they manage to survive for eight weeks in a lonesome hut in the eastern part of the country. The emotions are high (both for the family, as well as for the spectators) because although the participants were taking into consideration being moved back in time, they didn't expect being moved to the times of the Second World War (together with everything that this time brought in reality: inflation, starvation, compulsory German classes, censorship, indoctrination, interrogations, race proving, meetings with Gestapo, etc.).

The creator of the programme that is creatively called „(docu)reality show" claims: „this is the didactical form showing the history to the spectators in a more clear format" (Mocková 2015). The ‚only' problem is that the border between reality and fiction disappears dangerously, especially for the youngest participants of the ‚game' and senior family members, whose personal memories are being brought to life. Historical knowledge is here presented in the anachronistic form of old photos accompanied by a commentary that from time to time enriches the show. This educational aspect seems quite old-fashioned at the moment and surely is not correlating with the expectations of younger generation.

The author of the programme is quite enthusiastically (and lacking any afterthought) reflecting on the controversial Zimbardo experiment from the 1970s in which the students were given roles of guards and prisoners (cf. Mocková 2015). The experiment was stopped, *Holidays in the Protectorate* – not.

What is horrifying, is not only the ignorance, but also the unhealthy excitement of the creators triggered by the observation that after some days the family really started to hate its German molesters (that were played by Czech actors…). Is it really possible today to have a show testing how a modern family would survive in the dramatic conditions of the Protectorate, in a Europe united under the themes of integration and historical forgiving? Despite attempts at the most

---

[11] The programme was broadcasted by Czech TV during eight weeks in spring 2015. Detailed information, family and project description, or episodes are to be found on the website: http://www.ceskatelevize.cz/porady/10871520054-dovolena-v-protektoratu/ (15.2.2016).

adequate reconstruction of wartime reality, the show is lacking above all truth and respect for authentic testimony and memories of the survivors. Creators of the programme seem to be deaf to warnings about the necessity of remembering *not to let history re-occur*. One of the comments on the forum on official website of the show seems to be summarizing the situation quite well: „What next? Holidays in concentration camp?".

Writers, historians, painters, movie-makers, philosophers, and programmers are faced today with an ever-actual question: how far can we move in interpreting the reality, knowing that memory has apart from the cognitive and political dimension, also an aesthetic one. Not to mention ethical.

Details are decisive for the appropriateness of the chosen method: inverted coma before the word „to live through" in the game teaser, access to knowledge based on recognition and conversation, not on an attempt to pretend the feelings, engaging real witnesses of the time, not only the people who are „professionals".

And what about the motivation? The main character of Jáchym Topol's short story keeps on repeating: „we wanted to protect it, nothing else mattered to us". But this repetitive quote is turning into a line learnt by heart that is covering the obvious reasons for institutionalizing suffering. There are a bit too many similar declarations in the real world. In the present era of *popmemory*, there is luckily some space for memory that is not only reasonable, but returns as a responsible task. This is confirmed, against all the artificial festive events and reality show-like projects, by truthful artistic, literature and cultural events. They prove that there *is* a popular face of the memory about the Holocaust and the war that is not based on imaginations, myths, legends and stereotypes, but on testimony and experience. Literature, art, film, even computer games, consciousness of time passing by, are returning to a conversation with a survivor. And for this reason, regardless of the ‚pop' suggested by myself, in many cases the culture of memory go round the circle, stays classical and traditional despite the modern methods. Because the truth is, what Cathy Caruth claims: „history, like the trauma, is never simply one's own, that history is precisely the way we are implicated in each other's traumas" (Caruth 1995, 192).

Bibliography

Aksamit, Bożena 2014: „Pizza w Auschwitz". Polecamy dokument. http://wyborcza.pl/duzyformat/1,142470,17104015,_Pizza_w_Auschwitz___Polecamy_dokument.html (15.2.2016).

Assmann, Aleida 2009: Przestrzenie pamięci. Formy i przemiany pamięci kulturowej. Transl. from German Piotr Przybyła. In: Pamięć zbiorowa i kulturowa współczesna perspektywa niemiecka. Ed. by Magdalena Saryusz-Wolska. Kraków, pp. 101-142.

Caruth, Cathy 1995: Explorations in Memory. London.

Chmielewski, Henryk Jerzy 2012: Tytus, Romek i A'Tomek jako warszawscy powstańcy 1944. Warszawa.

Dobrovský, Pavel 2014: Hry se nedají od politiky oddělit. Rozhovor s Vítem Šislerem. In: Level 248, pp. 34-41.

Fantová, Jana – *Polouček*, Jan (eds.) 2011: Ještě jsme ve válce. Příběhy dvacatého století. Praha.

Grupińska, Anka 2014: Wysłuchiwanie Zagłady i rozmawianie o schedzie pozagładowej. In: Grynberg 2014, pp. 7-15.

Grynberg, Mikołaj 2012: Ocaleni z XX wieku. Po nas nikt już nie opowie, najwyżej ktoś przeczyta. Warszawa.

id. 2014: Oskarżam Auschwitz. Opowieści rodzinne. Wołowiec.

Hejl, Vilém 1990: Rozvrat. Mnichov a náš osud. Praha.

Hirsch, Marianne 2012: The Generation of Postmemory. Writing and Visual Culture after the Holocaust. New York.

Jacobson, Sid – *Colón*, Ernie 2013: Anne Franková – komiks. Transl. Miroslava Ludvíková. Praha.

Kaźmierczak, Marek 2012: Auschwitz w Internecie. Przedstawienia Holokaustu w kulturze popularnej. Poznań.

Kokoszka, Iwona 2010: Popyt na pop-historię. http://www.forbes.pl/artykuly/sekcje/sekcja-strategie/popyt-na-pop-historie,3376,1# (15.2.2016).

Kwieciński, Bartosz 2012: Obrazy i klisze. Między biegunami wizualnej pamięci Zagłady. Kraków.

Mocková, Zuzana 2015: Dovolená v protektorátu není o koncentrácích, říká režisérka. Rozhovor s autorkou a režisérkou televizního pořadu Dovolená v protektorátu o kritických recenzích, předpojatosti diváků i podstatě reality show. http://magazin.aktualne.cz/televize/nechteli-jsme-jim-hrozit-koncentraky-rika-reziserka/r~f300ab40085411e59d310025900fea04/ (15.2.2016).

Otto, Wojciech 2011: Prawda, prowokacja, propaganda. Obrazy Holocaustu w internetowych serwisach plików wideo. In: Images 8,15/16, pp. 67-80.

Saltzman, Lisa 2004: Awangarda i kicz raz jeszcze. O etyce reprezentacji. Transl. from English Katarzyna Bojarska. In: Literatura na Świecie 1/2, pp. 201-216.

Szpociński, Andrzej 2007: O współczesnej kulturze historycznej Polaków. In: Przemiany pamięci społecznej a teoria kultury. Red. Bartosz Korzeniowski. Poznań, pp. 25-42.

Topol, Jáchym 2009: Chladnou zemí. Praha.

Zwischen *Post-* und *Popmemory*.
Erzählen über den Holocaust in der Gegenwartskultur –
Versuch einer Exemplifikation

Der Artikel greift die Frage nach den gegenwärtigen Veränderungen der Erinnerung an den Holocaust und des Erzählens darüber in der polnischen und tschechischen Kultur und Kunst auf. Noch immer bleibt die Frage unbeantwortet, welche Erinnerungen die Repräsentanten der dritten Generation haben, unter denen sich immerhin junge Leute befinden, die sich eine KZ-Nummer auf den Arm tätowieren lassen. Welche Erinnerung symbolisiert die Armee der ‚Pritschensucher' in Jáchym Topols Novelle *Die Teufelswerkstatt*? Was gibt der jungen Generation ein Film wie *Dancing in Auschwitz*, in dem am Ende Jugendliche und Holocaust-Überlebender mit einer KZ-Baracke im Hintergrund tanzen? Was bedeuten heute die Worte der Tochter des ehemaligen KZ-Häftlings aus dem Film *Pizza In Auschwitz*: „we've got enough Holocaust, be happy, that we don't understand you"? Sind die unter dem bedeutungsvollen Titel *Ještě jsme ve válce* (*Wir sind noch im Krieg*) gesammelten Versuche, einzelne Holocaust-Schicksale als Comic darzustellen, möglicherweise eine andere Art des Sprechens in einer Zeit, in der man des Themas müde geworden ist und nicht mehr weiß, was und wie über Krieg und Holocaust geredet werden soll? Wie funktioniert heute der Holocaust im Dialog und welche Generationen nehmen an diesem Dialog teil? Wo verläuft die Grenze zwischen *memory*, *postmemory* und *popmemory* über den Holocaust in einer Zeit, in der die Bildkultur dominiert? In welche Richtung geht in der heutigen Entwicklung des Holocaust-Verständnisses die Diskussion über die Kommunikation mit Bildern? Kann eine Erfahrung virtualisiert werden? Dürfen die Zeugnisliteratur, Gespräche usw. durch Simulationen, ‚Bildungsprogramm' oder Computerspiele ersetzt werden?

Die Transzendierung der Geschichte durch die Poetisierung der Darstellung in Jiří Weils Prosazyklus *Barvy (Farben)*

Andreas Ohme, Jena

> Die Geschichte des Holocaust ist nicht vorbei.
> Er ist ein Präzedenzfall, der ewig währt,
> und seine Lektionen haben wir noch nicht gelernt.
> (Snyder 2015, 12)

Einleitung

Auch wenn die nationalsozialistischen Verbrechen, die im Massenmord an den europäischen Juden gipfelten, bereits während des Zweiten Weltkriegs nicht unbemerkt bleiben konnten, herrschte nach dessen Ende zunächst ein erhöhtes Informationsbedürfnis, welches nicht nur der Dimension dieser Verbrechen galt, sondern auch ihrer konkreten Planung und Durchführung. Eine zentrale Rolle spielten dabei Augenzeugenberichte in Form von Ego-Dokumenten, doch auch die thematisch einschlägige Belletristik aus der unmittelbaren Nachkriegszeit weist eine starke Tendenz zum sachlichen Bericht auf, wie etwa die Erzählungen von Tadeusz Borowski und Zofia Nałkowska belegen.[1] Eine vergleichbare Stilisierung in Richtung des Dokumentarischen findet sich auch in der tschechischen Nachkriegsbelletristik, die diesem Thema gewidmet ist, worauf bereits Reinhard Ibler (2012, 65) hingewiesen hat.

Vor diesem Hintergrund erscheint der 1946 publizierte Prosazyklus *Barvy (Farben)* des tschechischen Schriftsteller Jiří Weil (1900 – 1959), der als Jude die Shoah nur deshalb überlebte, weil er sich dem Transport ins Lager durch einen fingierten Suizid entziehen konnte, als eine der wenigen Ausnahmen von

---

[1] Vgl. die Erzählsammlungen *Byliśmy w Oświęcimiu* (1946; *Wir waren in Auschwitz*) und *Kamienny świat* (1945; *Die steinerne Welt*) von Borowski und *Medaliony* (1946; *Medaillons*) von Nałkowska. Es ist deshalb auch kein Zufall, dass diese Erzählungen immer wieder als standpunktgebundenes Sprechen ihrer konkreten Autoren (miss-)verstanden worden sind. Trotz der in ihnen zum Tragen kommenden diversen Authentisierungsstrategien, zu denen eben auch die Nüchternheit der Darstellung zählt, handelt es sich bei ihnen jedoch um fiktionale Texte, die als Kunstwerke wahrgenommen werden wollen. Zur künstlerischen Gestaltung der Texte, insbesondere unter dem Aspekt des Emotionalen, vgl. die jüngst erschienenen Beiträge von Krystyna Jakowska (2016) und Andrea Meyer-Fraatz (2016).

dieser Regel, da für ihn ein völlig anderer Zugang zur literarischen Gestaltung der nationalsozialistischen Gewaltverbrechen charakteristisch ist.[2] Statt mit einer präzisen und sachlichen Schilderung von Ereignissen wird der Rezipient hier mit verschiedenen Verfahren der Stilisierung und Poetisierung konfrontiert, die die Texte trotz der Verankerung ihres Gegenstandes in der brutalen Realität dezidiert als Schöne Literatur ausweisen und damit auch ihren Kunstcharakter bewusst machen. Im Folgenden soll daher der Frage nachgegangen werden, um welche Verfahren es sich dabei im Einzelnen handelt und welche Funktion sie in den jeweiligen Texten erfüllen. Daraus lassen sich sodann Rückschlüsse auf Weils spezifischen Umgang mit der Holocaustthematik in seinem Zyklus *Barvy* ziehen.

Der Zyklus *Barvy*

Er besteht aus zehn Prosatexten, die jeweils mit den Bezeichnungen zweier Farben betitelt sind. Die Texte, von denen nach Aussage des Autors einige während seiner klandestinen Existenz verloren gegangen waren und deshalb später neu geschrieben werden mussten (vgl. Weil 1966, 91), entstanden in den Jahren zwischen 1943 und 1945 und haben jeweils einen Umfang von lediglich drei bis fünf Druckseiten. Diese relative Kürze hat erhebliche Konsequenzen für den Textaufbau, da durch sie die Entfaltung einer längeren Handlungsfolge per se ausgeschlossen ist. An ihre Stelle tritt, wie bereits Jiří Opelík (1966, 192) in einem der immer noch vergleichsweise wenigen Forschungsbeiträge zu Weils Kurzprosa festgestellt hat, die Schilderung einzelner Situationen. Diese Situationen sind alles andere als alltäglich, vielmehr geht es in den meisten von ihnen – durchaus im Wortsinn – um Leben und Tod, wie einige Beispiele verdeutlichen mögen. In *Zelená a rudá* (*Grün und Rot*) soll ein Mann dazu gezwungen werden, jemanden zu verraten, doch entzieht er sich dieser Zwangslage durch Selbstmord; in *Hnědá a bílá* (*Braun und Weiß*) versucht ein Flüchtling seinen

---

[2] Der Begriff Shoah wird hier für die Planung und Durchführung des nationalsozialistischen Massenmords an den europäischen Juden verwendet, während der Begriff des Holocaust auch die anderen Opfergruppen, also etwa Sinti und Roma, Homosexuelle und Menschen mit Behinderung, einschließt. Zu dieser nicht unproblematischen terminologischen Frage vgl. Feuchert 2004, 17-30.

Häschern zu entkommen; in *Žlutá a černá* (*Gelb und Schwarz*) begibt sich ein Mann nach einer entsprechenden Aufforderung widerstandslos in die Hände seiner Mörder, ohne dabei seine Würde zu verlieren; und in *Fialová a černá* (*Lila und Schwarz*) wird – letztlich erfolglos – ein Haus gegen Angreifer verteidigt. Die geschilderten Situationen lassen also durchaus einen Rest an Ereignishaftigkeit erkennen, doch ist sie bisweilen nahezu auf ein Minimum reduziert.

Eine weitere Eigenart der Texte besteht darin, dass die jeweiligen Situationen weitgehend isoliert dargeboten werden, indem sie aus dem kausal-temporalen Handlungsgefüge gleichsam herausgeschnitten sind. Zwar ist in einzelnen Fällen ein möglicher Ausgang des geschilderten Konflikts immerhin angedeutet, doch fehlt grundsätzlich die Vorgeschichte. Dem Rezipienten wird auf diese Weise eine Erklärung, wie es zu den einzelnen Situationen überhaupt kommen konnte, konsequent vorenthalten. Durch diese Dekontextualisierung des Geschehens wirken die dargestellten Situationen weniger wie Teile eines singulären Handlungszusammenhangs, sondern nehmen eher den Charakter des Typischen an.

Diese Tendenz zur Typisierung wird noch dadurch verstärkt, dass die Figuren in aller Regel keine Namen tragen und dass auch Orts- und Zeitangaben nahezu vollständig fehlen.[3] Auch im Hinblick auf die raum-zeitliche Situierung des Geschehens findet also eine Dekontextualisierung statt, die freilich durch einige klar identifizierbare lebensweltliche Bezüge immer wieder unterlaufen wird. So ist etwa wiederholt die Rede von Nummern, die auf das Handgelenk tätowiert bzw. eingebrannt sind (vgl. Weil 1966, 112, 119 und 126), in *Žlutá a černá* wird ein aufgenähter Stern in eben diesen Farben erwähnt (vgl. ebd., 112), und auch wenn die Verbrennungsöfen und Massengräber nicht direkt als solche benannt sind, werden die entsprechenden Konzepte durch die jeweiligen Umschreibungen dennoch eindeutig aufgerufen (vgl. ebd., 97, 119 und 121). Gleiches gilt für das „gebrochene Kreuz" („lomený kříž"; ebd., 113), das unschwer als Hakenkreuz zu identifizieren ist. Ein weiterer Realitätsbezug wird über Paratexte hergestellt, da jeder der zehn Texte einer historischen Persönlichkeit gewidmet ist, die auf die eine oder die andere Art Opfer der nationalsozialistischen Gewalt

---

[3] Neben *Žlutá a modrá* (*Gelb und Blau*), ein Text, auf den im Weiteren noch ausführlich einzugehen sein wird, gibt es lediglich zwei weitere Ausnahmen, nämlich *Zelená a rudá*, wo die Namen Jana Marie und Karel genannt werden, sowie *Černá a bílá* (*Schwarz und Weiß*), wo der Name der oberfränkischen Stadt Hof fällt.

geworden ist, wie beispielsweise Milada Frantová, Pavel Eisner oder auch Milena Jesenská. Alle direkten Benennungen, wie etwa Jude, Deutscher oder Nationalsozialist, sind dagegen konsequent ausgespart.[4] Eine historische Situierung ist mithin durchaus gegeben, doch erfolgt sie lediglich indirekt über das beim Leser vorausgesetzte Kontextwissen, über das die zeitgenössischen Rezipienten unzweifelhaft verfügten und das bis heute zumindest in Europa zum Allgemeinwissen gezählt werden kann.

In den zehn Texten aus *Barvy* sind mithin zwei gegensätzliche Tendenzen erkennbar: Aufgrund bestimmter Realien kommt es bisweilen zu einer Verankerung der dargestellten Situationen im historischen Kontext, auf den ein dem Zyklus vorangestellter Paratext sogar explizit hinweist. Hier ist zu lesen, dass es sich um Erzählungen aus der Zeit der Okkupation handle (vgl. ebd., 91). Bezeichnenderweise wird aber auf eine explizite Nennung der Täter- und Opfergruppen verzichtet. Dieser Umstand gehört bereits zur zweiten Tendenz, nämlich der doppelten Dekontextualisierung des dargestellten Geschehens, die diesen Situationen den Charakter des Einmaligen nimmt und sie stattdessen als typisch ausweist. Diese zweite Tendenz wird durch stilistische und/oder intertextuelle Verfahren noch verstärkt, sodass sie zweifellos als die dominantere von beiden zu gelten hat. Die Analysen der Texte *Žlutá a modrá* sowie *Stříbrná a zlatá* (*Silbern und Golden*), die im Hinblick auf die Bandbreite das Zusammenspiels der genannten Tendenzen als die zwei Extreme in *Barvy* anzusehen sind, sollen diese These belegen.

Exemplarische Analyse I: *Žlutá a modrá*

Innerhalb des Zyklus besteht die Spezifik dieses Textes darin, dass er nicht nur mit Figuren- und Ortsnamen operiert, sondern auch eine vergleichsweise umfangreiche Ereignisfolge aufweist, die sich folgendermaßen paraphrasieren lässt: Der ehemalige Prager Goldschmied Kafka, seine Frau und ein gewisser Haase werden zusammen mit 997 weiteren Personen über das polnische Zamość nach

---

[4] Einen identischen Umgang mit Ortsangaben sowie mit den Bezeichnungen für die Täter- und Opfergruppen findet sich auch in Weils Roman *Život s hvezdou* (*Leben mit dem Stern*) aus dem Jahr 1949, worauf in der Forschung wiederholt hingewiesen worden ist (vgl. etwa Mercks 1995, 574; Heftrich 2000, 365f.; Hříbková 2014, 141).

Berdyčiv in der Ukraine deportiert, wobei Kafkas Frau noch auf dem Weg dorthin verstirbt. Während sich Kafka nach der Ankunft bei der Zwangsarbeit aufreibt und von den Wächtern geschlagen wird, gelingt es Haase, sich in der Ausgabestelle für das Werkzeug vergleichsweise bequem einzurichten. Bereits während des Transports hatte Kafka Haase anvertraut, dass er bei einem Prager Bekannten eine ansehnliche Menge Goldes versteckt hat, und Haase hat keinerlei Skrupel, sich dieses Wissen nun zunutze zu machen. Unter Verwendung von Kafkas Namen und unter tätiger Mithilfe eines Kollaborateurs lässt er sich Geld nach Berdyčiv schicken, um sich damit einen neuen Pass und somit eine neue Identität zu erkaufen. In der Tat gelingt es ihm auf diese Weise, sein Leben zu retten, während Kafka infolge der Zwangsarbeit umkommt.

Die Wahl Berdyčivs für dieses Geschehen ist zweifellos nicht zufällig. Hier wurden in nur wenigen Monaten des Jahres 1941 über 18.000 Juden und damit ca. ein Drittel der Gesamtbevölkerung der Stadt ermordet (vgl. Christ 2011, 12f.), worauf der Text eher allgemein mit dem Verweis auf Tausende von Toten rekurriert (vgl. Weil 1966, 102). Kafkas Schicksal wird durch den Handlungsort also in einen größeren historischen Zusammenhang gestellt, wodurch auch die Täter- und die Opfergruppe eindeutig identifizierbar werden.[5] Auf diese Weise verfügt *Žlutá a modrá* über ein hohes Maß an historischer Konkretheit sowie über ein kohärenzstiftendes Prinzip in der Texttiefenstruktur, nämlich über eine problemlos extrahierbare Narration bzw. eine kausal-temporale organisierte Fabel im Sinne der Vertreter des Russischen Formalismus.[6]

Diese Eigenschaft des Textes wird jedoch durch die Gestaltung seiner Oberfläche, also auf der Ebene des Sujets, auf vielfältige Weise konterkariert. Ersichtlich wird dies bereits am Texteingang, der deshalb hier in Gänze zitiert werden soll:

> Stín modře přechází v žluť podvečera. Okno se otevřelo, aby vydalo hlas v cizí skřehotavé řeči. Vůně Berdyčeva, vůně šafránu, vonného koření a skořice se vznášela přes můstek nad kalnou a špinavou vodou.

---

[5] In anderen Texten des Zyklus ist die Opfergruppe hingegen nicht eindeutig identifizierbar, wie etwa in *Zelená a rudá*, wo die geschilderte Situation in Verbindung mit der Farbsymbolik aber am ehesten auf eine kommunistische Widerstandsgruppe hindeutet. In *Fialová a černá* wiederum fehlen auch solche indirekten Hinweise, sodass die Gruppenzugehörigkeit des Opfers letztlich im Dunkeln bleibt.

[6] Vgl. dazu Tomaševskij 1985, 214f.

Přišel jsi, aby ses vlil do řeky, potoku. Obrazy planoucích svěc budou odneseny do neznámých moří, těžký, čadivý smutek, propletený pachem smažené sváteční ryby, dorazí k cizím břehům. A zdá se, že brzy vyjde strašidlo Vij z doupěte a kdosi mu zvedne víčka, aby padla hrůza do lidských srdcí. (Weil 1966, 100)

Blau geht der Schatten in das Gelb des frühen Abends über. Das Fenster hat sich aufgetan, um eine Stimme in einer fremden kreischenden Sprache herauszulassen. Der Duft Berdyčivs, ein Duft von Safran, duftendem Gewürz und Zimt stieg über die Brücke über dem trüben und schmutzigen Wasser auf.

Du bist gekommen, Bach, um dich in den Fluss zu ergießen. Die Bilder der lodernden Kerzen werden in unbekannte Meere fortgetragen werden, eine schwere, rußige Trauer, verwoben mit dem Geruch des gebratenen Feiertagsfisches, wird an fremden Ufern anlangen. Und es scheint, dass bald das Gespenst Vij aus seinem Bau herauskommen wird, und jemand wird ihm die Lider anheben, auf dass das Grauen in die menschlichen Herzen falle.[7]

Auch wenn hier durchaus einzelne Ereignisse zur Darstellung gelangen, so ist diese Textpassage doch dominiert von einer Reihe von Impressionen, die schließlich in eine Art Meditation übergehen. Dabei ist die Zurückdrängung der Narration zugunsten der Deskription und der Reflexion bereits an den Verbaltempora abzulesen: Der Text setzt im Präsens ein, wechselt dann in das für das Erzählen konventionelle Präteritum, um schließlich im Futur zu enden. Dementsprechend werden die Sachverhalte auch nicht dominant kausaltemporal miteinander verknüpft, sondern eher assoziativ, wobei zunächst visuelle, akustische und olfaktorische Sinneseindrücke vorherrschen, die strukturell durch das Äquivalenzprinzip des Kontrastes miteinander verbunden sind. Wirkt die über die titelgebenden Farben Gelb und Blau eingebrachte temporale Bestimmung weitgehend neutral, führt die Rede von einer fremden kreischenden Stimme zweifellos negative Konnotationen mit sich. Die Düfte Berdyčivs dürften dagegen positiv konkretisiert werden, das trübe und schmutzige Wasser wiederum eher negativ. Dieser Kontrast wird im zweiten Absatz fortgeführt mit dem Gegensatz des Feiertagsessens und der Trauer mit den jeweils dazugehörigen Epitheta, wobei die Passage durch die Verbindung der Trauer mit der Vorstellung von unbekannten Meeren und fremden Ufern geradezu einen elegischen Ton annimmt.

Aufgrund der rein assoziativen Verknüpfung der einzelnen Sätze und der Relationierung ihrer Teile nach dem Prinzip des Kontrastes, fehlt dem Texteingang

---

[7] Alle Übersetzungen stammen vom Verfasser.

jedwede Kontiguität und damit auf der Ebene der Semantik ein kohärenzstiftendes Prinzip, sodass er nachgerade dunkel anmutet. Infolgedessen muss die Kohärenz anderweitig gestiftet werden, soll der Text nicht als Nonsens aufgefasst werden. Genau dies ist auch der Fall, nämlich auf der Ebene seiner Faktur. Verantwortlich hierfür sind Wort- und Lautwiederholungen, sei es in Form von Alliterationen oder von wiederkehrenden Phonemen bzw. Phonemgruppen im Wortinneren. Beides findet sich paradigmatisch im Syntagma „*Vůně* Berdyčeva, *vůně* šafránu, *vonného koření* a skořice". Bereits in den ersten beiden Sätzen taucht allein fünfmal die Lautverbindung <ře> auf (modře, přechází, otevřelo, skřehotavé, řeči). Derartige Wiederholungen im Wortinneren, nicht zuletzt auch in Verbindung mit den Alliterationen (etwa „*p*ropletený *p*achem *s*mažené *s*váteční") oder der Häufung einzelner Vokale („*o*kn*o* se *o*tevřel*o*, aby vydal*o*"), betonen die akustische Qualität der Sprache und lenken die Aufmerksamkeit des Lesers auf sich.

Der Text weist also eine deutliche stilistische Markierung auf, die jedoch nicht zu einer Individualisierung der vermittelnden Instanz führt, da sie auf dialektale, soziolektale oder idiolektale Elemente gänzlich verzichtet.[8] Ihr Ergebnis ist vielmehr eine Art Lyrisierung der Prosa, zu der neben dieser Markierung natürlich auch die bereits angesprochene assoziative Verknüpfung von Impressionen und Reflexionen, die Dominanz des Äquivalenzprinzips über kausaltemporale Strukturen und schließlich auch die Apostrophe des Baches, die zu dessen Anthropomorphisierung führt, gehört.[9] Deshalb ist Eva Štědroňová (1989, 83) zweifellos zuzustimmen, wenn sie den Gesamtzyklus als lyrische

---

[8] Růžena Grebeníčková (1965, 4) und im Anschluss daran Eva Štědroňová (1990, 129) haben darauf aufmerksam gemacht, dass eine solche Stilgebung in unterschiedlich starker Ausprägung für eine Vielzahl der Texte Weils charakteristisch ist. Mit der fehlenden Individualisierung auf der Ebene des Stils korrespondiert auch der Umstand, dass *Žlutá a modrá* mit einem nichtfiguralen Erzähler operiert.

[9] Bereits Jiří Opelík (1965, 63) hat diese Tendenz zur Lyrisierung in *Barvy* ausgemacht und nennt in diesem Zusammenhang als weitere relevante Verfahren für den Zyklus insgesamt die Personifizierung einzelner Gegenstände, anaphorische Aufzählungen und syntaktische Parallelismen sowie den generell hohen Stil bei der Beschreibung banaler Alltagsdinge. Schließlich erwähnt er auch noch die raffinierte Verwendung der Farbsymbolik, auf die bei der Analyse von *Žlutá a modrá* noch zurückzukommen sein wird.

Prosa charakterisiert, doch lässt sich seine Spezifik aus narratologischer Perspektive mit dem Begriff der ornamentalen Prosa noch präziser fassen.[10]

Zur oben angesprochenen Dunkelheit des Texteingangs trägt freilich noch ein weiteres Element bei, nämlich die Nennung des Gespenstes Vij, welches sicherlich nicht allen Lesern ein Begriff sein dürfte. Es handelt sich dabei um die titelgebende Figur aus Nikolaj V. Gogol's gleichnamiger Erzählung, die 1835 im Rahmen des Zyklus *Mirgorod* erschienen ist.[11] Dort wird sie in einer Anmerkung des Erzählers zum Titel folgendermaßen charakterisiert:

> Vij – est' kolossal'noe sozdanie prostonarodnogo voobraženija. Takim imenem nazyvaetsja u malorossijan načal'nik gnomov, u kotorogo veki na glazach idut do samoj zemli. (Gogol' 1994, 321)
>
> Vij – das ist ein kolossales Geschöpf der folkloristischen Einbildungskraft. Mit diesem Namen bezeichnet man bei den Kleinrussen [d.i. den Ukrainern, A.O.] den Obersten der Gnome, dessen Augenlider bis hinunter zur Erde reichen.

Will der Vij seine Lider öffnen, dann müssen sie von anderen Dämonen angehoben werden, weil sie so schwer sind. Wen dann aber der Blick des Vij trifft, der ist des Todes, so wie auch der Philosophiestudent Choma Brut, der Protagonist aus Gogol's Erzählung. Mit diesem intertextuellen Verweis wird in den ersten beiden Absätzen von *Žlutá a modrá* ein weiterer Kontrast etabliert: der lebensweltlichen Verankerung des Geschehens durch dessen geographische Verortung in Berdyčiv steht die Betonung des Kunstcharakters des Textes durch die implizite Metafiktion in Form der Intertextualität entgegen.[12]

Bezeichnenderweise wird der Text unter Anknüpfung an diesen zweiten Pol des Gegensatzpaares, also der Metafiktion, fortgeführt. Es folgt nämlich eine

---

[10] Zur ornamentalen Prosa, die sich eben dadurch auszeichnet, dass bei ihr die kausaltemporale Verknüpfung in der Texttiefenstruktur zugunsten der Kohärenzstiftung durch Äquivalenzen und Wiederholungen an der Textoberfläche abgeschwächt ist, vgl. ausführlich Schmid 2008a, 160-167 und 2008b.

[11] Weil darf zweifellos als Gogol'-Kenner gelten, hat er doch sein Studium der Slavistik und der Vergleichenden Literaturgeschichte mit einer Arbeit über Gogol' und den englischen Roman des 18. Jahrhunderts abgeschlossen. Weil verfasste auch später noch literaturwissenschaftliche Studien, übersetzte darüber hinaus Texte russischer Avantgardedichter ins Tschechische und war auch mit den Theorien der Russischen Formalisten bestens vertraut (vgl. dazu Stolz-Hladká 2000/01, 175f.). Weil kann also getrost als Poeta doctus bezeichnet werden.

[12] In diesem Zusammenhang sei darauf hingewiesen, dass in Gogol's Erzählung gerade die Farben Gelb und Blau besonders häufig genannt werden (vgl. Gogol' 1994, 329, 330, 335, 336, 338, 343 und 346).

ausgedehnte Erzählerreflexion, in der darüber räsoniert wird, wie die Geschichte von Kafka und Haase denn überhaupt adäquat vermittelt werden könne. Sie beginnt mit einem Satz, der den mit der Holocaustthematik auf das Engste verknüpften Unsagbarkeitstopos zu evozieren scheint („Vypravovat tento příběh je hořké a nemožné" (Weil 1966, 100; „Diese Geschichte zu erzählen ist bitter und unmöglich")[13], doch macht der Erzähler umgehend klar, dass es ihm darum gerade nicht geht. Als Ursache für die Schwierigkeit, eine angemessene Ausdrucksform zu finden, erscheint hier vielmehr der Umstand, dass die tschechische Literaturtradition seit der Nationalen Wiedergeburt in der 1. Hälfte des 19. Jahrhunderts durch einen Idyllendiskurs geprägt ist, der vor der Beschreibung solcher Verbrechen zwangsläufig versagen muss[14]:

> Neboť zvykli jsme příběhům prostým, pramenícím ve vysokých horách a rozlévajícím se po nížinách, zvykli jsme olšoví a vrbinám, udicím se splávkem, hučícím jezům a sladkým tůním. (ebd.)
>
> Denn wir sind einfache Geschichten gewohnt, die in den hohen Bergen entspringen und sich in das Tiefland ergießen, wir sind Erlen- und Weidengehölz gewohnt, Angeln mit Schwimmer, tosende Wehre und süße Tiefen.

Dieser allgemeine Verweis auf die tschechische Literaturtradition wird bezeichnenderweise abgeschlossen mit einer konkreten intertextuellen Bezugnahme auf Karel Čapeks Roman *Válka s Mloky* (*Der Krieg mit den Molchen*), der im Jahr 1936 erschienen ist: „A vyšli-li mloci z hlubin země, pohrdli jsme jejich slepotou a odvraceli tváře" (ebd.; „Und als die Molche aus den Tiefen der Erde hervorgekommen sind, missachteten wir deren Blindheit und wandten unser Antlitz ab"). Diese Aussage legt nahe, dass Čapeks Warnung vor den Nationalsozialisten, für die die Molche in seinem Roman u.a. stehen[15], von den Tschechen auch deshalb überhört wurde, weil sie von ihrem Hang zum Idyllischen eingelullt waren.

---

[13] Zum Unsagbarkeitstopos in Bezug auf den Holocaust vgl. die äußerst erhellenden Überlegungen von Daniel Fulda 2013, 138-148.

[14] Zum Idyllendiskurs in der tschechischen Literatur und Kultur vgl. beispielsweise die Beiträge in Kaiserová/Martinovský 1999.

[15] Durch diesen intertextuellen Verweis findet auch eine textinterne Kohärenzstiftung statt, da in Čapeks Roman im Zusammenhang mit einer Radioübertragung der Molche wörtlich von einer „kreischenden Stimme" („skřehotavý hlas", Čapek 1981, 219) die Rede ist. Die im zweiten Satz von *Žlutá a modrá* erwähnte kreischende Sprache wird auf diese Weise mit den Molchen assoziiert und infolgedessen auch mit dem Deutschen.

Implizit wird damit die Frage aufgeworfen, mit welchen kommunikativen Strategien die tschechische Leserschaft angesichts der Vorliebe für die Gattungstradition der Idylle mit Blick auf die Holocaustthematik überhaupt zu erreichen sei. Der Text beantwortet sie, indem er drei Strategien nutzt, die den potentiellen Rezipienten bestens vertraut sind und damit auch geeignet erscheinen, das Gelingen der Kommunikation sicherzustellen. Die erste von ihnen ist in einem weiteren intertextuellen Verweis zu sehen, dessen Verständnis nun aber keineswegs ein Spezialwissen erfordert wie etwa bei der Figur des Vij oder möglicherweise auch hinsichtlich der Symbolik der Molche. Vielmehr kann der Prätext als allgemein bekannt vorausgesetzt oder notfalls nachgeschlagen werden, da er in Weils Text explizit genannt wird. Es handelt sich um die Offenbarung des Johannes, die allerdings insofern aktualisiert wird, als in *Žlutá a modrá* das Tier nicht die Zahl 666 auf der Stirn trägt, sondern das Wort „Transport" (ebd., 101). Die Bezugnahme auf die Apokalypse, in der der archetypische Kampf des Guten mit dem Bösen geschildert wird, etabliert für Weils Text einen klaren moralischen Rahmen, innerhalb dessen sich die geschilderte Handlung problemlos deuten lässt.

Mit der Ansiedlung des Konflikts auf einer solch abstrakten moralischen Ebene korrespondiert wiederum die Präsentation des oben paraphrasierten Geschehens. Die einzelnen Sachverhalte werden wie Fakten lediglich benannt und einfach aneinandergereiht. Der Text verzichtet somit auf jegliches Detail, das den einzelnen Ereignissen Anschaulichkeit verleihen könnte, ebenso wie auf Erklärungen, die diese in einen größeren historischen Bezugsrahmen einordnen würden. Dieser chronikartigen Darstellungsweise entspricht auch die Figurenkonzeption. Über das Äußere der Figuren erfährt der Leser ebenso wenig wie über ihre inneren Regungen, ein Umstand, der angesichts der existenzbedrohenden Situation besonders auffällig wirkt. Lediglich durch ihre Handlungsweise werden die Figuren indirekt charakterisiert.[16] Eine derartige Figurenkonzeption

---

[16] Die Entpsychologisierung der Figuren stellt einen zentralen Charakterzug der Poetik Weils dar, wie Růžena Grebeníčková (1967, 15) bereits im Zusammenhang mit dessen Romanwerk konstatiert hat.

ist aus dem Märchen bestens bekannt. Aufgrund des Fehlens jeglicher Tiefendimension spricht man hier von flächenhaften Charakteren.[17] Nicht nur die Figurenkonzeption in *Žlutá a modrá* ruft die Gattung des Märchens in Erinnerung, sondern auch die Bezeichnung von Kafkas Gold als „Zaubermittel" („kouzelný prostředek"; ebd., 102), die märchentypische Ortsangabe „hinter den sieben Flüssen und den sieben Bergen" („za sedmi řekami a sedmi horami"; ebd.) sowie die explizite Nennung der prototypischen Märchensammlung *Tausendundeinenacht* (ebd., 101).[18] Mit dem Rekurs auf das Märchen erscheint auch die Wahl des dargestellten Geschehens plausibel: Anstelle des mit dem Namen Berdyčiv verbundenen Massenmords fokussiert der Text das Handeln zweier Figuren, die sich in einer Notlage befinden, aus der sie sich befreien wollen.[19] Beide gehören also der Opfergruppe an. Die Täter, die die märchentypische Funktion des Schädigers erfüllen, bleiben dagegen anonym, und ihre Grausamkeit und Brutalität wird gleichsam poetisiert, so z.B. wenn der Tod von Kafkas Frau nicht in seiner ganzen Drastik beschrieben, sondern anhand der Figur des Vij personifiziert wird.[20] Als drastisch ist allerdings das Ende des Textes zu bezeichnen, welches folgendermaßen lautet:

> Hle, to je onen příběh o žluti šafránu a modři večerního stínu.
> Mrtví z něho civí důlky lebečních kostí, zlato se v něm třpytí a křiví tváře, modrá mlha se vznáší nad černými bažinami, mlýny melou žluté kosti na fosfát a odstředivky vylučují z modrého tuku žlutý glycerín.

---

[17] Vgl. dazu Lüthi 1997, 13-24.

[18] Der Begriff des Zaubermittels als literaturwissenschaftlicher Terminus geht zurück auf die strukturale Märchenanalyse Vladimir Propps (vgl. Propp 1975, 47). Angesichts der Vertrautheit Weils mit den Arbeiten der Russischen Formalisten entbehrt die Annahme, dass er auch Propps Studie aus dem Jahr 1928 gekannt haben könnte, durchaus nicht der Plausibilität.

[19] Nach Propp (1975, 36) ist es in jedem Zaubermärchen ein Verlust oder die Schädigung des Helden, die die Handlung in Gang setzt.

[20] Auch dort, wo der Massenmord immerhin angedeutet wird, geschieht dies in metaphorischer Form: „O řeko, jejíž ryby se mění v lidi podle barev a náboženství, jak se o tom vypravuje v ‚Tisíci a jedné noci'! Vrší, jež je do tebe ponořována, jsou vytahovány na pánve, aby se tam smažily k svému zatracení. A kuchaři zlých činů stojí opodál, aby pozorovali jejich smrtelné křeče" (Weil 1966, 101; „Oh Fluss, dessen Fische sich nach den Farben und der Religion in Menschen verwandeln, wie in ‚Tausendundeinernacht' erzählt wird! Mit einer Reuse, die in dich eingetaucht ist, werden sie herausgezogen in eine Pfanne, damit sie dort zu ihrer Verdammnis braten. Und die Köche der bösen Taten stehen unweit, um ihre Todeskrämpfe zu beobachten"). Der im zweiten Absatz des Textes (vgl. oben) genannte Feiertagsfisch erhält durch diese Passage eine ganz neue Konnotation.

A vůně Berdyčeva, vůně šafránu, vonného koření, smíšená s čadivým kouřem voskovic, stoupá v kruh mrtvých, za něž již nikdo neodříká kaddiš, modlitbu pohřební. (ebd., 104)

Siehe, das ist jene Geschichte vom Gelb des Safrans und vom Blau des abendlichen Schattens.

Die Toten starren aus ihr durch die Höhlen ihrer Schädelknochen heraus, das Gold in ihr glänzt und verzerrt die Gesichter, der blaue Nebel schwebt über den schwarzen Sümpfen, die Mühlen mahlen die gelben Knochen zu Phosphat und die Zentrifugen sondern aus dem blauen Fett das gelbe Glyzerin ab.

Und der Duft Berdyčivs, ein Duft von Safran, von duftendem Gewürz, vermischt mit dem rußigen Rauch der Wachskerzen, steigt in den Kreis der Toten, für die niemand mehr das Kaddisch, das Totengebet, hersagt.

Dieses Ende macht die Spezifik von *Žlutá a modrá* noch einmal besonders deutlich. Die Gräuel der Shoah werden poetisiert, nicht nur durch die Wortwiederholungen und die Lautinstrumentierung, die in dieser Passage gehäuft auftreten, sondern auch durch die Übercodierung der Farbsymbolik, die zunächst einmal durch die Nationalfarben der Ukraine sowie durch die intertextuelle Relation zu Gogol's ebenfalls in der heutigen Ukraine angesiedelter Erzählung motiviert erscheint. Werden die Farben Gelb und Blau dann zunächst mit zu ihnen passenden Naturphänomenen assoziiert, dienen sie schließlich dazu, das Grauen des Todes und die Verwertung der Leichen plastisch zu veranschaulichen. Gleichzeitig wird das historisch Konkrete, das durch den Ortsnamen evoziert wird, auf der Textoberfläche durch die Wiederaufnahme des Texteingangs konterkariert. Der linearen Zeitstruktur der Geschichte wird somit eine zyklische Zeitkonzeption an der Textoberfläche entgegengesetzt. Genau hier wird auch die Funktion der Stilisierung im Sinne der Ornamentalisierung deutlich, liegt der ornamentalen Prosa doch ein mythisches Denken zugrunde, das sich dadurch auszeichnet, dass es den individuellen Fall nicht als Teil einer teleologischen Abfolge auffasst, sondern als Ausdruck überzeitlicher stets wiederkehrender Abläufe.[21] Nicht dem historisch einmaligen Massenmord von Berdyčiv gilt damit das Interesse, vielmehr wird das Geschehen um Kafka und Haase als exemplarisch ausgewiesen.

Die Konzeption des Textes als Exemplum wird, nach dem Verweis auf die Apokalypse und der Bezugnahme auf das Märchen, auch durch die dritte der

---

[21] Zum Zusammenhang von ornamentaler Prosa und mythologischem Denken vgl. Schmid 1992, 15-28.

oben angesprochenen Kommunikationsstrategien gestützt, die der Text zur Verständnissicherung nutzt. Ergänzend zu den bisherigen Ausführungen ist nämlich hinzuzufügen, dass die Figuren nicht nur durch ihre Handlungsweisen indirekt charakterisiert werden, sondern auch durch ihre Namen. In Form eines Erzählerkommentars, der quasi einem Taufakt gleichkommt, wird dieser Umstand explizit gemacht:

> Dejme tomuto zlatníkovi jméno Kafka, jež znamená smutného ptáka s ustřiženými křídly. A onen člověk z lesních doupat nechť se jmenuje Haase, na paměť časů zlého plížení a kličkování. (ebd., 101)
>
> Geben wir diesem Goldschmied den Namen Kafka, der einen traurigen Vogel mit herabhängenden Flügeln bezeichnet. Und jener Mensch aus den Waldhöhlen soll Haase heißen, in Erinnerung an die Zeiten des bösen Schleichens und Hakenschlagens.

Auch wenn die Namen leicht verfremdet sind (<f> für <v> in tschechisch „kavka (Dohle)" und die Verdoppelung des Vokals <a>), ist doch offenkundig, dass sie über ihre Motivierung aus der Tierwelt Gefühlszustände oder Charaktereigenschaften ihrer Träger versinnbildlichen.[22] Auf diese Weise kommt die Gattungstradition der Fabel ins Spiel, auch wenn dort die Tiere nicht nur als Vergleichspunkt und Namensgeber, sondern als selbständige Handlungsträger auftreten. Gerade die Fabel aber kann zweifellos als jene Gattung angesehen werden, in der es darum geht, anhand der Tiercharaktere anthropologische Konstanten zum Ausdruck zu bringen. Und in eben diesem Sinne funktioniert auch *Žlutá a modrá*. Während Kafka, wie in der Namensgebung bereits angedeutet, sich in sein Schicksal ergibt, zeichnet sich Haase durch seine Verschlagenheit aus, die ihm schließlich auch die Flucht ermöglicht.[23]

---

[22] Vergleichbares gilt auch für die Täterseite, da die Organisatoren des Transports mit Raubtieren gleichgesetzt werden (vgl. Weil 1966, 100f.).

[23] Der Name Kafka ist darüber hinaus natürlich auch als ein weiteres metafiktionales Element anzusehen. Weil war mit Franz Kafka persönlich bekannt und hat in einer ersten Fassung von *Život s hvězdou* auch direkt auf dessen Roman *Das Schloss* Bezug genommen (vgl. dazu Holý 2014, 69f., vor allem aber Hříbková 2014, 136). Auch wenn Jiří Opelík (1966, 194) völlig zu Recht darauf hingewiesen hat, dass es Weil in keinem seiner Werke um die existenzielle Geworfenheit des Menschen an sich gehe, sondern stets um die existenzielle Bedrohung, die aus der konkreten historischen Situation erwachsen ist, so lässt sich doch immerhin konstatieren, dass die parabolischen Züge der Texte aus dem Zyklus *Barvy* eine gewisse poetologische Nähe zum Werk Kafkas aufweisen.

Resümierend lässt sich damit festhalten, dass in *Žlutá a modrá* trotz der konkreten Lokalisierung und der damit verbundenen zeitlichen Kontextualisierung des Geschehens keine historisch verbürgten Ereignisse der Shoah zur Darstellung gelangen, sondern bestimmte moralische Qualitäten oder Charaktereigenschaften, die als Aktualisierungen des ewigen Kampfes zwischen Gut und Böse aufzufassen sind. Etabliert wird der entsprechende Bezugsrahmen durch den Verweis auf die Apokalypse, doch werden hierfür auch Allusionen an Gattungskonventionen des Märchens, in dem es in säkularisierter Form um eben diesen Kampf geht, sowie der Fabel, die das Geschehen als Exemplum ausweist, genutzt. Dabei ist das Böse absolut, wie durch das Bild des apokalyptischen Tieres verdeutlicht wird. Bei den Opfern ist hingegen zu differenzieren: hier der bedauernswerte Kafka, dort der betrügerische Haase.

Diese Qualifizierung ist keineswegs in das Belieben des Rezipienten gestellt, sondern erfolgt durch den Akt der Namensgebung im Text selbst. *Žlutá a modrá* vermittelt somit eine rigorose moralische Position, die erneut an die Gattung des Märchens erinnert und damit auch den Modellcharakter des dargestellten Geschehens deutlich macht. Das Exemplarische dieses Geschehens wird ferner durch die Stilisierung in der Tradition der ornamentalen Prosa unterstrichen, durch die gleichzeitig im Sinne der Formalisten die Sprache in Gestalt ihrer Lyrisierung fühlbar gemacht wird. Auf diese Weise wird zudem der Kunstcharakter des Textes in das Bewusstsein des Lesers gehoben. Dieselbe Funktion erfüllt auch die Metafiktion in Form von intertextuellen Verweisen und der Selbstreferentialität der Erzählerkommentare. Durch all dieses Verfahren sowie die fehlende direkte Benennung der Täter- und Opfergruppen wird in *Žlutá a modrá* das historisch Konkrete in Richtung des Allgemeinen, ja des Archetypischen transzendiert, sodass nicht die Singularität der nationalsozialistischen Verbrechen in den Blick rückt, sondern die Fähigkeit des Menschen, derartige Verbrechen überhaupt zu begehen.

Exemplarische Analyse II: *Stříbrná a zlatá*

Wenn *Žlutá a modrá* in der Terminologie Schmids als ein typisches Beispiel für das ornamentale Erzählen anzusehen ist, dann hat man es in *Stříbrná a zlatá* mit einem Fall der rein ornamentalen Prosa zu tun.[24] Bei ihr ist die kausal-temporale Verknüpfung der zur Sprache gebrachten Sachverhalte so weit reduziert, dass „die Iterationsverfahren die einzigen Garanten der Textkohäsion" darstellen (Schmid 1992, 21). Genauso verhält es sich in *Stříbrná a zlatá*, auch wenn der erste Absatz den Anschein erweckt, dass eine bestimmte Handlung zur Darstellung gelangen würde:

> Z plakátů stékala krev, crčela v malých proudech a stékala do kanálů, bledly plakáty natřené červenou barvou, aby se staly podobnými plakátům jiným s hudbou, tancem a vřeštěním. Nepřehlušily plakáty mrtvé ticho, jen krev kanula pomalu. (Weil 1966, 125)

> Von den Plakaten floss Blut, rieselte in kleinen Strömen und floss in die Kanäle, die mit roter Farbe gestrichenen Plakate wurden bleich, um anderen Plakaten mit Musik, Tanz und Kreischen ähnlich zu werden. Die Plakate übertönten die tote Stille nicht, nur das Blut rann langsam.

Ungeachtet der auch in diesem Text vorzufindenden poetisierenden Verfahren wie Laut- und Wortwiederholungen sowie der Synästhesie implizieren die beiden durchgängig im Präteritum gehaltenen Sätze, dass hier die Folgen eines Gewaltverbrechens geschildert werden. Dadurch wird die Erwartung geweckt, dass alsbald die Hintergründe der Gewalttat aufgedeckt, mithin das Opfer und der Täter mit seinem Motiv genannt werden. Doch nichts dergleichen geschieht, stattdessen kommt es im nächsten Satz zu einem abrupten Themenwechsel, der durch die rein formale, da semantisch dysfunktionale anaphorische Bezugnahme zusätzlich in das Bewusstsein des Lesers gehoben wird: „Tak chodila zvířata polními cestami, zalézala do nor, unikala léčkam, vyhýbala se pastím, ulétala před čihadly" (ebd.; „So gingen die Tiere auf Feldwegen, verkrochen sich in Erdlöchern, entgingen den Schlingen, wichen den Fallen aus, flogen von den Vogelherden davon").

Statt eine fest umrissene Anzahl individueller Handlungsträger wird ein Figurenkollektiv eingeführt, das jedoch nicht in Menschengestalt auftritt, sondern als Tiere. Dass es sich dabei um eine metaphorische Bezeichnung handelt, wird daran ersichtlich, dass sich die Tiere in Menschen verwandeln können: „A plakáty

---

[24] Vgl. Schmid 2008b, 27. Ausgehend von Aage A. Hansen-Löves Dichotomie von Wortkunst und Erzählkunst beschreibt Schmid die ornamentale Prosa als ein Interferenz-Phänomen zwischen diesen beiden Grundformen. Während die rein ornamentale Prosa dem Pol der Wortkunst näher stehe, seien im ornamentalen Erzählen die Elemente der Erzählkunst noch deutlich erkennbar.

červeně označené mluvily o krvi. Neboť krev proměňovala zvířata v jména, jen krví bylo rušeno zakletí" (ebd.; „Und die rot eingefärbten Plakate sprachen vom Blut. Denn das Blut verwandelte die Tiere in Namen, nur durch das Blut wurde der Zauberbann gebrochen"). Spätestens an dieser Stelle wird erkennbar, dass es in *Stříbrná a zlatá* nicht um ein singuläres Gewaltverbrechen geht, sondern dass von der Gewalt eine ganze Gruppe von Figuren betroffen ist, wobei die Rede von einem Zauberbann und die Vorstellung von der Verwandlung von Tieren in Menschen erneut die Gattung des Märchens alludieren, wodurch das Geschehen auf eine symbolische Ebene überführt wird. Allerdings zeigt sich hier noch eine zweite Funktion der Tiermetaphorik. Sie verweist auf die mit der nationalsozialistischen Gewalt einhergehende Vertierung, die im Bild der blutrünstigen und scharfzähnigen Frettchen einen plastischen Ausdruck für die Täter findet. Deren Opfer werden dagegen ihrer Menschlichkeit beraubt, so dass sie unter den herrschenden Bedingungen ganz auf ihre tierischen Instinkte angewiesen sind. Dennoch können sie ihren Verfolgern offenbar häufig nicht entkommen, so dass sie von ihnen, um in der Logik der Bildsprache des Textes zu bleiben, gerissen werden.

Allerdings insinuiert *Stříbrná a zlatá* gleichzeitig, dass ihr Tod nicht umsonst ist. Zum einen werden sie erst durch ihn wieder zu menschlichen Individuen und erlangen auf diese Weise ihre Würde zurück, zum anderen wird ihr Tod als heroisches Opfer für die Befreiung von der herrschenden Bedrohung entworfen. Jedoch wird dies nicht diskursiv im Sinne eines Erzählerkommentars vermittelt, sondern in poetische Bilder gefasst, wie lediglich zwei Beispiele verdeutlichen sollen, die zugleich die titelgebenden Farben aufgreifen, anhand derer der Opfertod symbolisch glorifiziert wird[25]:

> Olovo a ocel jste změnili v stříbro a zlato. (ebd., 127)
> Blei und Stahl habt ihr in Silber und Gold verwandelt.

> Povstaňte, mrtví, a pohlédněte na své dílo. Jak zlatý most se klene nad stříbrnou řekou, jak zlaté cimbuří stříbrného hradu se tyčí v modři nebes. (ebd.)

---

[25] Durch ihre Symbolik tragen die Farben einerseits zur Bedeutungskonstitution der Texte bei, sind andererseits aber auch eines der zentralen Mittel, um den Zykluscharakter zu verstärken, indem sie immer wiederkehren. So tauchen Gold und Silber als Metalle bereits in *Šedá a fialová* (*Grau und Violett*; vgl. Weil 1966, 105) auf, während Rot, nicht nur als Farbe des Blutes, bereits im Eingangstext von *Barvy* eine zentrale Rolle spielt.

Steht auf, ihr Toten, und seht Euer Werk an. Wie sich eine goldene Brücke über den silbernen Fluss wölbt, wie goldene Zinnen einer silbernen Burg in das Blau des Firmaments emporragen.

Die Apostrophe der Toten, die wiederholt auftritt und in einzelnen Textpassagen noch deutlich ausgeweitet ist, sowie der fünfmalige refrainartige Ausruf „Salva na vaši počest!" (ebd., 126f.; „Eine Salve Euch zu Ehren!") verleiht dem Text dabei einen gleichsam hymnischen Charakter. Nicht nur durch diese Verfahren, sondern auch durch die Klang- und Wortwiederholungen sowie die Annäherung des Erzählers an ein lyrisches Ich, die durch die rein assoziative Verknüpfung einzelner Metaphern zustande kommt, tendiert *Stříbrná a zlatá* deutlich in Richtung eines Langgedichts in Prosaform. Unterstützt wird dieser Effekt zudem durch das von der Bildsprache ausgehende Pathos, das nicht an die Ratio des Lesers appelliert, sondern an dessen Emotionen. Da dieser Text den Zyklus beschließt, wird der Rezipient trotz des Motivs des massenhaften Todes mit einem Gefühl der Hoffnung auf ein Ende des Schreckens und eine bessere Zukunft entlassen, wie gerade in seinen letzten Zeilen deutlich wird:

> Salva na vaši počest! Květiny, jimiž podestlána je svoboda, jsou květinami vašich hrobů, světla, jež zaplašují tmu, jsou pochodněmi vašich pohřebních průvodů, dunění děl a rachocení tanků je vaší hudbou smuteční.
> Tak hořte a sviťte v zlatě požárů, stříbrnou polnicí zpívejte píseň svobody. (ebd., 127f.)
>
> Eine Salve Euch zu Ehren! Die Blumen, mit denen die Freiheit bestreut ist, sind die Blumen Eurer Gräber, die Lichter, die die Dunkelheit verjagen, sind die Fackeln Eurer Begräbniszüge, das Donnern der Geschosse und das Rattern der Panzer ist Eure Trauermusik.
> So brennt und leuchtet im Gold der Brände, mit silbernem Signalhorn singt das Lied der Freiheit.

Resümee

Bezeichnenderweise wird in *Stříbrná a zlatá* weder ein Toponym verwendet noch das Geschehen historisch verortet. Lediglich der Hinweis auf die in den linken Unterarm tätowierten Nummern (vgl. ebd., 126) stellt einmal mehr einen eindeutigen lebensweltlichen Bezug her. Lässt sich daraus auch die Opfergruppe ablesen, so bleibt sie doch eine anonyme Masse, aus der kein individueller Handlungsträger hervortritt. Ist dies, wie etwa in *Žlutá a modrá* und in einigen anderen Texten des Zyklus, doch der Fall, werden die Figuren konsequent entpsychologisiert, sodass ihre Geschichte nicht als konkreter Einzelfall erscheint, sondern als Exemplum. Verstärkt wird dieser Eindruck durch die in nahezu allen Texten vorzufindende Tiermetaphorik, die eine doppelte Funktion erfüllt. Zum einen steht sie für die aus den nationalsozialistischen Gräueltaten resultierende Entmenschlichung, wobei, wie bereits Jiří Opelík (1965, 62) zutreffend festgestellt hat, die Täter mit Raubtieren, die Opfer hingegen mit Beutetieren oder mit Schlachtvieh assoziiert werden. In der Regel ist es in den dargestellten Situationen erst der Tod, der den Menschen ihre Würde zurückgibt, wobei dieser Umstand im Bild der Rückverwandlung von Tier zu Mensch verdeutlicht wird. Zum anderen ruft sie die Gattungskonvention der Fabel auf, die noch durch ein weiteres Verfahren ins Spiel gebracht wird, welches in einzelnen Texten Verwendung findet. Diese sind nämlich bisweilen mit kurzen Eingangspassagen versehen, die eine vergleichbare Funktion erfüllen wie das Promythion in der Fabel, das die Thematik des jeweiligen Textes vorgibt. In Weils Zyklus geschieht dies erneut nicht diskursiv, sondern, ganz im Sinne der Ornamentalistik, in Form einer poetischen Meditation, wie das folgende Beispiel aus dem ersten Text mit dem Titel *Zelená a rudá* zeigt:

> Být stromem, stát pevně na svém místě. A přijde-li vítr, zachvěti se jen, shoditi několik listů, růsti do rodného nebe s kořeny pevně zapuštěnými v zemi. A vytrvati, když se blíží požár uprostřed rudých plamenů, vzpínati se větvemi a padnouti nakonec jako ohořelý trup, rozsypati se v jiskrách a zčernati v uhlících. (Weil 1966, 92)

> Ein Baum sein, fest an seinem Platz stehen. Und kommt der Wind, nur schwanken, ein paar Blätter abwerfen, fest in der Erde verwurzelt in den heimatlichen Himmel wachsen. Und ausharren, wenn sich der Brand inmitten der roten Flammen nähert, sich mit den Ästen aufbäumen und schließlich fallen wie ein verbrannter Rumpf, in Funken zerstieben und sich in schwarze Kohle verwandeln.[26]

Im Symbol des fest verwurzelten letztlich aber verbrennenden Baumes klingt bereits jene Standfestigkeit an, die der namenlose Protagonist des Textes an den Tag legt, wenn er sich lieber das Leben nimmt als seine Gefährtin Jana Marie ihren Häschern auszuliefern. Damit ist auch schon ein weiteres Strukturmerkmal der Texte angedeutet. Gemäß den Konventionen der ornamentalen Prosa wird die kausal-temporale Verknüpfung der Sachverhalte massiv geschwächt und an

---

[26] Die Heimatverbundenheit stellt einen immer wiederkehrenden Topos in den Texten von *Barvy* dar, der in *Černá a bílá* sogar zum zentralen Thema avanciert.

ihre Stelle tritt in *Barvy* die Schilderung einzelner Situationen, die bestimmte Charaktereigenschaften evozieren. Für diese Charaktereigenschaften wird als moralischer Interpretationsrahmen die Dichotomie von Gut und Böse etabliert, zu deren Fundierung die biblische Heilslehre dient, auf die in vielen der Texte explizit oder implizit Bezug genommen wird, sei es auf die Offenbarung des Johannes in *Žlutá a modrá* oder auf die Vorstellung von der Auferstehung der Toten in *Stříbrná a zlatá*.[27] Auf diese Weise gelangen in den einzelnen Texten des Zyklus nicht Ereignisse zur Darstellung, die als individueller Fall aufzufassen sind, sondern menschliche Verhaltensweisen, die als archetypisch ausgewiesen sind. Nicht die historische Einmaligkeit des Holocaust rückt somit in den Blick, vielmehr bietet er lediglich den Anlass, um anthropologische Konstanten vorzuführen.

Es wäre allerdings verfehlt, wenn man in dieser Transzendierung des historisch Konkreten ins allgemein Anthropologische eine Banalisierung des Holocaust sehen wollte. Vielmehr öffnet sie den Blick dafür, dass der Mensch ganz grundsätzlich zu Gräueltaten fähig ist, wie sie in der Zeit des Nationalsozialismus begangen worden sind. Die Einsicht in diesen Umstand formulierten der Historiker George M. Kren und der Psychologe Leon Rappoport gut 35 Jahre nach der Publikation von *Barvy* in ihrer Studie *The Holocaust and the Crisis of Human Behaviour* von 1980 folgendermaßen:

> If it could happen on such a massive scale elsewhere, then it can happen anywhere; it is all within the range of human possibility, and like it or not, Auschwitz expands the universe of consciousness no less than landings on the moon. (Kren/Rappoport 1994, 138)

Und erst unlängst hat der Historiker Timothy Snyder (2015, 13) mit Blick auf den Holocaust darauf hingewiesen, dass sich zwar Geschichte nicht wiederholt, dass sich aber bestimmte Konstellationen, wie sie aus der Geschichte bekannt sind, durchaus wiederholen können. Dessen war sich Jiří Weil offenbar bereits

---

[27] In *Černá a bílá* findet sich in Bezug auf die Heimat die Formulierung „posvěť se jméno tvé" (Weil 1966, 98; „dein Name sei geheiligt"), eine Abwandlung der entsprechenden Zeile aus dem *Vaterunser* („buď posvěceno tvé jméno", Matthäus 6,9). In *Šedá a fialová* dient die Geschichte von der Auferstehung des Lazarus als Bezugspunkt und in *Žlutá a černá* Petrus' dreimalige Verleugnung Christi nach dessen Gefangennahme. In *Hnědá a bílá* wiederum wird auf das Schicksal von Lots Frau angespielt. Dabei ist in einzelnen Fällen durchaus eine Abweichung von den biblischen Prätexten festzustellen, deren Spezifik und Funktion aber sinnvollerweise in einer gesonderten Studie nachgegangen werden müsste.

als Zeitzeuge des Holocaust bewusst. In diesem Sinne erweist sich sein Zyklus *Barvy* als eine Mahnung zu beständiger Wachsamkeit, dass sich ein Genozid wie der Holocaust eben nicht wiederholt. Doch erfolgt diese Mahnung nicht in Form einer Erinnerung an konkrete historische Ereignisse oder deren literarischer Darstellung mit quasidokumentarischen Mitteln, sondern als kunstvolle Konfrontation des Lesers mit negativen Facetten der menschlichen Natur.

Literaturverzeichnis

Čapek, Karel 1981: Spisy IX: Válka s Mloky. Praha.
Christ, Michaela 2011: Die Dynamik des Tötens. Die Ermordung der Juden von Berditschew. Ukraine 1941 – 1944. Frankfurt am Main.
Feuchert, Sascha 2004: Oskar Rosenfeld und Oskar Singer. Zwei Autoren des Lodzer Gettos. Studien zur Holocaustliteratur. Frankfurt am Main.
Fulda, Daniel 2013: Ein unmögliches Buch? Christopher Brownings *Remembering Survival* und die „Aporie von Auschwitz". In: Den Holocaust erzählen. Historiographie zwischen wissenschaftlicher Empirie und narrativer Kreativität. Hrsg. v. Norbert Frei u. Wulf Kansteiner. Göttingen, S. 126-150.
Gogol', Nikolaj V.: 1994: Sobranie sočinenij. Tom 1/2: Večera na chutore bliz Dikan'ki; Mirgorod. Moskva.
Grebeníčková, Růžena 1965: Wcilův Žalozpěv. In Tvář 5, S. 4-5.
dies. 1967: Jiří Weil a moderní román. In: Weil, Jiří: Život s hvezdou. Praha, S. 7-34.
Heftrich, Urs 2000: Der Unstern als Leitstern. Jiří Weils Werk über den Holocaust. In: Weil, Jiří: Leben mit dem Stern. München – Stuttgart, S. 360-386.
Holý, Jiří 2014: Jiří Weils Roman *Život s hvězdou* und seine kritische Rezeption. In: The Representation of the Shoah in Literature and Film in Central Europe. The Post-War Period. Red. Grzegorz Gazda, Małgorzata Leyko, Paweł Rutkiewicz. Łódź, S. 65-74.
Hříbková, Hana 2014: On the Emergence of the Novel *Život s hvězdou* (*Life with a Star*). In: The Representation of the Shoah in Literature and Film in Central Europe. The Post-War Period. Red. Grzegorz Gazda, Małgorzata Leyko, Paweł Rutkiewicz. Łódź, S. 129-144.
Ibler, Reinhard 2012: Zur Darstellung des Holocaust in der tschechischen Literatur des Prager Frühlings. Josef Škvoreckýs Erzählzyklus *Sedmiramenný svícen* (*Der siebenarmige Leuchter*). In: Ausgewählte Probleme der polnischen und tschechischen Holocaustliteratur und -kultur. Materialien des Internationalen Workshops in Gießen, 27.-28. Mai 2010. Hrsg. v. Reinhard Ibler. München – Berlin, S. 65-80.
Jakowska, Krystyna 2016: Ironie als Ausdruck von Emotionen in der polnischen Holocaustprosa. Tadeusz Borowski und Hanna Krall. In: „Ich kann es nicht fassen, dass dies Menschen möglich ist". Zur Rolle des Emotionalen in der polnischen Literatur über den Holocaust. Hrsg. v. Andrea Mayer-Fraatz u. Thomas Schmidt. Stuttgart, S. 100-125.
Kaiserová, Kristina – Martinovský, Ivan (red.) 1999: Idyla a idyličnost v kultuře 19. století. Sborník příspěvků ze symposia uspořádaného 9. a 10. března 1995 v Státní vědecké knihovně v Plzni. Ústí nad Labem.

Kren, George M. – *Rappoport*, Leon [2]1994: The Holocaust and the Crisis of Human Behaviour. New York.
Lüthi, Max [10]1997: Das europäische Volksmärchen. Form und Wesen. Tübingen – Basel.
Mercks, Kees 1995: Zur Rezeption des Romans *Das Leben mit dem Stern* von Jiří Weil. Sinn und Unsinn. In: Russian Literature 37, S. 561-578.
Meyer-Fraatz, Andrea 2016: Die Rolle des Emotionalen in Zofia Nałkowskas *Medaliony*. In: „Ich kann es nicht fassen, dass dies Menschen möglich ist". Zur Rolle des Emotionalen in der polnischen Literatur über den Holocaust. Hrsg. v. Andrea Meyer-Fraatz u. Thomas Schmidt. Stuttgart, S. 126-146.
Opelík, Jiří 1965: Weilovy povídky z let 1938 – 1948. In: Česká literatura 13, S. 61-68.
ders. 1966: Hodina pravdy, hodina zkoušky In: Weil, Jiří: Hodina pravdy, hodina zkoušky. Praha, S. 191-206.
Propp, Vladimir 1975: Morphologie des Märchens. Hrsg. v. Karl Eimermacher. Aus d. Russ. v. Christel Wendt. Frankfurt am Main.
Schmid, Wolf 1992: Ornamentales Erzählen in der russischen Moderne. Čechov – Babel' – Zamjatin. Frankfurt am Main [u.a.].
ders. [2]2008a: Elemente der Narratologie. Berlin – New York.
ders. 2008b: „Wortkunst" und „Erzählkunst" im Lichte der Narratologie. In: Wortkunst, Erzählkunst, Bildkunst. Festschrift für Aage A. Hansen-Löve. Hrsg v. Rainer Grübel u. Wolf Schmid. München, S. 23-37.
Snyder, Timothy 2015: Black Earth. Der Holocaust und warum er sich wiederholen kann. Aus d. Engl. v. Ulla Höber, Karl Heinz Siber u. Andreas Wirthensohn. München.
Štědroňová, Eva 1989: Jiří Weil – jeden lidský a umělecký osud české literatury. In: Literární měsíčník 18,10, S. 81-85.
dies. 1990: Dialektika umělecké metody a reality v díle Jiřího Weila. In: Česká literatura 38,2, S. 126-140.
Stolz-Hladká, Zuzana 2001/02: Jiří Weil a pravdivost slova. In: Literární archiv 32-33 (Narozeni na přelomu století…), S. 175-186.
Tomaševskij, Boris 1985: Theorie der Literatur. Poetik. Aus d. Russ. v. Ulrich Werner. Wiesbaden.
Weil, Jiří 1966: Hodina pravdy, hodina zkoušky. Praha.

Transcending History by Poeticizing Representation in Jiří Weil's Prose Cycle *Barvy* (*Colours*)

In his cycle *Barvy* (1946), consisting of ten relatively short prose-texts dealing with various aspects of the Holocaust, Jiří Weil (1900-1959) uses different means of poetization amongst them the most important ones are 1. the linking of the texts to specific generic traditions such as the fable and the fairy tale and 2. the ornamentalization of the narrative voice. By the use of features of the fable and the fairy tale the depicted situations are freed from their historic context and transformed into more or less abstract examples of human behaviour. This corresponds to the devaluation of narration in favour of description and reflection that comes along with an ornamentalization being achieved for example by the repetition of sounds and words as well as by the ambiguity of symbols. Thus the narrative voice loses all features of individual characterization and gains a kind of universal validity. This by no means implies a denegation of the singularity of the Holocaust but focuses on the fact that a crime like this can be repeated for the simple reason that man has proved to be able and willing to commit such a crime.

Jiří Weil: *Žalozpěv za 77 297 obětí*

Hana Hříbková, Praha

More than 80 000 Bohemian and Moravian Jews perished during the Second World War. One of the places where people over the last few decades have come to honour the memory of them is the Pinkas Synagogue, as this heritage site was chosen in the 1950s to become a dignified memorial to the victims of the Shoah.[1] The walls of the synagogue nave and its adjoining areas were continuously covered between 1954 and 1959[2] by Academy artists Jiří John and Václav Boštík with the known names of the Bohemian and Moravian victims of the Nazi final solution, totalling 77 297 in all.

During the alterations[3] to the new Pinkas Synagogue interior, writer Jiří Weil[4], who at that time was also a research worker at the State Jewish Museum in Prague, decided to write a new literary work to remind the broad public of those who had died in the extermination and concentration camps, including his parents, sister and a number of close friends. He called his latest work *Žalozpěv za 77 297 obětí* (*Lament for 77 297 Victims*).[5]

---

[1] The Pinkas Synagogue also has a permanent exhibition of drawings by the most innocent of the Shoah victims – the children; drawings which Jiří Weil, while organizing the archive material from Theresienstadt concentration camp, evaluated as valuable documentary material. Together with poems by children from Theresienstadt concentration camp he promoted their first joint postwar exhibition in 1955 as a warning against the possible return of antisemitism and as a reminder of the horrors of war. For details see Hříbková 2012.

[2] Michal Frankl, head of the Shoah History Department at the Jewish Museum in Prague, points out the discrepancy of a Holocaust memorial being allowed during a highly anti-semitic period in communist Czechoslovakia, following the show trial and execution of Rudolf Slánský and other party officials, the majority of them Jewish. „In this context, talking about the Holocaust – or anything Jewish – might even be dangerous and hardly anyone did it, but my interpretation of this is that the Pinkas Synagogue was seen as a purely religious space that belonged to the Jewish community, but didn't belong to or speak to the public space" (Stein 2016). However, the regime soon closed it down. The necessary reconstruction of the synagogue in 1968 was used as an excuse to close it down entirely to the public until 1989. During repairs in 1974 all the plaster was knocked off including the elaborate inscriptions.

[3] Such valuable but in many respects exhausting work was performed by Boštík in his subsequent creative activities. For details see the book by Karel Srp (2011).

[4] Jiří Weil was not the only writer, in whose work this interior and its inscriptions can be found. For examples see the *Žalozpěvy* chapter in the book by Hana Volavková (1966).

[5] Hereafter abbreviated to *Žalozpěv*.

The Literary Archive of the Museum of Czech Literature holds the proof-reading to *Žalozpěv*[6] in the personal papers of the editor Květa Drábková, together with preparatory notes for the printer regarding the selected font and minor editorial interventions.[7] In contrast to Weil's other manuscripts, several versions of which were always preserved, or even several alternative proofs, *Žalozpěv* is, at the Literary Archive of the Museum of Czech Literature, only accompanied by this single version of editing interventions, which were accepted without reservations for the final version, as can be seen from the 1958 edition.

Žalozpěv is a montage of three interlinking *sections* (which differ to a large extent both stylistically and graphically[8]). Throughout this work the reader has the option to progressively view the persecution and genocide of the Czech Jews[9]; from the invasion of the Nazi army to the mass murders in the extermination camps. The work oscillates on the genre boundary of poetry and prose, while straddling the interface between non-fiction (facts soberly documenting historical events) and literature.

The first section has a retrospective chronological composition, where the introductory and concluding passages create the framework for the retrospective narrative.

> Kouř blízkých továren zahaluje krajinu rovnou jako stůl, krajinu, která ubíhá do nekonečna. Pokrývá ji popel miliónů mrtvých. A rozsety jsou v ní drobné kostičky, jež nestačily spálit pece. Když přichází vítr, pozvedá popel do oblak, popel se vznáší k nebi a drobné kostičky leží stále na zemi. A déšť padá na popel a déšť jej proměňuje v dobrou

---

[6] Typescript with handwritten notes (Literary Archive of the Museum of Czech Literature, Květa Drábková fonds, 27/80).

[7] Deletions were only made in the case of several words, which were entirely removed or in exceptional cases replaced by words or expressions that were more apposite. These interventions did not in any way involve intrusions of censorship which otherwise were frequent and routine in Weil's case.

[8] For the sake of distinction italics and two kinds of font were used – Plantin and Garamond.

[9] As a researcher Jiří Weil had access to all the collected material documenting the Holocaust in the State Jewish Museum in Prague. He came across the first material and testimonies just after the liberation of Prague in 1945, when he joined in the activities of the restored Prague Jewish Museum. In the same year he also visited liberated Terezín. During the subsequent 1949 – 1958 period he was curating the Documentation of Jewish Persecution archive, spoke with witnesses, helped organize exhibitions on the persecution of Jews and subsequently became Chief Librarian.

a úrodnou prsť, jak se sluší u popelu mučedníků. Kdo může najít popel těch, kdož pocházeli z mé rodné země a jichž bylo 77 297? Nabírám rukou trochu popelu, neboť jen ruka se ho smí dotýkat, a sypu jej do plátěného pytlíku, tak jako kdysi nabírali ti, kdož odcházeli do cizí země, rodnou hlínu, aby nikdy nezapomněli, aby se k ní vždycky vraceli. (Weil 1958, 7)[10]

A hrstka těch, kdož přežili, vidí stíny,stíny svých blízkých, nepohřbených, jichž popel se smísil s hlínou. Mlčenlivě stojí stíny jako výčitka a stráž. Avšak jejich popel se změnil v úrodnou prsť, dobrou zemi, z níž roste obilí a kvetou stromy. Kráčíte po ní, a země je krásná v rozbřesku dne, kdy vody hučí po lučinách a bory šumí po skalinách, a stíny vás provázejí, jdou s vámi ruku v ruce. Neboť i jejich je tato země v pokoji a míru. (ibid., 28)[11]

Within this framework the space of the former concentration camp is described, where in front of the personal narrator the shadows of the unburied dead emerge, accompanying the survivors. Within this description the dominant motif of the landscape is a clear symbol of the Jewish nation, which like the landscape itself is gradually recovering from the ordeal it has suffered. At the same time, however, the motif of ash swirling in the wind and the omnipresent shadows point to the weight of the past, which the survivors will always carry with them. At the end of this reflective framework the author addresses the reader and by alluding to the Czech national anthem points to the imprescriptibility of the crimes committed.

---

[10] „Table-like, the smoke from nearby factories covers the landscape, a landscape that converges on infinity, veiling it in the ash of millions of the dead, while scattered around are the tiny bones that the ovens did not manage to incinerate. When the wind blows it raises the ash in a cloud, the ash rises skyward, while the tiny bones stay down on earth. And the rain falls on the ash, and the rain transforms it into good, fertile soil, as befits the ash of martyrs. Who can find the ash of those who came from my native land, of whom there were 77 297? I scoop up a little ash in my hand, as only my hand may touch it, and I pour it into a canvas bag, just as at one time those who were leaving for foreign lands scooped up their native soil, so as never to forget, so as always to come home" (Translations from Czech by Melvyn Clarke).

[11] „And a handful of those who survived see the shadows, the shadows of those dearest to them, unburied, whose ash was mixed with the clay. In silence the shadows stand like a reproach and a vigil. However, their ash has turned into fertile soil, good earth from which the corn will grow and the trees will blossom. You walk on it, and the earth is beautiful at the break of day, when the waters murmur through the meadows and the pinewoods rustle among the crags, and the shadows walk hand in hand together with you. For this land is also theirs in peace and harmony".

A retrospective narrative is inserted within this framework, its three parts are linked not only by the chronology, but also by the omniscient narrator, who here and there presents in poetic form general information on the distinct stages of the Holocaust.[12]

The first part includes texts[13] charting the invasion of the Nazis, people's attempts to emigrate, the gradual introduction of written and unwritten laws persecuting the Jewish population, people's attempts to adapt to the degrading living conditions and the arrival of the „hangman"[14], who began to speed up the killing process.

> Smrt vstoupila onoho dne do města, doprovázena pištci, nosiči koňských ohonů, smrtihlavy a rachocením bubnů. Lidé se snažili před ní utéci, ale smrt měla rychlejší nohy, dostihovala je na cestách, ve vlacích a u pohraničních závor. (ibid., 9)[15]

In the second part the narrator describes the fates of the Jews from their arrival at the Prague assembly point in Rádiotrh and their journey by freight train to the railway station and from there to the Theresienstadt concentration camp and the everyday lives of prisoners, in which death, hunger and Nazi terror were the order of the day. This is followed by information on the first transports to the east, when people did not know where this journey into the unknown would lead. The second part ends with a reference to the ‚Potemkin's villages' built in Theresienstadt concentration camp to deceive the visitors from the Red Cross Committee.

During the third part the narrator falls silent and the liquidation of the Jewish population in the extermination camps is portrayed purely as a prose poem. The

---

[12] In addition to the imagery of allegory, metaphors and symbols, the principles of contrast and parallels are often used in the text. Some parts of the section can be considered as a prose poem.

[13] Individual texts follow on one after the other in some sections, though this cannot be said to be a single continuous text that was subsequently divided into several short parts. The texts are linked by a chronologically ordered time line.

[14] In the parallel second section the name is pronounced in its entirety – the hangman is Reinhard Heydrich.

[15] „Death came to town that day, accompanied by pipers, ponytail wearers, death's heads and a roll of drums. People tried to escape it, but death had faster legs and caught up with them on their travels, in trains and at border gates".

symbol of human hands is used in the poetic image to emphasize the contrast between life before the war and the suffering and death during the war. The retrospective in the first section ends with a symbolic image:

> Ruce matky, hladící dítě po vlasech, ruce milenců, do sebe spletené, ruce žehnající nad pohárem vína, [...] jemné ruce vyšívačky, tvrdé uzlovaté ruce starců, malé pěstičky dětí. A ruce vztyčené z hrobů, ruce zkrvavené ranami, ruce se servanými nehty, ruce rozdrcené okovanými botami. (ibid., 27)[16]

The second section in *Žalozpěv* concretizes the general information[17] gained from the first section. Precise figures, dates and terms are presented[18], while the sober form of the text comes close to that of a newspaper report.[19] Again this section has a retrospectively chronological structure, but this time it is not housed within a framework, and the narrator is suprapersonal throughout the entire section.

The first episode explains the choice of the figure 77 297 and informs the reader of the recently established memorial at the Pinkas Synagogue. This introduction is followed by retrospective views of the past, which in terms of time

---

[16] „The hands of a mother caressing her child's hair, lovers' hands entwined, hands blessing a goblet of wine, [...] the soft hands of embroiderers, the gnarled, hardened hands of the elderly, the little fists of children. And hands raised from the graves, hands bloody with wounds, hands with the nails torn out, hands crushed under hobnailed boots".

[17] In contrast to Weil's other works, *Žalozpěv* definitely does not need any supplementary historical commentary. The author himself has inserted the factual element directly into the work. Thematically, *Žalozpěv* also covers Weil's entire work on the topic of the Holocaust. Individual motifs from *Žalozpěv* are presented in detail in *Život s hvězdou* (*Life with a Star*), *Na střeše je Mendelssohn* (*Mendelssohn is on the Roof*), the unfinished novel *Zde se tančí Lambeth-walk* (*Here they dance the Lambeth-walk*) and in his short stories. What is unique and untypical for Weil, who survived the war in Prague, but necessary for the overall composition and the intellectual purport of the work, is the location of Auschwitz selected for the work, which Weil only described in 1947 in one of his reportages from Poland. This work covers Weil's entire creative activity to date in terms of both the form and content of his other works on the Shoah. With the first section of the work Weil returns cyclically to the early origins of his work – carrying on from his wartime short stories *Barvy* (*Colours*) and his early poetic work. With the second section, as detailed above, Weil covers his postwar novel output. A question mark remains over the third section – psalms, which previously had not appeared in Weil's work. The specific inspiration in Weil's compositional plans for *Žalozpěv* might have been the psalms that make up the decoration in the Old New Synagogue, which were and still are part of the Jewish Museum in which he was employed.

[18] Rádiotrh, Terezín, Auschwitz, R. Heydrich, Hitler, Mengele etc.

[19] Though in some cases this style is breached by the use of colloquial words. For more details see Grebeníčková 1995, pp. 404 et seqq.

and space match the narrative of the first section. A lot of the episodes are focused around one of the specific figures[20], whose fate humanizes and concretizes the general text of the first section. It is these episodic views of the life of individuals that literally draw readers into a world they could barely imagine.

The texts of the second section can again be divided into three chronologically ordered parts. The first part has regularly alternating episodes focusing around a single character[21] with group scene episodes depicting the deliberate ongoing degradation of the Czech Jewish population as a whole – the selection of people standing in the queue for the papers required to emigrate, the beating and forced ejection of Jews from a cafe, the growing number of written orders sent to every household from the Jewish religious community. This first part ends with the appointment of Reinhard Heydrich as the Acting Reich Protector, who ordered the declaration of martial law and the start of the organized systematic liquidation of the Jews.

> Josef Friedmann, čtyřiačtyřicetiletý, emigrant z Vídně, skočil z čtvrtého patra činžovního domu. Umíral dlouho na ulici, sanitní vůz nemohl pro něho přijet, protože ulice byly uzavřeny vojskem. Když se konečně vůz zastavil u domu, byl Friedmann mrtev. Bylo to dne 15. března ve dvě hodiny odpoledne. (ibid., 8)[22]
>
> Lidé stáli v dlouhé frontě před policejním ředitelstvím na Perštýně. Stáli tam od ranních hodin, přišli ještě za tmy. V devět hodin se otevřela vrata. Vystoupil esesák v černé uni-

---

[20] The style of description for individual characters is similar to that in Weil's other work. For the most part this time we only know about the characters what was only known about the real victims from the card files – i.e. their names and towns of residence, and in some cases their age and details of death. The internal and external characteristics of the characters are left out, and they never comment in any way on the situation around them (with one exception). Only in certain cases does the narrator portray their external reactions, e.g. crying and in some important cases the character's main interest before the occupation. As the characters' past interests cease to be mentioned, so in parallel they themselves lose their will.

[21] Brief episodes successively depict four characters. Three of them die when they find there is no reason for living, i.e. the previous freedom, money or music. The fourth character tries to reconcile himself to the new situation, but not even that is a solution, because then he becomes defenceless before the Nazis.

[22] „Josef Friedmann, a forty-four-year-old emigrant from Vienna jumped from the fourth floor of a tenement block. He took a long time to die on the street; the ambulance could not reach him, because soldiers had closed off the street. When the vehicle finally got to the building, Friedmann was dead. This was at two o' clock in the afternoon on 15th March".

formě. Řekl: Židé z řady ven! Řekl to německy, rozkročen na chodníku, a český strážník to přeložil. (ibid., 9)[23]

In the second part Weil included characters who were already reconciled to their compulsory transportation to Theresienstadt concentration camp and their aim in life is now to stay alive there as long as possible. The first three consecutive episodes focus on individuals[24], followed by four group scenes[25], whose denouements prepare readers for the final third part, which takes place at the Auschwitz extermination camp.

Auschwitz is presented to readers in two episodic images. In the first one the character of Doctor Mengele decides on life and death with a wave of his hand, while in the second one the family camp in Auschwitz is liquidated and people going to their deaths sing the Czech national anthem.

This final scene comes to serve as a link with the framework of the first section – symbolizing the strength and courage of the Czech Jews tied to their homeland, which at the hour of death finds human heroism and banishes fear with a song from the native land:

> Dne 7. března 1943[26] byl likvidován tak zvaný rodinný tábor v Osvětimi. Osm tisíc mužů, žen a dětí bylo posláno do plynových komor. Věděli, jaký osud je čeká, věděli, že jdou na smrt. Šli a zpívali hymnu své rodné země. Byla to píseň *Kde domov můj*. (ibid., 28)[27]

---

[23] „People stood in a long queue in front of the police directorate at Perštýn. They had been standing there since the early hours before it was light. At nine o' clock the gates opened. An SS man in a black uniform appeared. He said: ‚Jews, get out of the line!' Standing on the pavement with his legs apart, he spoke in German, and the Czech policeman translated it".

[24] The narrator observes a lame man die, a woman being robbed and an exhausted old man starving. Four episodes follow with group scenes.

[25] The handicapped waiting for the transport, the execution of the innocent, an inventory of transports from Terezín in 1942 (in combination with precise figures showing how many people left and how many came back, i.e. taking the future into account) and children being led off to their deaths immediately after a theatre performance for the Red Cross.

[26] The incorrect date in the 1958 edition (and in the second edition of 1999) and in the typescript proofreading which is preserved in the Literary Archive of the Museum of Czech Literature, is most probably a typo and was not used deliberately; the correct date is 1944.

[27] „On 7th March 1943 what was known as the family camp at Auschwitz was liquidated. Eight thousand men, women and children were sent to the gas chambers. They knew what fate awaited them. They knew they were going to their deaths. They went and they sang their national anthem. It was the song *Where is my home?*".

The third, final section is made up of sensitively selected quotes from *Kralice Bible*, mostly from *Kniha žalmů*, and is closely related with text from the second section. These quotes also invite the reader to contemplation over what has just been read: „Pročež hodím vámi z země této do země, o níž nevíte vy, ani otcové vaši, a sloužiti budete tam bohům cizím dnem i nocí. Jeremiáš, 16,13" (ibid., 9).[28]

The linkage of all three sections results in a meeting among texts that were written thousands of years apart. Hence the *Žalozpěv* text is resurrected in new contexts that are relatable to present-day events.[29]

The text of the first edition (published as a bibliophile edition by Československý spisovatel publishers in a print-run of 700 copies) comes together with three art prints by the painter Zdeněk Seydl, who also designed the cover and the typographic arrangement of the text.

The uniquely sensitive lay-out of what was undoubtedly the author's supreme work was unfortunately not preserved in the second edition in 1999[30], as the work was artistically devalued with regard to the interlinking text composition and external lay-out of the book. Hence a significant part of the composition is lost to the contemporary reader, as its division was often also internally connected with the inclusion of prints in the three separate units freely inserted in the cover[31], printed with a monochrome copy of a photograph of part of the already completed painting of the Pinkas Synagogue walls.[32]

---

[28] „Therefore will I cast you out of this land into a land that ye know not, neither ye nor your fathers; and there shall ye serve other gods day and night. Jeremiah, 16,13".
[29] The photographer Věra Koubová included the final passage of *Žalozpěv* in her series of illustrations for Weil's short stories (see Koubová 2006).
[30] That same year *Žalozpěv* was also published in Germany under the title *Elegie für 77297 Opfer. Jüdische Schicksale in Böhmen und Mähren 1939 – 1945* (Aus d. Tschech. v. Avri Salamon. Konstanz).
[31] The exceptional nature of the cover is mentioned e.g. by Rudolf Iltis in his analytical article. Inter alia Iltis writes that the cover „in one small section indicates an endless chain of the names of the dead inscribed on the wall of the Pinkas Synagogue, the dead ‚whose shadows walk hand in hand together with us...' And these crowds of victims raise their voices together with us survivors in a crushing accusation! They appeal: ‚Don't forget us' [...]" (Iltis 1959). The title of the work is incorrectly quoted in the title of the article.
[32] The entire memorial with the names was not completed until after the publication of *Žalozpěv*.

Hence the new format of the new edition of *Žalozpěv* (most probably due to the financial cost of reprinting the original work) was unfortunately not the long-expected dignified successor of what is today the practically unavailable 1958 edition, and it can only be hoped that future editions will pay greater attention and respect to the lay-out, which this exceptional work undoubtedly deserves.

With its special lay-out, content and title *Žalozpěv* has, over the last few decades, appealed to several creative artists to consider its subsequent artistic re-presentation. Several dramatic and literary-musical adaptations have been created.

One of the best-known of these was a performance by the Miriam Theatre, first presented in 2002 to mark the 60th anniversary of the first transports of Jews to the Theresienstadt concentration camp.[33] A sensitive interpretation of individual sections was presented by Elena Strupková, Ester Janečková (both co-script-writers) and Rudolf Kvíz; the recitation was accompanied by composer Petr Traxler with impressive compositions based on the synagogue chants of Shalom Katz (a Romanian cantor who survived Auschwitz thanks to singing the Kaddish prayer). This performance with a minimum of props and an outstanding cast and musical accompaniment has been reprised many times.

No less impressive are the radio adaptations by Český rozhlas (Czech Radio) in 1990 and 1991. The recitation of individual sections in 1990 was undertaken[34] by Hana Kofránková, Pavel Soukup and Josef Červinka[35], while the reading is accompanied by a synagogue chant[36] from the record *A Dohány Utcai Zsinagóga Liturgiája*. In 1991 the work was recited by Jana Hlaváčová, Josef Somr and Petr Kostka. One of the most recent adaptations is a chamber interpretation by Czech Radio – Vltava recited by Michal Pavlata, and accompanied by piano compositions by Ervín Schulhoff.

---

[33] For more details see http://katalog.terezinstudies.cz/cz2/TI/newsletter/newsletter20_ special /weil (1.1.2016).

[34] A specific feature of the radio genre, which brings the written word to life, sets high demands in the context of the Shoah not only regarding the correct choice of the reciter, but also of the accompanying music.

[35] The libretto is from 1968, but for political reasons it was not staged until after 1989.

[36] Another research point might be the frequency of use of synagogue chants in connection with adaptations of works on the Shoah.

In the 21st century we are looking for some specific way to introduce the Shoah to modern society and the young generation. Numerous modern devices, computers and special visual effects are often used in Europe as well as in America. Jiří Weil's *Žalozpěv* speaks to readers without these complex effects. It is an essential work about the Shoah. This piece which started as a heartfelt remembrance of the next-of-kin has become truly timeless.

Bibliography

Grebeníčková, Růžena 1995: Weilův *Žalozpěv*. In: id.: Literatura a fiktivní světy. Praha, pp. 404-407.

Hříbková, Hana 2012: Jiří Weil: A Scientist and Initiator of Exhibitions of Children's Drawings from Terezín. In: The Representation of the Shoah in Literature, Theatre and Film in Central Europe: 1950s and 1960s. Ed. by Jiří Holý. Praha, pp. 51-63.

Iltis, Rudolf 1959: Žalozpěv na 77 298 obětí. In: Věstník ŽNO, 21,3, p. 5.

Koubová, Věra 2006: Návrh ilustrací k povídkám Jiřího Weila. In: Revolver Revue 65, p. 86-89.

Srp, Karel 2011: Václav Boštík. Praha.

Stein, Michael 2016: Prague Jewish Museum Marks 70th Anniversary of Terezín Deportations. http://ceskapozice.lidovky.cz/prague-jewish-museum-marks-70th-anniversary-of-terezin-deportations-1gv-/tema.aspx?c=A111123_161121_pozice_45488&setver=touch(1.1.2016).

Volavková, Hana 1966: Příběh židovského muzea. Praha.

Weil, Jiří 1958: Žalozpěv za 77 297 obětí. Praha.

id. 1999: Život s hvězdou. Na střeše je Mendelssohn. Žalozpěv za 77 297 obětí. Praha. http://katalog.terezinstudies.cz/cz2/TI/newsletter/newsletter20_ special /weil (1.1.2016).

Jiří Weil: *Žalozpěv za 77 297 obětí*

Diese Studie ist dem zeitlosen Werk *Žalozpěv za 77 297 obětí* (*Klagegesang für 77 297 Opfer*) des bekannten tschechischen Schriftstellers, Übersetzers, Journalisten, Literaturkritikers und Wissenschaftlers Jiří Weil (1900 – 1959) gewidmet. Die Studie enthält eine ausführliche Analyse des Werks, die um Informationen aus dem Archiv des Tschechischen Rundfunks, des Nationalarchivs und des Literarischen Archivs des Denkmals für das Nationale Schrifttum erweitert wurde (alle Institutionen sind in Prag ansässig). Im abschließenden Teil dieser Studie werden Informationen zur Publikationsgeschichte dieses Werks, zu den Unterschieden zwischen den einzelnen Ausgaben sowie eine kurze Übersicht über die bekanntesten Adaptionen dieses Werks geliefert.

This article was supported by grant GAČR 13-03627S *Reprezentace Židů a židovství v literatuře českých zemí ve 20. století*.

„Und, da das Schweigen Gift mir wird im Munde, / Gebe ich weinend von der Schande Kunde".
Karl Schnogs (1897 – 1967) satirische Holocaustdichtung

Charlotte Kitzinger, Gießen

Bereits im Oktober 1933 hatte der österreichische Schriftsteller, Publizist und Satiriker Karl Kraus in der 888. Nummer seiner Zeitschrift *Die Fackel* die Möglichkeit der Satire angesichts des Nationalsozialismus verneint. Satire (und Literatur an sich) könne keine treffenden Worte über und gegen den Nationalsozialismus finden. „Kein Wort, das traf" (Kraus 1933, 4), dichtete er in einem zehnzeiligen Gedicht mit dem Titel *Man frage nicht*, dessen letzter Vers lautete: „Das Wort entschlief, als jene Welt erwachte" (ebd.). Dennoch zeichnet sich ein nicht unerheblicher Teil der Literatur und Kunst über den Nationalsozialismus und Holocaust, gerade aus dem Exil, durch ihre satirische, komische, groteske und absurde Gestaltung aus. Die Erfahrung der Unangemessenheit der Worte und das Unvermögen, „was als Zivilisationsbruch unsere Epoche bestimmt hat […] tatsächlich erkennbar zu machen" (Braese 2005, 15), teilen sich diese satirischen Werke mit den meisten Zeugnissen und Werke über den Holocaust.

Der jüdische Autor und Künstler Karl Schnog hatte sowohl eigene Erfahrungen als sog. politischer Häftling, als verfolgter Jude, als Emigrant und nicht zuletzt auch als Überlebender der Konzentrationslager. All diese Phasen und Erlebnisse hat er dichterisch und satirisch verarbeitet. Eine sehr wichtige Funktion für die Niederschrift seiner Gedichte scheint dabei in der Bedeutung des Zeugnisablegens zu liegen. „Und da das Schweigen Gift mir wird im Munde, / Gebe ich weinend von der Schande Kunde" (Schnog 1947, 47), dichtete er kurz nach Kriegsende.

Auch das Gedicht *Nackte Aussage* widmete er dem Zeugnisdruck des Überlebenden, der nur so wieder ‚vom Schmutz gereinigt' werden kann:

> Ich habe so tief im Elend gesteckt,
> Ich schien verloren, verkommen, verdreckt.
> Gejagt ward ich und gepeinigt.
> Erst, wenn ich sage, was ich sah,

Erst wenn ich schreibe, was geschah,
Bin ich vom Schmutz gereinigt.
(ebd., 62)

Das Gedicht stammt ebenfalls aus dem 1947 erstmals veröffentlichten Band *Jedem das Seine*. Der Band ist in vier Abschnitte unterteilt, die in chronologischer Abfolge Gedichte aus den Jahren 1926 bis 1946 enthalten. Darunter sind auch Verse über Schnogs Haft in den Konzentrationslagern Dachau und Buchenwald von 1940 bis 1945. Ergänzt wird der Band durch einige Illustrationen von Herbert Sandberg, der als Grafiker und Karikaturist bekannt war. Aufgrund seiner illegalen Tätigkeit in der KPD war Sandberg von 1934 bis 1938 im Gefängnis und ab 1938 bis Kriegsende im KZ Buchenwald inhaftiert. Im Dezember 1945 gründete er zusammen mit Günther Weisenborn die Zeitschrift *Ulenspiegel* sowie den gleichnamigen Verlag, in dem 1947 auch der Gedichtband *Jedem das Seine* von Karl Schnog in einer Auflagenhöhe von 5.000 Exemplaren herausgeben wurde. Karl Schnog war zeitweise Chefredakteur des Blattes.

Schnog begann jedoch nicht erst nach dem Krieg zu schreiben und zu dichten. Er gehört nicht zu den Autoren, die einmalig über ihre Erlebnisse im Holocaust berichteten und sich weniger als Schriftsteller denn als Zeugen und Chronisten der Ereignisse verstanden wissen wollten. Er sah sich – soweit man das nachvollziehen kann – sowohl als Künstler als auch als politischer Mensch.

Schnog, der am 14. Juni 1897 in Köln geboren wurde, stammte aus einer jüdischen Handwerkerfamilie.[1] Er diente im Ersten Weltkrieg und gründete nach dessen Ende 1918 einen Arbeiter- und Soldatenrat in Hagenau. Er nahm außerdem Sprech- und Schauspielunterricht und trat (unter anderem in Erwin Piscators Revue *Roter Rummel*) als Conférencier und Rezitator in namhaften Kabaretts auf. Ab 1925 war er freier Schriftsteller und Mitarbeiter von Zeitungen wie *Die Weltbühne*, *Simplizissimus* und *Stachelschwein*, und ab 1927 fungierte Schnog zudem als Sprecher beim Rundfunk. Im gleichen Jahr begründete er die Gruppe Revolutionärer Pazifisten in Berlin mit. Schnog verwendete als Künstler

---

[1] Alle Angaben zur Biographie Karl Schnogs stammen aus folgenden, im Literaturverzeichnis aufgeführten Quellen: Dokumente des Archivs des International Tracing Service (ITS) Bad Arolsen; Kühn 2007, 340f.; Dokumente aus dem Landesarchiv Berlin; Autorenlexikon des Literaturport; Luxemburger Autorenlexikon.

zahlreiche Pseudonyme wie Anton Emerenzer, Carl Coblentz, Ernst Huth, Kornschlag, Tom Palmer und Charly vom Thurm. Nach der Machtübernahme der Nationalsozialisten wurden zwei Haftbefehle gegen Schnog erlassen und er wurde auf offener Straße schwer misshandelt. Im Mai 1933 emigrierte er in die Schweiz und im Oktober nach Luxemburg, wo er jeweils in Kabaretts Anstellung fand. Er war außerdem Mitarbeiter deutscher Exilzeitungen wie dem *Pariser Tagblatt* und dem *Neuen Vorwärts*, aber auch verschiedener Luxemburger Zeitungen.

Am 3. Dezember 1936 wurde Schnog die deutsche Staatsbürgerschaft aberkannt. Versuche, in die USA auszuwandern, scheiterten, und nach dem Einmarsch der Wehrmacht in Luxemburg wurde er am 25. Mai 1940 verhaftet und als politischer Häftling im Konzentrationslager Dachau festgehalten. Seine Haft in Dachau wurde durch eine vorübergehende Inhaftierung im KZ Sachsenhausen von August bis September 1940 unterbrochen, bevor er am 12. Juli 1941 dann endgültig von Dachau in das KZ Buchenwald deportiert und im Mai 1945 von dort befreit wurde. Er kehrte nach Luxemburg zurück, wo er bei Radio Luxemburg arbeitete. 1945 erschien zudem sein kurzer Erinnerungsbericht *Unbekanntes KZ* über seine fünfjährige Konzentrationslagerhaft. 1946 zog er nach Ostberlin und wurde Chefredakteur des *Ulenspiegel*. Ab April 1947 war er Mitglied einer Theatertruppe, die in jiddischer Sprache für das Durchgangslager der Hilfsorganisation United Nations Relief und Rehabilitation Administration (UNRRA) in Berlin spielte. 1947 veröffentlichte er zudem seine satirischen Gedichte zum Nationalsozialismus und Holocaust unter dem bereits genannten Titel *Jedem das Seine*. Er war von 1948 bis 1951 Redakteur für Kabarett und Satire beim Berliner Rundfunk und trat der Sozialistischen Einheitspartei Deutschlands (SED) bei. Ab 1951 arbeitete er als freier Schriftsteller und war unter anderem für das Ostberliner Kabarett *Die Distel* tätig. Er starb am 23. August 1964 in Berlin.

Karl Schnog war also vor und nach dem Krieg Schriftsteller, Radio-Sprecher, Kabarettist und Schauspieler. Doch vor allem die Wut und Fassungslosigkeit angesichts der Geschehnisse im Nationalsozialismus und Holocaust war ein zentraler Antrieb für seine Dichtung in den ersten Nachkriegsjahren. So erklärt er am Ende des Gedichtbandes in einem „Selbstgespräch eines satirischen Dichters auf der Brücke der Zeit" (Schnog 1947, 92) ein weiteres Mal sein Bedürfnis, das Erlebte sowie seine Gedanken und Empfindungen in Versform zu fassen:

> Ich forme Reime, – nur kaum aus Freude, meist aus Zorn, und der entstellt sie manchmal, weil der Stachel in das Fleisch der Satten fahren muß, die sich nicht um Blut und Tränen scheren, ob vergangen, gegenwärtig oder künftig. (ebd., 93)

Er sei sich ebenfalls sicher, heißt es weiter, dass

> der Trieb nach Recht und Freiheit lebt – […], mag er entstellt, verhärmt, verkümmert und von den Falten vieler Interessen gezeichnet, ja wohl sogar überdeckt sein. Ich glaube an die Bruderschaft von allen, die irgendwo in ihrem Innern noch guten Willens sind. Bin ich ein Narr?! Mein Beitrag, der Beitrag des Satirikers, soll es mir erweisen … (ebd., 94)

An dieser Stelle nennt Schnog seine Dichtung also – ebenso wie im Untertitel des Werks – explizit satirisch. Als solche wollte er sie verstanden wissen, und in diese Gattungstradition, die ihren Ursprung in der römischen Antike hat – zunächst als Spottdichtung in Form eines Hexametergedichts (vgl. Brummack 1977, 601) – stellte er sein Werk. Heute werden unter dem Begriff gattungsübergreifende Literaturformen und Werke beschrieben, die Zustände, Ereignisse, Missstände und Personen in sprachlich überspitzter, pointierter, verspottender oder aggressiver, ironischer und sarkastischer Form bloßstellen, entlarven und aufdecken (vgl. ebd., 602ff.).

Satire ist immer auch ein Zerrspiegel der Wirklichkeit, wie Erich Kästner – der ein weitaus bekannterer Verfasser als Karl Schnog von zeitkritischen und politisch-satirischen Gedichten und anderen Textformen war und der wie dieser für den *Simplicissimus* und *Die Weltbühne* tätig war – 1947 in einem Beitrag mit dem Titel *Eine kleine Sonntagspredigt. Vom Sinn und Wesen der Satire* schrieb (vgl. Kästner 1959). Der satirische Schriftsteller stelle die Dummheit, die Bosheit, die Trägheit und verwandte Eigenschaften an den Pranger in der Hoffnung, so eine Änderung der Menschen herbeizuführen, heißt es dort weiter. Die Ausführungen Kästners weisen auf zwei wesentliche Funktionen der Satire hin: Sie ist Ventil und Waffe, da sie als gesellschaftliches Regulativ und zur Verteidigung der Kultur dienen kann (vgl. Brummack 1977, 603).

Auch bei Schnog liegt die Funktion seiner satirischen Gedichte im Wesentlichen in der Kritik an der mangelbehafteten Wirklichkeit und Bloßstellung des – in diesem Fall nationalsozialistischen – Gegners. Wie bei aller Satire ist auch bei ihm die Zeitgebundenheit wesentlich, seine Gedichte beschäftigen sich mit ganz konkreten gesellschaftlichen, politischen, aber auch persönlichen Themen und stellen historische Personen – etwa Adolf Hitler – an den Pranger.

So bescheinigt Eugen Kogon, der vor allem durch seinen 1946 veröffentlichten Bericht über die Konzentrationslager *Der SS-Staat* bekannt geworden ist und der mit Schnog im KZ Buchenwald inhaftiert war, Schnogs Gedichten in einem Nachwort am Ende des Bandes, dass dessen Satire „gegen die übelste Abart der Schergen Hitlers" (Schnog 1947, 94) sie bei ihren illegalen Veranstaltungen im Lager mit befreiendem Lachen erfüllt habe. Schnogs satirische Gedichte trügen ihre Rechtfertigung in sich, „auch wenn die Getroffenen dagegen toben mögen" (ebd.). Gelegentlich erscheine es ihm, schreibt Kogon weiter, als ob ein „Hieb nicht so ganz sicher im Objekt" (ebd., 95) sitze, und manchmal frage er sich: „Ob's nützen wird?" (ebd.). Aber wer wüsste so genau, was im Durcheinander der Gegenwart angemessen sei oder was nicht, schließt er. Darum fordere er Schnog auf: „[L]os: sag's, was zu sagen ist" (ebd.).

Auch Kurt Wolter schrieb 1948 in der Zeitung *Welt und Wort*:

> ‚Vorher' – ‚Von draußen' – ‚Inmitten' – ‚Und heute' sind die Abschnitte des über zwanzig Jahre langen Weges, auf dem Karl Schnog Menschen und Ereignisse mit seiner spitzen Feder festhielt. Nicht von ungefähr ist diese Sammlung im ‚Ulenspiegel'-Verlag erschienen: sind es doch Spiegelbilder, die, dem Menschen vorgehalten, zur Besinnung auffordern. (Wolter 1948, 306)

Schnog verwischt die Grenzen zwischen Täter und Opfer nicht, sondern grenzt sie klar voneinander ab. Daher zeichnen sich die Gedichte oft durch eine einseitige Stellungnahme und Parteilichkeit aus, die manchmal agitativ und aggressiv, aber häufiger eher traurig und resigniert vorgebracht wird. Nicht ganz so deutlich und verhältnismäßig selten sind wirklich komische Elemente. Schnog kontrastiert viel mehr in einem ironischen und sarkastischen Ton – der ja auch ein Mittel der Distanzierung von eigenem Leid und ein häufiges Stilmittel in Texten der frühen Holocaust- und Lagerliteratur ist – Wirklichkeit und Ideal und gibt so den bedichteten Gegenstand der Lächerlichkeit preis, wie sich an einzelnen Beispielen zeigen lässt.

Der erste Teil des Bandes trägt die Überschrift *Vorher* und enthält Gedichte aus den Jahren 1926 bis 1930. Darin thematisiert Schnog gesellschaftliche und politische Themen und die Kriegsbegeisterung im deutschen Volk wie etwa in *Lob des Krieges*.

> LOB DES KRIEGES
> Zwischen Zotenreißen, Skat und Saufen
> Wird mit Schlachtenglück geprunkt:
> „Wie die Hasen sind die Kerls gelaufen.
> Unsre Artillerie traf auf den Punkt.
> Mensch, da türmten sich die Leichenhaufen.
> Wir natürlich: immer reingefunkt!"
> Und sie lauschen diesem Lob der Schlachten,
> Dem der üble Duft von Aas entquillt.
> Und im Horchen, Lügen und Betrachten
> Wird verborgner, dunkler Trieb gestillt.
> Bis sie den als schlapp und schlecht verachten,
> Dem das Morden nicht als Höchstes gilt.
> Und es ragt schöngefärbter Heldenschwindel
> Aus der Zeiten Trümmer wie ein Fels.
> Die im Pschorrbräu oder Münchner Kindl
> Loben Gasgranaten und Schrapnells.
> (Und im Kriege lag das in der Windel,
> Oder voll gefressen in Bordells.)
> (Schnog 1947, 9)

Hier wird die prahlerische Dummheit der Kriegsbefürworter und Kriegstreiber vorgeführt, die – wie in der letzten Zeile deutlich wird – niemals an einer Schlacht beteiligt waren und den Krieg nicht aus eigenem Erleben kennen, aber am Stammtisch mit Heldengeschichten und Kampfesbegeisterung prahlen. Wie in fast allen Gedichten Schnogs sind Versstruktur und Reimschema einfach gestaltet, hier durch einen einfachen Wechselreim, es kommt ihm offenbar nicht so sehr auf die Form, sondern auf den Inhalt an. Charakteristisch ist auch der deutliche und umgangssprachliche, bisweilen etwas saloppe Ton, der sich in einigen der Gedichte findet.

Der zweite Teil ist mit *Von Draussen 1933 bis 1940* überschrieben und beinhaltet Gedichte aus und über die Emigration. In *Naziführer sehen Dich an* nimmt Schnog Bezug auf das 1934 von Walter Mehring – einem deutschjüdischen Schriftsteller und einem der bedeutendsten satirischen Autoren der Weimarer Republik[2] – unter diesem Titel anonym veröffentlichte Buch, das 33

---

[2] Zur Biographie Walter Mehrings vgl. Emmerich 1990 sowie den Online Artikel „Walther Mehring" (s. Literaturverzeichnis).

Biografien über führende Nationalsozialisten enthielt. Das Buch spielte auf die antisemitische Schmähschrift *Juden sehen dich an* von 1933 an und sollte anhand dokumentarischen Materials zeigen, wie viele Kriminelle und Psychopathen unter den Führern des Dritten Reichs waren. Schnog widmet Mehrings Buch ein Gedicht, indem er eine Rezension in Reimform verfasst. Man sehe „nackt und dokumentarisch", heißt es, das „Spezial-Verbrechertum" mit seinem hemmungslosen Willen zur Zerstörung. Gleichzeitig warnt er vor „den braunen Horden" und ruft zum „Zusammenschluss zur Rettung der Kultur" (alle Zitate S. 27) auf.

> ZUM BUCH: *NAZIFÜHRER SEHEN DICH AN*
> Hier sieht Europa nackt, dokumentarisch
> Spezial-Verbrechertum, bewußt und arisch,
> Das – unbekümmert um die Menschheit – haust.
> Unfug und Untat im verworr'nen Knäuel;
> Kein Greuelmärchen, sondern echte Greuel.
> Die Welt verwundert sich, Europa graust.
>
> Nur keine Hemmung oder Lustverdrängung:
> Entführung, Überfall, Zerstörung, Sprengung.
> Weg mit der Menschlichkeit – es gilt die Tat
> (Die Wahrheit gegen Propagandadichtung)!
> Hier seht das Werk: Bedrohung und Vernichtung.
> Wer glaubt ans Endziel, an den – Musterstaat?
>
> Und wer dies las und vor dem Tun erstarrte,
> Der wisse: Dies ist nur die Musterkarte,
> Ist nur ein Rinnsal von der blut'gen Spur.
> Darum, sich wappnend gegen braune Horden,
> Ist der Entschluß in allen reif geworden:
> Zusammenschluß zur Rettung der Kultur!
> (ebd., 27)

Die bisher aufgeführten Gedichte stammen aus der Zeit vor Schnogs Konzentrationslagerhaft. Der dritte Teil *Inmitten 1940 bis 1945* enthält Gedichte über die Konzentrationslager Dachau und Buchenwald, die durch die jeweils kleingedruckte Angabe zum jeweiligen Konzentrationslager sowie zum Jahr ergänzt werden. In diesen Gedichten geht es nicht mehr wie in den früheren Versen darum, vor dem Nationalsozialismus zu warnen und ihm etwas entgegenzusetzen, nun geht es darum, über die Lager zu berichten und als Überlebender Zeugnis abzulegen.

Ein wesentliches Merkmal der Satire ist die Übertreibung, wie auch schon Kurt Tucholsky 1919 in seinem Aufsatz *Was darf die Satire?* feststellte. Aber wie übertreibt man die systematische und massenhafte Vernichtung von Menschen, die eigene Lagererfahrung? Die Übertreibung kann hier nicht in den Tatsachen liegen, nicht in dem was bedichtet wird, sondern in dem, wie es in Form gebracht wird. In *Erledigt* thematisiert Schnog etwa das Sterben eines ‚Muselmanns' in Dachau 1940.

> ERLEDIGT
> Was sollten sie mit dem Toten auch tun?
> So haben sie ihn denn angepackt,
> Im Winkel vom Waschraum liegt er nun,
> Mager und wächsern und nackt.
>
> Er kam ganz kräftig in das KZ
> Und war immer munter und laut.
> Erst verlor er die Laune, dann verlor er das Fett.
> Jetzt liegt da nur Knochen und Haut.
>
> Um die spitzige Nase ein bitterer Zug,
> Den Mund halb auf, wie zum Schrei.
> Es ist, als wollte er rufen: „Genug"!
> Doch, mit dem Protest ist's vorbei.
>
> Sie schlagen ihn in ein dreckiges Tuch
> Und schleppen ihn endgültig fort.
> Dann streicht man den Namen in einem Buch.
> Und einer geht ab beim Rapport.
> *Dachau 1940*
>
> (ebd., 51)

In diesem Gedicht wird das, was einen körperlich und psychisch gesunden Menschen zu großen Teilen ausmacht – genügend Körperfett und ein stabiles Gemüt –, mit dem, was von einem Menschen im KZ übrig bleibt – seelische Zerstörung, Haut und Knochen –, kontrastiert. Das Reimschema besteht auch hier aus einem einfachen Wechselreim mit jeweils vier Versen. Bereits der erste Satz des Gedichts ist eine rhetorische und zugleich ironisch-sarkastische Frage, die deutlich macht, dass hier keine Beschreibung eines würdigen Umgangs mit Verstorbenen zu erwarten ist. Die spitze Nase mit dem bitteren Zug und der halb zum Schrei geöffnete Mund gestalten ein verzerrtes, nahezu groteskes Bild eines toten Menschen. Kontrastiert wird dieses überzeichnete Bild mit der Alltäglichkeit und Bedeutungslosigkeit des Geschilderten durch die lapidaren Worte „Und einer geht ab beim Rapport".

In dem titelgebenden Gedicht *Jedem das Seine* von 1943 werden die Zeilen über dem Tor zum KZ Buchenwald in Rachephantasien des lyrischen Ichs umgedeutet:

> JEDEM DAS SEINE
> Die Herren haben wirklich Humor
> In diesen bitteren Zeiten:
> „JEDEM DAS SEINE" steht höhnisch am Tor,
> Durch das die Häftlinge schreiten.
>
> So leuchtet, erhaben und arrogant,
> Was sie an das Höllentor schmieden.
> Uns ist auch ohne das Sprüchlein bekannt,
> Was jedem im Lager beschieden:
>
> Dem Häftling – das Stehen in Sonne und Sturm,
> Erfrieren und klatschende Güsse,
> Dazu vom todesdrohenden Turm
> Das ernste Versprechen der Schüsse.
>
> Den Henkern – die Ehre, der schmackhafte Schmaus,
> Das Gleiten auf federnden Felgen;
> Die Ruhe und das behagliche Haus,
> Die Wollust, die Macht und das Schwelgen.
>
> Dem Häftling – der Hunger, die Angst und die Last,
> Die Marter, die viehischen Witze;
> Das Essen, das Baden, das Schlafen in Hast
> Und schließlich die mordende Spritze.
>
> Ihr Herren, die ihr heute noch grient,
> Glaubt mir, was ich schwörend beteure:
> Einst holt sich der Häftling, was er verdient.
> Und Ihr? Ihr bekommt dann das Eure!
> *Buchenwald 1943*

(ebd., 54)

Auch hier bedient sich Schnog eines jeweils vierversigen Kreuzreims, um zunächst das harte, menschenunwürdige und in jeder Sekunde lebensbedrohende Häftlingsdasein in Buchenwald mit der Überlegenheit und der Macht der Nationalsozialisten und SS zu kontrastieren. Bereits die erste Strophe klingt wie ein aus Verzweiflung und Wut geborener ironisch-sarkastischer Ausruf: „Die Herren haben wirklich Humor". Erst im letzten Vers werden die Machtverhältnisse und auch das Motto „Jedem das Seine" in eine herbeigesehnte Zukunft umgewertet: „Einst holt sich der Häftling, was er verdient. / Und Ihr? Ihr bekommt dann das Eure!". Der zynische Ton des Gedichts bezieht seine satirischen Elemente hier vor allem aus der Kontrastierung und Zuspitzung zwischen Täter und Opfer.

Der letzte Abschnitt des lyrischen Werks ist mit *Und Heute* betitelt und enthält teilweise im Berliner Dialekt verfasste Gedichte aus der unmittelbaren Nachkriegszeit. Vorsichtig optimistisch blickt Schnog im *Lied des Heimkehrers* in die Zukunft. In *Es ist alles wieder da* ist dieser Optimismus der Resignation gewichen: „Es ist, als wär nichts geschehen, / Ich mein, was die Menschheit betrifft" (ebd., 73). Andere Gedichte setzen sich mit der Schuldfrage der Deutschen auseinander, etwa in *Sind nur die toten Nazis schuldig?* In *Die Opfer rufen* thematisiert Schnog die Notwendigkeit von Sühne und Erinnerung. Die Opfer sprechen die Deutschen und die Welt darin direkt an und mahnen sie, sie nicht zu vergessen:

> Wenn diese Welt die Qual vergaß, / Dann sind wir nur ein stinkend Aas, / Dann sind wir nur ein modernd Fell. / Dann wird die Erde nie mehr hell // […] Nur, wenn ihr uns aus unserm Dunkel reißet, / Nur, wenn wir wieder sind, werdet ihr sein! (ebd., 85)

Mit dem Gedicht *Die neuen Kriegshetzer* schließt sich ein Kreis zum Gedicht *Lob des Krieges* aus dem ersten Teil des Gedichtbandes. Denn die neuen Kriegshetzer sind „eigentlich die alten", wie Schnog im Paarreim dichtet.

> DIE NEUEN KRIEGSHETZER
> Eigentlich sind es die alten,
> Immer dieselben Gestalten:
> Söldner, bestochene Schreiber,
> Tratsch- und auch andere Weiber,
> SS-Mann und Koltschak-Russe,
> Pfiffi- und Syndikusse.
> Sie haben's von „wichtigen Leuten"
> Und „wissen die Zeichen zu deuten",
> Verbreiten zu gerne die Hiobspost:
> „West gegen Ost!" …
>
> Sie wittern „bestimmte Gefahren"
> (Warum taten sie das nicht vor Jahren?),
> Sie haben „private Spione"
> Stets in der „anderen Zone".
> Und jede Ex-Schlachtfeld-Hyäne

Kennt „künftige Aufmarschpläne".
Wunschbildstrategen, Kriegsphilosophen,
Raunen sie nur von Weltkatastrophen.
Es stinkt ihrer Gerüchte Pest:
„Ost gegen West!" ...
Die Herren Atombombenflüstrer,
Sie sehen die Zukunft nur düstrer;
Raketen und Bomben sie hexen
Aus Minderwertskomplexen.
Von jedem, der's Pöstchen verloren,
Wird neu ein Weltkrieg beschworen.
Und wirklich muß sehr bald auf Erden
Ein neuer Krieg entfesselt werden:
Bekämpft die Kriegsgerücht-Industrie!
Wir gegen sie!

(ebd., 76)

Dieses Gedicht zeichnet sich durch die polemische Bloßstellung und Vorführung der „neuen" und gleichzeitig „alten Kriegshetzer" aus, deren Gesinnung und Geisteshaltung gleich geblieben ist. Es sind die ewig Gestrigen, denen es im Dritten Reich besser ging als jetzt und die scheinbar kein echtes Interesse an der Gestaltung einer neuen friedlichen Zukunft haben, sondern lieber Gefahren wittern und diese so – befürchtet Schnog – erst heraufbeschwören. Um ihnen mit ihren eigenen Mitteln entgegenzutreten, gibt ihnen der Dichter am Ende scheinbar Recht: Es müsse tatsächlich ein neuer Krieg entfesselt werden, der gegen die Kriegsgerüchte-Industrie nämlich. Außerdem klingt hier deutlich bereits der heraufziehende Kalte Krieg durch die Zeilen „West gegen Ost!" und „Ost gegen West!" an.

Dem Gedicht ist eine Karikatur Sandbergs an die Seite gestellt. Man sieht ein bürgerliches und trotz des Krieges gut genährtes „Tratschweib" oder auch ein „anderes Weib", wie es im Gedicht heißt, das Zeitung liest und dem offenbar nicht gefällt, was sie erfährt. Die Frau trägt eine Art kariertes Tuch vor den Augen, das ihre kleinkarierte Sicht auf die Welt andeuten mag.

Zusammenfassend bleibt zu sagen: Satire vereint in unterschiedlicher Ausprägung Kritik, Polemik, Didaktik und Unterhaltung. Das alles bietet auch Schnog in seinen Versen. Er übernahm vor, während und nach dem Nationalsozialismus mit und in seinen Gedichten angesichts eines übermächtigen Feindes das Amt des moralisch überlegenen Anklägers, des Kritikers und Warners. Er wollte Stellung beziehen und Stellungnahme provozieren und nicht zuletzt Zeugnis von den Ereignissen und seinen eigenen Verfolgungs- und Konzentrationslagererlebnissen ablegen.

Literaturverzeichnis

Archiv des International Tracing Service (ITS) Bad Arolsen: DOK-Id: 10290532, 10290533, 7051457, 7051456, 38030077, 12268001, 4095194, 8030068, 38030067, 38030090.

Braese, Stephan 2005: Selbstbegegnung: Zur Radikalisierung des Satirischen in der Konfrontation mit dem Nationalsozialismus. In: Hitler im Visier. Literarische Satiren und Karikaturen als Waffe gegen den Nationalsozialismus. Hrsg. v. Viktoria Hertling, Wulf Koepke u. Jörg Thunecke. Wuppertal, S. 15-24.

Brummack, Jürgen 1977: Satire. In: Reallexikon der deutschen Literaturgeschichte. Bd. 3. Hrsg. v. Werner Kohlschmidt u. Wolfgang Mohr. Berlin – New York, S. 601-614.

Emmerich, Wolfgang 1990: Mehring, Walter. In: Neue Deutsche Biographie 16, S. 626-628. Online: http://www.deutsche-biographie.de/sfz59843.html (10.2.2016).

Kästner, Erich 1959 [1947]: Eine kleine Sonntagspredigt. Vom Sinn und Wesen der Satire. In: ders.: Gesammelte Schriften. Bd. 5: Vermischte Beiträge. Köln, S. 119.

Kogon, Eugen 1946: Der SS-Staat. München.

Kraus, Karl 1933: Man frage nicht. In: Die Fackel 10,888, S. 4.

Kühn, Volker 2007: Schnog, Karl. In: Neue Deutsche Biographie 23, S. 340-341. Online: www.deutsche-biographie.de/ sfz114749.html (8.6.2015).

Schnog, Karl 1947: Jedem das Seine. Satirische Gedichte. Berlin.

Tucholsky, Kurt 1919: Was darf die Satire? In: Berliner Tagblatt v. 27.1.1919, Nr. 36., [o.S.].

Wolter, Kurt 1948: Schnog, Karl: Jedem das Seine. In: Welt und Wort 9, S. 306.

[o.A., o.J.] Materialien zu Karl Schnog. Aus: Landesarchiv Berlin C Rep.118-01, Nr. 19828, [o. Bl.].

[o.A., o.J.]: Walther Mehring. Online: http://walter-mehring.info/ (10.2.2016).

[o.A., o.J.]: Karl Schnog. In: Autorenlexikon des Literaturport. Online: http://www.literaturport.de/index.php?id=26&no_cache=1&user_autorenlexikonfrontend_pi1[al_aid]=1821&user_autorenlexikonfrontend_pi1[al_opt]=1 (6.10.2014).

[o.A., o.J.]: Karl Schnog. In: Luxemburger Autorenlexikon. Online: http://www.autorenlexikon.lu/page/author/111/1116/DEU/Schnog%2C%20Karl.pdf? (6.10.2014).

[o.A., o.J.]: Herbert Sandberg Biographie. Online: http://www.herbert-sandberg.de/bio.htm (19.1.2016).

Karl Schnog's (1897 – 1967) Satirical Poetry about the Holocaust

Karl Schnog, born in 1897 in Cologne into a Jewish family, was an author, radio announcer, cabaret artist and actor before and after the Second World War. Being Jewish and a political opponent to the National Socialists he was persecuted and – after attempts to emigrate to the US had failed – arrested in Luxembourg and put into a concentration camp. He transferred all these traumatic experiences into his satirical poems which he published in East Germany in 1947 under the title *Jedem das Seine* (*To Each his Own*). The title refers to the cynical inscription placed by the National Socialists on the entrance gate to Buchenwald concentration camp, where as well Schnog had been held captive.

The book is divided into four parts and the poems are arranged in chronological order from 1926 to 1947. The first part titled *Before* contains poems dealing with pre-war political and social topics. The second part *From Outside* includes satirical verses about exile and emigration. *Within* deals with Schnog's own concentration camp experiences and the last part *And Today* contains poems from the immediate post-war period which show Schnog's disappointment that the Germans didn't seem to have learned anything from the very recent catastrophe.

One important aspect of his satirical poetry was the exposure of and opposition to National Socialism. The poems are his attempt at telling the Germans about the true nature and intentions of National Socialism. The main goal with his writing, however, was bearing witness to the atrocities he had seen and experienced in the concentration camps where human beings were degraded into barely living creatures and most often finally murdered, as many of the poems testify of. „And because being silent turns to poison in my mouth, crying I announcethe shame", he wrote in one of the poems.

Satire combines political and social criticism, polemics, didactics and entertainment. All this can be found in Schnog's poems to varying degrees and combinations. His poems are often agitative and aggressive, but more often sad and full of resignation.

Humour and Irony as Forms of Aestheticization of Shoah Narrations: the Play *Doma u Hitlerů* by Arnošt Goldflam

Agata Firlej, Poznań

In discussions about an aestheticization of the Shoah the main concern usually is the fear of depreciating the victims' experience (the question of truth). Berel Lang (Cynthia Ozick or Alvin Rosenfeld alike) argues that the „discourse of history", as something opposite to the „discourse of memory", helps to resist a literary temptation to burst into a world that should be closed for ever (Lang 2000, 11). Frank Ankersmit, addressing the accusations of kitsch raised against Moshe Safdie's Children's Memorial, writes that artistic works commemorating the Holocaust may manipulate memories of the survivors. Anxiety of manipulation is connected with the imperative to seek the truth – though in the case of the Holocaust witnesses it is not necessary a historical truth (Ankersmit 2002, 180). Anka Grupińska writes: „We were writing down different versions of the same events. They could not be verified. Each was bringing its own truth and it was full-fledged" (Grupińska 2014, 12). And Elaine Scarry states that both victims and witnesses of terror lose the ability to describe a situation adequately – and all narratives are dictated by authorities or „priests of angry God" (Scarry 1985, 45). Protest against an aestheticization of the Shoa may be also a result of an earlier, post-war rejection of aesthetics – like in the case of Tadeusz Różewicz. Also one should not overlook the respective considerations by Jacques Derrida, Hayden White or the Polish theatre expert Grzegorz Niziołek who underline the presence of literary tropes and cultural symbols in the organization of the Holocaust and the attempts to describe it. A rejection of culture as a complicit in wrongdoing would be connected to the rejection of an attempt to describe what has happened, but repeated efforts of speaking out are associated with the fear to familiarize the evil. Primo Levi, as one of the opponents of an aestheticization of the Holocaust, used literary figures himself in his text, as proven by Hayden White (1999). There is simply no other language.

Hanna Krall – survivor of the Holocaust – seems to underline this when she says:

Historie z czasów Zagłady mają wielką moc uogólnienia, tak jak Biblia czy greckie opowieści. Ludzie poprzez takie historie będą opowiadali o miłości, o zdradzie, o tchórzostwie, o bohaterstwie. Powstaną komiksy, filmy, może opera albo balet? I dobrze.
Na wszystkie sposoby trzeba opowiadać. (Wodecka 2013, 14)

Stories from the Holocaust time have a great power of generalisation, like the Bible or Greek myths. People through such stories will speak about love, betrayal, cowardice and heroism. There will be comics, films, maybe opera or ballet? So be it.
It must be told by all means..[1]

The same author elsewhere speaks out words that are designations of the imaginary (as understood by Charles Taylor):

Myślę, że naprawdę zmienia się tylko sceneria i rekwizyty, ale ludzie wciąż odgrywają te same role. Tak jak gdyby te role zostały raz na zawsze rozdane. Gdyby się ta sama rzecz dzisiaj zdarzyła – getto, Umschlagplatz, powstanie, to ktoś byłby policjantem żydowskim, ktoś byłby granatowym, polskim policjantem w komisariacie niedaleko dworca, ktoś by się ukrył, ktoś byłby na barykadzie. Trzeba mieć świadomość, że te role istnieją, że można je znowu odegrać. I trzeba wiedzieć, do czego prowadzi odgrywanie każdej z nich ... (Krall 2014, 5)

I think it is really only a stage and props that change, but people keep playing the same roles. As if those roles were assigned once and for all. If the same thing were to happen again today – ghetto, Umschlagplatz, uprising, someone would be a Jewish policeman, another would be a Polish blue policeman in a police station by a railroad, someone would hide, someone would stand on a barricade. One must be aware these roles exist, they can be played again. And it must be understood where playing them leads...

Hanna Krall uses theatre language. The roles identified by the writer (policemen, fugitives, fighters) resemble Raul Hilberg's well-known scheme „perpetrators-victims-bystanders" and it leads to a trope rarely expressed in a public discourse, maybe unaware motivations of the opponents of an aestheticization of the Shoa, which will be explained below.

Aestheticization is connected with transferring attention from victims and events to the viewers that are put in the place of the former witnesses (bystanders) and forcing them to introspect. The scope of awareness in a given triangle „perpetrators – victims – witnesses" undergoes in such a way a significant transformation. Raul Hilberg, examining properties and degree of „visibility" of each of the earlier mentioned groups, proved that perpetrators and witnesses of the Holocaust are „the least" visible whereas the victims (who in turn see the least)

---

[1] All translations into English in this article by AF.

are the most exposed (cf. Hilberg 1993). The witnesses are not fully invisible but generally remain in a shadow – just as contemporary receivers who listen to the factual (historical) account separated from it by time and psychological distance. An aestheticization of the relation by focusing the attention on how the narration is led makes recipients visible to themselves. A ‚transparent', non-artistic communiqué does not demand a reply as ostentatiously as an artistic text or work which seems to speak to its reader: „What do you feel? How do you receive it?". Avoidance of discomfort caused by confrontation with his or her own reactions and discrepancy between expectations from himself or herself and real reactions is, as I see it, one of the reasons of fear of an aestheticization of Shoah history. It would be proven by a characteristic selection of vocabulary by the participants of a discussion especially often using words such as ‚impropriety' or ‚gaffe'.

An adequate reaction is a social taboo: one who sees reality in a different way than others, ‚improperly' brings to his or her attention many and risky exclusions. It is difficult to imagine a more inappropriate reaction than laughter when faced with the stories of the Holocaust – as long as it is not laughter of a man who lost his senses out of despair. Humour and comical irony in Shoah narrations are such examples of an aestheticization that really effectively force a reader/viewer to confront himself or herself with his or her inner self. And like metonymic representations of the Holocaust in art (works of Christian Boltansky or Horst Hoheisel or Jochen Gerz), like the kitsch of the Children's Memorial according to Frank Ankersmit (2006, 177) – humour in literary coverage of Shoah may reveal an impossibility of representation and painfully making recipients aware of his or her status of a by-stander. And what is even more difficult to bear: it reminds every person of being a lonely island, unavoidably lonesome in the face of calamity.

In the above mentioned Hilberg's triad the only thing that remains unchanged is the status of a perpetrator: the most hidden one, identified with fate, plight. In translation to Nazi reality that ‚hiding' of wrongdoers was just spreading and dividing responsibility by establishing a network of offices – like in Kafka's novel – where hosts of clerks were performing duties that all together formed a plan of the Holocaust (see also Bauman 2009). As long as the wrongdoers are hidden from the odium of being ‚different', ‚alienness' is laid on their victims, irrevocably connected with them. Faith in a mysterious fatality that dooms certain people, families or societies gives the others a sense of inner peace („it has nothing to do with me, I will not be hurt") and – through the ‚dehumanization' of the victims – sanctions passivity toward their cry for help. When the perpetrators emerge from the shadow it becomes clear that the fate of a victim can fall to anyone and this choice is purely accidental. And raising awareness of this causes confusion, frightens and forces to make a decision about activity or passivity. Essentially this fear is the most primordial, atavistic one – it is a fear of death.

In a theatre play, that will be a subject of my pondering, its author Arnošt Goldflam (born in 1946) strikes two sensitive strings: he forces a reader (viewer) to laugh, which is not an adequate reaction and brings forth from the shadows perpetrators of the Holocaust to dedemonize them, to tear off a nimbus of superhuman fatality.

Doma u Hitlerů was created in 2006 and a year later it had its premiere in the Brno theatre HaDivadlo, directed by Luboš Balák, and has been staged ever since under the title *Doma u Hitlerů aneb Historky z Hitlerovic kuchyně* (*At Home with Hitlers: Tales from Hitlers' Kitchen*). The text consists of 6 episodes bound by the figure of Adolf Hitler shown as a megalomaniac, sexual deviant, home tyrant, hysteric, and at the same time a mediocre, somewhat wimpy burgher, keen on spending afternoons on a sofa with cake and violin music (here by Himmler).

Goldflam, a Brno drama writer, actor and director, profusely uses both traditional Jewish humour, a tradition of the Czech satire (in the spirit of *Osvobozené divadlo*, the *Liberated Theatre*) and his own experience as a member of the artistic Brno bohemia of the late sixties influenced by Jan Novák. This ‚universal genius', as he was jokingly called, a poet, performer, mystificator, author of the opera *Novák mesiáš* (*Novák, the Messiah*), gathered around him young makers (apart from Goldflam also the writer Pavel Řezníček, the director Karl Fuksa, the composer Miloš Štědroň, the actress Eva Trúda Vidlářová and others). All were joined by a predilection for surrealistic comic quality and playfulness in the style of pre-war *recesse*.

Under this mysterious name is hidden a type of humour based primarily on happening, generally improvised, perfidy on the border of insolence, responding to current events and in some way similar to the provocative avant-garde performances (especially by dadaists and surrealists) against hypocrisy. *Recesse* is usually connected with the names of Vladimír Bor and Pavel Kropáček, Hugo Hušek, Rudolf Jaroš, co-authors of the *Prague Recessist' Club* (during the war it turned into the *The Circle of Friends of Reich KOLABORA*). In the sixties and seventies *recesse* revived in the student environments of various cities, for examples as circles named *Dr. Římsa's Antialcohol Team* or *Křižovníks' School of Pure Humor without Wit* (see Pořízková 2012) and also in the above mentioned Novák group. Radko Pytlík, a literary scholar, characterizing this type of comic irony, emphasizes its connection with a specific situation and notes that the source is usually a conviction of being in a hopeless position (Czechs describe such a position as ‚kafkárna'– from the name of Franz Kafka, *nota bene*: one of Goldflam's favourite writers; cf. Pytlík 2000). This kind of humour, saturated with arrogance and refusal to accept thoughtlessly the course of events, the blank rituals, pathos – all this constitutes this indomitable student (Monty Python style) temperament.

Recesse humour is ironic: the apparent acceptance of certain events or attitudes brought to the absurd reveals their emptiness or even the potential of evil that lurks in them. Goldflam uses the duality that constitutes irony to stage the stories of the Holocaust – plays about with its sources, such as *Doma in Hitlerů*, or about with its mechanisms like in *Sladký Theresienstadt* (1996; *Sweet Theresienstadt*).

In one of the interviews the playwright talks about the inspiration for *Doma u Hitlerů*:

> Teď' jsem napsal takovou aktovku o Hitlerovi a Stalinovi, jak se shodou okolností potkají v Brně […]. A já jsem přesvědčen, že i ten Stalin i ten Hitler vlastně veškeré zlo začali konat z takzvaně dobrých pohnutek. Že to byli velcí idealisti a v tom duchu jim se zdálo, že ideál, který si vytýčili, posvěcuje veškeré jejich činy, a to i ty nejhorší, kterých se dopustili. Oni ovšem byli asi přesvědčeni, že jdou tou nejlepší možnou cestou. (Goldflam 2010b, 547)

> Now I wrote a play about Hitler and Stalin, as they by accident met in Brno […]. And I'm convinced that Stalin and Hitler, all this evil, started with so-called good motives. They were just grand idealists and in the spirit of this idealism they were convinced that

purpose will justify all their means, and even the worst things they would commit. They were sure that everything went the best possible way.

The problem that inspired Goldflam reminds of a famous observation by Albert Camus that every revolutionary ends by becoming either an oppressor or a heretic and also Leszek Kołakowski's opinion that Nazism was a fruit of degenerated romantic ideas, and Communism that of the Enlightenment. The thin border between idealism and cruelty, between pathos and ridiculousness, an easy transition from zealous faith to fanaticism, a change from victim to oppressor – these subjects contain an ironic potential (and a tragic one as well – Friedrich Schlegel tied *ironisch* with *tragisch*).

One of Goldflam's favourite tricks is confronting pathos with a comic punch line in the spirit of *recesse*. In one of the scenes Adolf and Eva talk about having children: Hitler presents her a pathetic view of procreating a son on a mountain meadow with Nordic warriors standing guard with torches and Wagner's music in the background. As the story goes on the aggregation of Nazi symbols contradicted with the act of procreation reaches a level of absurd and at the end Hitler and Eva ascend to heaven – literary: lifted to a helicopter.

In a similar way a scene where Hitler presents himself as a Grand Sower of Nations – after a lofty introduction he starts copulating with eighty-eight Czech cows. The literalness of Goldflam's punch line resembles self-defensive wartime humour, jokes provocative towards the occupier and also – and it is a stream of which Goldflam is an artistic heir – satires of Werich's and Voskovec's *Osvobozené divadlo* with their cheeky creations of Hitler as a führer-donkey who speaks with donkey's voice to his people in a play *Osel a stín* (*The Donkey and the Shadow*) of 1933 or that of Mussolini being a Caesar (see *Caesar*, 1932).

Ironic creations of Hitler as a conservative, short-tempered, neurotic townsman form a distinctive style cropping up in various countries' culture from pre-war times until today – just to mention *Pacijent Doktora Freuda* (1994; *Doctor Freud's Patient*) by the Croatian Miro Gavran, *Ganesh Versus the Third Reich* from 2012 by the Australian company *Back to Back Theatre*, Monty Python's Flying Circus' sketch *Mr. Hilter and the Minehead by-election* (series 1, episode 12, 1969) or the novel *Er ist wieder da* by Timur Vermes of 2012 and its theatrical adaptation under the same title of 2015 based on a similar idea like the play by Howard Brenton *Hitler Dances* of 1972. In Brenton's play a German solder raised from the dead talks about his fate during World War II, in Vermes' work Hitler himself wakes up to life. George Tabori's play *Mein Kampf* of 1987 is also important and surely inspiring for Goldflam.

The characteristic cover of Timur Vermes' bestseller resembles a logo and goes along with the aesthetic preferences of the Facebook generation. Such aesthetics stir up controversies among art critics and readers, arising from the fear of introspection but also from the anxiety of pop cultural ethical indifference and mistrust of cognitive competitions of the young generation of recipients. Irony is, as we know, „an area of risky talk" (Głowiński 2002, 9) (and thus Alcanter de Brahm's idea to introduce a new punctuation mark describing irony).

In one of the scenes in *Doma u Hitlerů* Eva Braun chats with Magda Goebbels on the rules of healthy eating. Mrs. Goebbels boasts of her children's appetite and describes it with pride:

> „A já jim říkám, děcka, kdybych vám na to Vitello nasypala jed, vy to zblajznete jako malinu!" (Goldflam 2010a, 453)
>
> „And I tell them: kids, even if I sprinkle this Vitello with poison you will eat it anyway like raspberries!"

A viewer must decide whether it makes him or her laugh – or rather – if it is allowed for him or her to laugh at Magda Goebbels' allusion, who really poisoned her children – and cannot be hidden for himself or herself any longer. When spoiled Eva Braun says to Hitler:

> Třeba v tom, že mně držíš pořád doma. Proč bys mě nemohl vzít s sebou, když někam jedeš? Například na nějakou inspekční cestu. Třeba do té… Brzezinky. […] No máš tam přece nějaký tabor nebo lázně nebo co. A přitom tam musí být krásně! (ibid., 437)
>
> You keep me at home. Why don't you take me with you at one of your inspections? To that… Birkenau. […] Where you've got that camp or a bath. It must be wonderful there!

A recipient again must decide whether he or she would laugh about the idyllic image of a horrible camp where a million people have been murdered and how he or she would react to this laughter. And again he or she cannot hide this from himself or herself.

Another source of a comic quality in Arnošt Goldflam's plays is the long tradition of Jewish humour. Michał Mosze Chęciński, an expert in the Central European version of this humour, skilfully grasped irony and ambivalence rooted in it:

> Jest w tym humorze wiele sarkazmu, głębokiego smutku wyrosłego z wielowiekowej beznadziejności i trwających prześladowań. Nawet sukces, taki czy inny, był w jakimś sensie chwilowy, nietrwały, wiszący między bolesnym wczoraj a niepokojącym jutrem. Ambiwalentność ich uczuć i myśli jest w jakiejś formie obecna w ich anegdotach i żartach. (Chęciński 2002, 7 et seq.)
>
> There is a lot of sarcasm in this humour and deep sorrow grown up from ages of hopelessness and persecutions. Even success, this and that, was in a sense temporary, inconstant, hung between a painful yesterday and fearful tomorrow. Ambivalence of their feelings and thoughts is present in some form in their anecdotes and jests.

Arnošt Goldflam takes in self-ironic Jewish humour in one of the first scenes when Eva and Adolf talk about sex:

> *Eva* A co máš rád, tak to řekni. Vždyť by si lidi měli říct, co mají v lásce rádi, teda jako v sexu, rozumíš... jak to rádi dělají, za světla, potmě, při svíčkách, zepředu, zezadu...
> *Hitler* Já tohle nebudu poslouchat! Dost už těch lascivností. Já nejsem žádný... tento... Žid.
> *Eva* Proč Žid?
> *Hitler* Protože ti jsou perversní. (Goldflam 2010a, 427)
>
> *Eva* Tell me, what you like. People should talk about what they like about love, about sex, you know what I mean... how they would like to do it, in light or in dark, with candles, front side or back side...
> *Hitler* I will not listen to it! Stop these smuts. I am not... this... Jew!
> *Eva* Why Jew?
> *Hitler* Because they are perverts.

Comic quality close to *szmonces* (that is, as Michał Mosze Chęciński defines it, a joke of anti-Semitic meaning) is also a vehicle of much more serious ideas. In the first scene young idealists overwhelmed by revolutionary enthusiasm – Hitler and Stalin – meet at a rail station in Brno and start talking while waiting for a train to arrive.

Their dialogue – the comic quality of which is based on the confrontation between what has been said and the ‚pre-knowledge' of the recipient – covers not only anti-Semitism that Stalin and his cronies showed but also subtle, ‚general' xenophobia expressed by the benign expression: „I somehow don't trust such..." And this kind of presumably innocent, anti-Semitic discourse Stalin pours to his listener who, years later, will become a sponsor for the industrial killing of Jews.

Goldflam's concept has also got a deeper meaning: it is his argument in the discussion about what is allowed in public language and what is not. The Czech author, a representative of the generation of descendants of those who survived the Holocaust indicates that the tolerance of a wide spread, subtle, thoughtless rejection (dehumanization) of strangers made Auschwitz possible.

Hitler's character as created by Goldflam owes a lot to Dušan Hamšík's biography *Génius průměrnosti* (*The Genius of Mediocrity*), and it is also based on opinions about the „banality of evil" as formulated by Hannah Arendt. Vermes is led by similar motivations when he defends himself against accusations of relativizing and explains:

> Books don't have to educate or turn people into better human beings – they can also just ask questions. If mine makes some readers realize that dictators aren't necessarily instantly recognizable as such, then I consider it a success. (Oltermann 2014)

Interpreting this way of thinking that seems to be close to Goldflam (and Vermes) one can repeat according to Zygmunt Bauman:

> Zagładę obmyślono i przeprowadzono w naszym nowoczesnym racjonalnym społeczeństwie, w zaawansowanym stadium jego cywilizacyjnego rozwoju, w szczytowej fazie rozkwitu naszej kultury i dlatego Zagłada jest problemem tego społeczeństwa, tej cywilizacji i tej kultury. (Bauman 2009, 13)

> The Holocaust was invented and carried out in our modern, rational society in the advanced stage of its civilizational development, in the highest phase of our culture and that is why the Holocaust is a problem of this society, this civilization and this culture.

Goldflam takes Hitler and Eva Braun to a middle-class sitting room, hands in everyday props, lets them utter common phrases and collide with a background (existing only in the minds of the recipients) that is full of crematories with their smoking chimneys and barbed wires of concentration camps.

The piece of Goldflam's play quoted above allows seeing its dichotomy. It is necessary to separate the acting of Hitler and his co-workers (perpetrators of the Holocaust) from allusions to the Shoah („nation is not a stew – no admixtures"; „wonderful Birkenau"; doctor Mengele's „new medical discoveries",Albert Speer's „architectural activity"); one should also detach the situational and oral humour from irony that sustains the structure of the work. This ironic structure – that is based on constant exchange or even fight between that what is ‚seen' and 'presupposed' by the audience and what is shown – is in a way a skeleton for verbal and situational humour.

Despite the fact that a kind of 'Daumier's' caricatural showing of Hitler has its own tradition, the figure of the „Führer" is tabooed within wide artistic circles and in social discourse, going together with the view of the Shoah as a 'temporary madness', 'epoch of fall'. Adhering to those conventions authors and survivors in a sense found themselves locked within an existential 'ghetto', unwillingly supporting a narration about the 'superhuman' dimension of the Holocaust and additionally hiding perpetrators by surrounding the victims with the nimbus of fate.

Arnošt Goldflam, taking advantage of his status of a representative of the second generation and of the tradition of satire in Czech culture, breaks conventions – leaves the 'ghetto' and forces his audience to leave the old paths. The Czech author turns Hilberg's triangle upside down by hiding the victims and accentuating the perpetrators and – mainly – witnesses being ourselves, readers and spectators.

Bibliography

Ankersmit, Frank 2002: Remembering the Holocaust. Mourning and Melancholia. In: id.: Historical Representation. Stanford, pp. 176-194.
Bauman, Zygmunt 2009: Nowoczesność i Zagłada. Kraków.
Chęciński, Michał Mosze 2002: Przedmowa. In: id.: Humor żydowski. Toruń, pp. 5-12.
Głowiński, Michał 2002: Ironia jako akt komunikacyjny. In: Ironia. Red. Michał Głowiński. Gdańsk, pp. 17-56.
Goldflam, Arnošt 2010a: Doma u Hitlerů. In: id.: Písek a jiné kousky. Brno, pp. 423-468.
id. 2010b: A. G. jako Voyeur a Masochista. Rozhovor s Vladimírem Hulcem a Zdenko Pavelkou. In: id.: Písek a jiné kousky. Brno, p. 545-556.
Grupińska, Anka 2014: Wysłuchiwanie Zagłady i rozmawianie o schedzie pozagładowej. In: Mikołaj Grynberg: Oskarżam Auschwitz. Wołowiec, p.7-15.
Hilberg Raul 1993: Perpetrators, Victims, Bystanders. The Jewish Catastrophe 1933 – 1945. New York.
Krall, Hanna 2014: Hanna Krall w Poznaniu. In: Gazeta Wyborcza Poznań 3/4.1.2014, p.5.
Lang, Berel 2000: Holocaust Representation. Art Within the Limits of History and Ethics. Baltimore.
Oltermann, Philip 2014: Germany Asks: Is It OK to Laugh at Hitler? In: The Guardian 23.3.2014. www.theguardian.com/books/2014/mar/23/germany-finally-poke-fun-hitler-fuhrer (23.6.2016).
Pořízková, Lenka 2012: Protialkoholní společnost doktora Řimsy. Praha.

Pytlík, Radko 2000: Fenomenologie humoru aneb Jak filozofovat smíchem. Praha.
Scarry Elaine 1985: The Body in Pain. The Making and Unmaking of the World. New York.
White, Hayden 1999: Figural Realism. Studies in the Mimesis Effect. Baltimore.
Wodecka, Dorota: Polonez na polu minowym. Warszawa.

Humor und Ironie als Formen der Ästhetisierung des Erzählens über die Shoah: Arnošt Goldflams Drama *Doma u Hitlerů*

Der Beitrag stellt einen Versuch dar, die von Arnošt Goldflam in seinem Stück *Doma u Hitlerů* (*Zuhause bei Hitlers*) verwendeten Typen von Humor und Ironie zu charakterisieren und Antworten auf die Frage nach Funktion, Wirkung und Interaktion dieser Verfahren im Hinblick auf den Leser zu finden. Der Verortung von Goldflams Stück auf der Landkarte der (pop)kulturellen Tradition erlaubt es uns, den Wert der vom Dramatiker intendierten Ästhetik (und die Kontroverse darum) zu sehen.

Arnošt Goldflam schrieb das Stück 2006, und ein Jahr später feierte es am Brünner HaDivadlo Premiere unter der Regie von Luboš Balák. Seit dieser Zeit läuft es erfolgreich unter dem Titel *Doma u Hitlerů aneb Historky z Hitlerovic kuchyně* (*Zuhause bei Hitlers oder Geschichten aus der Küche der Hitlers*). Als Werk eines nach dem Krieg geborenen Autors, der einer jüdischen Familie entstammt, die im Holocaust viele Opfer zu beklagen hatte, kann das Drama entsprechend der Terminologie von Marianne Hirsch der Strömung des sog. post-memory zugeordnet werden. Das Interesse moderner Künstler an der Gestalt Hitlers – beispielhaft erwähnt seien das Drama *Pacijent Doktora Freuda* (1994; *Der Patient des Doktor Freud*) des Kroaten Miro Gavran oder der Roman *Er ist wieder da* (2012) des deutschen Autors Timur Vermes – hat zu Kontroversen geführt, die auf der Angst vor ethischer Indifferenz innerhalb der Popkultur beruhen. Goldflam, der sich der Mittel des schwarzen Humors, der satirischen Übertreibung und des reinen Nonsens bedient, zeigt Hitler als einen Idealisten, der zum Größenwahnsinnigen, sexuellen Perversling, Haustyrannen und Hysteriker wird. Hitler ähnelt auch auf gefährliche Weise dem Durchschnittsbürger, der nachmittags gerne auf der Couch liegt und den Klang von Geigenmusik (die von Himmler komponiert wurde) sowie ein gutes Stück Kuchen mag. Bei seiner Hitler-Figur wurde Goldflam in starkem Maße von Dušan Hamšíks Biographie *Génius průměrnosti* (*Der Genius der Durchschnittlichkeit*) inspiriert, es findet sich aber auch viel von jener ‚Banalität des Bösen', die Hannah Arendt in ihrem berühmten Buch über den Eichmann-Prozess aufgedeckt hat. Die Darstellung Hitlers als gewöhnlicher Mensch wird bei Goldflam regelmäßig von grotesken und absurden Bildern im Geiste von Monty Python kontrastiert.

Holocaustdichtung zwischen Poetizität und Prosaisierung

Holocaust Poetry between Poeticity and Prosaization

Lyrische Grüße an Deutschland –
Manfred Herzfeld und andere ‚ungeübte' Verfasser
von Holocaustgedichten 1945 bis 1949

Christiane Charlotte Weber, Gießen

Spricht man von Gedichten über den Holocaust, fallen meist zwei Namen: Nelly Sachs und Paul Celan. Sicherlich gilt Celans *Todesfuge* als eines *der* zentralen Gedichte über den Holocaust. Bereits Schülern und Schülerinnen wird an diesem Gedicht verdeutlicht, wie die Verfolgung und Ermordung in Konzentrationslagern künstlerisch bewältigt bzw. dargestellt werden können.

Doch es gibt neben diesen großen Namen auch Lyriker, die aus dem kulturellen Gedächtnis verschwunden sind. Einer von ihnen ist Manfred Herzfeld mit seiner 1947 in Israel publizierten Gedichtsammlung *Gruss an Deutschland. Eine Abrechnung in Versen*. Herzfeld steht repräsentativ für jene Gruppe von Autoren, die man als ‚ungeübte' Dichter bezeichnen kann. Manfred Herzfeld hatte – wie etwa auch Bruno Marcuse[1] – vor der Publikation seiner Gedichte keine Erfahrung als Schriftsteller oder speziell als Lyriker gesammelt und trat als solcher auch nicht öffentlich in Erscheinung. Er und die anderen ‚ungeübten' Autoren griffen für die Schilderungen ihrer Erlebnisse im Holocaust zum ersten Mal zu Papier und Stift, um Gedichte zu verfassen. Der bereits erwähnte Bruno Mar-

---

[1] Der Kaufmann Bruno Marcuse (geb. 6.1.1878 in Berlin, gest. 27.12.1948 in Temmenhausen) war – u.a. als Direktor – in verschiedenen Berliner Firmen tätig, die sich auf Maschinenbau spezialisiert hatten. Auf Grund seines jüdischen Glaubens wurde er am 21. Januar 1944 nach Theresienstadt deportiert, wo er seine Gedichte verfasste, die 1946 unter dem Titel *Erlebnisse im KZ Theresienstadt* publiziert wurden. Marcuse kehrte nach seiner Befreiung aus dem Getto nach Deutschland zurück. Da eine geplante Auswanderung wegen seines schlechten gesundheitlichen Zustands nicht in Frage kam, lebte Marcuse bis zu seinem Tod im Dezember 1948 im Kreis Ulm mit finanzieller Unterstützung der Israelitischen Kultusvereinigung Württemberg.
Bruno Marcuse verfasste seine Gedichte zunächst für sich selbst; der größte Teil entstand bereits während seiner Zeit in Theresienstadt. Mit der Publikation übergab er sie „auf Anraten von Freunden hiermit einem weiteren Kreise" (Marcuse 1946a, 6), um Aufklärungsarbeit zu leisten.
Die gesammelten Gedichte über seine Erfahrungen in Theresienstadt erschienen in einer einmaligen Ausgabe 1946. Vgl. Marcuse 1946a sowie die Biografie zu Bruno Marcuse unter www.geobib.info (1.12.2015).

cuse, der erst während seiner Zeit im Getto Theresienstadt zu schreiben begann, hielt dies in einem mit *Persönliches* betitelten Gedichten fest. Dort heißt es in der letzten Strophe:

> Sonderbar, höchst sonderbar!
> Über 65 Jahr
> Gab ich dem Erwerb mich hin,
> Hatt' für Dichten keinen Sinn.
> Aber die Natur nicht träge,
> Macht die Abwehrkräfte rege,
> Die wir brauchen, um den Dingen
> Unser Wollen aufzuzwingen.
> (Marcuse 1946a, 10)[2]

Die Gedichte der ‚ungeübten' Dichter verfügen zumeist – vorsichtig formuliert – nur über geringe künstlerische Qualitäten. Man findet in ihnen keine unauflöslichen Metaphern und Chiffren wie Celans ikonographische „schwarze Milch der Frühe", keine Sprachspiele oder Leerstellen. Sie haben also keinen genuin künstlerischen oder überzeitlichen Wert. Stattdessen nutzten diese Autoren die Lyrik, um ihre persönliche Sichtweise der Dinge darzustellen und zu propagieren. Im Fall von Herzfeld ist dies der Ärger über die Situation im Nachkriegsdeutschland, die er nicht in Zeitungsartikeln oder Pamphleten aufgreift – was man bei der Thematik eventuell hätte erwarten können –, sondern die er in Verse kleidet.

Gedichte in der Nachkriegszeit

Bereits während des Krieges begann die Jüdische Historische Kommission im besetzten Polen mit der Sammlung und Veröffentlichung von Gedichten, die direkt das Erlebte reflektierten. Die Literaturwissenschaftlerin Barbara Breysach weist auf die Bedeutung dieser ‚offiziellen' Publikation hin und betont dabei den hohen Stellenwert, der den Gedichten von der Kommission beigemessen wur-

---

[2] Wie tiefgreifend der Wandel im Selbstbild war, deutet ein Fragebogen an, den Marcuse nach dem Krieg für die Israelitische Kultusvereinigung Württemberg ausfüllte. Darin gibt er als Beruf „Schriftsteller, früher Kaufmann" an (Mitgliedsfragebogen, in: 1236_001, Archiv der Israelitischen Kultusvereinigung, heute Israelitische Religionsgemeinschaft Württemberg in Stuttgart, Personenakte Bruno Marcuse).

de.[3] Sie sollten – neben den Berichten aus den Konzentrationslagern – die Leser aufrütteln und zum Handeln bewegen. Selbstverständlich setzt sich das Gros der Publikationen über den Holocaust in der Zeit bis 1949 nicht aus Gedichtsammlungen zusammen, sondern es überwiegen eindeutig die Erinnerungsberichte und Dokumentationen. Im Rahmen des GeoBib-Projekts zur Erforschung der frühen Holocaust- und Lagerliteratur, die zwischen 1933 und 1949 auf Deutsch und Polnisch publiziert wurde, wurden über 350 dieser Texte untersucht.[4]

Eines der grundlegendsten Forschungsergebnisse des GeoBib-Projekts ist, dass viele Holocaustüberlebende ihre Erinnerungen schon unmittelbar nach der Befreiung niederschrieben, um sie so zu verarbeiten. Die Texte – ob Lyrik, Berichte, Dramen, Novellen oder Romane – erfüllten im Grunde immer eines der vier folgenden Hauptmotive[5]: Erstens sollten die gemachten Erfahrungen an die Zeitgenossen und die Nachwelt übergeben werden, um so vor dem Vergessen bewahrt zu werden. Zweitens wollten die Autoren die Leser über das aufklären, was in den Jahren der NS-Diktatur passiert war. Daher liefern diese Autoren oft genaue Zahlenangaben oder Fotografien als Belege. Drittens stellten die untersuchten Texte der Holocaust- und Lagerliteratur eine Mahnung an die Zeitgenossen dar, dass Verfolgung und Ermordung wie im nationalsozialistischen Deutschland in der Zukunft nicht mehr vorkommen dürfen und dass man dafür kämpfen müsse. In diesen Texten herrscht sehr oft eine klare Kampfrhetorik vor. Viertens fungierten diese Texte auch oft als literarische Grabsteine für verstorbene Familienmitglieder, Freunde oder Mithäftlinge. In dieser Gruppe von Texten werden viele Namen genannt und einzelne Schicksale geschildert.

---

[3] Barbara Breysach auf der Abschlusstagung des GeoBib-Projekts zum Thema *Texte, Karten, Erschließungsmethoden — Neue Perspektiven auf frühe Holocaust- und Lagerliteratur* am 4. und 5. Mai 2015 in Gießen, veranstaltet vom Zentrum für Medien und Interaktivität, der Arbeitsstelle Holocaustliteratur der Justus-Liebig-Universität und dem Herder-Institut für historische Ostmitteleuropaforschung Marburg.

[4] Für Informationen zum GeoBib-Projekt, in dessen Rahmen auch der hier vorgestellte Manfred Herzfeld untersucht wurde, vgl. www.geobib.info (1.12.2015). Der Beitrag von Charlotte Kitzinger zu Karl Schnog und seinen sarkastischen Gedichten, der ebenfalls im vorliegenden Band abgedruckt ist, entstammt demselben Projekt.

[5] Auf die Funktion der Texte weisen die Autoren durchaus selbst in den jeweiligen Vorworten deutlich hin.

Die Drucklegung von Gedichtbänden unterlag von 1945 bis 1949 denselben prekären Publikationsbedingungen wie andere Texte auch (vgl. Binsch 2015). Da Herzfeld im Jerusalemer Verlag Lychenheim & Sohn publizierte, stellt er in diesem Punkt eine Ausnahme dar. Andere ‚ungeübte' Autoren wie Bruno Marcuse mussten sich aber auf dem deutschen Markt durchsetzen. Dieser war geprägt von einer herrschenden Papierknappheit und den Kontrollen der Alliierten im Nachkriegsdeutschland, die eine Papiervergabe auch immer an der politischen Unbedenklichkeit der Autoren und einem demokratisch-aufklärenden Charakter eines Buches maßen. Neuerscheinungen mussten die Hürde nehmen, dass sie etwas zur Verbesserung der gegenwärtigen Situation beitragen konnten.

Gedichte wurden – ebenso wie andere Texte auch – demnach nicht wegen ihrer künstlerischen Qualität gedruckt, sondern um eine politisch-moralisch-gesellschaftliche Aussage zu transportieren. Da nur wenig Papier zur Verfügung stand, musste das gedruckt werden, was man unbedingt benötigte (Zeitungen, Kalender, Formulare) oder was von Kontrollorganen gefordert wurde. Letzteres war in erster Linie keine selbstreferenzielle oder schöngeistige Lyrik, sondern eine Lyrik mit klaren Aussagen. Gedichte wurden so in der Nachkriegszeit zu einer Art von Gebrauchstexten und der Stil trat bei den ‚ungeübten' Dichtern hinter die Funktion.

Definition ‚ungeübte' Autoren

Die Gruppe der ‚ungeübten' Autoren umfasst nur wenige Autoren. Sie zeichnen sich dadurch aus, dass sie keine Erfahrung in der Publikation von Gedichten hatten und vor 1945 nicht öffentlich als Lyriker oder Autoren anderer Texte in Erscheinung traten. So war Marcuse vor der Verfolgung durch die Nationalsozialisten Direktor einer Baufirma und Herzfeld ein kulturell assimiliert lebender Richter. Ihre Gedichtbände sind ein singuläres Phänomen, da sie ihre einzigen eigenständigen Publikationen bleiben.[6] Da ihnen die Übung fehlt, nutzen sie ein-

---

[6] Bruno Marcuse veröffentlichte zeitgleich mit seiner Gedichtsammlung unter dem Titel *Julius Berger und das Dritte Reich* (Marcuse 1946b) einen kurzen Band über den jüdischen Bauunternehmer Julius Berger, der im Getto Theresienstadt verstarb. Dies sind die beiden einzigen Publikationen von Marcuse, Gedichte finden sich nur in *Erlebnisse im KZ Theresienstadt* (Marcuse 1946a), weshalb er zur Gruppe der ‚ungeübten' Dichter gezählt werden kann.

fache literarische Stilmittel und reduzieren Gedichte zumeist auf den Reim, die Rhythmik und die Kürze. Statt literarischer Experimente findet man bei ihnen bekannte und vergleichsweise einfache stilistische Strukturen vor. Thematisch zeichnen sich die Gedichte durch einen hohen Realitätsbezug aus und es findet kaum etwas auf einer Metaebene statt. Dies ist entscheidend: Die Gedichte der ‚ungeübten' Autoren haben einen hohen dokumentarischen Charakter. Es gibt beispielsweise die Gedichte von Bruno Marcuse, die das Getto Theresienstadt und die dort herrschenden Bedingungen beschreiben. Dabei werden die täglichen Sorgen im Getto sowie die Krankheiten und Transporte in Vernichtungslager klar benannt. Eine Entschlüsselung von Metaphern muss vom Leser nicht erbracht werden.

Die ‚ungeübten' Autoren werden kaum von ihren Zeitgenossen wahrgenommen. Sie werden nicht rezensiert, es gibt keine größere Nachfrage, die eine weitere Auflage nötig machen würde, und es sind auch keine öffentlichen Lesungen überliefert.

Als biographisches Merkmal eint diese Autoren ein (groß-)bürgerlicher familiärer Hintergrund. Sie haben demnach eine entsprechende kulturelle Erziehung durchlaufen, die zumeist mit einem Studium abschloss. Auffällig ist auch, dass sie bei der Publikation ihrer Gedichte in einem höheren Alter waren: Herzfeld war 60 Jahre alt und Marcuse 68 Jahre alt bei der Veröffentlichung ihrer Gedichte. Der biografische Referenzrahmen der ‚ungeübten' Autoren lässt sich am Lebenslauf von Manfred Herzfeld verdeutlichen.

Manfred Herzfeld – eine Biographie[7]

Dr. Manfred Herzfeld wurde 1887 in Hannover geboren und wuchs als ältestes von fünf Kindern eines gut situierten jüdischen Kaufmanns in Hannover auf. Er studierte in München, Berlin und Göttingen Jura und legte 1911 seine Doktorarbeit vor. Seit 1921 arbeitete er als Rechtsanwalt in Celle und als Richter am dortigen Oberlandesgericht. Mit seiner Familie lebte er assimiliert und nahm am kulturellen Leben in Celle und vor allem in Hannover teil. Herzfeld war gebil-

---

[7] Zur Biografie Herzfelds vgl. Loewy o.J., Rohde 2010 sowie die Onlinebiografie unter http://www.celle-im-nationalsozialismus.de/stadtrundgang/rechtsanwalt-manfred-herzfeld (10.9.2015).

det, konnte Latein sowie Griechisch lesen und verehrte die großen deutschen Dichter wie etwa Goethe.[8] Er engagierte sich in der Zionistischen Vereinigung in Deutschland; der jüdischen Gemeinde seiner Heimatstadt stand er allerdings eher fern.

Nach der Machtergreifung 1933 verschlechterte sich die Lage Herzfelds: Er durfte seine Kanzlei zunächst nur weiterführen, da er als Teilnehmer des Ersten Weltkriegs unter die ‚Frontkämpferregelung' fiel. Bald blieben die Klienten allerdings ganz fern. Im August 1935 folgte Herzfeld nach einem Zusammenstoß mit der lokalen SA seiner Frau und seiner Tochter nach Jerusalem. Diese waren bereits zwei bzw. ein Jahr zuvor emigriert. Die Emigration stellte eine deutliche Verschlechterung des Lebensstandards dar. Die Familie konnte sich in Jerusalem nur eine kleine Kellerwohnung leisten und war auf Unterstützung von Hilfsvereinigungen angewiesen; auch Herzfelds Gesundheitszustand verschlechterte sich stark.

1947 – also mit 60 Jahren – veröffentlichte Herzfeld in Israel seinen einzigen Gedichtband. Nachdem er 1948 in Rente gegangen war, widmete sich Herzfeld der Weiterbildung, beschäftigte sich mit der hebräischen Sprache und las viel. 1950 kehrte er nach Deutschland zurück, um sich als Jurist in Wiedergutmachungsfragen für Juden einzusetzen. 1953 zog er nach Berlin-Dahlem, von wo aus er ab 1958 als Rechtsanwalt für die United Restitution Organization (URO) arbeitete und mit großen deutschen Firmen wie Thyssen oder der Deutschen Bank um Wiedergutmachungszahlungen verhandelte. Zahlreiche Publikationen in Zeitschriften wie der *Neuen Juristischen Wochenschrift* und eigenständige Werke zum Thema Wiedergutmachung folgten bis zu seinem Tod im Juli 1968. Weitere Gedichte publizierte er hingegen nicht mehr.

Gruss an Deutschland (1947) – eine Werkanalyse

Manfred Herzfeld verfasste in seiner Exilheimat Jerusalem Gedichte, die geprägt sind von Wut und Enttäuschung über die Tatsache, dass Deutschland bereits kurz nach dem Krieg durch die internationale Gemeinschaft, aber auch durch ehemals verfolgte Juden wieder politisch und gesellschaftlich akzeptiert zu wer-

---

[8] Die Verehrung der deutschen Klassiker wie Goethe schlägt sich auch in seinen Gedichten nieder, wie im Folgenden zu zeigen sein wird.

den schien. In einzelnen der insgesamt 22 Gedichte thematisiert er die Kollektivschuld der Deutschen und ruft dazu auf, das deutsche Volk weiterhin als „innerlich nicht gewandelt" (Herzfeld 1947, o.S.) zu behandeln. Bereits im Vorwort macht Herzfeld die Motivation für sein Schreiben deutlich:

> In einer Zeit, in der man den Deutschen wieder umwirbt, weil man sein Tun und Lassen nicht unter ewigen und sittlichen, sondern unter vergänglichen und machtpolitischen Gesichtspunkten betrachtet, ist es Sache des Juden – und gerade des aus Deutschland stammenden Juden, der den Deutschen so gut kennengelernt und so Schweres von ihm erlitten hat –, die Dinge ins rechte Licht zu rücken. (ebd.)

Die Gedichtform wählte Herzfeld dabei wegen der „Prägnanz der Darstellung, die bei prosaischer Behandlung desselben Gegenstandes nicht zu erreichen ist" (ebd.).

Die Gedichte gleichen dem Vorwort in ihrer Direktheit und Schonungslosigkeit. Ohne Umschweife beginnt Herzfeld in seinem ersten Gedicht *Vergeltung* mit der Aufzählung der Geschehnisse während des Holocaust:

> Sie haben Millionen erschossen und vergast,
> Sie haben – wilde Bestien – gebrandschatzt und gerast;
> Sie haben ihre Opfer geschändet und gequält,
> Sie haben Henkersknechte zu Führern sich erwählt.
>
> Sie haben Menschenwürde und Menschenrecht verlacht,
> Sie haben sich zum Götzen des eigenen Wahns gemacht;
> Sie haben schon die Kinder auf Raub und Mord gedrillt,
> Sie haben tief erniedrigt der Menschheit edles Bild.
>
> (ebd., 7)

Herzfeld ruft den Leser dazu auf, kein Mitleid mit den Deutschen zu haben, da sich alle, sowohl Männer als auch Frauen, schuldig gemacht haben. So heißt es im Gedicht weiter:

> Nun winseln sie um Gnade, nun betteln sie um Brot,
> Nun wollen sie Euch ködern mit ihrer grossen Not.
> Sie haben keine Regung des Herzens je gespürt –
> Und Ihr seid durch ihr Flennen gewandelt und gerührt?!
>
> (ebd.)

Bereits in diesem Gedicht wird deutlich, wie klar sich Herzfeld auf die gegenwärtige Situation bezieht und sie kritisch anmahnt. Das Gedicht ist nicht überzeitlich, sondern an das momentane Weltgeschehen gebunden. Es zeigt sich auch, dass das Gedicht einen dezidiert dokumentarischen Charakter hat: Es wird nicht versucht, für die Verfolgung und Ermordung neue Begriffe zu finden, sondern es werden ohne Umschweife die Erschießungen und Vergasungen dem Leser – zudem noch in der ersten Zeile des ersten Gedichts – vorgeführt. Noch etwas lässt sich an diesem Gedicht aufzeigen: Es herrscht stilistisch eine einfache Struktur vor, da das Gedicht aus regelmäßigen Jamben und Paarreimen besteht.

An wen wandte sich Herzfeld mit seinen Gedichten – wen wollte er mahnen? Herzfeld spricht in den meisten Gedichten Politiker und Menschen außerhalb von Deutschland an. Dies ist umso beachtlicher, als er dennoch auf Deutsch publiziert. In *Und schon vergessen?!* wendet sich Herzfeld zudem dezidiert an die überlebenden Juden, die seiner Meinung nach bereits die Geschehnisse der letzten Jahre verdrängt haben. Hierfür zählt er alle Maßnahmen und Schritte der Verfolgung von der Stigmatisierung durch den Judenstern über die Grabschändungen bis hin zur Ermordung von verwandten Kindern und Alten auf. Die ersten beiden Strophen des Gedichts lauten:

> „Sie ist am Ort das grösste Schwein,
> Sie liess sich mit 'nem Juden ein"
> Ich habe diese Aufschrift einst gelesen,
> In meiner Vaterstadt ist es gewesen.
> So haben sie sich frech vermessen
> Und schon wollt Ihr vergessen?!
>
> Sie jagten Euch von Strassen und von Flüssen,
> Ihr habt den gelben Schandfleck tragen müssen.
> Man hat Euch zum Gespött gemacht,
> Verfolgt, bespieen und verlacht!
> So haben sie sich frech vermessen,
> Und schon wollt Ihr vergessen?!
> (ebd., 21)

Doch auch die deutsche Nachkriegsbevölkerung sieht Herzfeld offenbar als seine potentiellen Leser an, denn in dem Gedicht *Anklage* adressiert er sie direkt. Abschließend heißt es dort: „Ihr tatet die ärgste der Taten: / Ihr habt Euch verkauft an den Dämon der Macht, / und den Geist habt ihr schmählich verraten" (ebd., 8). Gerade das Verstellen der Deutschen und das Leugnen von Taten nach dem Krieg beobachtet Herzfeld in vielen seiner Gedichte voller Schrecken. Den angepassten Deutschen bezeichnet er daher auch als „Chamäleon" (ebd., 10), das sein Erscheinungsbild ständig an die jeweilige Situation anpassen kann.

Herzfeld ist sich seiner harschen Kritik in den Gedichten durchaus bewusst, doch sieht er in allen Deutschen Schuldige. Konsequent zählt er die Vergehen der Deutschen ohne weitere Einleitung im Gedicht *Warum Kollektivschuld* auf:

> Weil sie Verbrechen schweigend toleriert,
> Weil sie die Wahrheit nicht erkennen wollten,
> Weil sie die Knechtschaft dankend akzeptiert,
> Weil sie den braunen Henkern Beifall zollten.
> Weil sie den „Führer" an die Macht gebracht,
> Weil sie ihm zugejubelt Jahr um Jahr,
> Weil sie die armen Opfer kalt verlacht,
> Weil nur Gewalt, nicht Recht, ihr Leitstern war.
> (ebd., 9)

Die Strafe beispielsweise für Richter, die während des NS-Regimes Schuldsprüche gegen Unschuldige verhängten und denen er ein eigenes Gedicht widmet, ist für den Juristen Herzfeld klar: „Verjagt die feigen Knechte, / Nehmt ihnen Robe und Brot! / Sie waren Verräter am Rechte – / Ihr Schicksal sei: Schande und Not!" (ebd., 12). Herzfeld fordert hier ein klares Vorgehen und begründet dies mit der Schuld eines jeden Einzelnen. Das Gedicht wird dadurch zur Meinungsäußerung und zum Aufruf zum Handeln.

Auf einen Punkt soll abschließend noch eingegangen werden: Herzfelds Verehrung der deutschen Klassiker. Auf den Aspekt, dass Deutschland jahrhundertelang als Land der Dichter und Denker galt, geht der Autor in verschiedenen Gedichten ein. Immer wieder nennt er daher Goethe, aus dessen Gedichten er auch zitiert, Hölderlin, Bach oder Hegel. Damit verweisen die Gedichte inhaltlich auf Herzfelds bildungsbürgerlichen Hintergrund. Im Gedicht *Einst und Jetzt* stellt er beispielsweise die ältere und die jüngere deutsche Vergangenheit in einen Kontrast zueinander: Goethe, Hölderlin, Kant, Bach und Mozart stehen für das Vergangene, das wertzuschätzen ist.

> Aber dem Deutschen von heute rühmet nicht nach,
> Was die Ahnen Grosses geschaffen.
> Machtwahn und Hass und Verblendung
> Prägten ein neues Geschlecht.
> Ach, das Deutschland von Weimar und Jena
> Ist längst schon dahin...
> Und statt seiner erstand
> Schaurig die Hölle von Auschwitz.
> (ebd., 13)

Auschwitz wird so bei Herzfeld zum Kontrapunkt zu Goethes Weimar. Die kulturellen Höhepunkte von einst haben mit dem Ist-Zustand 1947 nichts mehr gemein.

Es bleibt daher festzuhalten, dass in Herzfelds Gedichtband *Gruss an Deutschland* der sprachliche Stil der Gedichte nur selten komplex oder metaphorisch ist. Es herrscht in ihnen vielmehr ein deutlicher und anklagender Ton samt dokumentarischer Funktion vor, die nicht durch literarische Experimente verstellt werden. Es ist – wie der Untertitel des Gedichtbands es bereits sagt – eine deutliche zeitgeschichtliche Abrechnung.

Fazit

Die Gedichte von Manfred Herzfeld und Bruno Marcuse stellen ein Schreiben fern der ikonographischen Holocaustgedichte einer Nelly Sachs oder eines Paul Celan dar. Die ‚ungeübten' Lyriker der Nachkriegsjahre funktionalisierten ihre Gedichte zu dokumentarischen Zwecken. Neben Ästhetisierungstendenzen tritt zunächst der Versuch, mit Gedichten aufzurütteln und die Leser zum Handeln zu animieren bzw. zu überzeugen.

Die schwierige Frage, warum Manfred Herzfeld sich dafür entschied, gerade Gedichte zu schreiben, um seine Wut über die Situation im Nachkriegsdeutschland zu thematisieren, wird nicht geklärt werden können. Herzfeld hätte sicherlich mehr Leser gefunden, wenn er seine Entrüstung in einer Zeitung publiziert hätte und nicht in einem Gedichtband, noch dazu einem deutschsprachigen, der in Jerusalem verlegt wurde. Aber dennoch wählte Herzfeld die Lyrik, da er glaubte, damit etwas bewegen zu können. Allerdings – das zeigt die ausbleibende Rezeption seiner Gedichte und der anderer ‚ungeübter' Autoren – hatten Überlebende der NS-Verfolgung wie Herzfeld kaum Möglichkeiten, mit ihrer Botschaft an die Öffentlichkeit zu dringen, obgleich sie einen immensen Mitteilungsdrang verspürten.

Literaturverzeichnis

Benz, Wolfgang 2013: Theresienstadt. Eine Geschichte von Täuschung und Vernichtung. München.
Binsch, Anika 2015: Vom Manuskript zum Leser? Der Produktions- bzw. Publikationsprozess früher deutschsprachiger Holocaust- und Lagerliteratur unter amerikanischer Besatzung

1945 bis 1949. In: Als der Holocaust noch keinen Namen hatte. Zur frühen Aufarbeitung des NS-Massenmords an Jüdinnen und Juden. Hrsg. v. Regina Fritz, Béla Rásky, Éva Kovács. Wien, S. 339-356.

Celle im Nationalsozialismus. http://www.celle-im-nationalsozialismus.de/stadtrundgang/rechtsanwalt-manfred-herzfeld (10.9.2015).

Georeferenzierte Online-Bibliographie früher Holocaust- und Lagerliteratur (GeoBib). www.geobib.info (10.9.2015).

Herzfeld, Manfred 1947: Gruss an Deutschland. Eine Abrechnung in Versen. Jerusalem.

Loewy, Miriam [o.J.]: „Wer niest denn da?". http://www.oxfort.de/family.htm (29.10.2014).

Marcuse, Bruno 1946a: Erlebnisse im KZ Theresienstadt. [o.O.].

ders. 1946b: Julius Berger und das Dritte Reich. Ulm.

Mitgliedsfragebogen. In: Archiv der Israelitischen Kultusvereinigung, heute Israelitische Religionsgemeinschaft Württemberg in Stuttgart, Personenakte Bruno Marcuse, Signatur 1236_001.

Rohde, Reinhard 2010: Manfred Herzfeld – und sein *Gruß an Deutschland*. In: Um-Brüche. Celler Lebensgeschichten. Celle (= celler hefte. 5-6), S. 9-28.

Theresienstadt 1941 – 1945. Ein Nachschlagewerk. http://www.ghetto-theresienstadt.info/pages/d/dormitzere.htm (10.9.2015).

Lyrical Greetings to Germany – Manfred Herzfeld and Other ‚Untrained' Authors of Holocaust Poems 1945 – 1949

In the early period after the Holocaust – that is from 1945 to 1949 – many survivors reached for paper and pen to write down their memories in order to save them for the following generations, to vocalize a warning to their contemporaries or to set a literary gravestone for their deceased family members, friends, and inmates from the camps and ghettos. Only few of them, however, chose the genre of poems. Next to drama, lyric is the least represented form of literary coping. Nevertheless – or maybe especially because of this fact – academic engagement with the few collections of poems which were published between 1945 and 1949 by authors like Manfred Herzfeld and Bruno Marcuse is more than worthwhile. Members of this group who can be described as ‚untrained' authors published only one collection of their poems. This singular phenomenon of authors that never found their place in cultural memory as well as their biographical, stylistic and topic wise similarities are shown in the article. It mainly focuses on Manfred Herzfeld who published his collection of poems titled *Gruss an Deutschland. Eine Abrechnung in Versen* (*Greetings to Germany. A Vengeance in Rhymes*) in Israel in 1947. In his poems he accused Germans, fellow Jews and the Allied Forces of forgetting the Holocaust too easily. He chose a strict and very formal style without any tendencies towards an aesthetic approach which is – as the article will show – very typical for many ‚untrained' lyrical poets. This analysis is meant to highlight the lyrical output remote from the iconographic Holocaust poems by Nelly Sachs or Paul Celan.

Czech Bystanders Writing Poetry about the Shoah. Different Ways of Poetic Languages in the First Post-War Literary Reactions

Štěpán Balík, České Budějovice/Praha

The so-called *bystander effect*, *bystander apathy* or *bystander involvement* represents a psychological phenomenon which is characterized by not helping a victim because of the fact that there are more people present who could step in (cf. VandenBos 2007, 141; Greenberg 1994, 187 et seq.; Nolen-Hoeksema 2012, 712 et seqq.). A literary example par excellence is Czesław Miłosz's famous poem *Campo di Fiori* in which Poles are enjoying the carousel ride while the Warsaw Ghetto is burning during the uprising in the spring of 1943. This narration is confronted with a story about burning Giordano Bruno to death with an unconcerned Italian audience watching.

This poem and other post-war verses by Miłosz, such as *Biedny chrześciajanin patrzy na ghetto* (*The Poor Christian Looks at the Ghetto*), inspired Jan Błoński. They are both part of a book with his critical essay on Polish-Jewish war relation *Biedni Polacy patrzą na getto* (*The Poor Poles Look at the Ghetto*) which was published in the renowned catholic weekly magazine *Tygodnik Powszechny* for the first time in the late 1980s. He assumes – as most of the Shoah victims were from pre-war Poland – that Poles are responsible for the Polish complicity („współ-wina"), but not for a participation („współ-udział") because they could help their neighbours, with whom they had lived for many centuries, but they did not (cf. Błoński 2008, 11-33).

Although the war situation in the Polish and the Czech territories is very different (including the number of victims) during the World War II, it elicits a very similar question: How Czechs defended their Jews from going to Terezín and then Auschwitz? Thus, the memory of texts, written by well-known Czech poets, is not just a witness of the outstanding brutality of Nazis, but also at least partly a witness of the lyrical subjects' guilt for doing nothing or acting insufficiently.

In my paper I concentrate on Czech poetic bystanders writing in the 1940s and 1950s (Kamil Bednář, Josef Hiršal, František Halas, Konstantin Biebl, František Branislav, František Hrubín and Jiří Kolář). Apart from Kolář and partly Bednář and Halas, who return to the theme of Shoah repeatedly, all other named poets – as far as I know – wrote rarely about the Jewish war fate. Formulating the traumatic experience, the sudden loss of friends or neighbours etc. they used different ways of poetic languages. Generally speaking, there are two modes. Writers either chose classical rhythmical metre even with rhymes, or they come with a new form which brings the structure closer towards prosaic language. However, both are stylistic devices!

Preferring the prosaic style, Adorno's well-known statement questioning the artistic utterances after the Shoah plays the key role. However, doubts about the artistic means which could be used were in the air even before Adorno formulated it in 1949 and published it in 1954 (cf. Holý 2011, 201-224). Such a case is present in the poetry of KAMIL BEDNÁŘ (1912 – 1972), who represented the leading personality of a literary formation with Jiří Orten, Ivan Blatný etc. in the 1930s and 1940s. Soon after the end of the war he still sticks to the classic iambic verse with rhymes a-b-a-b in a mourning poem *Nezvěstnému* (*To the Missing One*) commemorating his close friend and poet Jiří Daniel (real name František Schulmann), who fell victim to the Shoah.[1]

> Po celou válku tajná rekviem jsem psal,
> teď ještě za tebe zas nové píši,
> tys umíral, já jen tvou hrůzu ssál
> a teď ji tiším – za všechny, kdo už neuslyší.
>
> V prach polských silnic navracím se teď,
> po paměti tam tvoji zhublou ruku hledám,
> v pochodu smrti šli jste – šeď, samá šeď –
> a tupí k životu a tupí k bědám.
>
> Byls mrtev již – had nad kolony se plazil dál,
> surový úšklebek na tváři vraha visel
> z vás jeden po druhém tak odpadal,
> v příkopech zbyla řada mrtvých čísel.
>   (Bednář 1945, 7 et seq.)
>
> All the war-time I spent writing secret requiems,
> now I'm writing one more,
> you were dying, I was only sucking your terror

---

[1] This poetic obituary was published in Černý's *Kritický měsíčník* (*Critical Monthly*) in the first post-war issue of the renewed magazine.

and now I'm relieving it – for all those who can't hear anymore.

Now I'm returning to the dust of Polish roads,
feeling around where your thin hand could be,
you walked in a death march – greyness, just greyness –
numb to the life and numb to the suffering.

You had already died – the snake crawled on above the convoys,
a brutish grimace hung on the murderer's face
you dropped behind one after another,
dead numbers were left in the ditch. [2]

Apart from such a personal dimension of the Shoah, the lyrical subject comes up with a more general and very revolutionary topic. (The poem slightly loses the structure of classic iambic verse and rhyme structure.) He asks himself – in another poem called *Poselství míru* (*The Message of Peace*) – how he can write poetry about the Shoah after having witnessed all the World War II cruelty, i.e. in Bednář's words after Pandora's Box of evil had been opened. The lyrical subject exclaims over and over:

Smrt jejich příliš těžká je,
než aby slovo uneslo ji –
[...]
Ach, mistře slov, jenž jimi zacházeje
změřiti umně chtěl bys otvor bezedný,
kam všichni propadli se!
[...]
Ti všichni rvou
z mých rukou tento list,
jenž písmem slepeckým je psán,
[...]
Vždyť nejsem víc
než komín, kterým stoupá
dým spalovaných těl,
mé písmo – provaz přissátý
tam na popravčí kůl,
já promluvit jen chtěl,
když z rukou tonoucích
pojednou život unikl – i nám –
a v prstech zaťatých
nám z vody moří živoucích
zbyla jen sůl.
        (Bednář 1946, 81 et seq.)

---

[2] Non-artistic translation of the extracts by Alexandra Šípová.

Their death is too heavy
for a word to be able to bear it –
[...]
Oh, you master of words, who knows how to use them
you want to measure the bottomless hole,
where everybody has fallen!
[...]
All of them are trying to rip
this sheet of paper out of my hands,
that is written in Braille,
[...]
After all I am not more
than a stack through which the smoke of
burning bodies is rising,
my writing – a rope coiled tightly
around the stake over there,
I only wanted to be heard,
when their lives – and ours, too –
broke loose from their drowning hands
and from all the water of living seas
in our clenched fists
just salt was left.

Another immediate post-war reaction was written by JOSEF HIRŠAL (1920 – 2003), who was mainly related to the artistic group *Skupina 42*. He published the poem *Terezín* in the collection of contemporary literature *Ohnice* (*Wild Radish*) in 1947 (2nd part). This annual was edited by Kamil Bednář mentioned above.

In his poem the description of the abandoned ghetto of Terezín just after the war is brief and simple. Although the text is written in a rather classical style: four strophes in regular iamb with rhymes: a-b-a-b, his concise or rather curt language and enjambments destroy the harmonic structure.

Postele, kufry vyházené
před dveře prázdných baráků.
Okna jak oči zahmouřené.
Pár ruských vojáků

tu drží stráž. A město dřímá.
Jen zářijový vítr žene
sem papíry. A je jen zima
v ulici vylidněné – –

Tak stál jsem. A tu se mi snilo
všecko, co paměť ví,

jak se zde před nedávnem žilo
nablízku šílenství,

jak ruce život objímaly
jejž v zmatek měnil strach,
jak večer děti usínaly
už jako v rakvičkách – –.
(Hiršal 1947, 6 et seq.)

Beds, suitcases thrown out
outside the door of empty houses.
Windows like narrowed eyes.
A couple of Russian soldiers

are on guard here. And the town is drowsing.
Just the October wind is blowing
papers here. And it's just cold
in the desolate street – –

So here I stood. And suddenly I had a dream
about everything that memory held
how we lived here not long ago
close to insanity,

how arms hugged life
the life turned into chaos by fear
how children fell asleep at night
already like in little coffins – –

FRANTIŠEK HALAS (1901 – 1949) already comments on the persecution of Jews – probably in connection with the growing persecution in Nazi Germany – before the war. Poem *Židům* (*To the Jews*) apparently remained only in the form of a manuscript (cf. Halas 1981, 322, 392). In the time of the Nazi occupation Jewish topics are depicted only covertly for many good reasons. Shortly after Jiří Orten's death (1/9/1941) František Halas published a cryptonymic poem-obituary *Za básníkem* (*Mourning for the Poet*) in *Kritický měsíčník* (cf. Halas 1941, 264 et seqq.).[3]

The Shoah is also implicitly depicted in Halas's poem *Ztracená* (*The Lost*) from the collection of poems *V řadě* (1948; *In Line*), and is only decipherable through the dedication „Na paměť Ireny Krausové" („To the memory of Irena

---

[3] During the war it was also published in the collection *Ladění* (1942, *Tuning*) under the name *Zmlklému* (*To the Silent One*), in the post-war publications of this collection and in other works by Halas under the name *Za Jiřím Ortenem* (*Mourning for Jiří Orten*) (cf. Halas 1957, 374 et seqq.; Halas 1983, 202).

Krausová"). This woman, one of Halas's friends, who died in Auschwitz in the autumn of 1944, is also briefly remembered in *Židovská ročenka* (1988/89; *Jewish Annual*), where the aforementioned poem was published in reverse order – the first two strophes come to the end (cf. Žantovský 1988/89, 131 et seq.).

> Vidím Tě Zůstalas
> A bděla k chropotům
> těl vychládajících
> když opouštěly je
> už i ty vši už i ty vši
> Tam v peklech zůstalas
> (Halas 1983, 65 and 1988/89, 131)

> I Can See You Stayed
> And stayed awake until the death rattle
> of bodies cooling down
> when even the lice even the lice
> were abandoning them
> You stayed in the hell down there

However, most of the poems in this collection are dedicated to Czech, Slovak and Soviet war martyrology, including the poem *Lidice* (cf. Halas 1983, 75).

The poem *A co básník* (*And What Does the Poet Say*) is written in a free verse partially in a iambic style with no rhymes, similarly to Halas's poetry mentioned above. The text, which was published twice, in 1946 and 1947, symbolizes the climax of the collection *A co?* (*And what?*) published posthumously in 1957 (cf. Penkala 2006, 51et seq.; Halas 1957, 472 et seqq.; Halas 1983, 111 et seqq.; Halas 2006, 37 et seqq.). The lyrical subject refuses the role of a poet as an announcer of the contemporary political opinion or mainstream oblivion too soon after the war cruelties were over, on the contrary, he proclaims freedom of speech and points out how difficult it is to resist the mainstream and superficial reader's perception. In this context a passing reference to the Shoah can be noticed.

> Byl čas přišitých hvězd
> Mařenek zmařených
> rozkopaných dětí
> (Halas 1983: 112)

There was a time of stars sewn on
Little Maries littered
Children kicked around the place

KONSTANTIN BIEBL (1898 – 1951) also belongs to the older generation. He was already a well-known poet before World War II. His poem *Žalm* (*Psalm*) was published in the collection of poems *Bez obav. Básně z let 1940 – 1950* (*No fear. Poems from the years 1940 – 1950*). It presents various Jewish topics. The Jews are depicted here without their enemies who are responsible for the Jewish bitter lot. Nevertheless, a final hope for a Zionist departure to Palestine appears at the end. The style in which he writes about the Middle East cultural and natural environment reminds us of Biebl's pre-war poems. Classic iambic rhymed verses almost form a sonnet (4+4+7).

Jehovův národe vy rabíni vy židovičky
Starého zákona obětní beránci
V co ještě doufáte za přimrzlými víčky
V tmě vagonu když usínáte s rukou na ranci?

Vstříc komu zavřely se oči vaše
V jezerech zledovělých řas?
Po věky čekáte na Mesiáše
Jenž nikdy nepřichází včas

Snad přece ještě přijde vkrátku
Pěšky
Nebo na oslátku
S nákladem datlí
Oliv
Vína
Všeho co rodí v dálce Palestina
         (Biebl 1951, 31 et seq.)

Jehovah's nation you rabbis you little Jewish women
Old Testament's scapegoats
What do you still hope for behind your frozen eyelids
In the darkness of the railway car while you're falling asleep, your hand on the bundle?

Towards whom have your eyes closed
In the lakes of icy eyelashes?
For ages you've been waiting for Messiah
Who is never on time

Hopefully, he'll come before long
On foot
Or on a donkey foal's back

Loaded with dates
Olives
Wine
With everything faraway Palestine bears

The poem is placed in the part called *Panychidy* (*Memorial Ceremonies*) together with the double poem *Válečné ticho* (*The War Silence*). The former is written in a free verse; the latter begins with a trochaic and ends in an irregular iambic verse. In the context of the official communist martyrology (poems about Julius Fučík or V. I. Lenin etc.), it shows the perspective of the contemporary official style: In the concentration camps no Jews are present, just Czechs, Poles and Russians. The black-and-white mindset is supported by a picture of a Nazi enemy, who is swept away by „the Red snowstorm".

Který Polák Čech a Rus je ještě živý
V koncentračním táboře
Jako z lesa přivezené dříví
Házeli je z vozu jenž stál v noci na dvoře

[...]

Už slyšíte ji fičet gestapáci
Na vaše kosti hraje pravá ruská vánice
Vršíc nad vámi bílou mohylu za vaši černou práci
Za poslední váš benzin jimž v noci vzplála
Na zasněženém dvoře ta svatá hranice
                                        (Biebl 1951, 34 et seq.)

Which Pole Czech and Russian is still alive
In the concentration camp
Like wood brought from the forest
They threw them off the wagon standing in the yard at night

[...]

You can hear it whistling now gestapo guys
The genuine Russian snowstorm
Playing your bones
Building up a white burial mound over you for your black labour
For your last petrol which set it on fire at night
That holy funeral pyre in the snow-covered yard

The poem *Birkenau* written by FRANTIŠEK HRUBÍN (1910 – 1971) is rather unknown. It is present just in the 2nd edition of Kraus and Schön's[4] *Továrna na*

---

[4] He changed his name to Kulka later on.

smrt (1950; *The Death Factory*), where they both, in the introduction, thank the author for the poem (December 1948). Probably because of Hrubín's political problems, his poem was removed from the other editions of their book about Auschwitz.

The verses without rhymes, but iambic tendencies are introduced in the motto by Hermann Hesse. His poem *Harte Menschen* describes a child's deprived psyche after endured suffering. The text focuses on revealing a child's world in different perspectives. In the surrealistic collage three narrations are intertwined with each other: slaughtering of a chicken; trying to get a Czech boy to sleep and thirdly, the process of killing children in Birkenau.

In general, the poem is based on shocking parallels. For example the contrast of an oven in a cosy home and the ovens used for cremation in Birkenau points out the phenomenon of Nazi brutal misuse of things, people, death and of course, words themselves. In the semantically ambiguous text there are no explicit Jewish motifs, apart from the name Birkenau itself. In contrast, the burning of gassed children victims is followed by the lyrical subject's desperate exclamation to the Virgin Mary.

Houpy, hou, houpy, synku náš –
(a zítřek matku celou prostupuje,
větrání, nákup, dříví
svět, na němž milionkrát žil
s maminkou malý živý) –
přikryj se hezky, celý, celý!
Hlavu ne! Chceš se udusit?

... daleko v Birkenau
maminky písek pláčí,
nacpány s dětmi v strašných komorách.
Už přirazili dveře. Na živáčky
čeká plyn – škrtič, smrtka – vrah...
(Hrubín 1950, 8)

Rock-a-bye, our son –
(and tomorrow penetrates the mother through and through,
airing, shopping, wood,
the world in which he has lived young alive million times
with his mum) –
cover yourself properly, from head to toe!
Not the head! Do you want to get smothered?

> ... far away in Birkenau
> mums are crying sand
> stuffed with their children into terrible chambers.
> They've already slammed the door shut. For the poor alive
> the gas – strangler, the Death – murderer are waiting...

In 1950 FRANTIŠEK BRANISLAV (1900 – 1968) published his collection of poems *Pozdrav Polsku* (*Greeting to Poland*). Like Biebl, most of his text depicting war scenes and narratives reveal the official heroic style, however, Branislav's fictional universe is more diverse. In comparison with the rest of the poems, the text *Ghetto v kamenech* (*Ghetto in Stones*) is written in a very sophisticated form. The poem is based on the contrast between an image of the Prague Jewish Cemetery and a view of the destroyed Warsaw Ghetto, which is called *Hřbitov hřbitovů* (*Cemetery of all cemeteries*). In addition, Branislav uses an asterisk (*) to show a change of scene (similar to separating the various shots during filmmaking).

The first two strophes about the Prague Jewish Cemetery are formed by 4 verses (rhyme a-b-a-b) in dactyl. The third one, introducing the theme of destroyed Warsaw Ghetto, continues in the identical structure. The fourth and most dynamic part, devoted to the detailed picture of post-war piles of stones of former Warsaw Ghetto, is built by 7 rhyming double verses in iambic style. The last two strophes with the topic from the beginning (Prague Jewish Cemetery) are again formed by 4 verses (rhyme a-b-a-b) in dactyl.

A formal drastic word game with the substantive *kámen* (*stone*) is present in the ‚Polish' part and makes the verses dynamic. Those repeatedly mentioned piles and ruins of stones symbolize the countless number of murdered Jewish people in an implicit way. In the ‚Czech' part such a reading is also stressed by the presence of a Jewish tradition consisting in lying pebbles on gravestones to commemorate those who passed away. At the end of the poem a metaphysical hope of something finally alive is accentuated and a commemorated rosehip in autumn may become a wild rose in spring.

> Nechtějme nikdy sčítat kámen za kamenem,
> nesčitatelný počet záhy zapomenem.
>
> Kamení, kámen nad kamenem u kamene
> kamenným mořem oči k smrti unavené.

Přijď, sestro zimo, přijď, ty znalá utěšení,
kameny mrtvých přikryj rouchem zasněžení.

*

Na starém hřbitově v židovské čtvrti
až jednou stát budu nad hroby,
nad cestou podzimu rozběhlou k smrti,
snad ruka hrob šípky ozdobí.

Až přijdou z jara klást kamínky prosté
za děti, za ženy, za muže,
užasnou pojednou, že tady roste
alespoň jedna noc do růže.
(Branislav 1950, 21 et seq.)

Let's not want to count up a stone after stone,
the number impossible to count will soon be forgotten.

The heap of stones, stone over the stone next to the stone,
eyes tired to death with the sea of stones.

Come, sister winter, come, well versed in consolation,
cover the stones of the dead under the robe of snow.

*

In the old cemetery in the Jewish neighbourhood
when I stand still for a while over the graves one day,
over the autumn road running to the death,
hopefully the hand will decorate the grave with rosehips.

When they come in spring to lay simple stones
for the children, for the women, for the men,
suddenly, they'll be astonished to see
at least one night grow into a rose.

The poetic style of JIŘÍ KOLÁŘ (1914 – 2002) contrasts with the classically structured verses mentioned above. He was member of the artistic group *Skupina 42*. Until 1989 Kolář was in the position of an unofficial artist, whose work was allowed to be published during times of political liberalization. This can be seen, for example, when taking a look at his poems devoted to the topic of the Shoah, with figures of Jews explicitly being present.[5] *Prométheova játra* (*Prometheus's Liver*), in which Zofia Nałkowska's short story *Przy torze kolejowym* (*On the Track*) is present in the translation of Helena Teigová (*Na trati*), was

---

[5] Only in the immediate post-war reaction *Sedm kantát* (*Seven cantatas*) (Kolář 1945) he conformed to the contemporary communist martyrdom.

written in 1950. It was published in 1970, but then confiscated and afterwards published again in exile by Sixty-Eight Publishers in 1985; in Czechoslovakia at last in 1990 (Kolář 1990). Not accidently it is focused on the bystander effect phenomenon, i.e. depicting people who are unwilling or scared to help a wounded Jewish woman. The theme of the Shoah also appears in the poem *Starý žid seděl na podlaze a modlil se...* (*An Old Jew Was Sitting on the Floor Praying*) from the collection *Dny v roce* (*Days in a Year*) (Kolář 1992, 283). The theatre play *Mor v Athénách* (*Plague in Athens*), where the author uses also fragments of the aforementioned book *Továrna na smrt*, was written in 1961. It was published in 1965, but just as a copy (Kolář 2000). Only his last work *Záznamy* (*Records*), where he exposes the Shoah to other genocides of the twentieth century, was not postponed, but published immediately after his death (Kolář 2002).

The history of his poem *1944* is not simple, either. Although it was published in 1966 in the collection *Černá lyra* (*The Black Lyre*) for the first time, it was written after his visit to the museum in Auschwitz (1954). As Kolář said, this experience confirmed him in his sceptical view of artistic instruments serving as tools of provocation (i.e. artistic exhibitionism). He gave up his original intention and placed the verses about the Shoah at the beginning of the collection. In *Dovětek autora* (*Author's Postscript*) to *Vršovický Ezop* (*Aesop from Vršovice*; 1966) Kolář comments on this as follows:

> Celá sbírka měla být dějinami lidské podlosti, ukončenými svědectvími z koncentračních táborů. Napřed jsem se pokoušel vtáhnout tyto výpovědi do mlhy literatury, ale brzy jsem poznal nesmyslnost svého počínání a rozhodl jsem se ponechat jim jejich autentičnost. Proto jsem také tyto básně nazýval „autentickou poezií". A proto bych si také přál, aby nebyly považovány za nic jiného [...] než jakési „knižní podání", neboť v těch letech bylo mým největším přáním pomoci těm, kdo je zaznamenali, donést je dál (Kolář 1993, 245).

> The whole collection was intended to be the history of human wickedness, finished with the evidence from concentration camps. At first I tried to draw these into the fog of literature, but soon I realized how ridiculous my actions were and decided to leave them their authenticity. That is why I called these poems „authentic poetry". And that is why I wish they were considered to be nothing [...] but some kind of „literary presentation", as in those years my greatest wish was to help those, who kept record of them, pass them on.

He was inspired by the elimination of a so-called family camp of Czech Jewish prisoners. Poem *1944* was made into verses according to the fragment from

Kraus' and Schön's *Továrna na smrt* mentioned above. Kolář's non-poetic style or literal poetry is distinguished by a prosaic narration in verses without punctuation. Such an attitude allows him to make a sarcastic transposition of Nazi newspeak.

Velitel krematorií nařídil
vykopat kolem hranic příkopy
pro stékající tuk škvařících se těl
tímto sádlem poručil mrtvé polévat
Tak šla práce kupředu rychleji
Sám se bavil tím
že házel do vřícího omastku děti
nebo tam skopával starce a stařeny
Protože živých bylo tolik
že všechno vraždění nestačilo
Vybírali nejzdravější a hnali je po tisících do bloků
[...]
Tam jim brali krev a nutili je psát:
<u>Buďte bez obav, daří se nám dobře, na shledanou!</u>
V srpnu dosáhly plynové komory špičkového výkonu
za dvacet čtyři hodin
bylo zahubeno
dvacet tisíc maďarských židů
                    (Kolář 1993, 16)

The head of the crematorium ordered
to dig ditches around the pyres
for the fat trickling down the burning bodies
he ordered to pour the lard over the dead people
This way the work moved on faster
He entertained himself
throwing children in the boiling grease
or he kicked in old men and women
Because there were so many of those who were alive
that all the killing wasn't enough
they chose the healthiest ones and drove thousands of them to the blocks
[...]
They took their blood there and forced them to write:
<u>Don't worry, we're fine, see you!</u>
In August the gas chambers reached the peak output
within twenty-four hours
twenty thousand Hungarian Jews
were exterminated

In 1955 Kolář wrote *Očitý svědek. Deník z roku 1949* (*The Eye Witness. The Diary of 1949*). Under the date of 19th February a separated incipit „Jestliže v roce dvaačtyřicátém" („If in the year forty-two") is to be found and the poem continues with Kolář's history of human wickedness, which ends, however, with a chance of hope.

> usedla žena s knihou k lampě
> se stínidlem z kůže z lidských zad,
> je to znamení muži, aby si pospíšil
> vynajít něco nepřirozenějšího,
> neboť hodina, kdy jiná žena
> zatouží po rukavicích nebo obuvi
> nevídanější –; muž, nebude-li znát
> jiný prostředek, sáhne po staré
> zkušenosti a zbude mu jen volit
> kůži z rukou dítěte nebo
> nohou rodičky. Ale toto všechno
> je jen zdáním posledního soudu.
> [...]
> Je tu jen jedna možnost,
> že pozná marnost svého úmyslu
> a odejde, aniž splnil přikázání.
> (Kolář 1997, 137)

> a woman sat down with a book next to a lamp
> with a shade made from people back's skin,
> it is a sign for a man to hurry up
> to find something more unnatural,
> as the hour when another woman
> starts longing for gloves or shoes
> more extraordinary –; the man if he doesn't know
> another means, he will go for his old
> experience and will only have to choose
> between the skin of a child's hand or
> an expectant mother's feet. But all this
> is a mere illusion of the last judgement.
> [...]
> There is only one chance
> that he will see how purposelessly he tries
> and will leave without carrying the order.

Despite the fact that Kolář's shocking prosaic narration in verses is unique in the context of Czech poetry about the Shoah, Hiršal's curt style approaches the experimental artistic utterance of his colleague. Moreover, Bednář is probably the first Czech poet who – in 1946 – raised the major issue of asking about the form in which the Shoah is literarily graspable. Kolář's writings seem to be an answer either to Bednář's appeal or the later Adorno's proclamation which is set in a more general way.

Most of the aforementioned poets, writing usually just a single poem about the Jewish annihilation, used traditional ways of poetic language in iamb and rhymes. However, Bednář already loosed the iambic and rhymed structure. In addition, Branislav chose dactyl (apart from dynamic verses in iamb), which could be considered as a way to the free verse used e.g. by Jaroslav Seifert in *Koncert na ostrově* (*Concert on Island*) in the mid-60s.

Biebl, Branislav and Halas equalized the picture of the Jewish tragedy by war verses meeting requirements of the official period martyrdom. Only Kolář was continuously returning to the theme of the Shoah in an explicit way. He was far from being only a quiet bystander, he was a poetic witness who systematically shouted out loud words about the horrible factory cruelty committed on Jewish neighbours the majority of whom had been lost forever.

Bibliography

Bednář, Kamil 1945: Nezvěstnému. In: Kritický měsíčník 6,1, pp. 7-9.
id. 1946: Poselství míru. In: Kritický měsíčník 7,4-6, pp. 81-83.
Biebl, Konstantin 1951: Bez obav. Praha.
Błoński, Jan 2008: Biedni Polacy patrzą na getto. In: id.: Biedni Polacy patrzą na getto. Kraków, pp. 11-33.
Branislav, František 1950: Pozdrav Polsku. Praha.
Greenberg, Martin S. 1994: Bystander Involvement. In: Encyclopedia of Psychology. Ed. by Raymond J. Corsini. New York [etc.], pp. 187-188.
Halas, František 1941: Za básníkem. In: Kritický měsíčník. 4,7, pp. 264-266.
id. 1957: Básně. Praha.
id. 1981: Časy. Praha. (= Dílo Františka Halase II).
id. 1983: A co básník. Praha. (= Dílo Františka Halase III).
id. 1988/89: Ztracená. In: Židovská ročenka 5749, Praha, p. 131.
id. 2006: A co? Praha.
Hiršal, Josef 1947: Terezín. In: Kamil Bednář (red.): Ohnice. Sborník současné literatury. I. Praha, pp. 6-7.
Holý, Jiří 2011: U nás v Auschwitzu... Osvětimský tábor v literatuře a v reflexi filozofů. In: Miroslav Petříček (red.): Moderní svět v zrcadle literatury a filosofie. Praha, pp. 201-224.
Hrubín, František 1950: Birkenau. In: Ota Kraus – Erich Schön: Továrna na smrt. Praha, pp. 7-9.

Kolář, Jiří 1945: Sedm kantát. Praha.
 id. 1990: Prométheova játra. Praha.
 id. 1992: Křestný list; Ódy a variace; Limb a jiné básně; Sedm kantát; Dny v roce; Roky v dnech. Praha (= Dílo Jiřího Koláře I).
 id. 1993: Černá lyra; Návod k upotřebení; Marsyas; Z pozůstalosti pana A.; Vršovický Ezop; Česká suita. Praha. (= Dílo Jiřího Koláře III).
 id. 1997: Černá lyra; Čas; Očitý svědek. Praha. (= Dílo Jiřího Koláře II).
 id. 2000: Chléb na vezdejší; Mor v Athénách. Praha – Litomyšl. (= Dílo Jiřího Koláře V).
 id. 2002: Záznamy. Praha – Litomyšl. (= Dílo Jiřího Koláře XI).
Kraus, Ota – *Schön*, Erich 1950: Továrna na smrt. Praha.
Nolen-Hoeksema, Susan [et al.] 2012: Psychologie Atkinsonové a Hilgarda. Praha.
Penkala, Vít 2006: Ediční poznámka. In: František Halas: A co? Praha, pp. 51-60.
Seifert, Jaroslav 1965: Koncert na ostrově. Praha.
VandenBos, Gary R. (Ed.) 2007: APA Dictionary of Psychology. Washington, DC.
Žantovský, Jiří 1988/89: Vzpomínka z Čáslavě na Terezín. In: Židovská ročenka. 5749, Praha, pp. 131-133.

Die Dichtung tschechischer ‚bystanders' über die Shoah.
Unterschiedliche Formen dichterischer Gestaltung in den ersten literarischen Reaktionen der Nachkriegszeit

Inspiriert durch den psychologischen Begriff des *bystander effect* konzentriere ich mich auf ausgewählte nichtjüdische tschechische Dichter der vierziger und fünfziger Jahre (Kamil Bednář, Josef Hiršal, František Halas, Konstantin Biebl, František Branislav, František Hrubín und Jiří Kolář), die man als ‚bystanders' bezeichnen könnte. Außer Kolář und teilweise Bednář und Halas, die das Thema der Shoah wiederholt aufgegriffen haben, schrieben alle anderen genannten Dichter – soweit ich weiß – eher selten über das Schicksal der Juden während der Nazidiktatur. Bei der dichterischen Gestaltung traumatischer Erfahrungen, wie etwa des plötzlichen Verlustes von Freunden und Nachbarn u.ä., verwendeten sie unterschiedliche poetische Ausdrucksmittel. Die Autoren setzten entweder klassische rhythmische Versmaße ein (in der Regel Jamben), und dies auch mit Reimen, oder aber ganz neue Formen, die sich der Prosasprache annähern (Kolář). Jedenfalls gab Bednář die jambische und gereimte Struktur auf und Branislav wählte den Daktylus, was als erster Schritt hin zum freien Vers gedeutet werden könnte, den etwa Jaroslav Seifert in *Koncert na ostrově* (*Konzert auf der Insel*) Mitte der sechziger Jahre verwendete. Auch Hiršals gedrungener Stil steht Kolářs experimentellem künstlerischem Ausdruck nahe.

Bednář ist vielleicht der erste tschechische Dichter, der – im Jahre 1946 – intensiv nach Formen suchte, mit denen die Shoah literarisch dargestellt werden könnte. Kolářs Texte erscheinen wie eine Reaktion sowohl auf Bednářs Bemühungen als auch auf Adornos späteres, allgemeiner formuliertes Diktum. Auf der anderen Seite relativierten Biebl, Branislav und Halas das Bild der jüdischen Tragödie mit Versen über den Krieg, die der damaligen offiziellen Martyrologie entsprachen. Nur Kolář war weit davon entfernt, nur ein stiller ‚bystander' zu sein; er war ein dichterischer Zeuge, der deutlich und systematisch Stellung bezog zum grausamen Schicksal seiner jüdischen Nachbarn, von denen die meisten ermordet worden waren.

Tadeusz Różewicz's Poetics of Testimony

Arkadiusz Morawiec, Łódź

> From two films
> and a few books
> I construct a landscape without color
> Tadeusz Różewicz, *Stone Imagination*[1] (1976b, 11)

In his article published on 16 June 1947 in *Dziennik Polski*, Jalu Kurek described his visit to the museum which had been opened two days earlier in the former Auschwitz concentration camp. He wrote:

> I am looking at thousands of brushes and shoe polish boxes, heaps of human hair stiffened by lethal gas, baby shoes, suitcases, prostheses, artificial arms and legs, and trusses – to whom did these items belonged? So many cripples were brought here! What did those people look like? [...] This evidence of torment and murder activates a writer's imagination. How many more artists will have their imagination fertilized by this monstrous, horrifying *Lager*, as it will be gradually losing its realistic appeal and fading out in time, and will only be seen as a decontextualized vision? (Kurek 1947)[2]

Kurek was not the only Polish writer who visited the former *Konzentrationslager* while it was being transformed into a museum or soon after the museum was opened. Another report from a visit to the Auschwitz-Birkenau State Museum was published by Juliusz Kydryński (1946), a former Auschwitz prisoner. Reportages and articles related to this memorial place were written by, for instance, Kazimierz Koźniewski (1948), Wanda Kragen (1947), Tadeusz Kudliński (1947), and Jerzy Putrament (1948).

This horrifying *Lager* „fertilized the imagination", to use Kurek's words, of the authors of innumerable literary texts (as well as of films, and other works of art and music) dealing with this topic. It is difficult to make a list of all the works inspired by or created in the former concentration and death camps, mu-

---

[1] „Z dwóch filmów / i książek kilku / układam bezbarwny krajobraz" (Różewicz 1948, 6).

[2] „Oglądam tysiące szczotek, pudełek od past, stosy zestrzyżonych włosów ludzkich stwardniałych od działania śmiercionośnego gazu, buciki dziecinne, walizki, protezy, sztuczne ręce i nogi, pasy przepuklinowe – do kogo to wszystko należało? Ileż tu kalek przywożono! Jak wyglądali ci ludzie? [...] Wyobraźnia pisarza pracuje, oglądając te fragmenty kaźni. Iluż artystów i twórców jeszcze zapłodni ten potężny wstrząsający lager, im bardziej będzie się oddalał od swego realistycznego sztafażu, przyblakły w czasie, polatujący tylko w oderwanym wizyjnym kształcie?".

seums, and memorial sites. As regards Polish literature, it suffices to mention the reportage entitled *A Sunday Afternoon in Dachau* (1964; *Niedzielne popołudnie w Dachau*) by Ryszard Wojna, Józefa Radzymińska's novel *The Night above Us* (1966; *Nad nami noc*), Zofia Romaniczowa's short story *Cuckoo* (*Kukułka*; in Romanowiczowa 1965), Andrzej Brycht's short story *Excursion: Auschwitz-Birkenau* (*Wycieczka Auschwitz-Birkenau*; in Brycht 1966), the play *My Wife's Parents' Trip to Treblinka* (2003; *Podróż rodziców mej żony do Treblinki*) by Marian Pankowski, and the poems: Andrzej Bursa's *Auschwitz – An Excursion* (*Oświęcim – Wycieczka*; in Bursa 1973), Julian Przyboś's *Auschwitz* (*Oświęcim*; in Przyboś 1961), and Adam Zagajewski's *The Swallows of Auschwitz* (*Jaskółki Oświęcimia*; in Zagajewski 2003). As Kurek predicted, opening museums and erecting monuments in those tragic places and, in general, turning them into memorial sites only reinforced their great inspirational power (see Morawiec 2009, 310 et seq., 372 et seq.).

One of the most important and, apart from Brycht's *Excursion: Auschwitz-Birkenau* (which was adapted to film), most well-known works of Polish literature which explores the theme of a concentration camp museum is Tadeusz Różewicz's short story *An Excursion to the Museum* (*Wycieczka do muzeum*), which was published in 1961 (Różewicz 1961; reprint in Różewicz 1966; an English translation in Różewicz 2002). In this context, one should also mention two other, earlier, and undoubtedly outstanding works by the same author: his poems *Massacre of the Boys* (*Rzeź chłopców*) and the canonical *Pigtail* (*Warkoczyk*), which has for years been on the syllabus for Polish schools and which was first published at the beginning of 1949 in the *Odrodzenie* weekly[3] (Różewicz 1949). I am not going to interpret these texts here, since this has been done before by many competent literature scholars (see, for example, Gancarczyk 1990, Tomaszewski 1993, Osborne 1997). I would only like to focus on the text which, in my opinion, greatly influenced these works. So far neglected, this source of inspiration suggests that the originality of Różewicz's poetry, whose characteristic feature is „the prosaicisation of lyrical speech" (Vogler 1949)[4],

---

[3] All the Polish quotations from these poems have been taken from this edition; in this article I will use the following abbreviations: *MB* for *Massacre of the Boys* and *P* for *Pigtail*.
[4] „prozaizacja żywiołu lirycznego".

does not exclusively derive from the author's personal, traumagenic war experience and the poetry he read (the critics have, among other things, pointed to the poetry of Leopold Staff, expressionists, Guillaume Apollinaire, surrealists, futurists, the representatives of the Cracow Avant-garde, Józef Czechowicz, and Czesław Miłosz; see, for example, Lam 1976, 88-98; Drewnowski 1990, 86-95). It also, if not mostly, has its source in other, often non-poetic texts read by Różewicz. I will return to this issue later.

The obvious, or at least unquestioned, source of inspiration for both of the above-mentioned poems – *Massacre of the Boys* and *Pigtail* – was Różewicz's visit to the Auschwitz-Birkenau museum. In *Pigtail*, this thesis, which I am not going to question, is supported by the reference to „hair [...] of those suffocated in gas chambers" (Różewicz 1997a, 19)[5], placed in large boxes under glass. The allusion is less obvious in *Massacre of the Boys*, in which Różewicz explores the motif of children's toys – little horses made of wire – which he might have seen among the exhibits at the museum. In fact, a few toys were displayed in a small room in block 6 soon after the museum was opened (see Kermisz 1947). The possible doubts concern *Massacre of the Boys*, rather than *Pigtail*, since tangled hair has been exposed to public view in block 4 since the very beginning of the museum's existence, becoming one of the icons of Auschwitz. These doubts, however, are dispelled by the caption under these poems which reads: „Museum-Oświęcim 1948" (Różewicz 1950, 11 et seq.). Informing the reader about the source of inspiration for the poems, rather than about the place where they were written, the caption was absent from the first edition, but was added to the poems when they were reprinted in 1950 in the collection entitled *Five Poems* (*Pięć poematów*) and can also be found in later editions.

Nevertheless, it appears that the above-mentioned literary works, which are among the most moving responses to the crimes committed in German Nazi camps and to the Holocaust, were not exclusively, or not mostly, inspired by a visit to the museum. These texts were also influenced by the testimony given in

---

[5] „włosy uduszonych w komorach gazowych" (*P*). This motif is also present in the short story entitled *My Little Daughter* (*Moja córeczka*): „A potem znalazłem wszystkie włosy kobiece, wszystkie włosy zebrane z głów żywych i umarłych za szkłem muzeum" (Różewicz 1966, 53; „And then I found all hair belonging to the women, all the hair shaved from the heads of the alive and the dead, behind the museum glass").

1945 to the Regional Jewish Historical Commission (Wojewódzka Żydowska Komisja Historyczna) in Cracow by Rudolf Reder, a former soap factory owner from Lviv (Lwów), to which Różewicz alludes in a surprisingly covert way. Reder was one of the only five people who escaped from Bełżec extermination camp (where around five hundred thousand people, mostly Jews, were killed in the period of seven months), of whom only two survived the war or rather: of whom only two are known to have survived the war (see Kuwałek 2005, 52 et seq., 63). Since August till November 1942 Reder, as a member of ‚death crew', was forced to remove corpses from the gas chambers and bury them in mass graves. His testimony is exceptional because it is the only evidence coming directly from a prisoner who was a member of Bełżec extermination camp support staff. It was written down by Nella Rost and included in the book entitled *Bełżec*, which was published in 1946 under Reder's name[6] (Reder 1946).

In Reder's testimony I found the strangely familiar words:

> When all the women from the transport had been shaved, four workers used brooms made of linden to sweep and gather all the hair. (Reder 1999, 128)[7]

The opening five lines of *Pigtail* are an almost accurate, or rather one should say a covert quotation, but written in verse with no punctuation:

> When all the women from the transport
> had been shaved
> four workers used brooms made of linden

---

[6] Reder's short testimony (or a short version of his full testimony) was published a year earlier, in the book entitled *Documents of Crime and Martyrdom* (*Dokumenty zbrodni i męczeństwa*) (Borwicz et al. 1945). Fragments of his another testimony, which concerned the gas chambers, are quoted by Eugeniusz Szrojt (1947) in his article *Belzec Extermination Camp* (*Obóz zagłady w Bełżcu*). Furthermore, on 30 September 1944, a text entitled *Belzec – A Way to Hell* (*Bełżec – droga do piekła*) was published. It was based on Reder's account and signed with the initials Z.W. (1944).

The quotations in the remaining part of the article come from the bilingual, Polish-English edition of *Bełżec* (Reder 1999). The English translation of Reder's words (by William Brand and Michael Jacobs) published in this edition has been modified by the translator of this article. The same concerns English translations of Różewicz's poems. The aim of this strategy is to convey the similarities between Różewicz's works and their non-literary source of inspiration – Reder's testimony, in which – as the Jewish Historical Commission states – „the form and manner in which the witness described things are preserved" (Reder 1999, 85).

[7] „Kiedy już wszystkie kobiety z transportu ogolono, czterech robotników, miotłami zrobionymi z lipy, zmiatało i gromadziło wszystkie włosy" (Reder 1999, 55).

		to sweep up
		and gather the hair
					(Różewicz 1997a, 19)[8]

Różewicz omitted only one word („wszystkie" = „all"), and modified another („zmiatało" = „swept" was replaced with „zamiatało" = „swept up"). These minute changes were probably made for stylistic reasons.

The first stanza of *Massacre of the Boys*:

		The children cried „Mommy!
		But I've been good!
		It's dark! It's dark!"
					(ibid., 21)[9]

was taken from another fragment of the testimony in which Reder describes the reactions of the ‚death crew' to „those horrible pleas of the people being suffocated each day, and the cries of the children" (Reder 1999, 141).[10] He states:

> Only, when I heard how the children cried out – „Mommy! But I've been good! It's dark! It's dark!" – our hearts were torn to shreds. And then we went back to not feeling anything. (ibid.)[11]

It is important to note that Różewicz used Reder's words in the opening lines of both poems. This suggests that the main impulse to write them came not so much from the visit to the museum in Oświęcim (Auschwitz), but rather from Reder's testimony.

The horrifying account given by the Bełżec survivor was published in a small number of copies. Thus, it was not, and still is not, well-known, also to the readers of Różewicz's works. This explains why many interpretations of *Pigtail* and

---

[8] „Kiedy już wszystkie kobiety / z transportu ogolono / czterech robotników miotłami / zrobionymi z lipy zamiatało / i gromadziło włosy" (*P*).

[9] „Dzieci wołały – ‚Mamusiu! / ja przecież byłem grzeczny! / Ciemno! Ciemno!'" (*MB*).

[10] „straszliwe skargi duszonych co dzień ludzi i wołania dzieci" (Reder 1999, 66).

[11] „Tylko kiedy słyszałem jak dzieci wołały: Mamusiu! ja przecież byłem grzeczny! Ciemno! Ciemno! – szarpało się w nas serce na strzępy. A później znowu przestawaliśmy czuć" (Reder 1999, 66). It is crucial to mention that the same shocking fragment was used by Jerzy Ficowski as a motto for his poem *The Seven Words* (*Siedem słów*): „‚Mummy! But I've been good! It's dark!' – words of a child being shut in a gas chamber at Belzec in 1942, according to the statement of the only surviving prisoner; quoted in Rudolf Reder, *Belzec* (1946)" (Ficowski 1981, 17) – „‚Mamusiu! Ja przecież byłem grzeczny! Ciemno! Ciemno!' (słowa dziecka zamykanego w komorze gazowej w Bełżcu 1942 r. – według zeznania jedynego więźnia, który ocalał). Rudolf Reder – *Bełżec*, 1946 r." (Ficowski 1979, 21).

Massacre of the Boys fail to take these allusions into account.[12] Feliks Tomaszewski's analysis of *Massacre of the Boys*, in which he states: „The image of extermination is evoked by the scream of the children forced into a gas chamber, heard in 1948 *in the Auschwitz Museum*" (Tomaszewski 1993, 86; italics mine – A.M.), can only be justified if we assume that the author did not want his readers to recognize the above-mentioned borrowed quotations. This line of thinking seems to be rather flawed. Instead, one should ask a different, well-founded question: why does Różewicz consistently hide this testimony, which is *the textual source* of the agonizing scream? Why does he conceal this source of inspiration, or rather does not reveal it?

In 1993 in a conversation about the 1982 play *The Trap* (*Pułapka*) Różewicz commented on the motifs explored in this drama and pointed to the source text which he used. He explained:

> The teeth, for instance, aren't only Felice's teeth, her gold dental crowns... Later these are the teeth from Auschwitz, the teeth of the dead. In the text I used a fragment of a prose work... an account from Majdanek. (Dębicz 1993, 92)[13]

Of course, in such a long text it is hard to find all intertextual references, especially that all of Różewicz's works, and mostly his late works, are highly intertextual (see Majchrowski 1992). I must admit that I have not found the account from Majdanek mentioned by Różewicz or the fragment which alludes to it. However, I have found a quotation in Tableau Ten, which is preceded by the following remark included in the stage directions: „A man appears against the

---

[12] Here are two examples of the interpretations of the opening stanza of *Pigtail*: „In the graphically separate first part of the poem we hear the voice of a person who uses the past tense to describe what happened in the concentration camp which now (in 1948) houses the Museum. [...] the voice that we hear in this place is similar to *the voice of the Museum guide*. The guide knows the text by heart, and he has repeated it so many times that he is no longer emotionally engaged with the content. He can be compared to a barrel organ, which has deformed the text – the stream of language has mechanically been divided into fragments, and thus the logical and syntactic structure of the texts has been destroyed. [...] At the same time, one may say that the voice of the guide becomes similar to the voice of history, which simply takes place and does not judge, but remains emotionless and indifferent to the meaning of the events, to human suffering" (Czaplejewski 1981, 228 et seq.; italics in original); „The first [stanza] *resembles a court testimony* – a dispassionate evidence given before an unknown tribunal" (Gronczewski 1982, 30; italics mine – A.M.).

[13] „Zęby, na przykład, to nie było tak, że to tylko zęby Felice, złote koronki... Potem są to zęby z Oświęcimia, zęby trupów. W tekście jest kawałek prozy... relacja z Majdanka".

black wall, holding a book. He opens it and reads" (Różewicz 1997b, 52). Put in inverted commas, the words read out by the man have been taken from Rudolf Reder's testimony. The fragment concerns the ‚dentists' from Bełżec and it deserves to be quoted in its entirety, because its echoes, albeit distant, can also be heard in the poem *Recycling*, and especially in the section entitled *Gold* (*Złoto*).[14] According to Reder,

> On the way from the gas chambers to the graves, and thus along several hundred meters, stood several dentists with pincers. They stopped each of the workers dragging corpses, opened the mouth of the cadaver, looked into it and pulled out the gold, and then threw it into a basket. There were eight dentists. Most of them were young, picked out of transports to perform this work. I got to know one of them better. His name was Zucker and he came from Rzeszów. The dentists had their own little barracks, together with the doctor and the pharmacist. At sundown they carried the baskets full of gold teeth to their barracks, when they separated the gold out and melted it down into bars. A Gestapo officer, Schmidt, guarded them and beat them when the work went too slow. Each transport had to be done in two hours. The teeth were melted into bars one centimeter thick, half a centimeter wide, and twenty centimeters long. (Reder 1999, 128 et seq.)[15]

---

[14] I am referring, for instance, to the following fragments: „gold laundered in Switzerland / decomposes and rots / in antiseptic Sweden // it contains gold teeth / gold caps gold rings", „ingots and bullion / bare their teeth skulls are silent / eye-sockets speaks" (Różewicz 2001, 35, 41) – „złoto ‚wyprane' w Szwajcarii / rozkłada się i gnije / w aseptycznej Szwecji // zawiera w sobie złote zęby / złote koronki złote pierścienie", „sztabki i sztaby złota / szczerzą zęby czaszki milczą / oczodoły mówią" (Różewicz 1998, 98, 101). Bleeding gold is the leitmotif of this poem, which was also, if not mostly, inspired by the following sentence from Kazimierz Wyka's essay entitled *The Excluded Economy* (*Gospodarka wyłączona*): „A gold tooth ripped from a dead body will always keep bleeding, even if no one remembers to whom it belonged" (in Wyka 1957, 131; "Złoty ząb wydarty trupowi będzie zawsze krwawił, choćby już nikt nie pamiętał jego pochodzenia"). This source of inspiration is, in fact, directly referred to in the poem. Another echo of Reder's testimony may be found in *Recycling* (on p. 94), in the reference to an orchestra playing the tune entitled *Highlander, Have You No Regrets?* (*Góralu, czy ci nie żal?*), which is alluded to in the context of the *Lager* motif. In *Bełżec* there is a mention of one of the SS men ordering the camp orchestra to play this tune „until they dropped" (Reder 1999, 138) – „w kółko do upadłego" (ibid., 64).

[15] „W drodze prowadzącej od komory gazowej do grobów, a więc na przestrzeni kilkuset metrów, stało kilku dentystów z obcążkami i zatrzymywali każdego ciągnącego trupy; otwierali usta zmarłego, patrzyli w nie i wyciągali złoto, po czym wrzucali je do kosza. Dentystów było ośmiu. Byli to na ogół ludzie młodzi, pozostawieni z transportów dla spełnienia tej roboty. Jednego z nich znałem bliżej, nazywał się Zucker, pochodził z Rzeszowa. Dentyści zajmowali osobny mały barak, wraz z lekarzem i aptekarzem. O zmroku przynosili oni całe kosze złotych zębów do baraku i tam oddzielali złoto i przetapiali na sztabki. Pilnował ich gestapowiec Schmidt i bił, kiedy robota szła zbyt powoli. Jeden transport musiał być gotów w

Here is an analogous fragment from *The Trap* (*Pułapka*):

> On the way leading from the gas chamber to the graves, that is the space of a few hundred metres, stood a group of dentists with pliers. They would open the corpse's mouth, inspect it and remove gold teeth and gold dental crowns which they threw into a basket. There were eight dentists. On the whole they were young people detained from the transports to perform these duties. One of them I knew quite well, his name was Zucker. He came from Rzeszów. The dentist were housed in a separate hut. In the evening they would bring basketfuls of gold teeth into the hut where they would separate the gold and turn it into slabs. They were guarded by a Gestapo man who beat them if they didn't work fast enough. The bars were 1cm. thick, ½ cm. wide and 20 cm. long. (Różewicz 1997b, 52)[16]

It seems that the „fragment of a prose work", which the author identified as an account from Majdanek, is the above-mentioned excerpt from Reder's testimony. The question remains: why does Różewicz mislead the interviewer, Maria Dębicz, and his readers? It seems that this is not due to Różewicz's amnesia, since apart from *The Trap* there are at least three other, earlier texts by Różewicz which allude to the testimony of the Bełżec survivor. Chronologically the third of these works is the 1960 short story entitled *In the Most Beautiful City of the World* (*W najpiękniejszym mieście świata*; Różewicz 1960b, reprint in Różewicz 1960a). Samuel – one of the characters in this story, whose plot is set in contemporary Paris – was modelled on Henryk Vogler, a former detainee of the labour camps in Rozwadów and Stalowa Wola, the Gross-Rosen concentration camp, and its sub-camp in Görlitz. Vogler was not only a writer, but also Różewicz's friend and a connoisseur of his work.[17] In *Gliwice Diary* (*Dziennik*

---

ciągu dwóch godzin. Przetapiano zęby na sztabki jeden centymetr grube, pół centymetra szerokie i 20 cm długie" (Reder 1999, 55 et seq.).

[16] „W drodze prowadzącej od komory gazowej do grobów, a więc na przestrzeni kilkuset metrów, stało kilku dentystów z obcążkami... otwierali usta zmarłego, patrzyli w nie i wyciągali złoto, złote zęby i koronki i rzucali je do kosza. Dentystów było ośmiu. Byli to na ogół ludzie młodzi, pozostawieni z transportów dla spełnienia tej roboty. Jednego z nich znałem bliżej, nazywał się Zucker, pochodził z Rzeszowa. Dentyści zajmowali osobny mały barak. O zmroku przynosili oni całe kosze złotych zębów do baraku i tam oddzielali złoto i przetapiali na sztabki. Pilnował ich Gestapowiec i bił, kiedy robota szła zbyt powoli. Przetapiano zęby na sztabki, jeden centymetr grube, pół centymetra szerokie i dwadzieścia centymetrów długie" (Różewicz 1982, 55).

[17] The short story *In the Most Beautiful City of the World* was inspired by the trip to Paris that the two writers took in 1957. Some information about this trip can be found in Vogler's autobiography entitled *Self-Portrait from Memory* (*Autoportret z pamięci*; Vogler 1981); on page 301 Vogler admits that Samuel was modelled on him.

gliwicki), in the entry of 30 June 1957, Różewicz recollects that „when he [Vogler] was in the camp, for a period he was with the *Leichenkommando*, burying corpses and those still living who were thrown into the pit" (in Różewicz 1999, 96). The final part of the short story *In the Most Beautiful City of the World* contains Samuel's monologue. It is partly composed of the words of another *Leichenträger*:

> we had leather belts with buckles which we fastened over the corpse's wrists. The ground was sandy, we had to pull the bodies out of the chambers and drag them as far as the graves. There was musical accompaniment when we dug the graves. What is music? Between the gas chamber and the graves a six-piece band usually played songs. (Różewicz 1964a, 352)[18]

The above-mentioned fragment is a modified compilation of the following excerpts from Reder's testimony:

> The ground was sandy. It took two workers to drag one corpse away. We had leather straps with buckles. We put the straps over the arms of the corpses and pulled. The heads often caught in the sand (Reder 1999, 131)[19]

> We dragged the bodies of people who had still been alive not long ago; we used leather straps to drag them to the huge, waiting mass graves, and the orchestra played during this. It played from morning to evening... (Reder 1999, 122)[20]

> The orchestra, made up of six musicians, usually played in the space between the gas chambers and the graves. (Reder 1999, 135)[21]

It is hard to explain why Różewicz obscures Rudolf Reder's words in his own works. We can no longer ask Różewicz to explain this strategy. However, even if this was possible, I doubt whether he would be willing to provide a satisfactory answer. The writer might intentionally have concealed the text which influ-

---

[18] „mieliśmy skórzane paski ze sprzączką, które zakładało się na ręce trupa, grunt był piaszczysty, trzeba było wyciągać zwłoki z komór, wlec je aż do grobów. Gdy kopaliśmy groby, przygrywała muzyka. Co to jest ‚Muzyka'? Orkiestra składająca się z sześciu muzyków grała zazwyczaj między komorą gazową i grobami piosenki" (Różewicz 1960b, 24 et seq.).

[19] „Grunt był piaszczysty. Jedne zwłoki musieli ciągnąć dwaj robotnicy. Mieliśmy skórzane paski ze sprzączką, które zakładaliśmy na ręce trupa, głowa często wrzynała się w piasek i ciągnęliśmy..." (Reder 1999, 58).

[20] „Ciągnęliśmy trupy ludzi jeszcze niedawno żywych, ciągnęliśmy je za pomocą pasków skórzanych do przygotowanych, olbrzymich masowych grobów, a orkiestra przy tym grała, grała od rana do wieczora..." (Reder 1999, 49).

[21] „Orkiestra, składająca się z sześciu muzykantów, grała zazwyczaj na przestrzeni między komorą gazową a grobami" (Reder 1999, 61).

enced him the most. Among many sources of Różewicz's „prosaicisation of lyrical speech", which has also been described as poetry „stuck in a lumpy throat"[22] or „antipoetry" (see Lam 1976), due to its allusions to everyday speech, the use of simplified syntax and reduction of metaphors, one may find the *testimony* of the horrible crime committed at Bełżec, which is described without exaltation, in a reserved, matter-of-fact way. Różewicz's first poems which were published in his debut 1947 collection *Anxiety* (*Niepokój*) were written and published in the press in 1945, while the poems that anticipate Różewicz's „prosaicised", reserved style, such as *The Survivor* (*Ocalony*), *Lament* (*Lament*), *Mother of the Hanged* (*Matka powieszonych*), and *The Rose* (*Róża*), were published in 1946 – in the same year when Reder's *Bełżec* was released. The earliest of these poems – *The Survivor* – was published in April (Różewicz 1946); *Bełżec* was put out earlier – in the first quarter of the year. It is worth mentioning that most of the

---

[22] This term, which is often used in relation to Różewicz's poetry, has its source in the poem *A Visit* (*Odwiedziny*):

I couldn't recognize her
when I came in here
just as well it's possible
to take so long arranging these flowers
in this clumsy vase

„Don't look at me like that"
she said
I stroke the cropped hair
with my rough hand
„they cut my hair" she says
„look what they've done to me"
now again that sky-blue spring
begins to pulsate beneath the transparent
skin of her neck as always
when she swallows tears

why does she stare like that
I think I must go
I say a little too loudly

and I leave her with
a lump in my throat
       (Różewicz 1976a, 26)

The original version of the final lines: „i wychodzę ze ściśniętym gardłem" (Różewicz 1948, 9).

poems that were published by Różewicz in the press in the years 1945 – 1946, the majority of which were later included in the collection entitled *Anxiety*, are stylistically refined and sophisticated. These poems serve as the evidence of Różewicz's fascination with avant-garde poetry, and especially with the works of Julian Przyboś. His antipoetry did not fully develop until the publication of his 1948 collection entitled *The Red Glove* (*Czerwona rękawiczka*).[23]

I leave the possible speculations about the reasons why Różewicz conceals his references to Rudolf Reder's testimony to others. The same concerns the problem whether in the poems *Massacre of the Boys* and *Pigtail* we are dealing with a collage or plagiarism. Or perhaps we should coin another term to describe the way in which Różewicz used Reder's text, since it does not belong to the canon of literature and, therefore, is largely unknown (and thus the allusion was not intended to be recognized). Perhaps Różewicz, who valued ethics over aesthetics and attempted to break with poetic diction, simply did not wish to reveal this essentially *poetic* gesture, which consists in the use of the simple speech of the *survivor*. It is a gesture which is – *horribile dictu* – artistic! In any case, Rudolf Reder's name should be added to the long list of the authors, such as Adorno, Celan, Heidegger, Kafka, Mickiewicz, Nietzsche, Norwid, Przyboś, Wittgenstein and many others, to whose works Różewicz openly alludes in his texts (see, for example, Ubertowska 2001). Reder's testimony serves as one of the most fundamental texts which shaped Różewicz's imagination – „stunted stone and implacable" (Różewicz 1976b, 13)[24] – and his poetic oeuvre, which was a unique and unparalleled turning point in the twentieth-century history of Polish poetry (see Kłak 2012, 7; Skrendo 2012, 16).

It may be possible to find more similar texts – testimonies, accounts, and diaries – which have little in common with romanticism, high modernism, or the classics of contemporary philosophy and which have influenced Różewicz's perception of the world and poetic style. As has been shown, his poetry *from the very beginning* fed on other voices, and often resembles *a testimony*, *a report*, or

---

[23] The *gradual* development of Różewicz's poetics was discussed by Jan Błoński (1956, 230). See also: „*Anxiety* is not the result of a transition from ,the language of the Muses' to ,the human language', but a collection of works in which this transition is progressing" (Pietrych, in print).

[24] „małą kamienną i nieubłaganą" (Różewicz 1948, 8).

an account. It may turn out that Różewicz did not begin his career as, to use the words from Andrzej Skrendo's book *Tadeusz Różewicz and the Limits of Literature* (*Tadeusz Różewicz i granice literatury*), „a person who is ostentatiously seeking to discover reality and who *turns away from everything that is textual*" (Skrendo 2002, 187; italics mine – A.M.). In the 1963 short story, or rather multi-generic text, *A Shield of Cobweb* (*Tarcza z pajęczyny*) we find the following words: „I read the letters of the executed at bedtime, and *The Auschwitz Notebooks* after lunch" (Różewicz 1964b, 6; reprint in Różewicz 1965). *The Auschwitz Notebooks* (*Zeszyty Oświęcimskie*) journal was first published in 1957. Apart from scholarly articles, it contained other texts, including camp memoirs. One may suspect that Różewicz read these numerous texts much earlier – already in 1945.

Różewicz's reflection on the world, as well as his works, including poems, were also shaped and certainly inspired by Tadeusz Borowski's concentration camp stories (Borowski's first two texts were published in April 1946 in the *Twórczość* literary magazine), which are often classified as documents, although they also have literary value. Some, albeit discreet, evidence of this influence is the above-mentioned short story *An Excursion to the Museum* (*Wycieczka do muzeum*), which is a peculiar sequel to Borowski's short story entitled *The People Who Walked On* (*Ludzie, którzy szli*). One may suspect that Różewicz's sources of inspiration were not limited to Borowski's writings. In the text entitled *Back to the Roots* (*Do źródeł*) Różewicz recalls: „In 1948 at the congress of young writers in Nieborów I talked a lot with Tadeusz Borowski. This was our second encounter. We talked about various things and about poetry" (in Różewicz 2004, 147 et seq.). It is very likely that these „various things" included issues related to the war- and occupation-time experiences of both writers, one of them being a former Polish guerrilla, and the other – a prisoner of a concentration camp. This personal encounter between Różewicz and Borowski took place rather late and was quite short. Apart from the poem entitled *Desire* (*Pragnienie*), written after Borowski's suicide, Różewicz devoted a lot of attention to the author of *Among us, in Auschwitz...* (*U nas, w Auschwitzu...*) on the „pages torn from" the *Gliwice Diary* (*Dziennik gliwicki*) and in the preface to the Swedish edition of his short stories (see Drewnowski 2001, 294).

Resembling a reportage, Różewicz's short story *An Excursion to the Museum* was originally published in *Nowa Kultura* weekly late in 1961 (Różewicz 1961). A slightly modified version of the text published in the 1966 collection of short stories, *An Excursion to the Museum* (*Wycieczka do muzeum*), is dated 1959 (Różewicz 1966). Despite this difference, one may suspect that the *actual* source of inspiration for the short story was, apart from Borowski's texts, Różewicz's visit (possibly not the first one) to the Auschwitz-Birkenau State Museum. In any case, the description of the museum given in the short story is both evocative and credible (see Morawiec 2013); thus, it seems to be based on the author's first-hand experience.

Translated by Katarzyna Ojrzyńska

Bibliography

Błoński, Jan 1956: Poeci i inni. Kraków.
Borwicz, Michał M. – Rost, Nella – Wulf, Józef (red.) 1945: Dokumenty zbrodni i męczeństwa. Kraków.
Brycht, Andrzej 1966: Dancing w kwaterze Hitlera. Warszawa.
Bursa, Andrzej 1973: Utwory wierszem i prozą. Kraków.
Czaplejewicz, Eugeniusz 1981: Poezja jako dialog. Warszawa.
Dębicz, Maria 1993: Co się dzieje w *Pułapce*? Rozmowa z Tadeuszem Różewiczem. In: Notatnik Teatralny 5, pp. 90-94.
Drewnowski, Tadeusz 1990: Walka o oddech. O pisarstwie Tadeusza Różewicza. Warszawa.
id. (red.) 2001: Niedyskrecje pocztowe. Korespondencja Tadeusza Borowskiego. Warszawa.
Ficowski, Jerzy 1979: Odczytanie popiołów. Wiersze. London.
id. 1981: A Reading of Ashes. Poems. Transl. by Keith Bosley with Krystyna Wandycz. London.
Gancarczyk, Anna 1990: Analiza i interpretacja wiersza T. Różewicza *Warkoczyk*. In: Polonistyka, no. 2-3, pp. 109-115.
Gronczewski, Andrzej 1982: Pogrzeb hrabiego Orgaza i ciała niczyje. In: Poezja, no. 5/6, pp. 17-40.
Kermisz, Józef 1947: Na największym cmentarzysku narodu żydowskiego. In: Opinia, no. 22, p. 7.
Kłak, Tadeusz 2012: O Tadeuszu Różewiczu. Studia i szkice. Kielce.
Koźniewski, Kazimierz 1948: Drażliwy problem. In: Przekrój, no. 179, pp. 3-4.
Kragen, Wanda 1947: Obóz koncentracyjny przeobraża się w muzeum. W dniu otwarcia muzeum w Oświęcimiu. In: Robotnik, no. 160, p. 4.
Kudliński, Tadeusz 1947: Czternasty czerwca.... In: Tygodnik Warszawski, no. 26, p. 8.
Kurek, Jalu 1947: Muzeum ludobójstwa. In: Dziennik Polski, no. 159, p. 1.
Kuwałek, Robert 2005: Obóz zagłady w Bełżcu. Lublin – Bełżec.

Kydryński, Juliusz 1946: W Oświęcimiu.... Odwiedziny po latach. In: Dziennik Polski, no. 200, p. 3.

Lam, Andrzej 1976: Z teorii i praktyki awangardyzmu. Warszawa.

Majchrowski, Zbigniew 1992: „Pustosząc pustkę słowa". O intertekstualności w poezji Tadeusza Różewicza. In: Między tekstami. Intertekstualność jako problem poetyki. Studia. Red. Jerzy Ziomek, Janusz Sławiński, Włodzimierz Bolecki. Warszawa, pp. 271-290.

Morawiec, Arkadiusz 2009: Literatura w lagrze, lager w literaturze. Fakt – temat – metafora. Łódź.

id. 2013: Tadeusza Różewicza wycieczka do muzeum (i biblioteki). In: Czytanie Literatury, no. 2, pp. 25-35.

Osoborne, John 1997: Tadeusz Różewicz: *Pigtail*. In: *Różewicz*, Tadeusz: Poezje wybrane. Selected Poems. Transl. by Adam Czerniawski, afterword by Tom Paulin and John Osborne. Kraków, pp. 321-329.

Pankowski, Marian 2003: Podróż rodziców mej żony do Treblinki. In: Dialog, no. 12, pp. 66-74.

Pietrych, Piotr in print: *Niepokój* – niemal zapomniany tom poetycki Tadeusza Różewicza z 1947 roku.

Przyboś, Julian 1961: Próba całości. Warszawa.

Putrament, Jerzy 1948: Notatki o Oświęcimiu. In: Odrodzenie, no. 23, p. 3.

Radzymińska, Józefa 1966: Nad nami noc. Lublin.

Reder, Rudolf 1946: Bełżec. Kraków.

id. 1999: Bełżec. 2nd ed. Kraków.

Romanowiczowa, Zofia 1965: Próby i zamiary. Londyn.

Różewicz, Tadeusz 1946: Ocalony. In: Odrodzenie, no. 15, p. 5.

id. 1948: Czerwona rękawiczka. Kraków.

id. 1949: Rzeź chłopców, Warkoczyk. In: Odrodzenie, no. 2, p. 4.

id. 1950: Pięć poematów. Warszawa.

id. 1960a: Przerwany egzamin. Warszawa.

id. 1960b: W najpiękniejszym mieście świata. In: Twórczość, no. 6, pp. 8-25.

id. 1961: Wycieczka do muzeum. In: Nowa Kultura, no. 52/53, pp. 6-7.

id. 1964a: In the Most Beautiful City of the World. Transl. by Adam Czerniawski. In: Introduction to Modern Polish Literature. Ed. by Adam Gillon and Ludwik Krzyzanowski. New York, pp. 331-353.

id. 1964b: Tarcza z pajęczyny. In: Twórczość, no. 5, pp. 5-22.

id. 1965: Przerwany egzamin. 2nd ed. Warszawa.

id. 1966: Wycieczka do muzeum. Warszawa.

id. 1976a: Selected Poems. Transl. with an introduction by Adam Czerniawski. Harmondsworth.

id. 1976b: *The Survivor* and Other Poems. Transl. and introduced by Magnus J. Krynski and Robert A. Maguire. Princeton.

id. 1982: Pułapka. Warszawa.

id. 1997a: Poezje wybrane. Selected Poems. Transl. by Adam Czerniawski, afterword by Tom Paulin and John Osborne. Kraków.

id. 1997b: The Trap. Transl. by Adam Czerniawski, with an introduction by Daniel Gerould. Amsterdam.

id. 1998: Zawsze fragment. Recycling. Wrocław.

id. 1999: Matka odchodzi. Wrocław.

id. 2001: Recycling. Transl. by Tony Howard and Barbara Plebanek, with an introduction by Adam Czerniawski. London.

id. 2002: An Excursion to Museum. In: *A Dream* by Felicja Kruszewska and *An Excursion to Museum* by Tadeusz Różewicz. Ed. and transl. by Jadwiga Kosicka. London – New York, pp. 77-84.

id. 2004: Utwory zebrane. Proza 3. Wrocław.

Skrendo, Andrzej 2002: Tadeusz Różewicz i granice literatury. Poetyka i etyka transgresji. Kraków.

id. 2012: Przodem Różewicz. Warszawa.

Szrojt, Eugeniusz 1947: Obóz zagłady w Bełżcu. In: Biuletyn Głównej Komisji Badania Zbrodni Niemieckich w Polsce. Vol. 3, pp. 29-45.

Tomaszewski, Feliks 1993: Poetycka refleksja nad losem narodu wybranego. Tadeusz Różewicz: *Rzeź chłopców*. In: Tematyka żydowska w lekturach szkolnych licealistów. Red. Alicja Krawczyk. Kielce, pp. 84-89.

Ubertowska, Aleksandra 2001: Tadeusz Różewicz a literatura niemiecka. Kraków.

Vogler, Henryk 1949: Rękawiczka czyli o wstydliwości uczucia. In: Odrodzenie, no. 2, p. 4.

id. 1981: Autoportret z pamięci. Vol. 3. Kraków.

Wojna, Ryszard 1964: Niedzielne popołudnie w Dachau. In: Życie Warszawy, no. 185, p. 4.

Wyka, Kazimierz 1957: Życie na niby. Szkice z lat 1939-1945. Warszawa.

Z.W. 1944: Bełżec – droga do piekła. In: Gazeta Lubelska, no. 53, pp. 2-3.

Zagajewski, Adam 2003: Powrót. Kraków.

Tadeusz Różewiczs Poetik des Zeugnisses

Eine lange Zeit übersehene (vom Autor verschwiegene) Inspiration für so bekannte Gedichte Różewiczs mit Holocaust-Bezug wie *Warkoczyk* (*Das Zöpfchen*) und *Rzeź chłopców* (*Das Abschlachten der Burschen*) wie auch für seine Erzählung *W najpiękniejszym mieście świata* (*In der schönsten Stadt der Welt*) und das Drama *Pułapka* (*Die Falle*) ist Rudolf Reders Bericht (Zeugnis) über das Todeslager Bełżec. Man kann davon ausgehen, dass sowohl dieser Text als auch andere Memoiren und literarische wie paraliterarische Werke, die von den Gräueln des Zweiten Weltkriegs handeln, zur Herausbildung von Różewiczs Poetik der „zugeschnürten Kehle" und seiner „Prosaisierung der lyrischen Rede" beitrugen, aber auch seine Weltsicht prägten. Die Spuren dieses und anderer Texte, die sich in Różewiczs Werken finden, belegen, dass der große polnische Dichter (oder Anti-Dichter, der versuchte, „Gedichte nach Auschwitz zu schreiben") nicht, wie allgemein angenommen, als Autor begann, der sich von dem abwandte, was textuell ist.

Heimrad Bäckers *Nachschrift* und/als Zeugnisliteratur[1]

Sascha Feuchert, Gießen

Als der Wiener Schriftsteller Oskar Rosenfeld im November 1941 in das Getto Łódź bzw. Litzmannstadt, wie die Nationalsozialisten die Stadt umgetauft hatten, deportiert wurde, stellte sich für ihn sofort eine Frage: Wie kann man sprachlich dokumentieren, was hier geschah, wie kann man nach-schreiben, was hier an Entsetzlichem verbrochen wurde, wie kann man Zeugnis ablegen? Rosenfeld fand für sich anfangs in der größtmöglichen Distanz ein Mittel:

> Umschreibend sagen: ganz sachlich, kurze Sätze, alles Sentimentale beseitigen, fern von aller Welt sich selbst lesen, ohne an Umgebung denken, allein im Raum, nicht für die Menschen bestimmt... Als Erinnerung für spätere Tage ... (Rosenfeld 1994, 36)

Die Rückbesinnung auf sich selbst, der Rückzug auf eine möglichst sachliche, offenbar ordnende Sprache, das Bezeugen für sich selbst – all das schien Rosenfeld kurz nach seiner Ankunft möglich. Neben seinen Alltagsbeschreibungen versuchte er sich auch an kurzen, offenbar fiktionalisierten Erzählungen, mithin an einer behutsamen Literarisierung der Ereignisse.

Spätestens ab dem September 1942, in dem die Kinder unter zehn Jahren und die Alten über 65 brutal aus dem Getto deportiert und ermordet wurden, um es zu einem reinen Arbeitsgetto zu machen, das keinen Platz hatte für – wie es verächtlich hieß – ‚unnütze Esser', spätestens ab dann gingen diese textlichen Strategien jedoch nicht mehr auf: Rosenfelds Sprache in seinen Tagebüchern zerfiel zusehends, verglühte zu Satzfetzen, die sich zu sträuben scheinen, zu beschreiben, was vor sich geht. Rosenfeld verzeichnet etwa das sich im Getto verbreitende Gerücht, die deportierten Menschen würden vergast:

> Kleiner Ort. Es kommen aus der Provinz 500-600 Juden. Entkleidet in einem großen Gebäude. SS sagt: „Es geschieht Euch nichts. Nur gebadet. Reinigung. Entlausung etc."

---

[1] Der nachstehende Text wurde als Festvortrag anlässlich der Verleihung der Heimrad-Bäcker-Preise am 2.. Juni 2008 in Linz gehalten. – Das Werk Bäckers zeigt exemplarisch, welche (literarischen) Folgen die Dokumente der Opfer des Holocaust haben, die in den Archiven nicht nur aufbewahrt werden, sondern denen so großartige Wissenschaftler wie Julian Baranowski im Staatsarchiv Łódź zu einer öffentlichen Geltung verhelfen. Der Beitrag ist Julian, der 2009 viel zu früh von uns gegangen ist, in tiefer Dankbarkeit für die jahrelange freundschaftliche, vertrauensvolle Zusammenarbeit gewidmet.

Gehen weiter. Schiefe feuchte Ebene. Kommen ins Rutschen. Gleiten herab. Eine Art Bassin. Dampf. Ersticken. *Fürchterliche Schreie...* Tot. (ebd., 206; Hervorhebung dort)

Auch wenn Rosenfeld nicht aufhört, sprachlich zu dokumentieren, was im Getto geschieht, so ist doch ein Erzählen oder Berichten in einer kohärenten Form für ihn nach den Ereignissen des September 1942 kaum mehr möglich: alles ist ihm nur „Nachklang, Echo, Zittern der Nerven" (ebd., 195).

Oskar Rosenfeld sollte den Holocaust nicht überleben. Im August 1944 wurde er nach Auschwitz-Birkenau gebracht und sofort in den Gaskammern getötet.

Sein Dilemma aber, die Ereignisse versprachlichen, bezeugen zu müssen und daran immer wieder notwendig zu scheitern, blieb und bleibt bestehen: Nicht zuletzt das Werk des österreichischen Dichters Heimrad Bäcker (1925 – 2003) ist Ausdruck dieses Dilemmas.

In den wenigen nachfolgenden Zeilen möchte ich ein wenig darüber nachdenken, wie Heimrad Bäckers überaus erfolgreiche Lyriksammlung *Nachschrift* (Bäcker 1993) sich mit dem Holocaust beschäftigt, genauer: Ich will zweierlei Dinge zu erfragen suchen: Zum einen was genau seine Texte selbst poetisch bezeugen, zum anderen wie sie mit dem, was wir Zeugnisliteratur nennen – also mit den Schriften von unmittelbar Beteiligten und Betroffenen –, umgehen. Diese Annäherungen möchte ich unter drei Stichworten unternehmen: 1. Opfer, 2. Täter, 3. Sprecher. Dabei werde ich ein besonderes Gewicht auf den ersten Punkt, also die Opferperspektive, legen.

Gleich zu Beginn möchte ich aber auch betonen, womit ich mich nachfolgend nicht oder doch nur am Rande beschäftigen werde: mit der Frage nach der Legitimität des Bäckerschen Unterfangens, denn sie stellt sich mir so prinzipiell nicht. Siegfried J. Schmidts (rhetorische) Frage, die er mit Bezug zu Bäckers *Nachschrift* stellte, ob man sich mit Monstrositäten dieses Ausmaßes überhaupt literarisch auseinandersetzen könne, ja dürfe, ist insofern obsolet, als es tausende, hunderttausende Male versucht wurde, oder besser, wie ich eingangs versucht habe zu zeigen: versucht werden musste (vgl. Schmidt 2001). Mein Interesse gilt also vor allem dem Wie, nicht dem Ob.

1. Opfer

Gleichwohl – und insofern ist Schmidts Frage dann natürlich doch nicht unklug – ertappe ich mich, wie ich bei der ersten Lektüre der *Nachschrift* anfangs ängstlich überprüfe, welchen Effekt es hat, dass Opfertexte poetisch – nennen wir es einmal so – ‚benutzt' werden. Denn Bäcker bedient sich bei diesen originalen Textzeugnissen und ‚verwertet' sie für seine eigenen Werke. Ist es etwa eine Folge der dichterischen Zurichtung der Originale, dass die Perspektive der Opfer vergleichsweise einfach einzuholen versucht wird? Oder dass Empathie durch die überdeutliche Dramatisierung, durch neue Arrangements der Opferworte erzeugt werden soll – und damit garantiert verloren ginge? Doch diese Ängste zerstreuen sich schnell, denn wie Friedrich Achleitner zurecht feststellt, lässt sich Bäcker „vom Material nicht verführen" (Achleitner 1993, 132). Sein Arbeiten mit den Texten zielt nicht auf einfache Effekte, noch hat es die „Übertreibung des Nicht-Übertreibbaren" (ebd., 131) zur Folge, um noch einmal Achleitner zu zitieren. Das aber liegt *gerade* in der dichterischen Bearbeitung begründet, die sorgsam darauf achtet, das Grauen im doppelten Sinne konkret zur Sprache zu bringen: konkret zum einen, weil sie ohne absolute Chiffren auskommt, sondern mit der Präsentation von Schriftspuren wirkt, und konkret zum zweiten, weil sie sich der Mittel der konkreten Poesie bedient. Die einzelnen Teile werden isoliert, herausgelöst „aus dem Kontext ihrer grausigen historischen Wahrheit" (ebd., 132) und eingestellt in eine Fläche, die ermöglicht, was Bäcker selbst den „Zusammenfall von Dokument und Entsetzen, Statistik und Grauen" (zit. nach ebd., 131) nennt. Es handelt sich bei Bäckers Poemen um Zitate, die allerdings kein bloßes Nachsprechen, kein bloßes Abschreiben, kein Imitieren sind, sondern – der Titel ist Programm – ein Nach-Schreiben im ganz wörtlichen Sinne, ein Nachziehen der Konturen. Das Verfahren lässt sich am besten illustrieren, wenn man es an einem konkreten Beispiel verfolgt: Der eingangs erwähnte Oskar Rosenfeld gehörte im Getto Łódź/Litzmannstadt zu einem Team von ca. 15 Autoren, das zwischen Januar 1941 und April 1944 täglich an einer Chronik schrieb – es entstanden so über 2000 Seiten eines kollektiven Tagebuchs, das neben einer Menge statistischen Materials viele Berichte, Reportagen und sogar kleine Feuilletons enthielt, die die Getto-Existenz sprachlich zu bannen versuchten. Im Juni 1944 schrieb Rosenfeld eine solche literarische Skizze, die – wie immer in der Chronik – unter der Überschrift *Kleiner Getto-Spiegel* erschien. Es handelt sich um einen der wenigen völlig kohärenten Texte Rosenfelds, die nach September 1942 bemerkenswerterweise auch Aufnahme in sein privates Tagebuch gefunden haben:

> Kleiner Getto-Spiegel.
> Zu spät. So vieles kommt im Getto zu spät. Kranke Menschen, geschwollen, Knochenentkalkt oder sonstwie siech, bemühen sich um verbesserte Nahrung, um Vigantol, um Tran. Ehe sie solch ein Heilmittel bekommen, sind sie rettungslos verloren.
> „Zu spät, nichts mehr zu machen", sagt kopfschüttelnd der Arzt. Aber nicht nur auf der jüdischen Seite hat dies „Zu spät" Geltung. Die Kripo fahndet nach einer 11-köpfigen Familie Szmulewicz. Sie klopft an die Tür, reisst die Tür auf, fragt den Insassen.
> Wohnt hier Szmulewicz?
> Hat gewohnt. Jetzt bin ich hier, Dawid Botwin. Ich hab die Wohnung der Szmulewicz bezogen.
> Mordko Szmulewicz? fragt der Beamte.
> Gestorben.
> Szaja?
> Gestorben.
> Lajzer und Sure Szmulewicz?
> Ausgesiedelt.
> Jankel?
> Hat sich zum Fenster heruntergestürzt. Tot.
> Chawe Szmulewicz?
> Ausgesiedelt.
> Ein 15 jähriger Mojsze Szmulewicz?
> Am Draht erschossen.
> Zwei Brüder Boruch und Hersz?
> Auf der Flucht nach Warschau umgekommen.
> Boruchs Sohn Josef?
> Weiss nicht. Ist garnicht ins Getto hereingekommen.
> Die zwei Beamten blicken in der Stube umher. Ein armseliges Bild. Von der Familie Szmulewicz keine Spur. Elf Menschen ausgelöscht. Nichts zu machen.
> Die Toten können nicht erzählen, wo sich gegebenenfalls ein ‚Päckel' befindet. Wären die Herren früher gekommen, hätten sie vielleicht etwas von dem durch reichsgesetzliche Regelung beschlagnahmten jüdischen Vermögen aufgespürt.
> Zu spät. Der Tod hat der Behörde ein Schnippchen geschlagen. Gegen den Tod ist sogar die schlagartigste Hand machtlos. (zit. nach Feuchert/Riecke/Leibfried 2007, 380f.)

Bäcker kürzt diesen Text erheblich ein, löst ihn aus seinem Umfeld und legt so seine Essenz frei:

> Wohnt hier Szmulewicz?
> Hat gewohnt.
> Mordko Szmulewicz?

> Gestorben.
> Lajzer und Sure Szmulewicz?
> Ausgesiedelt.
> Jankel?
> Hat sich zum Fenster heruntergestürzt.
> Tot.
> Chawe Szmulewicz?
> Ausgesiedelt.
> Ein 15jähriger Mojsze Szmulewicz?
> Am Draht erschossen.
> Zwei Brüder Boruch und Hersz?
> Auf der Flucht nach Warschau umgekommen.
> Boruchs Sohn Josef? (Bäcker 1997, 12)

Anders als Rosenfelds Ur-Text lässt Bäcker seine Version offen enden – das Fragen kommt buchstäblich nicht zum Ende, es könnte immerfort gehen, die Liste der Opfer ist unendlich. Bäcker tilgt alle Sprecher, nimmt die Verben, die den Dialog als solchen kennzeichnen, heraus und verlegt das Geschehen so aus seinem konkreten Kontext in den weiteren des umfassenden Schreckens. Aus einer gerundeten und damit auch wider Willen sinnvollen Erzählung Rosenfelds erarbeitet er ein Zitat, das – wie er selbst betont – außerhalb seiner selbst keine Literarizität mehr besitzt (vgl. Achleitner 1993, 131).

Bäcker hat mit seiner behutsamen Arbeit am Material ein Zeugnis zweiten Grades geschaffen: Es kann sich als Zitat auf die konkrete Zeugenschaft des Urtextes berufen und bezeugt selbst auf eigene Weise das allgemeine Geschehen. Diese Anverwandlung des Allgemeinen durch das Konkrete scheint sich mir durch Bäckers *Nachschrift* als Prinzip durchzuhalten. Ich will dies noch an einem Beispiel verdeutlichen: Wenn Bäcker aus Malvezzis und Pirellis (1955) berühmter Sammlung von Briefen zum Tode verurteilter Widerständler zitiert, dann tilgt er zum einen die konkrete Situation, ja sogar das konkrete Opfer, doch er gewinnt ein eindrucksvolles Zeugnis des umfassenden, des allgemeinen Schreckens:

> meine leiche befindet sich diesseits der schule beim straßenwärterhaus, wo albegno ist, diesseits der brücke. ihr könnt sofort mich holen kommen. (Bäcker 1993, 114)

Isoliert, in die Fläche der Seite platziert, sticht das radikale Auseinanderfallen gewohnter Ich-Konstruktionen und -Bezüge heraus: Das Ich wird sprachlich zum bereits toten Körper, jenseits dieses toten Körpers ist kein Ich mehr erkennbar. Das Possessivpronomen „mein", das Personalpronomen „mich" bezieht sich nur auf die Leiche des Sprechers. Was in anderen Zusammenhängen als paradoxes Spiel mit der eigenen Endlichkeit verstanden werden könnte, wird hier zum prinzipiellen Kennzeichen einer Existenz, wie sie der nationalsozialistische Terror millionenfach verursachte: Seine Opfer sind immer schon als Lebende Tote.[2]

Doch nicht nur dieser – so möchte ich das nennen – Ich-Entzug, der auf vielen Ebenen ein Kennzeichen des Holocaust war, wird von Bäcker in seinen Zitaten deutlich, auch der Verlust von Sprache, wie ihn etwa Oskar Rosenfeld erlebte und wie ich eingangs versuchte zu schildern. Es ist dies bei Bäcker ein tatsächliches, von außen kommendes Wegnehmen der Wörter, das hier konkret gemeint, doch natürlich auch metaphorisch zu verstehen ist:

> ich habe das mittlere normale leben eines mannes gelebt und habe nicht (zensuriert) ich bin sehr glücklich (zensuriert) es an der pforte des todes zu bestätigen und beizufügen, daß ich (zensuriert) was (zensuriert) immer (zensuriert) (ein ganzer abschnitt zensuriert) meinen zahlreichen kameraden und freunden (zensuriert) die (zensuriert) und das hatte ein (zensuriert) für (zensuriert) uns sagend (zensuriert) ich denke, daß (zensuriert) (ebd., 109)

Bäcker nutzt erneut ein konkretes Zeugnis[3], um abermals einen größeren Zusammenhang zu eröffnen: Die Sprache der Opfer wird beschnitten, zur Unkenntlichkeit verstümmelt, die gerissenen Lücken können nicht sinnvoll aufgefüllt werden, sondern allenfalls überschrieben durch die tödliche Begegnung mit einer neuen, einer anderen Sprache: der Tätersprache, einem organisierten, „das Leben kostenden Kauderwelsch" (Bäcker 1993, 133), um Bäckers eigene Formulierung zu verwenden.

In den Lagern war der Schock über die Begegnung mit diesem Kauderwelsch so groß, dass er nicht selten poetisch verarbeitet werden musste. Erinnert sei in diesem Zusammenhang an Jadwiga Leszczyńskas berühmtes Gedicht *Frauenlager*, das nur mit deutschen Wörtern, Befehlen, Ausrufen arbeitet und die Lagerexistenz zeigt (vgl. Zych/Müller-Ott 2001, 61).

---

[2] Vgl. in dieser Hinsicht auch den Essay *Die Tortur* von Jean Améry (Améry 1977, besonders S. 64).
[3] Bäcker spielt auch auf einen Topos von Lagerliteratur politischer Häftlinge an: der zensierte Brief, der nur aus Anrede und Grußformel besteht. Man findet das u.a. bei Staszek Hantz in seinen Erinnerungen *Zitronen aus Kanada* eindrücklich beschrieben (vgl. Graf 1998, 77).

Bäcker operiert meines Erachtens ähnlich, wenn er uns in der Nachschrift mit zahllosen Zitaten aus Tätertexten und Dokumenten konfrontiert, die uns auf mehreren Ebenen hart treffen.

2. Täter

Bäckers Zitate aus Täterdokumenten führen zum einen die sinnlose Formelhaftigkeit nationalsozialistischer Propaganda vor. Mit nur wenigen Schnitten und neuen Arrangements, etwa bei Texten Adolf Hitlers, wird das „Leben kostende Kauderwelsch" verdeutlicht, sinnentleerte Schlagworte zeigen die Psychopathologie der leeren und im doppelten Sinne toten Phrase. Gespiegelt wird diese Phrasendrescherei der Akteure während der Tat durch ihre gebetsmühlenartigen Formeln nach dem Krieg:

> ich kann darauf keine antwort geben
> darauf kann ich keine antwort geben
> ich erinnere mich nicht
> ich habe das nicht erklärt
> ich muß sagen, ich kann mich nicht erinnern
> ich kann mich nicht mehr erinnern
> nein (Bäcker 1993, 111 – Auszug)

Auch Freislers Gerichtsakten werden von Bäcker neu montiert und damit ihrer Sinnlosigkeit endgültig ausgeliefert. Die völlige Dehumanisierung wird auch durch Sprachreglung offenbar:

> unbeschadet der zu erwartenden gesamtanordnung hinsichtlich verwertung des beweglichen und unbeweglichen besitzes der umgesiedelten juden wird hinsichtlich des eingebrachten gutes, das künftig in allen anordnungen als diebes-, hehler- und hamstergut zu bezeichnen ist, schon jetzt folgendes bestimmt: (ebd., 69)

In der Isolierung als Zitat wird die Ungeheuerlichkeit dieser und anderer Verordnungen greifbar: Man spürt, dass solche Ver-Ordnungen das eigentliche Gegenteil von Ordnung sind, die menschliche Ordnung wird hier sprachlich verrückt, tödlich ver-wirrt.

Unablässig begegnet uns in Bäckers Werk die Banalisierung des Ungeheuerlichen durch seine Aktanten; die vielen Zahlen, die sich nur zu geometrischen Figuren ordnen lassen, verweisen nicht mehr auf die Toten. Die Zahlen bleiben als bloße Ergebnisse stehen, nicht als Repräsentationen der Tat oder ihrer Opfer.

Doch diese Unangemessenheit im Sprechen über den Massenmord zeigt sich nicht nur bei den Tätern, sondern auch – und das tritt besonders erschreckend in Bäckers *Nachschrift* hervor – auch in den Texten jener nachgeborenen ‚Sprecher', die den Holocaust beschreibend einordnen wollen und müssen. Damit komme ich noch kurz zum dritten und letzten Punkt meiner Ausführungen.

3. Sprecher

Wenn Bäcker aus dem Register einer Arbeit zur juristischen Aufarbeitung der Verbrechen in Konzentrationslagern zitiert:

arbeitslager	67f.
probevergasung	136f.
vernichtungsvorgang	63ff.
zahl der opfer	136 (ebd., 39 – Auszug)

dann wird gerade auch mir als betroffenem ‚Sprecher' (denn was anderes bin ich, der wissenschaftlich über Holocaust-Literatur zu sprechen versucht?) schlagartig bewusst, wie inadäquat die routinierte wissenschaftliche Beredsamkeit in Bezug auf den Holocaust ist.

Dieses in Bäckers *Nachschrift* an mancher Stelle herausisolierte Unbehagen am Sprechen über den Holocaust strahlt allerdings auch auf sein eigenes Werk zurück und wird damit auch zur Metakritik: Allerdings meint diese Einsicht in die Unmöglichkeit adäquaten Sprechens über den Zivilisationsbruch nicht, dass dieses nicht notwendig bleibt: Heimrad Bäcker hat belegt, dass der stete Versuch als Aufgabe fortbesteht.

Literaturverzeichnis

Achleitner, Friedrich 1993: Über die *Beschreibbarkeit des Unbeschreibbaren* oder der Versuch eines Nachworts zur *Nachschrift*. In: Heimrad Bäcker: Nachschrift. Graz, S. 131-132.
Améry, Jean 1977: Die Tortur. In: ders.: Jenseits von Schuld und Sühne. Bewältigungsversuche eines Überwältigten. Stuttgart, S. 46-73.
Bäcker, Heimrad 1993: Nachschrift. Hrsg. v. Friedrich Achleitner. Graz.
ders. 1997: Nachschrift 2. Hrsg. v. Friedrich Achleitner. Graz.
Feuchert, Sascha – *Riecke*, Jörg – *Leibfried*, Erwin (Hrsg.) 2007: Die Chronik des Gettos Lodz/Litzmannstadt. In Kooperation mit Julian Baranowski, Joanna Podolska, Krystyna Radziszewska und Jacek Walicki. Bd. 4. Göttingen.
Graf, Karin 1998: Zitronen aus Kanada. Das Leben mit Auschwitz des Stanisław Hantz. Oświęcim.

Malvezzi, Piero – *Pirelli*, Giovanni (Hrsg.) 1955: Und die Flamme soll euch nicht versengen. Letzte Briefe zum Tode Verurteilter aus dem europäischen Widerstand. Aus d. Ital. v. Ursula Muth u. Peter Michael. Mit einem Vorwort v. Thomas Mann. Zürich.

Rosenfeld, Oskar 1994: Wozu noch Welt. Aufzeichnungen aus dem Getto Lodz. Hrsg. v. Hanno Loewy. Frankfurt am Main.

Schmidt, Siegfried J. 2001: Literatur und Authentizität. In: Die Rampe. Hefte für Literatur. Linz, S. 27-32.

Zych, Adam A. – *Müller-Ott*, Dorothea (Hrsg.) 2001: Auschwitz Gedichte. Weg zum Himmel. Oświęcim.

Heimrad Bäcker's *Nachschrift* (*Postscript*) and/as Testimony

In his collection of poems with the meaningful title *Nachschrift* (*Postscript*), the Vienna poet Heimrad Bäcker tries to de- and reconstruct texts from victims, perpetrators and scholars of the Holocaust. He shortens the original texts, cuts everything away that hinders to see the horrible truth behind the testimonies or the real nature of the „deathly cant" of the Nazis. He also uncovers the linguistic brutality of later-born Holocaust-scholars when he just cites their book indices in a poem-like way. Bäcker's concrete poetry is always meta-poetry: it shows how important and at the same time how impossible poetry about the Holocaust is.

Towards the Unavoidable Silence:
on the Shoah Context in Andrzej Sosnowski's Poetry

Anna Maria Skibska, Poznań

> to – kto wie? – będziemy może jak ludzie,
> którym ostatni pociąg rzeczywiście
> uciekł, ale właśnie podstawia się specjalny
> i nagle wszystkie czapki wylatują w górę,
> ściskamy najbliższych i unosimy kciuki
> do tych, którzy stoją dalej i pewnie
> przyszli popatrzeć tylko na rozkład?
> (Sosnowski 2006, 94)
>
> (I pisze się tak samo,
> żeby ogrzać palce...)
> (ibid., 151)
>
> Are you going to fall precipitously into the trap?
> (Derrida 1986, 27]¹

The unexpected presence of Andrzej Sosnowski in the workshop dedicated to the theme of the Holocaust, a presence that I will tend to defense in the further passages of my writing, should be preceded by a brief biographical note. Sosnowski was born in Warsaw in 1959. A poet, translator, and essayist, he studied and later taught at the University of Warsaw. His collections include *Życie na Korei* (*Life in Korea*), *Sezon na Helu* (*Season in Hel*), *Stancje* (*Lodgings*), *Konwój. Opera* (*Convoy. Opera*), *Zoom, Taxi, Po tęczy* (*After the Rainbow*), *Nouvelles impressions d'Amérique* (*The New Impression of America*), and re-

---

[1] „so – who knows? – perhaps we will be like people, / who indeed missed the last / train, but the special one is already approaching / and suddenly all the hats are flying up, / we are hugging our loved ones and raising / our thumbs towards those, who are standing in the distance and probably / they have only arrived here to look at the timetable / decomposition?"; „One writes to warm one's fingers" (all translations into English, if not otherwise indicated, A.M.S.). The first epigraph, derived from the poem XII in *Sezon na Helu*, ends with the word „rozkład", which refers to two different meaning fields revealed by the contextual frame: on the one hand „rozkład" stands for ‚timetable', on the other – for ‚decomposition'. The simultaneous presence of both meanings assume an activity of syllepsis, which is a figure stimulating the realm of lingual aporias, due to which one simply cannot make a choice as for their further interpretation.

cently published (Feb. 2015) *Dom ran* (*House of Wounds*). He has translated many American and English poets of the so-called ‚other tradition', including Ezra Pound, John Ashbery, Ronald Firbank, and Edmund White. Regarded as the most significant poet of his generation, he has received significant literary prizes, including the Kościelski Foundation Prize and the Kazimiera Iłakowiczówna Prize. Due to his aesthetical choices and preferences, Sosnowski is rated among the postmodern poets as a socially inaccessible artist (cf. Turczyńska 2004), since his poetry of the „small devastations" is inhabited by the smouldering ruins of language. Considered as an extremely hermetic artist (cf. Cisło 1994, Śliwiński 1999), Sosnowski may be also interpreted as heir to modern Parnassianism (cf. Klejnocki 1995), the influence hereof transforming his poems into collections of sophisticated sentences (cf. Momro 2003). In this highly artistic cipher (consisted of the poet's ‚own' idiom and many multi-lingual borrowings; cf. Okulska 2011), one would not be able to come across the notions of the Holocaust, neither explicit nor implicit, however, Sosnowski's extra-ordinary concept of heterogeneous idiom, which is embroiled in many textual plays, exhibits a peculiar extermination of the conventional space of meaning.[2] And this lingual/linguistic extermination results in a poem drifting towards the strands of sounds, which is to remind us that the *eidos* of poetry is originally derived from music, and as such ought to be experienced as a structure of resistance against all discursive manipulations and usurpations[3].

In the first words of my essay, I am obliged to explicate the so-called ‚essence' of the titular provocation that manifests itself in the phrase „unavoidable silence", the phrase conjoined by me with the radical experience of the Shoah. The phenomenon of such a silence must be, therefore, considered as an ultimate gap between two different realities, of the language and of the world, since from the view-point of the initial context their incommensurable properties seem

---

[2] In the interview *50 lat po Oświęcimiu i inne sezony* (*50 Years after Auschwitz and Other Seasons*), Sosnowski (2010b, 28) claims that the concept regarding poetry focused on telling about its own end, its own catastrophe, inaugurated by Tadeusz Różewicz, remains somehow actual and almost obligatory in each ‚after-Auschwitz-generation' of Polish and Central European poets.

[3] The realm of sounds is to reveal the essence of language itself, which is a matter of its sonic ‚nature'. For it does exist beyond all secondary conventions stimulating the strategies of communication.

more than clear. Thus the general assumption, shared by the commented poetry, that none among possible languages is able to face up to the world, has to determinate the sphere of reference, of which immutable ‚fate' is to flee the force of representation. For this reason, Sosnowski, partly following the aesthetical decisions made by Paul Celan[4], often admits that all the events created from words constitute nothing but the unsuccessful tryst (date) between the language and the world (cf. Sosnowski 2001/02, 57). Perceived as such, the language itself fails to meet requirements of cognition, which regards the external reality as well as the human experience[5] – except for the experience of loss drifting towards a disintegration of the poetical self which tends to vanish among other voices and other sounds. Thus the effect of the commented poetry is a performative polyphonic spectacle consisting of various tones establishing the rhythm and of various fonts, syntax, and versification systems through which the graphic essence of the verses is achieved (cf. Nofikow 2012, 311). The other voices' presence should be understood as an intentional exposition of the intertextual game in which this poetry is necessary embroiled. Due to this game, the other voices, originated either from the archives of poetry or ephemeral sites of the Internet, are subjected to de-contextualization and re-contextualization thanks to which „pozostaje tylko nieczytelna potencjalność, co zamazywane słowa mi-

---

[4] This great poet claims that poetry should free itself from the conventional manners of poetical speaking, since they cannot anymore be applied to the forms of expressions, in which historical experience the unbearable event of the Holocaust is permanently inscribed. What is more, „Celan's atmosphere of decay or decomposition, also with a necessary reference to the body of the poems [...] must be dedicated only to the specters, shadows, phantoms, that is in other words, to all phenomena that must remain in the state of regained concealment, on the threshold of impenetrable darkness" (Skibska 2015, 45). The essential presence of Celan's influence is clearly exposed in the collection *Po tęczy* (Sosnowski 2007a): for Sosnowski, Celan embodies a master of grammatical insolubility determined by the tectonic movements of memory (cf. Orliński 2008), or by the waves of experience having a significant effect on the structure of notation conjoined with display. Furthermore, Celan (next to Adorno) is chosen by Sosnowski as an ideal partner of the impossible dialogue (cf. Pyzik 2015).

[5] „A thing from our past that comes back in memory, but also a problem for the future, an eternal problem, and above all a way toward poetry. Not poetry, but a way in view of poetry, one way only, one among others and not the shortest. ‚This would mean art is the distance poetry must cover no less and no more. / I know that there are other, shorter, routes. But poetry, too, can be ahead. *La poésie, elle aussi, brûle nos étapes*' [...]" (Derrida 1992, 377 et seq.).

ałyby znaczyć, co opisywać" (Sosnowski 2010b, 30).[6] The cited phrase comes from *poems*, in which the strategy of gathering other voices is streaked with a spectacular presence of Adam Mickiewicz and his famous 'dziady' ritual concerning the act of conjuring up the departed (cf. Próchniak 2010, 25]. It's worth emphasizing that this act resembles the last revisionist procedure assumed by Harold Bloom in his anxiety of influence that determines the so-called theory of poetry. Let me recall the epigraph by Ralph Waldo Emerson initiating the chapter devoted to the *apophrades* (in ancient Athens, a dark period of several days in which the departed were conjured): „No anchorage is. / Sleep is not, death is not; / Who seem to die live" (Bloom 2002, 181). The departed, or precursors in Bloom's terms, are the other voices with assistance of which the poet constructs his own verses, and becomes, via the paradoxical figure of transumption (or metalepsis), the 'inventor' of the 'dead poetry'. In *A Map of Misreading*, Bloom continues this transumptive mode by stating that „the price, as always in transumption, is the reality of the present moment, vanished between a lateness made early again, and a lost earliness now seen as belated" (Bloom 2003, 192). Several pages later, the scholar also adds what follows: „A subject, a mode, a voice; all these lead to the question: 'What, besides my death, is my own?'" (ibid., 198 et seq.). And Sosnowski perfectly knows that his own voice which remains at the poems' disposal does not belong to him; on the contrary, it loses itself among the other voices and, alike the other voices, gravitates towards the end of sounds. Yet the festival of the intertextual games conducted in the commented poetry also consists in strategies derived directly from the world of music such as like sampling or cover enabling the original fragments to be put in a completely new context (i.e. *Techno* as a cover of the double sestina by Sir Philip Sidney (cf. Gutorow 2003, 189)).

With reference to the English translation of his poems, made recently by Benjamin Paloff, Sosnowski musters the perverse courage to confess:

> I write in an utterly fallen, scrambled language, and it's possible that somewhere in this language of mine, in the language of these poems, there remain some fallen sparks of revelation [...] You translate my fallen language into an equally scrambled and fallen

---

[6] „[...] only remains an unreadable potentiality, what the blurred words should mean, what they should depict".

American idiom, and your only essential task [...] is to discover and lift up this lost spark. (Paloff 2011)[7]

In the above cited passage, the poet constitutes a new field of the interactional manoeuvres this time inscribing itself into the cabbalistic concept of the fallen language, elaborated by Walter Benjamin (cf. 1996). According to the author of *Illuminations*, the fallen language should be conceived as an imperfect device that serves both illusory projects of the human mind, communication and cognition.[8] Furthermore, it is established in a dazzling opposition to the lost language of creation, which must be comprehended as a realm of pure energy that has nothing in common with the alibi of meaning. The restitution (in the cabbalist idiom known under the name of *tikkun*) of this lost language is obviously impossible to achieve, however, the poetry under the banner of Sosnowski, through its struggle against the conventional manners of language, seems to be on the right way to this ‚aimless' aim.

In late Derrida terms the above mentioned alibi is identified with the army of unquestionably malevolent substitutions that is in other words, a forgery, falsification, fraud, counterfeiting, manipulation, distortion, etc.[9] Thus the alibi must

---

[7] The translator, in his note, acknowledges that: „[...] the beauty and challenge of Sosnowski's poems derive not from his elision of the rhetorical chains that might otherwise help us make sense if the whole – ‚this gadfly sense', as he writes in *The Walk Ahead* – but from their *inclusiveness*, the practiced diligence that allows him to name as much as he can in the time that he has, and the discipline and restraint that permit the naming to tell its own story again. Again, *inventory*. As he says in *What is Poetry*, itself a response to Ashbery's poem of the same name, ‚No need to regret delay, / for maybe it will sing?'" (Sosnowski 2011, x).

[8] „The paradisiac language of man must have been one of perfect knowledge; whereas later all knowledge is again infinitely differentiated in the multiplicity of language, was indeed forced to differentiate itself on a lower level as creation in name. For that the language of paradise was fully cognizant, even the existence of the tree of knowledge cannot conceal. Its apples were supposed to impart knowledge of good and evil. [...] The knowledge to which the snake seduced, that of good and evil, is nameless. It is vain in the deepest sense, and this very knowledge is itself the only evil known to the paradisiac state. Knowledge of good and evil abandons name, it is a knowledge from outside, the uncreated imitation of the creative word. Name steps outside itself in this knowledge: the Fall marks the birth of the *human word*, in which name no longer lives intact, and which has stepped out of name language, the language of knowledge, from what we may call its own immanent magic, in order to become expressly, as it were externally, magic. The word must communicate *something* (other than itself). That is really the Fall of language-mind" (Benjamin 1996, 71).

[9] Inscribed in history of lie, the phenomenon of the alibi is confronted with paralysis and aporia: „[...] paralysis is the negative symptom of aporia. Paralysis arrests, whereas aporia, at

be comprehended as a foundation for the so-called history of lie which results in the effect of paralysis, and this paralysis might be overcome by its transformation to aporia. The commented substitutions belong to the lingual reality, which is controlled by the authority of *signifié*, for reason of which the discursive spectacles of sense still are to be maintained in order to protect the false beliefs against the messianic perspective of restitution (revelation). In order to rethink this Gnostic idea of revelation in the context of poetry, one has to turn to the early poems of Sosnowski wherein the traditional relationship between the language and the world seems to be out of tune. In the poem entitled *Rozmowa na wycieczce* (*A Conversation on the Excursion*), there appears an anonymous ‚you' who becomes a centre of some intriguing persuasion, articulated by the poem: „spróbuj zapamiętać, gdy śpiew znad horyzontu / ściera zmarszczki z czoła i kołysze pamięć / przed dryfem umysłu w słabym prądzie nocy."[10] The quoted phrases ‚usurp' the right to establish a ‚deranged' opposition between memory and mind as if they belonged to different states of the poetical consciousness. In the second strophe of this poem, a necessity of deregulation regarding the language based on sense is even more significant: „Kiedyś na każdym kroku / cios obuchem sensu, dziś tylko niuanse, / związki między kometą i wielorybami / w nurcie Sacramento, akwenach Alaski."[11] This „blow with the blunt end of sense" refers to the past, and may be understood as a former experience of crisis stemming from the ‚fundamental' despair of the metaphysics of presence. Thus the only answer to the destitution of the intelligible order is a sphere of „nuances", which are to loosen and, in consequence, invalidate the semantic relations between words. For this reason, one cannot be surprised that the presence of a „comet" becomes a situation, which conditions another pres-

---

least as I interpreted it (the possibility of the impossible, the ‚play' of a certain excess in relation to any mechanical movement, oriented process, path traced in advance, or teleological program), would be the very condition of the *step* [pas], or even of the experience of path breaking, route (*via rupta*), march [*marche*], decision, event: the coming of the other, in sum, of writing and desire. [...] To transform the paralysis into aporia, to break a path for myself, I tried, gropingly, to find my voice [...]" (Derrida 2002, 140).

[10] „[...] try to remember when singing from above the horizon / wipes the wrinkles of one's forehead and sways memory / against a drift of one's mind in the week current of the night".

[11] „At one time a blow with the blunt end of sense / at every turn, today only nuances / relations between a comet and whales / in the current of Sacramento, the Alaska basins".

ence: of „whales". Such a declaration of war against the logical conventions of the language, and its motionless positions, appears in another poem entitled *Spacer przed siebie* (*The Walk Straight Ahead*), which turns out to be a specific exposition of the subjectivity's epistemological failures confirmed by the contradiction between the external realm of sounds and the helpless ‚self': „w rosnącym szumie nasłuchujesz / ... i rozum idzie w rozsypkę."[12] The transformation of the personal pronoun from ‚you' to ‚self' emphasizes the importance of the essential question: „Kiedy więc przestanę upadać w te światy?"[13] But what worlds are here to be considered? Since they are fallen, one may confront them with the idea of the fallen language, which means a multiplication of alibis, referring to the unlimited number of discourses making up a madness of the archive. Poetry cannot free itself from this archive, recognized so well by Derrida[14], nevertheless the same poetry should take a risk of meandering among all these idioms in order to break their ranks, to throw a spanner in their works, to demolish their apparent orders. „Multiplicity and migration, certainly, and within language, Babel within a *single* language" (Derrida 1992c, 407) is at stake. Sosnowski's conviction as for the necessary yet often inaccurate presence of the archive, being at the same time a risky challenge and undesired curse from the past, remains in conformity with the theses from *Archive Fever*, and expresses itself in the following words:

---

[12] „[...] and you are listening in the growing murmur / ... and the mind is running away in confusion".

[13] „So when will I stop falling to these worlds?".

[14] To the madness of the archive, one should also add the madness of the date, analyzed by Derrida in the context of Paul Celan's poetry and explicated in the following words: „A date gets carried away, transported; it takes off, takes itself off – and thus effaces itself in its very readability. Effacement is not something that befalls it like an accident; it affects neither its meaning nor its readability; it merges, on the contrary, with reading's very access to that which a date may still signify. But if readability effaces the date, the very thing which it offers for reading, this strange process will have begun with the very inscription of the date. The date must conceal within itself some stigma of singularity if it is to last longer – and this lasting is the poem – than that which it commemorates. This is its only chance of assuring its spectral return. Effacement or concealment, this annulment in this annulation of return belongs to the movement, this dating. And so what must be commemorated, *at once* gathered together and repeated, is, *at the same time*, the date's annihilation, a kind of nothing, or ash. / Ash awaits us" (Derrida 1992a, 396).

Mówisz o doświadczeniu tak, jak wiele innych osób mówi o innych doświadczeniach – używając tych samych słów, tej samej składni. I gdzie jest w twoich słowach niezwykłość twojego doświadczenia [...] Próbuję zatem, mówiąc inaczej, uniknąć naiwności wiary w to, że przy opisie własnych doświadczeń można dać sobie radę bez archiwum. Doświadczenie bez archiwum po prostu nie istnieje, bo ląduje poza językiem. (Sosnowski 2010c, 75)[15]

In such extra-ordinary circumstances, an apology of the side drift must be born (in the early poem *Wiersz dla twojej córki* (*A Poem for your Daughter*), there is an accurate confession in the first person singular: „to dlatego, że mnie poniosło, / to przez ten boczny dryf" (Sosnowski 2006, 11)[16], and it does substantiate Sosnowski's choice for the pre-Socratic philosophy of Heraclitus, who in his treatise *On Nature* presents the rather obscure and mysterious thought of the endless movement.[17] In consequence, the poet's decision to make the aquatic element, which obviously stands for this endless movement, a dominant driving force of this poetry results in a striking presence of the aquatic lexicon: next to the side drift, there are oceans, rivers, basins, clouds, steam, fog, snow, but also multi-directional navigation which always starts at a poetic latitude of zero.[18] It's worth emphasizing that this post-Heraclitus movement refers to the so called radical (or cold) hermeneutics promoted under the influence of deconstruction

---

[15] „You are talking about experience alike many other people talk about other experiences – by using the same words, the same syntax. And where in your words is your experience's peculiarity [...] Thus I keep trying, in other words, to avoid a naïve belief that one may manage without the archive in order to describe one's own experience. Experience without the archive simply does not exist since it lands beyond language".

[16] „it's because I got carried away / it's because of this side drift".

[17] The most common theses of Heraclitus are: „You cannot step twice into the same river, for other waters and yet others go ever flowing on. They go forward and back again" (in the critical commentary by William Harris, the phenomenon of continuum is emphasized: „It is not the same river obviously since the water has all moved along downstream. Nor is it the same YOU, since each instant your physical nature has replenished and recreated parts of itself"); „It is in changing that things find repose" (according to the translator: „In a world in which motion is the normal state, there may be an apparent but temporary state of what we see as static ‚repose', in other words there is a seeming ‚repose' but only as a by-product of the process of continual change"); „The fairest universe is but a heap of rubbish piled up at random" (In the translator's commentary: „This is a problem involving randomization finally yielding an entropic state, which we have learned to accept as our designed world. We are looking at the pleasantly solid and static world around us from the wrong end of the process, it is all a snapshot of randomized garbage taken at our specific moment in time" – Heraclitus [n.y.]).

[18] I am referring to the poem entitled *Szerokość poetycka zero* which initiates to the second collection of Sosnowski's poetry, *Sezon na Helu* (1994).

by John D. Caputo (1987). The radical hermeneutics introduces itself as a philosophy of kinesis, which reveals nothing but a condition of being-in-motion that inaugurates a realm of amorphousness:

> Cold hermeneutics does not believe in „Truth" – it renounces all such capitalization – something hidden by and stored up in a tradition which is groaning to deliver it to us. It has lost its innocence about that and is tossed about by the flux, by the play, by the slippage. It understands that meaning is an effect. This is not a hermeneutic we seek but one which is visited upon us against our will, against our *vouloir-dire*, which we would just as soon do without. It catches us off guard, in an unsuspecting moment, just when we were beginning to think all was well and the tremors had passed. Derrida's effect is to keep us *Angstbereit*, ready-for-the-*ébranler*, ready for the difficulty and the flux. We keep a stagecoach horn on our desk, like Constantin. Just when the metaphysics of presence is about to convince us that being clings to being, that truth is a well-rounded whole, a hermeneutical or eschatological circle, cold hermeneutics opens up an abyss. Heidegger's hyphen punches a whole in truth's well-rounded sphere. (Caputo 1987, 182)

Facing the cold hermeneutics, explored in the company of its active representatives, Heidegger and Derrida[19], Caputo presumes that the deceptive metaphysics of presence must be replaced with the apocalyptic thought, which conveys the structure of writing as it is (cf. Caputo 1986). In order to explicate the ‚proper' sense of this thought, one has to refer to the so called postal system (or postal principle), which is established by a phenomenon of message that is to be sent. The message itself suggests that there is some information to deliver, information promised by the sender (*destinateur*), and expected by the receiver (*destinaire*) (cf. Derrida 1981, 445). Thus the apocalyptic or eschatological thought, according to the radical hermeneutics, renders precisely this power of expectation, which subsequently mirrors both delusive desires, of meaning and of destiny. The moment of transgression, conjoined with the overcoming of the postal principle, manifests itself as an experience of crisis caused by the overwhelming complications with delivery. These complications, exposed by Derrida while reading the Revelation of St John the Divine[20], result in the phenomena of drift

---

[19] Caputo proposes an intriguing game between Heidegger and Derrida who are put in the role of the double agents attempting to deconstruct each other's systems: both of them are rooted in the realm of the radical hermeneutic thought and, as such, reveal different ways to overcome the paralyzing metaphysics of presence.

[20] Analysing the Scripture, Derrida comes across a pleat that complicates and, in consequence, deregulates the angelic postal system; the pleat (fold or drift) consists in increasing the num-

and of skid distorting the message itself. In consequence, the apocalyptic structure of writing becomes a sort of cipher impossible to decode, since one does not know any more who talks and to whom. We are to achieve, therefore, a level of the crucial tautology in accordance with which the references refer to each other, and there is neither decisive source nor soluble interpretation.

Let me turn back to Sosnowski's poetry perfectly reflecting the aforementioned collision of languages which follows the end of the postal system. Moreover, since the first book of poems, *Life in Korea*, Heraclitus's element of water has become a dominant image and constantly stimulates this quivering play of the language. Thus its only task is to miss the external, hence unreachable reality in order to invest in the creation that unfolds in the world of the language, understood as the medium of various impulses. In Sosnowski's poetry, according to Grzegorz Hetman (2015), all words, phrases, quotations, repetitions are to construct an extremely dynamic scenery, in which a polyvalent power of language is endowed with a permanent tendency to amorphousness that determinates the „shapeless", elusive or indiscernible structure of his poems. The energy of the side drift, exposing itself as a presentation of the language in a weightless environment, the very properties of Sosnowski's poetry makes visible. Among them one has to distinguish three fundamental principles, namely, rhythm (for each poem is a vocal event), non-intentional meanings *in statu nascendi*, and unconditional movement, which remains above the sphere of the logical predictability and acceptance. Without this side drift Sosnowski's poetry as a pure device of resistance would be impossible to consider. Regarding this, Karol Maliszewski speaks of „a line of fierce resistance" (Maliszewski 1995), according to which a chaotic precision of the commented poems is organized, and Maciej Maciejewski adds that Sosnowski's linguistic performance means the play of words, which consists in an activity of hijacking words.[21] Such an activity subsequently results in dissolving sense and reveals delusions of meaning. In consequence, the language of the side drift does not simply speak of the impossibility of sense (as well as the Shoah, pressed on it), it also constitutes innumer-

---

ber of voices belonging to Elohim, Jesus, angelus, and John. This confusion of voices effects the irremediable distortion of the apocalyptic message (cf. Derrida 1981, 470 et seq.).

[21] This strategy is necessarily related with meanings' effacement, since to hijack words is to free them from communication and cognition.

able spectacles regarding this impossibility. Thus the ‚essence' conditioning Sosnowski's poetry is revealed in the process of many lingual transformations, which aim to create a new idiom rendered by the words-in-distortion (cf. Nofikow 2012, 310). The new idiom, expressed by deregulations of the poet's own postal system (manifested ‚literally' in the phrase announcing that the system is overloaded: „Za dużo snu w systemie, system przeciążony. / Tak żyć. Można żyć. Dobry świat. Głęboki. / Kotek w przestronnym worku płynący Wisłą do Gdańska. / Nasłuch. Odsłuch, oddźwięk. Potem – zacichanie. Sasanka?" (Sosnowski 2006, 247)[22]), gives birth to the poems which should be considered as the artistic objects acting in the performative realm of art through the rhythm and through the sound. As the most essential properties of Sosnowski's style, the rhythm and the sound collaborate in order to produce the performative matter of poetry concentrated on hearing rather than showing. Furthermore, those poetical events establish the extra-ordinary ‚voice' intertextuality described as a postmodern fugue (cf. Nofikow 2012, 310), which paradoxically may be interpreted as an ironic return to the musical ‚sources' of poetry itself, or to the heteronomy presented in the polyphonic layers of the Scripture.[23] Thus each verse is born from the other verses, and by ‚other' one should conceive the other poets' works as well as works by Sosnowski. Quoting the others, the poet also quotes himself since in his elegiacally flowing view regarding poetry there is no substantial difference between his own voice and the others' idioms.[24] Furthermore, in his last

---

[22] „Too much of sleep (dream) in the system, the system overloaded. / To live. One may live. Good World. Deep. / In the Vistula, a kitten in the space sack floating to Danzig. / Watch, listening, response, later – dying away. A pasque flower?".

[23] Considering the polyphonic character of the (Hebrew) Bible, Bloom notices that its oldest parts of which authorship is attributed to the legendary J writer has nothing in common with traditional literary representation: „The representations of Yahweh by the Elohist, or by the Priestly writer, or by the Deuteronomist, or by the prophets: all these differ immensely from J's vision of God. ‚Vision of God' is not an accurate phrase to apply to J's mode of representing Yahweh, since his images of Yahweh are not visual but auditive, dynamic, and motor" (Bloom 1991, 5).

[24] To give an example of the poet's self-quotation, one may take into consideration two poems *Acte manqué* and *Wiersz (Trackless)*, since both of them are equipped with the very same phrase that belongs to the implicit motto of Sosnowski's poetry: „Wiersz wychodzi z domu i nigdy nie wraca" („The poem leaves the house and never comes back"). The first poem comes from *Sezon na Helu* (1994), the second one is placed in *Taxi* (2003): as might be easily seen, there is a distance of nine years between the indicated texts, yet this self-repetition tends to

collections of poems, next to the verbal balancing games there appears a phenomenon of inter-lingual ambiguity manifested by the fusion of different ethnical languages (Polish, German, English, Latin) with professional lexicons (of music, computer science, etc.) (cf. Okulska 2011).

One of the aforementioned spectacles expresses itself in the following poem, the title of which, *Małe dewastacje* (*Little devastations*), makes the assumption that any order, constructed and promised by the institution of the poetic language, is a matter of delusion:

> Wszyscy sobie szukają małych dewastacji
> w sobie i w innych. I po całym świecie.
> i winnych nie ma. Anielskie gehenny,
> geny jak w genezis. Lawsonia i henna.
>
> Głos jeży się w gardle. W sumie ciemne niebo
> i neonowe nici z grzybni w czarującym lesie
> jakby szedł zawsze z przodu i wykręcał grzyby
> jak żarówki, sprzątał światła, instalując wokół
> mrok dokumentny, szemrane płomyki,
> znikliwe runo, dyskretny wir pod stopy
> jak dyplomatyczny wykręt samej ziemi,
> szept, zmrużenie piasku w oku źródła.
> Kiedy układ z lasem zjeżdża do podscenia
> i nowa publiczność trzęsie się ze śmiechu
> jak niebo w mżawce spadających gwiazd,
> zachodzi zmiana w scenach mojego widzenia,
>
> jest ciepło, gorąco, wrzątek, ukrop, war, i to
>
> tu. Ktoś zanurzył rękę. Wessało.
> Biegał potem jak oparzony i próbował jeszcze
> drzeć powietrze, bo mu w końcu
> wszystko poznikało pod spodem,
> odciągnięte na krótkiej lince,
> podprowadzone.
>   (Sosnowski 2006, 199)[25]

---

cover more important phenomenon inscribed in Sosnowski's poetry, which might be expressed (after Victor Shklovsky) as a sophisticated ‚resurrection' of the poetical utterance, since in the new verbal environment, it regains a new life that is to die out (again) with the last sound of the poem.

[25] „Every one looks for little devastations / in the self and in the others. All over the world. / and there are no guilty ones. Angelic Gehennas, / genes like in genesis. Lawsonia and henna. / A voice is bristling in the throat. In essence, a dark sky / and neon threads from the mycelium in the charming forest / as if he walked always in front and unscrews mushrooms / like bulbs,

The cited poem comes from a rather small book entitled *Zoom*, and, alike all the other poetic events by Sosnowski, inscribes itself into a strategy of the impossible closeness to the reality, which is obviously not given but constituted by words. This constitution turns out to be more than symbolic, since it focuses on a scene of dismantlement, in which everything (that is, every single theme) is to disappear. The poem itself imitates a theatre declaring its own bankruptcy, and is ‚completed' by the dangerous supplement of hot water, due to which the army of ambiguous words vanishes in the end „at the bottom".[26] Thus the whole sphere of meaning drowns in the ‚deep' essence of words, which are to maintain only their own sonic ‚nature'.

The poetry of the little devastations, considered as a sophisticated manifestation of the „other tradition" (in terms of John Ashbery 2001[27]), tends to establish an intriguing lingual project. Its only task is to create a performative event focusing on the „walked off" signification. This event deals with all rhetoric manipulations exposed by the ironic mechanism, which is to undermine the expected realm of meaning. In the following fragment coming from the early poem entitled *Wiersz dla Becky Lublinsky* (*A poem for Becky Lublinsky*), the conventional order of the poetical expression is annihilated, and due to this we are fac-

---

he gathers lights to install around / a complete gloom, shady flames, / vanishing undergrowth (fleece), discreet whirl under the soles / like a diplomatic excuse of the soil itself, / whisper, squinting of sand in the eye of the spring. / When the set with the forest goes down under the stage / and a new audience is in convulsions / like the sky in the drizzle of shooting stars, / a change is occurring in the scenes of my seeing, / it's warm, hot, boiling, boiling, boiling water, and this / here. Someone plunged his hand. It was sucked up. / He was running off later like a scalded cat and still was trying / to tear the air, because in the end / everything disappeared to him at the bottom (underneath), / pulled away by the thin cord, / walked off".

[26] I am referring here to the concept of writing as a „dangerous supplement" elaborated by Derrida while reading Jean-Jacques Rousseau: „But the supplement supplements. It adds only to replace. It intervenes or insinuates itself *in-the-place of*. [...] As substitute, it is not simply added to the positivity of a presence, it produces no relief, its place is assigned in the structure by the mark of an emptiness" (Derrida 1992b, 83).

[27] In the introduction to *Other traditions*, John Ashbery states that „poetry has its beginning and ending outside thought. Thought is certainly involved in the process; indeed, there are times when my work seems to me to be merely a recording of my thought processes without regard to what they are thinking about. If this is true, then I would also like to acknowledge my intention of somehow turning these processes into poetic objects, a position perhaps kin to Dr. Williams's ‚No ideas but in things', with the caveat that, for me, ideas are also things" (Ashbery 2000, 2).

ing a sort of ‚emancipation' regarding every single element of the poetical material:

> W końcu wszystko jedno, który fragment pójdzie
> na pierwszy ogień; starczy byle słowo albo i sylaba,
> żeby dzień zacząć na dobre czy złe, a ten smutek,
> który cię bierze wieczorem jest może po prostu
> świadomością, że znów jedynie kurz ci został,
> pył z paru wydarzeń, kilka pajęczych nici,
> które jeszcze trzymasz w palcach, splątane
> i już niezdolne wprawić w ruch niczego.
> (Sosnowski 2006, 25)[28]

The motifs of „sorrow" and „consciousness", referring to the uncertain or even suspicious subject of the poem, suggest the presence of the so-called poetics of experience, which is exposed to the ‚erosive' action of the flying time. Yet this harmful and obstinate exposition may be overcome by the unique manner of speaking (which belongs, let me say it again, to the post-Celan tradition), since it is freed from communication along with its temporal involvements. The poem's textual tissue with which sonic ‚truth' one may commune regardless time and meaning (that is, regardless horrors of one's individual death and of the Shoah) refers to the secret world of music as well as to the soma „in a different state of matter". It is confirmed by the poet himself: in one of the interviews, Sosnowski states, that

> [...] język to jest głównie muzyka atmosferyczna i ciało, cielesność w innym stanie skupienia, w innym stadium materii. [...] czemu język nie miałby być subtelną, acz materialną formą obecności ciała w przestrzeni? Myślenie o języku zostaje drastycznie zubożone w momencie, kiedy zaczyna dominować pojęcie informacji, przekazu, komunikatu. [...] Zawsze chodzi raczej o choreografię. Wielość kroków i figur. Ponadto wielość dźwięków i głosów. (Sosnowski 2007c, 101)[29]

---

[28] „After all it doesn't matter, which fragment will / be sent to the frontline, any word or syllable is enough / to begin the day for better and for worse, and this sorrow / which catches you in the evening is perhaps a simple / consciousness, that you are left again with a dust only/ the dust from a few events, some cobweb threads / which you are still holding in your fingers, tangled / and already incapable to put anything in motion".

[29] „[...] the language is mainly the atmospheric music and body, corporeality in a different state of matter [...] why wouldn't be this language a subtle yet material form of the presence of the body in the space? Thinking about the language becomes drastically impoverished when the notion of information, message, or communication begins to dominate [...] It's al-

The timeless yet bodily presence of the language suspended in the air, as if it was a sequence of endless sounds, allows the reader to find consolation in a freedom from conventional interpretation. „I am here to comfort you since I am an event which belongs above all to the rhetoric of *dissuasion*", the poem seems to promise. The rhetoric of dissuasion, derived from the encounter between Harold Bloom and Kafka's Odradek, and inscribed to the commented poetry, should be regarded as an advice against interpreting Sosnowski.[30] For this reason, the quoted poems are a matter of negative contemplation rather than explication or constitution of sense. Thus the only „truth" of the poem, which acts as a „shadow" in order to cover the reader's eyes, is its own „experience" (signature in Derrida's terms) exposed to the experience of the reader (counter-signature).[31]

> Żeby wiersz podszedł
> cię jak cień i przesłonił oczy, ten
> wiersz – cień rzucony na prawdę z głębi
> łzy, odprysku światła, szklanej kropki
> kończącej rozmowę rozbitych luster?
> (Sosnowski 2006, 49)[32]

A peculiar deconstruction of depth, revealed in the cited passage, confronts the „truth" with the „activity" of a single tear which is to blur the outlines of the world since it „ends a conversation of the broken mirrors". The effect of „the broken mirrors" itself annihilates the possibility of communication, and frees the poem from the conventional manners of poetry according to which it should be perceived as a device serving ‚the art' of explicating and organizing the outside

---

ways a question rather of choreography. Multiplication of steps and figures. Besides, multiplication of sounds and voices".

[30] „If Odradek is fallen, he is still quite jaunty, and cannot be closely scrutinized, since he ‚is extraordinarily nimble and can never be laid hold of', like the story in which he appears. Odradek not only advises you not to do anything about him, but in some clear sense he is yet another figure by means of whom Kafka advises you against interpreting Kafka" (Bloom 1991, 177).

[31] In *This strange institution called literature* one may come across the following statement: „‚Good' literary criticism, the only worthwhile kind, implies an act, a literary signature or counter-signature, an inventive experience of language, *in* language, an inscription of the act of reading in the field of the text that is read. This text never lets itself be completely ‚objectified'" (Derrida 1992a, 52).

[32] „So that the poem would come up to / you as a shadow and obscure your eyes, this / poem – a shadow thrown on the truth from the depth / of a tear, a splinter of light, a glass dot / ending a conversation of the broken mirrors?".

reality. The Shoah experience has nothing in common with depth presentiment, dismayed by the poem, because it manifests a bare life only that faces its individual end (cf. Agamben 1998).[33] „Can you dive?", the question expressed by the undermentioned poem, sustains the absence of depth figuratively substituted by the word „sister" which, next to the phrase of a mysterious girl who holds the razor blade in her teeth („tam mała dziewczynka w bloku naprzeciwko / uśmiecha się z żyletką pomiędzy zębami" – Sosnowski 2006, 5)[34], stands for the poet's attitude towards writing. In addition to this, I am forced to remind you that the term of poetry is of the feminine gender. Thus the smile of the girl from the initial poem of Sosnowski, a smile absolutely impossible to perform, constitutes a ‚spectacular' opposition between the image and the rhythm, and reconstructs or decomposes the traditional order of our perceptive apparatus, or of our sensible being in the world, which is to relay on a blind spot rather than on the wounded thus elusive possibilities of seeing (cf. Welsch 2011).[35] They seem to be exhausted not only because the human eye saw too much and in effect became indifferent to all kinds of experience. The problems with contemporary perception also originate from the devaluation concerning traditional discourses of which a necessary reconsideration postulates breaking off the culture founded on the primate of the eyeball. For this reason, we are to abandon the apparently autonomous world of the light which sanctions the order of daytime and appreciates the laws of the *ratio* (their significant rejection one may find in Maurice Blanchot's *Madness of Day*)[36] in order to re-gain the heteronomous kingdom of

---

[33] Regarded as the centre of Agamben's bio-politics, incorporated in his post-philosophical thought from the famous theses of Michel Foucault, a phenomenon of bare life stems from the ideological reduction, of which total realization occurred in concentration camps.

[34] „there, in the opposite block, a little girl / smiles holding the razor blade in her teeth".

[35] „In the meantime, while the dominative patterns of perception and cognition underlying this privilege have been subjected to critique by authors like Heidegger, Wittgenstein, Foucault, Derrida, and Irigaray, we are currently experiencing the fact that vision is no longer the reliable sense for contact with reality that it was once held to be. The privilege of vision no longer holds in a world in which physics has become indemonstrable and in a world dominated by media" (Welsch 2011, 11 et seq.).

[36] „Blanchot przypomina o istnieniu dwóch rodzajów nocy: tej, której – używając słów poety – ‚czerń się zmywa jak lakier z paznokci acetonem światła', i tej, która ‚z pewnego oddalenia odsłania sens nie prawdą, lecz ciemnością'" (Kula 2007, 193; „Blanchot reminds of the existence of two kinds of nights: one whose – according to the poet's words – ‚blackness can be

the darkness, in which the ‚consolidated' subjectivity breaks into the other voices. As a result of this essential transformation, Sosnowski's poetry turns out to be an expression of the ambivalent state of weightlessness which creates favourable conditions for writing from now on, considered as a prayer articulated in a totally foreign language. Thus the poetical idiom communicates nothing but the void in which incomprehensible strands of words there is, however, a shadow of mutual communion between the sender and the receiver, who are to meet at the instant of the sonorous performance that necessarily happens above any scrutiny, above any knowledge.

> [...] communication becomes virtual only when its space is heterogeneous, when it is invaded by an alien, an inscrutable other that embodies a void, a nothing as the I-know-not-what, which I, having been invited into that space, cannot ignore. It is this alien invasion that creates a crisis in me, and it is this crisis that causes the event of communication to occupy me, to take its place in me – in spite of its nothingness, in spite of the void it induces in me. [...] The communication of a void therefore does not and cannot avoid communication. (Chang 1993, 225)

The poetical void, consisting of the alien voices, expresses itself in the middle of nowhere, „gdzie diabeł mówi dobranoc", and consequently loses its readable contextual frames that results in words which are to witness the lingual catastrophe announced by irony and death (cf. Kula 2007, 193).

> Gdzie ciemny port schron zamarły azyl
> snów lekkich jak kostka w szybkiej grze
> gdy opuszcza obręcz światła i leci
> gdy spada z sukna i nieruchomieje
> gdzie diabeł mówi dobranoc i znaczy
>
> lub nie znaczy lecz znika z oczu
> w świetle tunelu lunety jak studni
> przyłożonej rano do zatartego oka
> żeby wywołać kontur twarz
> kontynentu zachodzącego białą plamą
> na mapie nocnych i podwodnych lotów
>
> Na oślep przez biel do utraty tchu
> Umiesz nurkować? Umiesz skarby
> przynosić w zaciśniętej dłoni patrz
> te szare perły to są twoje oczy
> atlantydo?

---

removed like varnish from a nail with the acetone of light', and another one which ‚does not reveal its sense from a safe distance by truth, but by darkness'").

To co w nas umierało nie od razu
To w czym umieraliśmy nie od razu
czy inny świat? Ciemny schron
gdzie mienisz się nieobecnością
siostro?

(Sosnowski 2006, 58)[37]

In order to penetrate the sonic tissue of the above poem, I am to begin with the initial utterance, which proves Sosnowski's ability to make use of the multi-lexical borrowings. The term of anoxia is derived from the medical discourse and, as a manifestation of more general hypoxia, stands for condition in which the body or a region of the body is completely deprived of adequate oxygen supply. The gesture of intercepting the word, which previously was the property of a specialist vocabulary, in order to dismay its semantics by the incommensurable context born in the poetical laboratory of Sosnowski inaugurates a phenomenon of a *quasi*-encyclopaedic book in a state of dynamic disintegration. Taken in its colloquial meaning, anoxia might be understood as a lack of breath to which paradoxical cascades of words are the only response. The catastrophic effect of the breathless poetry suggests that its performance may cause a dyspnoeic attack from the excess of sounds which demand articulation. The theme of death organizing the space of the last strophe is associated with „dark bunker" and „sister sparkling with absence". These three motifs seem to condition the existence of Sosnowski's poetry, especially if one will conjoin them with the aspect of the sonic event, which disappears within the last word crushed by the silence.

Ogołacać się
I gubić drogę

Bo w zgubieniu ścieżka
Bo w zgubieniu ślad

---

[37] „Where a dark port bunker lifeless asylum / of the light dreams as a dice in the quick game / when it leaves a ring of light and flies / when it falls down from a cloth and freezes / in the middle of nowhere and it means / or doesn't mean but vanishes from one's sight / in the light of a tunnel of a telescope like a well / applied to a wounded eye in the morning / in order to recall a contour a face / of a continent misted over with a white stain / on a map of the night and underwater flights / Blindly through the white breathlessly / Can you dive? Can you bring / treasures in a clenched hand look / these grey pearls they are your eyes / atlantis? / This what was dying in us not at once / This in which we were dying not at once / another world? The dark bunker / where you sparkle with absence / sister?".

> Bo w zgubieniu nas
> Szary anioł
> I lekkość ponad pojęcie
>
> Żeby uszło z nas co jest martwe
> I co innego dotknęło do żywego
>
> Tak opadło z nas co było martwe
> I nie zostało jeszcze nic żywego
> (Sosnowski 2006, 93)[38]

In Sosnowski's poetry which follows the art of losing, said every day as if it was a last prayer, the colour of grey is elevated that is confirmed by the presence of the grey pearls (as the eyes of atlantis) in *Anoksja*, and of the grey angel in *Pięć sążni w dół* (*Five fathoms down*). The exposition of the grey colour creates favourable conditions for blurring the outlines of the images, which are to fall into the aporetic realm of sounds. Following the side erratic drift, the greyish poetry abandons the apparent world of vision in order to consolidate the chasm between writing/seeing and writing/hearing; the consolidation itself is often rendered by the presence of the catastrophic tone presented in the further poems. In *Tachymetria* (*Tacheometry*), the commented catastrophic annihilation of the visionary thus traditional representation occurs with participation of the four „elements": wind, light, frost, and fear. The sequence of the events articulated by the elegiac voice of the plural pronoun of „we" as it was belonged to the disintegrated projection of some lost generation maintains the domination of grey: this colour is attributed directly to such words like bread, bonfire, and fall, although its implicit presence also regards old letters, cobweb, ash, mould, etc.

> Kiedyś te domy przejdzie wiatr
> szyby nabiegną tęczą jak wodospad
> obudzimy się w zimnych pokojach
> zdjęcia sfruną ze ścian i rzecz
> nie przyzna się do rzeczy i głos
> załamie się gdy cyfry na tarczach
> zamienią się miejscami
> teraz tak jest że mamy wiatr
> niech już zostanie na zawsze

---

[38] „To clean oneself out / And to lose one's way / For in losing a path / For in losing a track / For in losing us / A grey angel / And a lightness beyond notion / So that we would escape what was dead / and something else would touch us on the raw / This is how we have lost what had been dead / And nothing alive has remained yet".

I na czworakach poszukamy starych
listów i jak pajęczyna będzie czas
na mojej twarzy jak zetlałe płótno
farba na twoich palcach Uważaj
nie skalecz się Pleśń jest dobra
siwy chleb pajęczyna i słońce
A słońce wejdzie po schodach
i wyskoczy przez wybite okna
teraz tak jest że mamy blask
niech już zostanie na zawsze

A życie będzie nocą na horyzoncie
łuną otoczoną pierścieniem neonów
i autostrad Saturn Dziecko bez tchu
przebiegnie nad krawężnik W oczach
błyśnie aureola z aut więc wróci
żeby nam śpiewać nowinę lecz my
będziemy przetrząsać pola i pleść
szare ogniska z folii
teraz tak jest że mamy mróz
niech już zostanie na zawsze

Czujesz ten błysk w węźle gardła?
To czułość Już nic nie pamiętam
Słońce leci z zachodu na wschód
stawia nam włosy na głowie i robi się
tak ciepło wyciągnij dłonie
W te domy w końcu włożą dynamity
i obłok będzie jak wzruszenie ramion
popielaty upadek jak ukłon
teraz tak jest że mamy strach
niech już zostanie na zawsze
    (Sosnowski 2006, 115 et seq.)[39]

---

[39] „Some day these houses will be passed by the wind / the windows will flush with rainbow like a waterfall / we will wake up in the cold rooms / the pictures will go flying down from the walls and / will crack when the numbers on the dials / will change places with each other / it is now that we own the wind / let it remain for ever / And on all fours we will look for the old / letters and the time will be like a cobweb / on my face as a decaying canvas / the paint on your fingers Be careful / don't hurt yourself The mould is good / a grey bread, cobweb and sun / And the sun will climb up the stairs / and jump out through the broken windows / it is now that we own the light / let it remain for ever / And life will be a night on the horizon / a glow surrounded by a ring of neon lights / and motorways Saturn Child out of breath / will come running at the kerb In the eyes / the cars' aureole will flash he will therefore come back / to sing news to us but we / will search the fields and weave / the grey bonfires out of foil / it is now that we own the frost / let it remain for ever / Can you feel this gleam in the knot of

The term of tacheometry playing the role of the title is borrowed from another specialist idiom and means a system of rapid surveying, by which the horizontal and vertical positions of points on the earth's surface relative to one another are determined without using a chain or tape, or a separate levelling instrument. In Sosnowski's poetry this term's usage is characterized by irony serving the map, which is charted by the endless multiplication of distances destroying a foundation for any measure. The only property of the tacheometry, which is not invalidated by the negative activity of irony, is its rapidness, with no doubt present in the commented poems. It's worth mentioning that the same irony permits the fragments of Sosnowski's poetical prose, which, as the following example tends to demonstrate, comments on an unbearable phenomenon of shrinking that concerns our current everyday language:

> aż do oślepnięcia, i skonstatujmy, że w istocie radykalizujemy tylko inną ogólniejszą tenedencję, bo czyż na każdym kroku nie znajdujemy przykładów kurczenia się języka, wyciekania języka z naszej społecznej przestrzeni, jego postępującej atrofii? A niby o czym mają świadczyć te wszystkie wesolutkie skróty, niefrasobliwe lingwistyczne kalectwa, komiczne komunikaty, w których absolutnie nikogo nie stać już na zdanie, ba, nawet na w pełni wyartykułowane słowo; co mają znaczyć pokurcze w rodzaju „reje", „obse", „omia" nie dalej jak trzy stroniczki temu, te propozycje pójścia na piwo, zredukowane do smętnego „pi", na które odpowiada się „mmmm", albo jeszcze gorzej „cze nie" (Że nie wspomnimy o banałach w rodzaju rzekomego prymatu obrazu nad rzewnym spadkiem po Fauście i Gutenbergu.) (Sosnowski 2006, 134)[40]

The drifting commentary concerning the undermentioned poem I ought to begin with the deeper or broader emphasis, which is put on the omnipresent and overpowering theme of loss spectacularly revealed in the *quasi*-etymological title

---

your throat? / It's tenderness I can't remember anything / The sun is flying from the West to the East / making our hair stand on end it gets / so warm hold out your hands / In the end they will put dynamite in these houses / and the cloud will be like a shrugging one's shoulders / the ashen fall like a bow / it is now that we own fear / let it remain for ever".

[40] „till to go blind, and let us state that in essence we only radicalize another, more general tendency, since do we not find on every step examples of shrinking of language, leaking of language out of our social space, its progressive atrophy? And for what else are to testify all those cheerful abbreviations, carefree linguistic disabilities, comical communicates, in which absolutely no one can afford a sentence, or even a fully articulated word; what are to mean shrimps like ‚reje', ‚obse', ‚omia' no farther than before three last pages, these propositions to go out to drink beer, reduced to a pitiful ‚be', to which one responses with ‚mmmm', or even worse ‚y not' (Not to mention about banalities alike the apparent primate of the image over the wistful inheritance from Faust and Gutenberg)".

Glossa. Its loss adheres to the experience of lot, and the clear proximity of both words located in two parallel verses suggests the activity of alliteration, which on the one hand stimulates the elegiac tone of poetical monotonous litany, and on the other announces a ‚real' event of loss happening to the poem within its own end. For the principle structure of Sosnowski's poetry is rendered extremely well by the mini-dialogue performed in Glossa, according to which the only answer to the question „And what does one do?" is „One loses". Another situation created in this poem, which deserves a special attention, is the phrase „Nie można się nie krzyżować", since its ambiguous power stems from the double negation, incorrect from the view-point of English syntax, and it can be easily lost in translation. Nevertheless the poet's erratic idiom allows the reader to construct an inaccurate yet necessary equivalent in English that is, „One mustn't not to cross". The idea of crossing might be obviously interpreted in the obligatory context of the idioms' fusion meaning the strategy of permanent interweaving or alternating codes, ciphers, and figures. What is more, one should also take into consideration the broaden semantics of the word „krzyżować" that assumes a presence of the act of crucifying, which carries with it a theme of an unhealed wound. The idea of a poem as the unhealed wound underlines, therefore, the already mentioned transformation of the perceptual apparatus, which, next to hearing, tends to privilege the sense of touch.

> Teraz bardziej z gołą głową i boso.
> Teraz zimniej na mieście i jaśniej.
> Śnieg. Ale nie myśli się o tej ozdobie
> na włosach, bo to nie nowy klimat: ta noc
> zimno i widno, syk lamp i strata z tytułu
> słówka *loss* w tytule wiersza „Glossa".
> Los. Sypie śnieg. A co się robi? Traci.
> Najpierw trzewiki. Ktoś zabiera sobie
> jeden na kołyskę. Drugi bez śladu
> ginie, z całą prostotą „bez śladu".
>
> Szczęść Boże. Nie można się nie krzyżować.
> Z nikim nie ranić, słowem, nie zabliźniać,
> to dawny klimat. Bo idzie się na noc
> z gołą głową i boso, a więc mając jeszcze
> coś po stronie strat, po tej stronie nocy,
> której czerń się zmywa jak lakier z paznokci
> acetonem światła, całkiem niepotrzebnie,

bo i tak jest coraz widniej i zimniej,
coraz bardziej z gołą głową i boso.
Śnieg. Coraz zimniej i jaśniej. Idzie się
bez śladu, z gołą głową i boso, idzie się
z całą prostotą w kąt między domami, się
siada, kurczy, nogi podciąga pod siebie,
bo baśń tak chce. „Z całą masą zapałek"
marznie się o niebo lepiej i – Ach – mówi –
jedna mała zapałka, jakby to dobrze było!
Baśń cię pochowa jak chłopca z zapałkami.
Gminna wieść zachowa jak małą dziewczynkę.
Pali się. Nowy Rok. Potrzeba słów i obrazów.
Nowych słów i obrazów, więc pali się jaśniej,
żeby rozgrzać palce (i pisze się tak samo,
żeby ogrzać palce: przy tej dziwnej świecy
zacny piec z drzwiczkami z mosiądzu i gęś
czołga się po podłodze jak wierna kobieta
z nożem i widelcem w grzbiecie) i – Ktoś umarł –
mówi się, i robi się jaśniej – ktoś umarł –
pisze się z niedopałkiem siarnika w ustach,
kiedy nikt nie wie, jak piękne rzeczy się widzi
i w jakim blasku wstępuje w szczęśliwość Nowego Roku.
(Sosnowski 2006, 151 et seq.)[41]

---

[41] „Now more bareheaded and barefoot. / Now colder in the town and brighter. / Snow. But one does not think about this hair decoration, / for it's not a new climate: this night / cold and bright, a hiss of the lamps and a loss by way of / word *loss* in the title of the poem ‚Gloss'. / Lot. It's snowing. And what does one do? One loses. / At first the bootees. Somebody takes one of them away / to make a cradle. The second one is lost / with no trace left, with the whole simplicity of ‚not a trace left'. / God bless you. One mustn't not cross. / Not to wound anyone, in a word, not to heal / it's the old climate. For one walks in the night/ bareheaded and barefoot, and thus still having / something on the side of losses, on this side of the night, / of which black washes off like a nail varnish remover /with the acetone of light, quite unnecessarily, / since it is brighter and colder / more and more bareheaded and barefoot. / Snow. It's still colder and brighter. One walks / with not a trace left, bareheaded and barefoot, one walks / with the whole simplicity to the corner between the houses / one sits down, shrinks, pulls one's knees under oneself, / as the fairy tale wants. ‚With a mass of the matches' / one freezes so much better and – ooh – one says – / a single tiny match, it wouldn't be so well! / The fairy tale will bury you as if you were a boy with the matches. / Rumour will retain you as you were a little girl. / It's burning. The New Year. One needs words and images. / The new words and images, thus it's burning brighter, / to warm one's fingers (and one writes for the same reason, / to warm one's fingers: with this strange candle / a good oven with a brass door and a goose / is crawling along the floor like a faithful woman / with a knife and fork in her body) and – Somebody died – / one speaks and it's getting brighter – somebody died – / one

The return to the melic poetry manifested in Sosnowski's poems results, as it has been already noticed, in deconstruction of the traditional hierarchy of senses. His poetry assumes the secret power of the blind spot, which should be understood as a consequent response to the crisis in the heart of history of representation.[42] Furthermore, the exhaustion of seeing carries with it an annihilation of the opposition between light and darkness, and subsequently conditions experience of warmth and cold. Both the issues, indicated in the aforementioned poem, may be interpreted in the context of the Shoah, since the "old climate" adheres to the definite past, which means a reservoir of the lost values. In the realm of the "new climate", light streaked with cold determines the presence of negativity that exposes helplessness of the subject, who strives to escape in vain.

In the further passages, I am to witness an evolution of the commented experiences which are to converge at the constant process of thwarting:

Weźmy teraz na warsztat koniec wszystkich rzeczy.
Na koniuszek języka. Ale bez histerii
spisać trzeba na straty coś, co nas niweczy

o czym się milczy w każdym ze znanych narzeczy
co nas domownie załatwia. Choć w niebieskiej feerii
ognia, co pilotuje koniec twoich rzeczy

to nacięcie w pół słowa. Ale nic nie przeczy
temu, co się nie liczy w dziennej buchalterii
która spycha na straty coś, co ją zniweczy

bo przetarg ograniczony. Od rzeczy do rzeczy
wiąże się koniec z końcem w osnowie materii.
Potem jazda pod młotek na sam koniec rzeczy

i dobija się wątek. Lecz co go kaleczy
tka się dalej nicując krawędzie scenerii
niwą świata bez światła, który cię niweczy

---

writes with a butt of sulphur in one's mouth, / when no one knows how beautiful things one sees / and in what brightness one enters to a bliss of the New Year".

[42] „Our aesthetic goal must be to develop a ‚culture of the blind spot' that recognizes its own inherent limitations and appreciates the fact that perceptional ways include non-perception just as insight is necessary tied to blindness. This knowledge, Welsch argues, helps us recognize a ‚postmodern aesthetics of resistance' within contemporary art. Art and contemporary culture literally improves ‚our health' by inoculating us against the simplistic hope for an easy reconciliation of differences in a totalizing (and totalitarian) aesthetic state: ‚The shell of aesthetics may become identified with design, but its […] core aims toward justice'" (Strathausen 2005, 232).

w pół słowa snu na aukcji bez akcji na rzeczy
zimny jak niwacja w polarnej austerii.
Świeży trop koniec końców kończy nasze rzeczy.
Aż spisze nas na straty coś, co nie zniweczy.[43]
(Sosnowski 2006, 180)

The only defence against thwarting, rendered by the catastrophically mad variation on the theme of the end, is writing which, paradoxically, keeps performing the loss effect. The cited poem seems to be incarnated in a form of apotropaic litany which serves the rhythmical incantation recited against the unavoidable experience of silence namely, death. Furthermore, the mortal horizon on which the poem is to vanish marks itself in the title introducing Sosnowski's incantation. The word „dożynki" stands for a ,harvest festival', however, considering also the necessary presence of the verb „dożynać", which means ,to saw through', or ,to finish off', or ,to botch something up hopelessly', the poem one more time focuses on the painful sensual repetition of the loss's experience.

Wiersz traci pamięć za rogiem ulicy
W czarnym powietrzu brzmią wołania straży
Szukałem siostry i nie mogłem znaleźć
Nie miałem siostry więc nie mogłem szukać

Nie miałem siostry jak sięgnąć pamięcią
Wstecz wzdłuż ulicy której dawno nie ma
W naszej okolicy zgubi się w podwórkach
Nie zna białego ranka Pije w suterenach

Marzy godzinami przy murku śmietnika
Moje ciemne powieki ciężkie są od wina
Wiersz wychodzi z domu i nigdy nie wraca
Wiersz nie pamięta domu którego nie było

---

[43] "Now we shall take the end of everything on the workbench / on the tip of our language. But no hysterics / one needs to write it off, this what thwarts us / on what one is silent in each of dialects one knows / that what rejects our matter. Though in the blue extravaganza / of the fire that pilots the end of your things / this incision in the middle of the word. But nothing denies / this what shows no consideration in the everyday book-keeping / which pushes something into the background, something that keeps thwarting it / for a limited tender. From one thing to another thing / the end ties itself to the end in the fabric of the matter. / Later a ride to go under the hammer in the very end of things / and the weft is driven in. But this what hurts it / one weaves further on turning the edges of the scenery / with a lea of the world without the light, which thwarts you / in the middle dream on the auction without the action of things / cold as a leation in the polar inn. / A new track ends our things in the end / till writes it off, this what thwarts us".

Dla tej ciemnej miłości dzikiego gatunku
Wstecz wzdłuż ulicy której dawno nie ma
Idzie bez pamięci i znika bez śladu
Nie ma wiersza pamięci siostry ani domu
 (Sosnowski 2006, 237)[44]

The cited poem tries to present an intriguing encounter of the titular poem with the ‚self', although at the first instant the poem is suffering from amnesia while the self turns out to be torn between presence and absence of some mysterious sister (who remains sister to all the previous sisters inhabiting Sosnowski's verses). Yet above the tautological poem (after all we face the poem about the poem), lyrical subject, sister, and memory there is an overriding motif of loss, which holds all the elements of the verse together. After the previous encounters with the presented verses it seems more than obvious that the loss, as a theme, catastrophic sense, and poetical strategy, sets the tone in every single poem of Sosnowski. What is more, each poetical situation might be regarded as a ‚mourning band' for words which passed away (the phrase coined in the already cited *Piosenka dla Europy*; Sosnowski 2006, 49). Their overwhelming existence may be maintained only during the act of performing, and exhausts itself within the last sound of the lyrical spectacle. Besides many associations with the polyphonic fugue, Sosnowski's poetry also evokes a canonical form of elegy along with its funeral motivation. For that reason, one ought to reconsider this poetry as a commentary to its own funeral. In this commentary, however, a crucial paradox must be exposed: through the permanent manner announcing the experience of loss, Sosnowski's verses, as a matter consisted of rhythms and sounds, keep protesting against their apocalyptic destiny. For to remain alive (a shadow of immortality desire is the eternal companion in art), even if such life stands for

---

[44] „A poem loses its memory around the corner of the street / The guards' calls resound in the black air / I was looking for the sister and I couldn't find her / I haven't got a sister so I couldn't look for her / I haven't got a sister as far as I remembered / backwards along the street which is gone for a long time / It will lose itself in the courtyards of our neighbourhood / It knows nothing about the white morning It drinks in the basements / It dreams for hours against the wall of the bin / My dark eyelids are heavy from wine / The poem leaves the house and never comes back / The poem doesn't remember the house which did not exist / For this dark love of the wild genre / Backward along the street which is gone for a long time / It walks with no memory and vanishes with no track / Neither poem memory sister nor house are existed".

brief yet unlimited intervals of reincarnation, poetry like music must be performed.

The quoted poem beguiles with its canonical form: it is constructed from the four regular quatrains, of which lines are impeccably parallel being confirmed by a tonal affinity. Through its graphical order, the poem inscribes itself into the archive which, however, remains somehow anonymous. This anonymity of what is called literary tradition comes from Sosnowski's peculiar map of poetry which is deprived of topography usually consisting of cardinal points of the lingual or textual horizon. This map, if only having existed, serves losing rather than gaining: all directions are blurred, all places, including the one occupied by the poetical self, remain unknown, and the poem, as a trackless event, must eventually vanish behind the corner of the street alike the heterogeneous strand of sounds, which is to die out... on its always returning way to the unavoidable silence.

In the essay devoted to John Ashbery's poem, Sosnowski claims that there are three methods of writing, in accordance with which:

> [...] można powiedzieć, że coś jest tym albo tamtym, można powiedzieć, że coś nie jest ani tym, ani tamtym, ale wciąż jest w przestrzeni możliwej wypowiedzi, i można mówić bezustannie wyzbywając się punktów odniesienia – ja, miejsca, świata – mimo woli pozostawiając margines ciszy, gdzie kryje się to, co niewypowiadalne. (Sosnowski 2007b, 67)[45]

One moment centred in the realm of the unutterable (providing that the unutterable itself might be thought in collision of any centre) also shapes the newest collection of poems entitled *Dom ran*, which proceeds with touching many unhealed wounds, among which one may silently assume the effect of the Shoah, the effect convincingly rendered by the following elegiac distich: „wymawiam głoski jak obrzękłe nuty / wyciągam wiersze jak żelazne druty" („I pronounce sounds like swollen tones / I pull verses out like iron wires"; Sosnowski 2015, 25). For the only experience, encapsulated in this poetry, is derived from the

---

[45] „[...] one may say that something is this or that, one may say that something is not this or that yet it still exists in the space of the possible utterance, one may say all the time avoiding the points of reference – the self, place, world – unwittingly remaining a margin of silence where is concealed what is unutterable".

overwhelming desire for an impossible reconciliation with the exposed or obscured loss.

Bibliography

Agamben, Giorgio 1998: Homo Sacer. Sovereign Power and Bare Life. Transl. by Daniel Heller-Roazen. Stanford, Cal..
Ashbery, John 2001: Other Traditions. Cambridge, Mass. – London.
Benjamin, Walter 1996: Writings. Vol. 1: 1913-1926. Ed. by Marcus Bullock, Michael W. Jennings. Cambridge, Mass. – London.
Bloom, Harold 1991: Ruin the Sacred Truths. Poetry and Belief from the Bible to Present. Cambridge, Mass. – London.
id. 2002: Lęk przed wpływem. Teoria poezji. Transl. by Agata Bielik-Robson, Marcin Szuster. Kraków.
id. 2003: A Map of Misreading. New York.
Caputo, John D. 1986: Cold Hermeneutics. Heidegger and Derrida. In: Journal of the British Society for Phenomenology 17,3, pp. 252-275.
id. 1987: Radical Hermeneutics. Repetition, Deconstruction and the Hermeneutic Project. Bloomington – Indianapolis.
Chang, Briankle G. 1993: Deconstructing Communication. Representation, Subject, and Economies of Exchange. Minneapolis.
Cisło, Maciej 1994: Flirt z Kaliope. In: Nowy Nurt, no. 6, pp. 10-18.
Derrida, Jacques 1981: D'un ton apocalyptique adopté naguère en philosophie. In: Les fins de l'homme. À partir du travail de Jacques Derrida. Colloque de Cerisy-la-Salle. Sous la direction de Philippe Lacoue-Labarthe et Jean-Luc Nancy. Ann Arbor, MI, pp. 440-482.
id. 1986: Glas. Transl. by John P. Leavey, Jr., Richard Rand. Lincoln – London.
id. 1992a: This Strange Institution Called Literature. An Interview with Jacques Derrida by Derek Attridge. In: id.: Acts of Literature. Ed. by Derek Attridge. New York, N.Y., pp. 33-75.
id. 1992b: That Dangerous Supplement. In: id.: Acts of Literature. Ed. by Derek Attridge. New York, N.Y., pp. 76-109.
id. 1992c: From Shibboleth. For Paul Celan. In: id.: Acts of Literature. Ed. by Derek Attridge. New York, N.Y., pp. 370-413.
id. 1996: Archive Fever. A Freudian Impression. Transl. by Eric Prenowitz. Chicago – London.
id. 2002: Without Alibi. Transl. by Peggy Kamuf. Stanford, Cal.
Gutorow, Jacek 2003: Dwa razy o Andrzeju Sosnowskim. In: id.: Niepodległość głosu. Szkice o poezji polskiej po 1968. Kraków, pp. 163-185.
Heraclitus [n.y.]: The Complete Fragments. Transl. by William Harris. community.middlebury.edu/~harris/Philosophy/Heraclitus.pdf (28.12.2015).
Hetman, Grzegorz [n.y.]: Gdzie życie staje się żyrandolem. http://www.biuroliterackie.pl/przystan/czytaj.php?site=260&co=txt_1681 (10.5.2015).
Klejnocki, Jarosław 1995: Za gardą. In: Nowy Nurt, no. 21, pp. 3-5.
Kula, Agata 2007: Pisze się, żeby ogrzać palce. In: Maurice Blanchot. Literatura ekstremalna. Ed. by Paweł Mościcki. Warszawa, pp. 185-194.

Maciejewski, Maciej 1997: Sytuacje języka, sytuacje podmiotu – o twórczości A. Sosnowskiego. In: Śladami człowieka książkowego. Ed. by Tomasz Mizerkiewicz. Poznań, pp. 99-115.

Maliszewski, Karol 1995: Precyzja chaosu. In: Nowy Nurt, no. 21, pp. 1-7.

id. [n.y.]: Nowa poezja. Mały przewodnik po tendencjach i stylach. http://bl.pl/przystan/czytaj.php?site=260&co=txt_1025 (10.5.2015).

Momro, Jakub 2003: Wśród świata nieograniczonego i martwego. In: Lekcja żywego języka. O poezji Andrzeja Sosnowskiego. Ed. by Grzegorz Jankowicz. Kraków, pp. 93-109.

Nofikow, Ewa 2012: Między językami, między głosami. O „poems" Andrzeja Sosnowskiego. In: Białostockie Studia Literaturoznawcze, no. 3, pp. 91-106.

Okulska, Inez 2011: Język (wy)grywa. Gry językowe poezji Andrzeja Sosnowskiego w przekładzie In: Kwartalnik Językoznawczy 1,5, pp. 33-69.

Orliński, Marcin 2008: Konkretne nadrealina. In: Twórczość, no. 7, pp. 95-101.

Paloff, Benjamin 2011: Fallen Language: In Conversation with Andrzej Sosnowski. In: Sosnowski, Andrzej: Lodgings. Selected Poems 1987 – 2010. Transl. by Benjamin Paloff. Rochester, N.Y. http://poems.com/special_features/prose/essay_paloff.php (24.6.2016).

Próchniak, Paweł 2010: Poema: widowisko. In: Wiersze na głos. Szkice o twórczości Andrzeja Sosnowkiego. Ed. by Piotr Śliwiński. Poznań, pp. 126-135.

Pyzik, Agata 2015: Szum centrali. In: dwutygodnik.com, p. 154.

Skibska, Anna Maria 2015: Between Reshimu and Messianic Actions. In: The Aspects of Genres in the Holocaust Literatures in Central Europe. Ed. by Jiří Holý. Praha, pp. 41-55.

Sosnowski, Andrzej 2001/2002: Czy jesteś w takim razie poetą ponowoczesnym? Interview by Michał Paweł Markowski. In: Nowy Wiek, no. 7/8, pp. 15-26.

id. 2006: Dożynki 1987-2003. Wrocław.

id. 2007a: Po tęczy. Wrocław.

id. 2007b: O poezji „flow" i „chart". In: id.: Najryzykowniej. Wrocław, pp. 62-78.

id. 2007c: Dziadowskie klimaty. In: Rozbiórka. Wiersze, rozmowy i portrety 26 poetów. Rozm. Magdalena Rybak. Wrocław.

id. 2010a: poems. Wrocław.

id. 2010b: 50 lat po Oświęcimiu i inne sezony. Interwiew by Mariusz Maciejewski, Tomasz Majeran. In: Trop w trop. Rozmowy z Andrzejem Sosnowskim. Selection, introduction, ed. by Grzegorz Jankowicz. Wrocław, pp. 25-35.

id. 2010c: Podróż przez archiwum. Interview by Stanisław Bereś. In: Trop w trop. Rozmowy z Andrzejem Sosnowskim. Selection, introduction, ed. by Grzegorz Jankowicz. Wrocław, pp. 73-86.

id. 2011: Lodgings. Selected Poems 1987-2010. Transl. by Benjamin Paloff. Rochester, N.Y.

id. 2015: Dom ran. Wrocław.

Strathausen, Carsten 2005: Adorno, or, The Ends of Aesthetics. In: Globalizing Critical Theory. Ed. by Max Pensky. Lanham, MD, pp. 221-240.

Śliwiński, Piotr 1999: Reakcje łańcuchowe. In: Res Publica Nowa, no. 11/12, pp. 107-110.

Turczyńska, Agata 2004: Andrzej Sosnowski – poeta społecznie niedostępny. www.polisemia.com.pl, no. 4.

Welsch, Wolfgang 2011: Aesthetics beyond Aesthetics. Towards a New Form of the Discipline. openjournals.library.usyd.edu.au/index.php/LA/article/viewFile/5251/5957 (4.3.2016).

Auf dem Weg zur unvermeidlichen Stille:
Über den Shoah-Kontext in Andrzej Sosnowskis Dichtung

Der vorliegende Beitrag zielt darauf ab, das eigenartige Phänomen der Übertragung aufzuzeigen, das bei einem der bedeutendsten Idiome der modernen polnischen Dichtung zu beobachten ist. Die Übertragung selbst betrifft den sog. Shoah-‚Effekt', da dieser sich gut in die Schichten der Sprache einfügt und dabei als radikale Hinwendung zur Erfahrung die mit der konventionell erfassten Bedeutung konfrontierte semantische Leere offenbart. Ich möchte daher einen neuen kontextuellen Rahmen vorschlagen, in dem die außergewöhnlichen Gedichte Andrzej Sosnowskis als implizite Repräsentanz der sprachlichen Shoah gesehen werden können, die alle Strukturen des künstlerischen Idioms durchdringt. In der aus der Lektüre dieses Idioms folgenden verworrenen Situation sollte unterstrichen werden, dass der Ausgangspunkt meiner Analysen die Akzeptanz der Notwendigkeit ist, die traditionelle Art des Lesens aufzugeben, was aus der Annullierung dessen folgt, was Referenz genannt wird. Um die Dichtung Sosnowskis, die mit diesem nicht alltäglichen Kontext der Shoah konfrontiert wird, zu verstehen, sei die ambivalente Figur der Wüste erwähnt, die von Jacques Derrida so überzeugend beschrieben wurde. In seinem Essay, der für das berühmte Symposium in Capri geschrieben wurde, führt Derrida aus, dass solche Orte wie eine Wüste, eine Insel oder auch das Gelobte Land zur Domäne der Aporie gehören, in deren Optik die Worte ihre (gegenüber der Sprache immer externe) Semantik verlieren, und zwar aus dem Grunde, um zu sich selbst zurückzukehren und ihre unlesbare Identität zurückzugewinnen. Die Rückkehr zu sich selbst bedeutet die Restitution der Laute und Töne (akustischen Wellen), die verletzen und Chaos bewirken. Die sprachliche Shoah verwandelt die Dichtung demnach in ein Gebet, das in einer völlig fremden Sprache artikuliert wird, deren Konsequenz eine Bewegung in Richtung der unvermeidlichen Stille ist. Es ist jedoch anzumerken, dass die enigmatischen Gedichte Sosnowskis, die meist aus postmoderner Perspektive und unter dem Einfluss der modernen angloamerikanischen Poesie interpretiert worden sind, bisher nicht im Kontext der Shoah gelesen wurden. Ich denke jedoch, dass das vorgeschlagene Idiom die Möglichkeit bietet, in die Worte-im-Zustand-des-Zerfalls einzudringen, die sehr wohl die ruinierte Welt der literarischen Wüste widerspiegeln können, die als diskretes Erbe der Shoah verstanden wird.

**Das Erzählen des Holocaust
zwischen Authentizität und Fiktionalität**

**Holocaust Narration
between Authenticity and Fictionality**

Zwischen Dokument und Kunst:
Josef Bors Werke über den Holocaust

Reinhard Ibler, Gießen

Für Erwin Wedel zum 90. Geburtstag am 9.4.2016

Im Kontext des literarisch-kulturellen Paradigmenwandels in der Tschechoslowakei, der Mitte der fünfziger Jahre mit dem ‚Tauwetter' (tschech. ‚tání') einsetzte und seinen Höhepunkt wie auch sein frühzeitiges Ende im Prager Frühling der späten sechziger Jahre erreichte, spielte die Thematisierung des Schicksals der Juden im Zweiten Weltkrieg eine zentrale Rolle. Der Völkermord der Nationalsozialisten, zu dessen bleibenden Symbolen das Ghetto bzw. Lager[1] im nordböhmischen Festungsstädtchen Theresienstadt (Terezín) gehört, war bereits in den vierziger Jahren Gegenstand zahlloser Texte gewesen, wobei hier allerdings Dokumente von Opfern, Überlebenden und sonstigen Zeitzeugen über das Leben in den Ghettos, Konzentrations- und Vernichtungslagern vorherrschten.[2] Über die Grenzen des Landes hinaus bekannt wurde das Buch *Továrna na smrt* (1946; *Die Todesfabrik*) der tschechisch-jüdischen Autoren Ota Kraus und Erich Schön (Kulka), eine der ersten ausführlichen Innenansichten von Auschwitz. Vereinzelte (im eigentlichen Sinn) literarische Werke über den Holocaust gab es in dieser Zeit zwar ebenfalls, für diese war aber dann in der antisemitisch gestimmten Atmosphäre des Stalinismus kein Platz, weshalb sie meist erst später (wieder)veröffentlicht werden konnten. Bekanntestes Beispiel hierfür ist Jiří Weils Roman *Život s hvězdou* (*Leben mit dem Stern*), der kurz nach seiner Erstveröffentlichung 1949 verboten wurde und erst in der liberaleren Atmosphäre am Beginn der sechziger Jahre (2. Auflage 1964) von einer breiteren literarischen Öffentlichkeit zur Kenntnis genommen werden konnte. Von den vielen tschechischen Autoren der jüngeren Generation, die sich im Jahrzehnt zwischen 1958 und 1968 zumeist in Romanen und Erzählungen mit dem Holocaust befassten, haben sich vor allem der jüdische Autor und Holocaust-Überlebende

---

[1] Zur Diskussion des Status von Theresienstadt vgl. Benz 2013, 9ff.
[2] Einen Überblick über die Entwicklung der tschechischen Holocaustliteratur bietet Holý 2011 (in deutscher Sprache: Holý 2012).

Arnošt Lustig und der nichtjüdische Schriftsteller Ladislav Fuks nachhaltig in das kulturelle Gedächtnis eingeschrieben.[3] Andere wie František Kafka, Ludvík Aškenazy oder Hana Bělohradská gerieten früher oder später aus dem Fokus des breiteren Interesses und damit beinahe in Vergessenheit.[4] Zu diesen seinerzeit sehr erfolgreichen, heute kaum mehr bekannten Autoren gehört auch Josef Bor, um den es im vorliegenden Beitrag gehen soll. Das Hauptaugenmerk soll dabei auf die beiden Werke gerichtet werden, mit denen sich Bor in die tschechische Literaturgeschichte eingeschrieben hat und die ihm nicht nur ein heimisches Renommee, sondern auch ein gewisse internationale Beachtung eintrugen. Es handelt sich hierbei um den Roman *Opuštěná panenka* (1961; *Die verlassene Puppe*) und die Novelle *Terezínské rekviem* (1963; *Theresienstädter Requiem*). Trotz großer thematischer Nähe gehen die beiden Werke mit der Problematik des Holocaust in unterschiedlicher Weise um. Dies ist insofern interessant, als diese Differenzen einen wichtigen poetologischen Entwicklungsschritt markieren, der sich damals in der internationalen Holocaustliteratur zu vollziehen begann. Man könnte diesen Prozess als den Übergang von der Dokumentarität zur Literarität bezeichnen.

Josef Bondy, wie er ursprünglich hieß, stammte aus einer tschechisch-jüdischen Familie und wurde 1906 in Ostrava geboren.[5] Er studierte Jura und wurde, wie sein Vater, ein erfolgreicher Rechtsanwalt. Mit dem Beginn des Zweiten Weltkriegs gelangte Bondys vielversprechende Karriere abrupt an ihr Ende. 1942 wurden er und seine ganze Familie, darunter seine Frau Edita und

---

[3] Arnošt Lustigs (1926 – 2011) bekannteste Werke dieser Zeit sind die Erzählsammlung *Démanty noci* (1958; *Diamanten der Nacht*) sowie die Novellen *Dita Saxová* (1962) und *Modlitba pro Kateřinu Horowitzovou* (1964; *Ein Gebet für Katharina Horowitz*). Von Ladislav Fuks' (1923-1994) frühen Werken mit Holocaust-Bezug sind neben der Erzählsammlung *Mí černovlasí bratři* (1964; *Meine schwarzhaarigen Brüder*) vor allem die Kurzromane *Pan Theodor Mundstock* (1963; *Herr Theodor Mundstock*) und *Spalovač mrtvol* (1967; *Der Leichenverbrenner*) zu nennen.
[4] Vgl. u.a. František Kafkas (1909 – 1991) dokumentarischen Roman *Krutá léta* (1963; *Grausame Jahre*), Ludvík Aškenazys (1921 – 1986) Erzählsammlungen *Psí život* (1959; *Ein Hundeleben*) und *Vajíčko* (1963; *Das Ei*) und Hana Bělohradskás (1929 – 2005) Roman *Bez krásy, bez límce* (1962; *Ohne Schönheit, ohne Kragen*).
[5] Eine ausführlichere Darstellung zum Leben und Schaffen Bors fehlt bis auf den heutigen Tag. Kurzgefasste Einführungen auf wenigen Seiten bieten u.a. Bolton 2004 und Schreiner 2007.

seine beiden kleinen Töchter Věra und Hana, nach Theresienstadt deportiert. 1944 erfolgte der Transport nach Auschwitz-Birkenau, wo alle Familienmitglieder in der Gaskammer den Tod fanden und nur Bondy, der für den Arbeitseinsatz im Lager der Buna-Werke im nahegelegenen Monowitz ausgewählt wurde, überlebte. Nach der Auflösung des Lagers wurden die Häftlinge auf einen über 40 km langen Todesmarsch getrieben. Obwohl todkrank, kam Bondy schließlich mit einem Transport nach Buchenwald. Nach einem weiteren Todesmarsch erlebte er im April 1945 seine Befreiung in der Nähe von Jena. Nach dem Krieg heiratete Bondy wieder und trat eine Stelle im tschechoslowakischen Verteidigungsministerium in Prag an. Da die Ministeriumsmitarbeiter mit deutsch oder anderen fremdländisch klingenden Namen verpflichtet wurden, diese durch tschechische Namen zu ersetzen, nannte er sich von dieser Zeit an Bor (vgl. Schreiner 2007, 2). Anfang der fünfziger Jahre geriet Bor im Zusammenhang mit den Säuberungsaktionen der Tschechoslowakischen Kommunistischen Partei und dem Prozess um Rudolf Slánský in politische Schwierigkeiten, weshalb er seinen Posten im Ministerium verlor. Nach diversen Bürotätigkeiten in Košice und Prag ging Bor 1966 aus gesundheitlichen Gründen in Rente. Bis zu seinem Tod 1979 in Prag widmete er sich intensiv dem christlich-jüdischen Dialog.

Bereits dieser kurze Abriss des Lebenswegs lässt erkennen, dass Bor kein professioneller Schriftsteller war, sondern sich seinen Lebensunterhalt primär auf andere Weise verdiente. Und der Antrieb, die beiden erwähnten Bücher zu schreiben, die ihm Anfang der sechziger Jahre literarischen Ruhm eintrugen, war auch nicht in erster Linie künstlerischer Natur. Als Holocaust-Überlebender, der fürchterliche Erlebnisse durchstehen musste, suchte er einen Weg, die eigenen traumatischen Erfahrungen zu verarbeiten und die Leserschaft daran teilhaben zu lassen. Interessant ist dabei vor allem die Frage, warum Bor ausgerechnet den Weg der *Literatur* beschritten hat. Dass er die Voraussetzungen zum Schriftsteller hatte, zeigt auch die Breite seiner literarischen Fähigkeiten: Denn, wenngleich beide Werke in die Welt der Lager, der Erniedrigung und Demütigung von Menschen, der Transporte und der Vernichtung eintauchen, bestehen dennoch große Unterschiede in der künstlerischen Bewältigung der Thematik.

Der Roman *Opuštěná panenka*[6] ist bereits von seiner Entstehungsgeschichte her sehr interessant. Obwohl das Werk erstmals 1961[7] publiziert wurde, waren größere Teile des Textes bereits zehn Jahre zuvor geschrieben worden. Denn man schrieb das Jahr 1951, als Bor, wie er in einem Interview aus dem Jahre 1965 rückblickend berichtet, die innere Notwendigkeit verspürte, der Öffentlichkeit zur Warnung vor den weiterhin drohenden Gefahren von Krieg und Faschismus etwas von seinen schlimmen Erfahrungen mitzuteilen:

> Tenkrát v tom roce [1951], tehdy prožitek, který léta ve mně zrál, musel na papír. Tehdy jsem prostě nemohl mlčet, protože jsem viděl, že s fašismem není ještě konec, že stále ještě není jistota, že se ty hrůzy nebudou opakovat... Tehdy jsem za tři měsíce napsal v hrubých obrysech svou první knihu – *Opuštěná panenka*. (Doboš 1965, 4)

> Damals in diesem Jahr [1951] musste das Erlebnis, das Jahre in mir reifte, zu Papier gebracht werden. Damals konnte ich einfach nicht schweigen, da ich gesehen habe, dass der Faschismus immer noch nicht an sein Ende gelangt war, dass es immer noch keine Sicherheit gab, dass sich die Schrecken nicht wiederholen würden... Damals habe ich innerhalb von drei Monaten in groben Zügen mein erstes Buch geschrieben – *Die verlassene Puppe*.[8]

Es muss betont werden, dass in den frühen fünfziger Jahren ein Werk über die jüdischen Leiden in den Konzentrations- und Vernichtungslagern aus o.g. Gründen keine Chance auf Veröffentlichung gehabt hätte. Aber Bor, im Schreiben ohnehin noch ungeübt, nutzte diese Zeit, um seinen Roman kontinuierlich zu erweitern und darüber hinaus stilistisch wie kompositorisch zu verbessern. Aktive Unterstützung fand er darin bei keinem Geringeren als Pavel Eisner, dem bekannten tschechisch-jüdischen Übersetzer und Journalisten (vgl. ebd.). Im deutlich liberaleren kulturellen Milieu der frühen sechziger Jahre konnte das Werk schließlich publiziert werden. Da das Holocaust-Thema damals auf ein breites Interesse stieß, blieb der Erfolg nicht aus, was sich auch in den Reaktionen der Literaturkritik widerspiegelt, die vor allem die außerordentliche Wichtigkeit der dargestellten Problematik und die Autorität des unmittelbaren Zeitzeugen, d.h. des selbst vom Holocaust betroffenen Schriftstellers hervorhob. Einige Zweifel geäußert wurden hingegen an der literarischen Qualität des Werks. So bezeich-

---

[6] Ausführlicher zu diesem Werk siehe Ibler 2015.
[7] Weitere Auflagen folgten 1962 und 1965 (deutsche Übersetzung 1964 u.d.T. *Die verlassene Puppe*).
[8] Übersetzungen aus dem Tschechischen hier und im Folgenden, wo nicht anders ausgewiesen, R.I.

nete der Literaturkritiker Jiří Opelík *Opuštěná panenka* als „wertvolles Zeugnis" („cenné svědectví"), bemängelte an dem Buch aber Folgendes:

> Kolísá se mezi dokumentem a beletrií, mezi mozaikou a vypravěčstvím. Kniha se těžko rozbíhá, zpočátku strhuje jen látkou, nikoli jejím uchopením. (Opelík 1961)
>
> Es schwankt zwischen Dokument und Belletristik, zwischen Mosaik und Erzählung. Das Buch kommt schwer in die Gänge, anfangs reißt es nur durch seine Stofffülle mit, nicht aber durch deren Bewältigung.

Die Auffassung, dass *Opuštěná panenka* primär ein Werk von dokumentarischem Wert sei, aber künstlerische Schwächen aufweise, zieht sich wie ein roter Faden durch die Rezeptionsgeschichte des Werks und wird auch in neueren Arbeiten vertreten.[9] Hier stellt sich allerdings die Frage, warum Bor sich dezidiert für eine *literarische* Gattung, den Roman, entschieden hat, wenn es ihm vor allem auf dokumentarische Genauigkeit und Verlässlichkeit ankam. Wir werden also nicht umhin können, in *Opuštěná panenka* neben der ‚dokumentarischen' auch die literarisch-künstlerische Ebene einer Betrachtung zu unterziehen, wobei es von Interesse ist, ob letztere wirklich jene Schwächen offenbart, wie sie bei Opelík anklingen.

Bei *Opuštěná panenka* handelt es sich um einen relativ umfangreichen Roman (die tschechische Ausgabe umfasst 330 Seiten), der aus vier Teilen besteht, die in kompositorischer wie stilistischer Hinsicht teils sehr unterschiedlich sind. Während die ersten drei Teile in eine Vielzahl kurzer Kapitel untergliedert sind und aus wechselnden Perspektiven erzählt werden, bietet der letzte Teil eine durchgehende und dabei fast homogene Narration.

Der Titel des 1. Teils ist *Šlojska (Die Schleuse)*. Darin geht es um das Schicksal der jüdischen Bevölkerung von Kutná Hora, die 1942 nach Theresienstadt deportiert wird. Im Zentrum des Geschehens steht der Protagonist des Romans, Jan (Honza) Breuer, mit seiner Familie. Die Handlung setzt mit der Ankündigung des Transports ein und erstreckt sich über einen Zeitraum, der von den Vorbereitungen dieses Unternehmens bis zur Ankunft der Deportierten in Theresienstadt reicht. In insgesamt 23 Kapiteln entfaltet sich in diesem 1. Teil eine große Vielfalt unterschiedlichster Szenen, u.a. aus dem Familienleben der

---

[9] So spricht z.B. Jiří Holý (2011, 29) von der „Dokumentarität" („dokumentárnost"), die in Bors Prosa generell vorherrschend sei.

Breuers, aus der Organisation und dem Ablauf des Transports, aber auch aus dem Leben in den Kommandostellen der nationalsozialistischen Unterdrücker. Breuer, ein Mann voller Energie und mit weitreichendem Einfluss innerhalb der jüdischen Gemeinschaft, wird mit der Organisation des Transports beauftragt. Nach der Ankunft in Theresienstadt gehört es zu seinen Aufgaben, die Verhandlungen mit den Judenältesten zu führen, die maßgeblichen Einfluss auf die Zusammensetzung der nach Auschwitz und in die anderen Todeslager führenden Transporte haben. Trotz intensivster Bemühungen kann Breuer es allerdings nicht verhindern, dass seine Schwester und deren Familie bald nach der Ankunft auf einen dieser Transporte gehen müssen, der für sie den Tod in der Gaskammer bedeutet.

Die Teile 2 und 3, *Terezínský pochod* (*Theresienstädter Marsch*) und *Na troskách ghetta* (*Auf den Trümmern des Ghettos*), drehen sich vor allem um das Leben Breuers und seiner verbliebenen Familie bis zum Ende des Ghettos 1944. Eingebettet sind diese Schilderungen wiederum in eine Vielzahl von Szenen aus dem Alltags- und Arbeitsleben in Theresienstadt. Wir erhalten Einblicke u.a. in die jüdische Selbstverwaltung, das Schmugglermilieu, die reichen kulturellen Aktivitäten im Ghetto (wo zahlreiche renommierte Künstler interniert waren), aber auch in die Wirkungssphäre der Nationalsozialisten und ihrer Untergebenen, z.B. der tschechischen Aufseher. Diese immense Vielfalt an Eindrücken, mit denen der Leser konfrontiert wird, macht die Lektüre des Werks in der Tat schwierig. Es wäre aber voreilig, dies als künstlerische Schwäche abzutun, solange man nicht nach der Funktion dieser Darstellungsform fragt. So glaubt etwa Vladimír Forst, dass hier ein bewusst eingesetztes Verfahren vorliegt, das für den Bereich der damaligen Holocaustliteratur eine Innovation darstellt:

> Románový charakter práce se ztrácí v pestrém kaleidoskopu nejrůznějších událostí z terezínského ghetta. Tyto záběry terezínského života mají svérázný a v literatuře o koncentračních táborech i nový charakter. (Forst 1961)
>
> Der Romancharakter des Werks verliert sich in einem bunten Kaleidoskop der unterschiedlichsten Ereignisse aus dem Theresienstädter Ghetto. Diese Aufnahmen vom Theresienstädter Leben haben einen eigentümlichen und in der KZ-Literatur auch neuartigen Charakter.

Der 4. und letzte Teil des Romans, *Temno před úsvitem* (*Dunkel vor der Morgendämmerung*), ist im Gegensatz zu den vorangehenden Teilen nicht in Kapitel untergliedert. Zudem nimmt der Erzähler fast durchgehend die Perspektive Jan Breuers ein, der nach der Ankunft des letzten Theresienstädter Transports in Auschwitz den Rest seiner Familie in der Gaskammer verliert, während er selbst zum Arbeitseinsatz abkommandiert wird. Wir werden Zeugen von Breuers Leidensweg durch die Lager von Monowitz, Gleiwitz und Buchenwald sowie auf mehreren Todesmärschen. Völlig entkräftet und schwerkrank erlebt er in der Nähe von Jena seine Befreiung. Breuer ist nach dem Verlust seiner Familie zu einer Person ohne jegliche Individualität degeneriert, die nur mehr vor sich hinvegetiert. Der Erzähler nennt Breuer deshalb auch nicht mehr beim Namen, sondern „Číslo" (die Nummer). In der Schlussszene, d.h. unmittelbar nach der Befreiung, macht Breuer eine Art Wiedergeburt durch: Er entdeckt allmählich wieder sein Menschsein und seine Individualität, ohne dass sich ihm freilich der Sinn all der entsetzlichen Geschehnisse, die sein Leben in den vorangegangenen Monaten und Jahren geprägt hatten, erschließen will.

> Vězni radostně jásají a mávají rukama. Někteří však mlčí a stojí nehybně.
> Mlčí i Číslo.
> Stojí tu vychrtlý, zavšivený, pokálený. Něco, zbavené duše a citu, vůle i touhy.
> Náhle jím otřese hrozná myšlenka.
> Proč?
> Proč on, a ne žena a děti? Proč to všechno?
> Proč?
> Otázky vnikají do mozku, divoce buší do všech nervů a křečovitě zalomcují celým jeho tělem.
> A Číslo pomalu poznává, že se stává opět člověkem.
> Pláče. (Bor 1962, 330)

> Froh jubelten die Häftlinge und winkten. Manche aber schwiegen und verharrten reglos. Auch die Nummer schwieg.
> Abgezehrt, verlaust, verunreinigt stand sie da. Ein Etwas, der Seele, des Gefühls, des Willens und der Sehnsucht beraubt.
> Plötzlich durchzuckte sie ein furchtbarer Gedanke.
> Warum?
> Warum sie, und nicht die Frau und die Kinder? Warum das alles? Warum?
> Fragen über Fragen drangen in den Verstand, zerrten wie wild an allen Nerven und schüttelten krampfhaft den ganzen Körper.
> Langsam erkannte die Nummer, dass aus ihr wieder ein Mensch wurde.
> Er weinte. (Bor 1964, 437)

Schon diese äußerst knappe Zusammenfassung macht deutlich, dass das in *Opuštěná panenka* dargestellte Geschehen in der Tat sehr viel mit Bondys/Bors eigenen Erfahrungen zu tun hat, was Kritiker wiederholt dazu veranlasst hat, hier von einer Autobiographie zu sprechen. Natürlich lässt es sich auch gar nicht abstreiten, dass das Geschilderte bis ins Detail (Personen, Namen, Lokalitäten, Ereignisse usw.) von Josef Bondys schrecklichen, durch die Deportation ausgelösten Erlebnissen inspiriert wurde. Aber es gibt eben auch eine Reihe signifikanter Unterschiede zwischen literarischer und biographischer Wirklichkeit. Das betrifft etwa, um nur ein Beispiel zu nennen, die Namen des Protagonisten (Jan Breuer statt Josef Bondy) und seiner Frau (Duška Breuerová statt Edita Bondyová), wohingegen die Vornamen der beiden kleinen Töchter in Fiktion und Realität dieselben sind: Věra und Hana.

Abgesehen von solchen Details, die für sich genommen nicht überbewertet werden müssen, soll hier noch einmal die entscheidende Frage gestellt werden: Warum hat der – zudem literarisch weitgehend unerfahrene – Autor nicht eine echte Autobiographie bzw. einen sonstigen dokumentarischen Text verfasst, sondern bewusst ein literarisches Genre gewählt, nämlich einen Roman? Die Antwort auf diese Frage liegt m.E. nahe, wenn man sich die komplexe Struktur des Werks betrachtet. Man kann die Überfülle an Szenen-, Orts- und Perspektivwechseln in den ersten drei Teilen natürlich als künstlerische Schwäche abtun, da es dem Leser tatsächlich nicht leicht gemacht wird, den Überblick zu bewahren. Bei näherem Hinsehen könnte man in diesem „Kaleidoskop" aber auch das Bemühen des Autors erkennen, ein umfassendes und detailliertes Bild vom Holocaust zu entwickeln, das diesen in seiner Totalität erfasst und möglichst viele Facetten des verbrecherischen Geschehens einbezieht. Denn erhält der Rezipient nicht gerade dadurch die Möglichkeit, das individuelle Schicksal des mit autobiographischen Zügen ausgestatteten Protagonisten auf das System des Holocaust in seiner ganzen Vielfalt und Komplexität zu projizieren? Zu diesem Zweck benötigte Bor allerdings zusätzliche, über seine eigenen Erfahrungen hinausgehende Einblicke, auch in Bereiche, die einem Häftling normalerweise nicht zugänglich waren. Dies betrifft im vorliegenden Fall z.B. die mitunter detailgenau geschilderten inneren Diskussionen und Streitigkeiten der Ältestenräte im Ghetto oder gar die Gespräche der Nazis in ihren Diensträumen oder Offizierscasinos, von den Reflexionen Eichmanns in seinem Berliner Büro ganz zu schweigen. Solche Perspektiven konnten nur mit Hilfe zusätzlicher, von außen stammender Informationen, vor allem aber mittels Imagination und Fiktion gewonnen werden. Wenn also in Rezensionen und literaturwissenschaftlichen Darstellungen vom dokumentarischen Charakter von Bors Werk gesprochen wird, dann sehe ich diesen weniger mit den persönlichen Erlebnissen des Autors im Sinne (auto)biographischer oder historischer Authentizität verknüpft, sondern eher als kreativen Impuls für Bors eigentliches Anliegen: dem Leser über den Leidensweg eines Einzelnen hinaus ein möglichst umfassende, detailgenaue und konkrete Vorstellung von den Strukturen und dem Funktionieren des Holocaust zu vermitteln. ‚Dokumentarität' ist in dieser Hinsicht also weniger als Verpflichtung zu historischer Wirklichkeitstreue denn als bewusst eingesetztes literarisches Verfahren zu verstehen. Um dies auch terminologisch zu präzisieren, schlage ich für *Opuštěná panenka* und vergleichbare Werke den Begriff ‚quasi-dokumentarische Prosa' vor.

1963, zwei Jahre nach *Opuštěná panenka*, wurde Bors zweites literarisches Werk, die Novelle *Terezínské rekiem*, publiziert.[10] Über das Genre hinaus unterscheidet diese sich in mehrerlei Beziehung deutlich vom Erstling. Auch *Terezínské rekiem* beruht teilweise auf den eigenen Erfahrungen des Autors in Theresienstadt, teils auf den Erzählungen von Bekannten. Die authentischen Ereignisse um die 1943 und 1944 erfolgte Einstudierung und Aufführung von Verdis *Messa da Requiem* im Ghetto durch den jüdischen Dirigenten Rafael Schächter (1905 – 1945) wurden für die Novelle jedoch in gewissem Umfang literarisch modifiziert. So wissen wir beispielsweise, dass der Chor bei den tatsächlich stattgefundenen Aufführungen des Werks nur auf dem Klavier begleitet wurde. In der Novellenhandlung gibt es hingegen ein ganzes Orchester, dessen Instrumente zudem größtenteils von außen ins Ghetto geschmuggelt wurden. Solche Schmuggelaktionen gab es tatsächlich, aber eben nicht im Zusammenhang mit Schächters Einstudierung von Verdis Requiem. Bor bedient sich hier gewissermaßen aus verschiedenen Bereichen der Theresienstädter Wirklichkeit, die für sich genommen nachweisbar und authentisch sind, die in ihrer spezifischen Selektion und Kombination aber eine ganz eigene künstlerische Wirklichkeit generieren. Dies betrifft auch andere Komponenten des Werks. So musste

---

[10] Weitere Auflagen 1964 und 1995 (deutsche Übersetzung 1964, 1966 u.d.T. *Theresienstädter Requiem*). Ausführlicher zu Bors Novelle siehe Udolph 2003 und Ibler 2016.

Schächter in der Realität sein Ensemble wegen der Verluste an Mitgliedern durch die Transporte dreimal neu zusammenstellen, wobei es das letzte dieser Ensembles sogar auf fünfzehn Aufführungen des Requiems brachte (vgl. Karas 1985, 139f.), wohingegen in der Novelle lediglich zwei Ensembles und insgesamt zwei Aufführungen erwähnt werden. Die letzte Aufführung fand bekanntlich vor Vertretern des Internationalen Roten Kreuzes statt, die über die Verhältnisse im Ghetto – wie überhaupt über den Holocaust – getäuscht werden sollten. An dieser Aufführung nahmen auch Eichmann und andere Nazi-Offiziere teil. In der Novelle wird das Motiv des Roten Kreuzes völlig ausgeblendet. Es ist lediglich von einer Sondervorstellung für die Nazi-Prominenz die Rede. Diese literarisch motivierte Reduktion bringt das zentrale Anliegen des Werks, in der direkten Konfrontation von Opfern und Mördern innerhalb der Aufführung die Überlegenheit der Kunst über Gewalt und Banalität zu demonstrieren, auf den Punkt. Freilich gab es Kritik an Bors Vorgehen. So gesteht die bekannte Musikwissenschaftlerin und Opernkritikerin Eva Herrmannová, die selbst Theresienstadt-Überlebende war, dem Autor seine künstlerischen Freiheiten zwar zu, bemängelt in ihrer Besprechung von *Terezínské rekviem* aber, dass die Unterschiede zwischen Realität und Fiktion im Buch nicht kenntlich gemacht worden seien: „Bývá dobrým zvykem autorů upozornit čtenáře na jisté záměny, úpravy skutečnosti, na jejich stylizaci či ‚přebásnění'" (Herrmanová 1965; „Es ist ein guter Brauch von Autoren, dass sie die Leser auf bestimmte Veränderungen oder Bearbeitungen der Realität, auf ihre Stilisierungen oder ‚Umdichtungen' aufmerksam machen"). In seiner direkten Antwort auf diesen Vorwurf unterstreicht Bor, dass ein fundamentaler Unterschied zwischen der Wahrheit im Leben und der Wahrheit in der Kunst bestehe:

> Nejevilo se mi důležité, zda se jednotlivé příhody ve skutečnosti udály právě při studování a provedení Verdiho Rekviem, nesnažil jsem se vykreslit skutečné postavy zpěváků, i když jsem mnohé z nich znal. Pokusil jsem se podat důkaz umělecké pravdivosti jiným způsobem než vysvětlováním, co je v novele skutečné a co smyšlené. (Bor 1965)
>
> Es erschien mir nicht wichtig, ob die einzelnen Geschehnisse sich wirklich gerade während der Einstudierung und Aufführung von Verdis Requiem ereigneten; ich habe mich nicht darum bemüht, die wirklichen Gestalten der Sänger darzustellen, obwohl ich viele von ihnen kannte. Ich trachtete danach, den Beweis künstlerischer Wahrhaftigkeit auf andere Weise zu erbringen, als zu erklären, was in der Novelle real und was fiktiv ist.

does not exclusively derive from the author's personal, traumagenic war experience and the poetry he read (the critics have, among other things, pointed to the poetry of Leopold Staff, expressionists, Guillaume Apollinaire, surrealists, futurists, the representatives of the Cracow Avant-garde, Józef Czechowicz, and Czesław Miłosz; see, for example, Lam 1976, 88-98; Drewnowski 1990, 86-95). It also, if not mostly, has its source in other, often non-poetic texts read by Różewicz. I will return to this issue later.

The obvious, or at least unquestioned, source of inspiration for both of the above-mentioned poems – *Massacre of the Boys* and *Pigtail* – was Różewicz's visit to the Auschwitz-Birkenau museum. In *Pigtail*, this thesis, which I am not going to question, is supported by the reference to „hair [...] of those suffocated in gas chambers" (Różewicz 1997a, 19)[5], placed in large boxes under glass. The allusion is less obvious in *Massacre of the Boys*, in which Różewicz explores the motif of children's toys – little horses made of wire – which he might have seen among the exhibits at the museum. In fact, a few toys were displayed in a small room in block 6 soon after the museum was opened (see Kermisz 1947). The possible doubts concern *Massacre of the Boys*, rather than *Pigtail*, since tangled hair has been exposed to public view in block 4 since the very beginning of the museum's existence, becoming one of the icons of Auschwitz. These doubts, however, are dispelled by the caption under these poems which reads: „Museum-Oświęcim 1948" (Różewicz 1950, 11 et seq.). Informing the reader about the source of inspiration for the poems, rather than about the place where they were written, the caption was absent from the first edition, but was added to the poems when they were reprinted in 1950 in the collection entitled *Five Poems* (*Pięć poematów*) and can also be found in later editions.

Nevertheless, it appears that the above-mentioned literary works, which are among the most moving responses to the crimes committed in German Nazi camps and to the Holocaust, were not exclusively, or not mostly, inspired by a visit to the museum. These texts were also influenced by the testimony given in

---

[5] „włosy uduszonych w komorach gazowych" (*P*). This motif is also present in the short story entitled *My Little Daughter* (*Moja córeczka*): „A potem znalazłem wszystkie włosy kobiece, wszystkie włosy zebrane z głów żywych i umarłych za szkłem muzeum" (Różewicz 1966, 53; „And then I found all hair belonging to the women, all the hair shaved from the heads of the alive and the dead, behind the museum glass").

1945 to the Regional Jewish Historical Commission (Wojewódzka Żydowska Komisja Historyczna) in Cracow by Rudolf Reder, a former soap factory owner from Lviv (Lwów), to which Różewicz alludes in a surprisingly covert way. Reder was one of the only five people who escaped from Bełżec extermination camp (where around five hundred thousand people, mostly Jews, were killed in the period of seven months), of whom only two survived the war or rather: of whom only two are known to have survived the war (see Kuwałek 2005, 52 et seq., 63). Since August till November 1942 Reder, as a member of ‚death crew', was forced to remove corpses from the gas chambers and bury them in mass graves. His testimony is exceptional because it is the only evidence coming directly from a prisoner who was a member of Bełżec extermination camp support staff. It was written down by Nella Rost and included in the book entitled *Bełżec*, which was published in 1946 under Reder's name[6] (Reder 1946).

In Reder's testimony I found the strangely familiar words:

> When all the women from the transport had been shaved, four workers used brooms made of linden to sweep and gather all the hair. (Reder 1999, 128)[7]

The opening five lines of *Pigtail* are an almost accurate, or rather one should say a covert quotation, but written in verse with no punctuation:

> When all the women from the transport
> had been shaved
> four workers used brooms made of linden

---

[6] Reder's short testimony (or a short version of his full testimony) was published a year earlier, in the book entitled *Documents of Crime and Martyrdom* (*Dokumenty zbrodni i męczeństwa*) (Borwicz et al. 1945). Fragments of his another testimony, which concerned the gas chambers, are quoted by Eugeniusz Szrojt (1947) in his article *Belzec Extermination Camp* (*Obóz zagłady w Bełżcu*). Furthermore, on 30 September 1944, a text entitled *Belzec – A Way to Hell* (*Bełżec – droga do piekła*) was published. It was based on Reder's account and signed with the initials Z.W. (1944).

The quotations in the remaining part of the article come from the bilingual, Polish-English edition of *Bełżec* (Reder 1999). The English translation of Reder's words (by William Brand and Michael Jacobs) published in this edition has been modified by the translator of this article. The same concerns English translations of Różewicz's poems. The aim of this strategy is to convey the similarities between Różewicz's works and their non-literary source of inspiration – Reder's testimony, in which – as the Jewish Historical Commission states – „the form and manner in which the witness described things are preserved" (Reder 1999, 85).

[7] „Kiedy już wszystkie kobiety z transportu ogolono, czterech robotników, miotłami zrobionymi z lipy, zmiatało i gromadziło wszystkie włosy" (Reder 1999, 55).

Indem er der künstlerischen Wahrheit eine eminent hohe Bedeutung beimisst, bezieht Bor in einer bis heute kontrovers geführten Debatte eindeutig Stellung: ob man sich dem Holocaust überhaupt von der künstlerischen Seite nähern darf. Josef Bor, der – wohl gemerkt – selbst die fürchterlichsten physischen und psychischen Qualen zu durchleiden hatte und deshalb die Realität des Holocaust aus eigener Anschauung kannte, gibt hier erneut eine eindeutige und unmissverständliche Antwort zu Gunsten der Kunst. Und im Falle von *Terezínské rekviem* ist es – im Unterschied zu *Opuštěná panenka* – nicht nur eine Entscheidung für ein literarisches Genre und die dieses Genre kennzeichnenden künstlerischen Mittel. Bors Novelle ist gleichzeitig ein Werk über die Kunst, und zwar die Kunst unter den spezifischen Bedingungen eines Ghettos bzw. Lagers.

In Theresienstadt gab es, wie bereits angedeutet, viele jüdische Künstler, darunter auch Personen von internationalem Renommee. Zu diesen gehörte zweifellos der Pianist und Dirigent Rafael Schächter, vormals Gründer und Leiter der Prager Kammerspiele, der in Theresienstadt bekanntlich mehrere aufsehenerregende musikalische Ereignisse organisierte, so u.a. eine Inszenierung von Bedřich Smetanas Oper *Prodaná nevěsta* (*Die verkaufte* Braut). Davon ist u.a. auch in *Opuštěná panenka* die Rede. Die Einstudierung und Aufführung von Verdis Requiem war eine weitere große Leistung Schächters, zumal der Dirigent seine ohnehin schon unter schwierigen Umständen zu realisierende Arbeit von zahllosen Rückschlägen begleitet sah, insbesondere durch die Transporte, die, wie erwähnt, die wiederholte Neubesetzung des Ensembles notwendig machten. Zudem gab es von Seiten jüdischer Intellektueller heftige Reaktionen, die es als Provokation betrachteten, dass Juden ausgerechnet eine alte katholische Totenmesse aufführen sollten. Aber für Schächter zählte dieser Aspekt nicht. Er sah in dem Werk in erster Linie den Ausdruck einer absoluten, jegliche nationalen, ethnischen oder religiösen Grenzen hinter sich lassenden Kunst. Dieser Aspekt, aus dem Schächter die Kraft schöpfte, allen Widrigkeiten zu trotzen, wird in der Novelle, in welcher der Erzähler fast durchgehend die Perspektive des Dirigenten einnimmt, besonders herausgestellt. Im Prozess der Proben erkennt Schächter zunehmend die dem Werk ebenfalls innewohnende Kraft zu Widerstand und Rebellion. Teile wie *Dies irae* oder das finale *Libera me*, in der katholischen Totenmesse Verweise auf das Gericht Gottes und die Hoffnung auf jenseitiges

Glück, nehmen aus jüdischer Perspektive und in der Lagersituation eine andere Bedeutung an. Das wird vor allem bei der Sonderaufführung des Requiems für die Nationalsozialisten sichtbar, bei der das Werk zunehmend zum – freilich nur symbolischen – Ausdruck von Wut und Widerstand gerät. Der Begriff der künstlerischen Wahrheit bekommt hier seinen ganz spezifischen Sinn. Denn das künstlerisch evozierte Aufbegehren vermag die Realität des Holocaust einerseits zwar nicht zu verändern: Auch wenn das Nazi-Publikum einschließlich Eichmanns von der Vorführung beeindruckt ist, geht das ganze Ensemble bald darauf auf den Transport nach Auschwitz – womit die Novelle endet. Andererseits – und dies ist die eigentliche Botschaft des Werks – wird die Kunst hier demonstrativ als diejenige Sphäre vor Augen geführt, in der die humanen, ethischen und ästhetischen Werte hochgehalten werden, an denen es dem nationalsozialistischen Vernichtungsapparat vollends mangelte. Diese Werte in Verdis Werk erkannt und die Gegner damit unmittelbar konfrontiert zu haben, ist in der Novelle Schächters besondere Leistung. Auch wenn *Terezínské rekviem* mit der Deportation des ganzen Ensembles Richtung Auschwitz endet, haben dessen Mitglieder einen ganz entscheidenden Sieg über das Terrorregime errungen. Darin liegen zumindest Ansätze von Trost und Hoffnung.

Josef Bor war ein tschechisch-jüdischer Schriftsteller aus der Opfergeneration, der sich in seinen beiden Hauptwerken über den Holocaust bewusst für die Literatur als Form der Auseinandersetzung mit dem von ihm selbst Erlebten entschieden hat. Die Literatur mit ihren zentralen Komponenten der Fiktion und Imagination half ihm einerseits, den Holocaust aus einer Vielzahl von Perspektiven und mittels zahlreicher konkreter Details in seiner Totalität zu erfassen. Andererseits benutzte er künstlerisch-literarische Strategien, um die Kunst als machtvolles Mittel im Widerstand gegen ein barbarisches, unmenschliches System erfahrbar zu machen.

Literaturverzeichnis

Benz, Wolfgang 2013: Theresienstadt. Eine Geschichte von Täuschung und Vernichtung. München.
Bolton, Jonathan 2004: Josef Bor (Bondy). In: Efraim Sicher (ed.): Holocaust Novelists (Dictionary of Literary Biography. Vol. 299). Detroit, S. 58-64.
Bor, Josef 1962: Opuštěná panenka. 2. Aufl. (1. Aufl. 1961). Praha.

ders. 1963: Terezínské rekviem. Praha.
ders. 1964: Die verlassene Puppe. Aus d. Tschech. v. Elisabeth Borchardt. Berlin (Ost).
ders. 1965: Zasláno. In: Literární noviny 14,23 (5.6.1965), S. 2.
Dobeš, Karel (= dk) 1965: A tu nemohl jsem mlčet... Pět minut hovoru a dlouhá doba mlčení s Josef Borem. In: Svobodné slovo 21,72 (14.3.1965), S. 4.
Forst, Vladimír 1961: Kniha bolesti a hrůzy. In: Tvorba 26, S. 547-548.
Herrmannová, Eva 1965: [Rez.] Josef Bor, *Terezínské rekviem*. In: Lidové noviny 14,22 (29.5.1965), S. 4.
Holý, Jiří 2011: Židé a šoa v české a slovenské literatuře po druhé světové válce. In: Jiří Holý [u.a.]: Šoa v české literární a v kulturní paměti. Praha, S. 7-65.
ders. 2012: Die Juden und die Shoa in der tschechischen Nachkriegsliteratur. In: Reinhard Ibler (Hrsg.): Ausgewählte Probleme der polnischen und tschechischen Holocaustliteratur und -kultur. München – Berlin, S. 17-34.
Ibler, Reinhard 2015: Josef Bors Roman *Opuštěná panenka* zwischen Faktizität und Fiktionalität. In: Slovo a smysl 12,23, S. 80-93.
ders. 2016: Kunst im Holocaust. Zu Josef Bors Novelle *Terezínské rekviem* und ihrer Rezeption. In: Poznańskie Studia Slawistyczne [im Druck]
Karas, Joža 1985: Music in Terezín 1941-1945. New York.
Opelík, Jiří (= J.O.) 1961: *Opuštěná panenka* Josefa Bora. In: Kultura 5,24, S. 7.
Schreiner, Stefan 2007: „Seine Taten sind sein Denkmal". Zur Erinnerung an Josef Bor (1906-1979). In: Orientierung 71,1, S. 1-4.
Udolph, Ludger 2003: Josef Bors *Terezínské rekviem* (1963). In: Walter Schmitz (Hrsg.): Erinnerte Shoah. Die Literatur der Überlebenden. Dresden, S. 326-337.

Between Document and Art: Josef Bor's Works about the Holocaust

The article focuses on some questions concerning the position of literary texts about the Holocaust between the spheres of document and art (or rather poeticity). This is exemplified by the works of Josef Bor, a Czech-Jewish writer who was very popular in the sixties, but is nearly forgotten nowadays. The author went through the hell of Terezín, Auschwitz and Buchenwald. At Auschwitz, he lost his wife and two little daughters in the gas chambers. Bor did not write about his suffering in the form of an autobiography or a documentary text. Although not a professional writer, he made a clear decision for literature as a means of dealing with his experiences. He published the novel *Opuštěná panenka* (*The Abandoned Doll*) in 1961, the novella *Terezínské rekviem* (*The Terezín Requiem*) followed in 1963. *Opuštěná panenka* is, on the one hand, clearly based upon Bor's personal history during World War II. But the literary devices used in this novel (fictional persons and scenes, changing perspectives, narrative strategies and so on) helped the author to give a broad and multiperspective picture of the functioning of the Holocaust. Similar strategies can be observed in *Terezínské rekviem*. In this novella about the rehearsal and presentation of Verdi's *Messa da Requiem* at Terezín by the Jewish director Rafael Schächter several artistic devices are used, too, thus modifying the real events. Additionally, the central subject of the novella – Schächter's indomitable will in pursuing his artistic goal – contributes in fulfilling the work's aim: to demonstrate the power of art when facing a barbaric, inhuman system.

Jerzy Kosinskis „Autofiction" –
eine mögliche Strategie, über den Holocaust zu schreiben?

Hans-Christian Trepte, Leipzig

> I am a story-teller. There's nothing in my novels
> that isn't derivated (of my life) in some way.
> (Jerzy Kosinski, zit. nach Abrams 1984)

Jerzy Kosinski[1] gehört zu jenen Schriftstellern, die sich zur ‚Autofiktion' als einer besonderen Schreibstrategie, als einer besonderen Konvergenz von historischen Fakten und literarischer Fiktion bekannten. Unter Berücksichtigung der Debatte über das Schreiben nach Auschwitz (Adorno, Różewicz, Grynberg), stellt sich auch in Bezug auf die Persönlichkeit und das literarische Werk von Jerzy Kosinski, in erster Linie den Roman *The Painted Bird* betreffend, die Frage, ob ein solches Verfahren angebracht und legitim sei. Kann ein solcher „autobiographischer Pakt" (Lejeune 1994), die Wahrheit des Holocaust betreffend, überhaupt zwischen einem Autor und seinen Lesern geschlossen werden? Der polnisch-jüdische Schriftsteller Henryk Grynberg hatte noch die Meinung vertreten, dass die Literatur in erster Linie in Form einer „dokumentarischen Prosa über den Holocaust" Zeugnis ablegen sollte (Grynberg 1979, 116). Thematisiert wird von Kosinski allerdings nicht die *Auto(tanato)grafie*, die die polnische Literaturwissenschaftlerin Aleksandra Ubertowska aus Jacques Derridas *Demeure. Fiction and Testimony* übernommen hat, sondern es geht vielmehr um den Zufall oder das Glück des wundersamen Überlebens als eine Narration über das Grauen, die Qualen und den Tod aus der Perspektive eines Holocaustüberlebenden in Form einer autobiographisch angelegten Fiktion (vgl. Ubertowska 2014, 10). Bereits Derrida hatte darauf verwiesen, dass die (Auto-)Fiktion in der Lage sein kann, über eine „wirkliche Existenz" Zeugnis abzulegen (Blanchot/Derrida 2000, 96). Fiktion kann ein wesentlicher, geradezu notwendiger Bestandteil einer Zeugenaussage sein: „Fiction of a testimony is more than a testimony in which the witness swears to tell the truth, the whole truth, and nothing but the

---

[1] Von mir wird im Text durchgehend die – international übliche – amerikanische Schreibweise des Namens verwendet (Kosinski), nicht die polnische (Kosiński).

truth. [...] The possibility of literary fiction haunts so-called truthful, responsible, serious, real testimony as its proper possibility" (ebd., 72f.). Hinzu kommen Narrationen über Traumata der Holocausterfahrung, die Gedächtnislücken, Nichtaussprechbares und bewusst Verschwiegenes beinhalten können (vgl. Tal 1996).

Kosinski nahm sich allerdings nicht sofort des Themas Überleben im Holocaust an. Unter dem Pseudonym Joseph Novak hatte er zunächst zwei Texte veröffentlicht, in denen er sich als Kenner und Verfolgter des in seinem Heimatland Polen herrschenden Stalinistischen Regimes darstellte: *The Future Is Ours, Comrade. Conversations with the Russians* (1960) und *No Third Path* (1962). Zweck und Ziel dieser Bücher war es, die englischsprachigen Leser im Westen über das kollektive Leben im kommunistischen Osten Europas aufzuklären. Sein erster, nunmehr unter dem Namen Jerzy Kosinski[2] veröffentlichter Roman, *The Painted Bird* (1965), war zuerst von mehreren Verlagshäusern abgelehnt worden, bis er schließlich, als ein authentisches Holocaustdokument anerkannt, die Erlebnisse eines Holocaustüberlebenden aus der Sicht eines verfolgten und misshandelten Jungen in das Bewusstsein der Amerikaner einbringen konnte. *The Painted Bird* fand als ein wichtiges und authentisches Beispiel über den Holocaust weltweit Anerkennung. Der Tod und das Töten gehören während der Odyssee des Jungen durch das östliche Grenzland zu den Hauptmotiven des Romans, stets ist der Ich-Erzähler Opfer und Beobachter zugleich. Kosinskis Protagonist gelingt es, alle Verfolgungen, Folterungen und Qualen zu überleben, er passt sich an, ist ständig auf der Flucht. Letztendlich gelingt es ihm „seine Opfer- in eine Täter-Identität" zu verwandeln und sich „seinerseits Opfer zu suchen" (Behring/Brandt/Dózsai/Kliems 2004, 348). Kosinski beschränkte in der Erstausgabe seines Romans *The Painted Bird* Angaben über sich und sein Werk auf ein gebotenes Minimum. Seinem Roman stellt er eine kurze Information über Handlungsort und Protagonisten voran:

> In the first weeks of World War II, in the fall of 1939, a six-year-old boy from a large city in Eastern Europe was sent by his parents, like thousands of other children, to the shelter of a distant village. (Kosinski 1965, 3)

---

[2] Kosinskis ursprünglicher Name war Josek Lewinkopf. Den polnischen Namen (Kosinski) hatte sein Vater zum besseren Schutz seiner Familie angenommen.

Kosinski hatte beim Einreichen seines Textes dem Verlag mitgeteilt, dass sein Manuskript auf eigenen Erfahrungen beruhen würde: „ [...] fictional as the material may sound, it is straight autobiography" (Myers 1996, 59). Dementsprechend wurde das Buch vermarktet, das in den USA zu einem der wichtigsten Bücher über den Holocaust avancierte. *The Painted Bird*, in mehr als 40 Sprachen übersetzt, gewann zahlreiche Preise und wurde zu einem absoluten Bestseller. Kosinski hatte, ähnlich wie zahlreiche andere Schriftsteller im Exil, seinen Schreibstil wie auch seine Schreibstrategie den Erwartungen und dem Geschmack seines neuen Leserpublikums in den USA angepasst. Seine Ankunft in Amerika hatte Kosinski als einen absoluten Neubeginn, als eine einschneidende Veränderung seiner kulturellen Identität, seines Ichs angesehen. Dabei spielte der von ihm in den USA vollzogene Sprachwechsel eine wichtige Rolle. Die neue Sprache schuf, nicht zuletzt auch in Form eines Filters, eine Distanz zu seiner Kindheit; Sprache und Sprachwechsel wurden zu einer „wichtigen Determinante" seines literarischen Schaffens (Kliems/Trepte 2004, 384).

> It seemed that the language of my childhood and adolescence – Polish and Russian – carried a sort of mental suppression. By the time I was 25, an American, my infancy in English had ended and I discovered that English, my stepmother tongue, offered me a sense of revelation, of fulfillment, of abandonment – everything contrary to the anxiety my mother tongue evoked [...]. In English I don't make involuntary associations with my childhood. I think it is childhood that is often traumatic, not this or that war. (Teicholz 1993, 46)

Die bewusst gewählte englische Schreibsprache scheint den Autor von den Traumen seiner (jüdischen) Kindheit zu erlösen. Einer Therapie gleichend, befähigte ihn der Wechsel zu einer anderen Schreibsprache, bisher durch die Angst im Gedächtnis Blockiertes freizugeben, es künstlerisch-literarisch zu artikulieren:

> I know that there are certain areas of the Polish or Russian or English language which touch me emotionally more than others. [...] I have adopted an outlook which I might never have aquired had I decided to write in my own language. (ebd., 47)

Mit Hilfe der anderen Schreibsprache beabsichtigt der Autor sich selbst zu kontrollieren, zugleich möchte er aber auch ein deutliches Signal an seine Leser senden: „Each page I write tells me: Listen Jerzy, try to see something you have not seen in your life or in the lives of others around you. By talking to myself I also talk to my reader" (Kosinski 1995, 8). Der Schreibprozess in der anderen Sprache wurde für Kosinski zu einem „Spiel zwischen den einzelnen Bestandteilen seines Ichs, die, von ihm in Syntagmata gefasst, das doppelte Totalitarismuserlebnis heraufbeschworen" (Kliems/Trepte 2004, 384f.). So spielte der Schriftsteller ganz bewusst mit verschiedenen „Facetten seiner kulturellen Identität", ließ sich auf entsprechende Rollenspiele und auf das Tragen unterschiedlicher Masken ein: „Larvatus prodeo. I walk disguised (Descartes). Easily said, Pa!" (Kosinski 1991, 482).[3] Auf diese Weise versuchte er einen besonderen Platz und spezielle Aufmerksamkeit für sich und sein ungewöhnliches Leben, seine Lebensfacetten und Identitätsspiele in der amerikanischen Öffentlichkeit zu sichern, ohne dabei je seine jüdische Identität in Frage zu stellen: „You can change a family name and you can change the language, but you can never undo circumcision. Never, ever" (Teicholz 1993, 57).

Fiktionale „Umformungen" wie bei Kosinski fallen bei der Bearbeitung von erlebter Geschichte unterschiedlicher Art immer wieder ins Auge. In schreibstrategischer Hinsicht begleiten „fiktionale Narrationen Prozesse des Umdenkens und der Neubewertung" (Behring, 2004, 442). Nicht selten gab es bei einigen Autoren, so auch bei Kosinski, einen „starken Impetus der kritischen Abnabelung" von tradierten Betrachtungs- und Schreibweisen, der häufig mit einem erfolgreich vollzogenen Sprach- und Adressatenwechsel einherging, die „rigorose Distanzierung von allen mitgebrachten Zwängen" kam einer persönlichen und künstlerischen „Befreiung" zwischen Sinnsuche und Dekonstruktion gleich (ebd., 488).

In seinen Nachbemerkungen, *Afterward* (Kosinski 1976), gibt Kosinski einige wichtige Geheimnisse über sich als einen unabhängigen Geschichtenerzähler preis, der sich nicht nur auf eigenes Erlebtes und Gehörtes, sondern auch auf andere Quellen stützt. „I decided I too would set my work in a mythic domain, in the timeless fictive present, unrestrained by geography or history" (Kosinski 1995, xiii). Den Entstehungsprozess seines Buches charakterisierte Kosinski wie folgt: „[t]he result of a slow unfreezing of a mind long gripped by fear" (Landesman 1972, 8). Kosinski hatte mit zahlreichen, häufig sich widerspre-

---

[3] Letter to the editor (ohne Angabe des Namens). In: Kosinski is worth our support (New York Times, Nr. 23 v. 28. November 1982, S. 6).

chenden Äußerungen selbst zu den Verwirrungen um seine Person und sein Werk beigetragen. Dem aus der Tschechoslowakei stammenden Filmregisseur Miloš Forman zufolge ist es tatsächlich extrem schwierig herauszufinden, wo Kosinski aufhört seine „persönliche Geschichte" zu erzählen und wo „literarische Fiktion" beginnt (Lavers 1982,15). Dennoch wurde *The Painted Bird* auch weiterhin als ein „traditioneller Holocaust-Roman" (Vande Wyngaerde 2006/07, 1) bzw. als lebendiges Beispiel der Holocaustliteratur angesehen. Eine solche Meinung wurde nicht nur in der Literaturwissenschaft zunehmend modifiziert und revidiert. Im Falle von Kosinskis *The Painted Bird* konzentrierte man sich dabei nicht nur auf Fragen der (Auto-)Fiktion, sondern zunächst auch auf den besonderen Reifeprozess des zentralen Protagonisten: „Kosinskis text is a kind of bildungsroman manqué; it traces the boy's maturation but it is a maturation to disillusionment and, finally, if not nihilism, cynism" (Kremer 2003, 698). Zunehmend setzt sich die Auffassung durch, dass der Roman ein literarisches Werk sei. „It is a *literary* work, one that works not in the mechanical ticking of standard narrative but in the symbolic realm of myth" (Baumann 2014, 1). Eine ähnliche Meinung vertritt James Parker Sloan, Verfasser einer umfassenden Biographie über Jerzy Kosinski. In Kosinskis „autofiction" erkennt auch er eine besondere Schreibstrategie des Autors (vgl. Sloan 1996, 34). Grundlage der Erzählungen, vor allem aber des Romans *The Painted Bird* von Kosinski bildet Sloan zufolge „transparently autobiographical material", das der Wahrheit entspricht bzw. „near autobiographical" sein kann und von „emotional truth" zeuge (ebd., 149). Zumeist wurde Kosinski von der Kritik angelastet, seine literarischen Werke als authentisch bzw. später autofiktional auszugeben. In diesem Kontext spielt ein polarisierendes Enthüllungsbuch der polnischen Journalistin Joanna Siedlecka, *Czarny Ptasior* (2011; etwa: *Der Schwarze Piepmatz*), eine wichtige Rolle, in dem sie nachweist, dass Kosinski in *The Painted Bird* wie auch in zahlreichen anderen literarischen Werke sein Leben während der deutschen Besatzung frei erfunden habe und nichts von den vom ihm vorgegebenen Dingen über sein Leben in Polen der Wirklichkeit entsprach.

Die Darstellung des Holocausts als Fake ist nicht allein Kosinski anzulasten. Eine besondere und nicht zu unterschätzende Rolle spielten seine Kritiker, Rezensenten, Fürsprecher und Mentoren:

> If there was a „hoax" being operated as regards *The Painted Bird*, it was being operated not by Kosinski but by Wiesel and those others who would have *The Painted Bird* be a Holocaust document – which is explicitly to say to have *The Painted Bird* be intentionally, directly, exclusively, a Holocaust text exclusively about the Jewish experience during the war. (Baumann 2014, 1)

Dem entspricht im Übrigen auch ein Statement von Kosinski selbst:

> They wanted to cast me in the role of spokesman for my generation, especially for those who had survived the war; but for me survival was an individual action, that earned the survivor the right to speak only for himself. (Kosinski 1976, xiii)

In der Tat war es kein geringerer als der international bekannte Holocaustüberlebende Elie Wiesel gewesen, der Kosinskis Roman *The Painted Bird* zunächst abgelehnt und ihn als reine Fiktion bezeichnet hatte und dann seine Meinung änderte. „I thought it [*The Painted Bird*, HCT] was a fiction, and when he told me it was autobiography I tore up my review and wrote one a thousand times better" (Vice 2000, 78). Erst nachdem Kosinski auf den autobiographischen Charakter verwiesen hatte, bezeichnete Wiesel das Buch als eine „Chronik der physischen Gewaltanwendung" und „des Horrors im Holocaust": „If we ever need proof that Auschwitz was more a concept than a name, it is given to us here with shattering eloquence in *The Painted Bird*" (Wiesel 1965, 46).

Nach einsetzenden Zweifeln und Anfechtungen, die Authentizität, den autobiographischen Wert und die damit im Zusammenhang stehenden literarischen Konfusionen seines Romans *The Painted Bird* betreffend, begann Kosinski seine eigenen Vorstellungen über „autofiction" darzulegen. Von ausschlaggebender Bedeutung war diesbezüglich ein in der New Yorker Zeitschrift *Village Voice* 1982 erschienener Artikel unter dem Titel *Tainted Words*. Die Verfasser, Geoffrey Stokes und Eliot Fremont-Smith, bezichtigten Kosinski des Plagiats und verwiesen darauf, dass sein Buch nicht auf eigenen Erlebnisse basiere (vgl. Stokes/Fremont-Smith 1982, 41ff.). In einem Interview hatte Kosinski zunächst allgemein seine Auffassung von Fiktion erläutert: „[…] fiction is a very democratic enterprise. It doesn't impose. It doesn't suggest. It merely says, ‚Suspend disbelief. My name is fiction.' I leave morality to the reader" (Tepa Lupack 2012, 166f.). In seinem Text *Death in Cannes* geht Kosinski schließlich näher auf den Begriff „autofiction" ein und verweist darauf, wie sich Fiktion und Autobiographie gegenseitig bedingen und überschneiden können (vgl. Kosinski 1986, 82). Selbst die authentischen Erinnerungen von Holocaustüberlebenden beinhalten für Kosinski stets auch fiktionale Elemente, Erinnerungen selbst können im Prozess des Erinnerns zur Fiktion werden (vgl. Sloan 1996, 217). Den Begriff „autofiction" bezieht Kosinski auf sein eigenes literarisches Werk, sowohl auf seinen Erfolgsroman *The Painted Bird* als auch auf sein letztes Werk, *The Hermit of 69th Street*:

> The premise for autofiction was established with notes I wrote as an appendix for my first novel in 1969. In the notes, I said that the writer incorporated the fragments of objective reality into a new literary dimension, but took from outside of himself only what he is capable of creating in his imagination anyhow. Perversely, I can also take from outside things that in my fiction can exist as a fact of my life, since clearly I exist only as a fiction writer. My personality, a certain vision of myself, and therefore I sell as a storyteller – is it a one-to-one-conversion? It is not, since no such transfer can take place in literature. Is it a revisitation of my life? No, it is not. Rather it's a vision. As I wrote back in 1965, *The Painted Bird* is a vison of myself as a child, not a reexamination or a revisitation. (Tepa Lupack 2012, 167)

Die Gründe für seine Wendung hin zur (Auto-)Fiktion begründete Kosinski folgendermaßen:

> The reason that I moved to fiction, however, was because fiction is a democratic form of conveyance of ideas. It identifies itself from the outset as fiction, not as fact. What it says to the reader is this: „It is up to you. Take it or leave it. Project yourself or not. Turn the page or not". (ebd., 113)

Eine umfassende Erwiderung auf alle gegen ihn gerichteten Vorwürfe sollte Kosinskis letztes großes literarisches Werk sein, *The Hermit of 69th Street. The Working Papers of Norbert Kosky* (1988, 1991), an dem er ca. acht Jahre gearbeitet hatte.[4] Auch hier nahm Kosinski noch einmal zum Problem der „autofiction" Stellung. Im Vorwort zu der vom Autor revidierten Ausgabe von 1991 heißt es:

> Dubbed an „autofiction by the author" […] It is a compulsive adventure in which Kosinski explores the complex universe of one Norbert Kosky, a survivor of the Holocaust, immigrant to America from the only slightly mythical country of Ruthenia, and successful but tortured writer in search of spiritual order and freedom, especially the freedom to be himself in the ultimate sense. (Kosinski 1991, 5)

---

[4] Kosinski beging im Mai 1991 auf spektakuläre Weise Selbstmord.

Das Buch kann als eine „postmodernistische Version der Migrationsliteratur" angesehen werden (Kliems/Trepte 2004, 384). Immerhin beabsichtigte Kosinski mit seinem Roman eine völlig neue Art von Literatur zu schaffen, eine Literatur, in der Geschichte, Kulturgeschichte, literarische Fiktion und Autobiographie scheinbar problemlos miteinander verflochten werden sollten. So lässt sich der Verfasser auch auf ein Spiel mit seiner eigenen Biographie ein, er erforscht eine Vielzahl von literarischen Bezügen, experimentiert mit eigenen literarischen Analysen und vielfältigen Bezügen auf andere literarische Werke. Durch häufig „überbordende Zitationen" trägt das Werk Züge eines „enzyklopädischen Nachschlagewerks" (ebd.). Der Name des Protagonisten, Norbert Kosky, deutet auf die Person des Autors selbst hin: „Der Holocaustüberlebende Kosky, ein in die USA emigrierter Pole, ist Kosińskis Alter ego (KO-sin-SKY) aus dessen Namen symbolhaft die Silbe ‚sin' (das engl. Wort für ‚Sünde') eliminiert ist" (ebd.). Bedingt durch den Tod von Kosky, kann kein Roman im eigentlichen Sinne entstehen, es muss zwangsläufig bei den „Arbeitspapieren" („working papers") Koskys bleiben. Das Vermischen von Wahrheit und Fiktion erfährt in *The Hermit of 69th Street* einen Höhepunkt. Der Holocaust wird in einen breiten, tiefschürfenden historischen und kulturgeschichtlichen Kontext gestellt. So weist das Buch zahlreiche Bezüge und Verweise auf den Judaismus, auf die Geschichte, Kultur und Sprache der osteuropäischen Juden und ihre komplizierten Beziehungen u.a. auch zu Polen auf.

Wie bereits erwähnt, kann die Auffassung, dass Kosinskis Roman *The Painted Bird* zur authentischen Holocaustliteratur gehört, heute nicht mehr gehalten werden. Dazu haben u.a. auch komparatistische Untersuchungen beigetragen (so z.B. Douglas 1995), die u.a. den ebenfalls aus Polen stammenden amerikanischen Autor Louis Begleys (Ludwik Begleiter) und dessen Erfolgsroman *War Time Lies* (1991; *Lügen in Zeiten des Krieges)*, auch unter dem Aspekt von „The Testimony Of The Liar/Survivor" (Douglas 1995, 385) vergleichend analysieren. In diesem Kontext kann auch Kosinskis autofiktionales Schreiben über den Holocaust als die „Profession eines Lügners" („the liar's profession") (Sloan 1996, 53) angesehen werden. Hinzu kommen weiterführende Forschungen zum autobiographischen Schreiben und zu „autofiction" (z.B. Czermińska 2000, Michineau 2010), aber auch entsprechende Einträge in Nachschlagewerken wie *Holocaust Literature. An Encyclopedia of Writers and their Works* (vgl. Kremer 2003, 265ff.).

Serge Doubrovsky, der versuchte, den Begriff „autofiction"[5] näher zu bestimmen, hatte u.a. darauf verwiesen, dass der Begriff bereits vor ihm existiert hat (vgl. Doubrovsky 2014). Unter „autofiction" verstand er „Mischungszustände zwischen Fiktion und Autobiographie" (Doubrovsky 2008, 123). Seine Auffassungen wurden durch Gérard Genette und seinen Schüler Vincente Colonna erweitert.[6] Einen wichtigen Forschungsbeitrag leistete Colonna mit seiner 2004 erschienenen Dissertation *Autofiction et autres mythomanies littéraires* wie auch mit seinem zuvor erschienenen Beitrag *L'autofiction (essai sur la fictionalisation de soi en Littérature* (= Colonna 1989). Im germanistischen Bereich beschäftigt sich u.a. Martina Wagner-Engelhaaf mit „Auto(r)fiktion" als einem „literarischen Verfahren zur Selbstkonstruktion" (Wagner-Engelhaaf 2013, 7).

Die Faszination für Jerzy Kosinski und sein literarisches Schaffen hält bis heute an. Davon zeugen u.a. die BBC-Dokumentation *The Passionate Life Eye: Sex. Lies and Jerzy Kosinski*[7] wie auch die Aufführung des Stücks *More Lies About Jerzy* 2001 am Vineyard Theatre in New York.[8] Verwiesen sei in diesem Zusammenhang aber auch auf das Buch von Janusz Głowacki *Good night Dżerzi* (2010), mit dem der Verfasser, der selbst lange Zeit im amerikanischen Exil gelebt hatte, einen wichtigen Beitrag zur weiteren Entmythologisierung Amerikas leistet. Zugleich scheint das Buch aber auch eine Art Abgesang auf die schillernde Persönlichkeit und das literarische Werk seines Landsmannes, über dessen Aufstieg und Fall zu sein. Kosinskis polnischer Vorname Jerzy ist im Titel von Głowackis Buch phonetisch der amerikanischen Aussprache angepasst und in polnischer Schreibweise wiedergegeben: Dżerzi. Unter dem Vorwand, einen Film über Kosinski zu drehen, hatte sich Głowacki auf eine Suche nach Wahrheit und Mystifikation begeben. Dabei geht auch Głowacki interessanter Weise auf die besondere Rolle ein, die Eli Wiesel in der ‚Holocaust-Fiktion' Kosinskis gespielt hat:

---

[5] http://www.autofiction.org/index.php?post/2008/10/17/DOUBROVSKY-Serge (10.2.2016).
[6] Vgl. den Konferenzband *Autofiction et Cie* (= Doubrovsky/Lecarme/Lejeune 1993).
[7] http://www.paleycenter.org/collection/item/?q=holocaust&p=4&item=T:41456 (10.2.2016).
[8] http://www.vineyardtheatre.org/more-lies-about-jerzy/ (10.2.2016)

[...] I Wiesel się podniecił, bo na tej podwiązce miałeś napis „Holocaust". I go przekonałeś, że to dokładnie twoja historia. [...] On podarł tę kiepską recenzję i napisał nową, entuzjastyczną. [...] I co się stało? Taki drobiazg, że książka się do razu zrobiła arcydziełem... [...] I wtedy wszyscy krytycy sie za nim ruszyli, zostałeś Beckettem, Genetem, Kafką i Dostojewskim w jednej osobie. (Głowacki 2010, 51)[9]

„Autofiction" ist inzwischen als eine bevorzugte Schreibstrategie immer mehr zu einer anerkannten und weitverbreiteten Tendenz, auch in der zeitgenössischen polnischen Literatur über den Holocaust, geworden. Dabei reichen die angebrachten künstlerisch-literarischen Mitteln von der Phantastik über die Groteske und das Absurde bis zur „Problematik Holocaust und Comic" (vgl. Trepte 2015). Immer häufiger wird das jüdische Thema bzw. der Holocaust auch als *einer* von vielen Handlungssträngen und Motiven in einem breiten historischen, gesellschaftspolitischen und ästhetischen Kontext vorgestellt (u.a. Joanna Bator, Bożena Keff, Igor Ostachowicz). Dabei versuchen nicht nur die Vertreter der Kinder- und Enkelgeneration von Holocaustüberlebenden, sich einen eigenen, unverstellten Zugang zum „jüdischen Thema" und zum „Holocaust" zu verschaffen. Nicht selten kommt es dabei auch zu einer Selbstdarstellung und Selbstvermarktung, zu beabsichtigten wie „unbeabsichtigten Autofiktionen". Das ermöglicht u.a. auch Rückschlüsse auf die Intentionen des Autors selbst (Lubas-Bartoszyńska 2005, 634). Um Zugang und Verständnis für den Holocaust bei der jüngeren Generation zu wecken, reichen dokumentarische Aufzeichnungen und Interviews von Überlebenden nicht mehr aus. Das Ungeheuerliche, das Unbegreifliche kann nicht mehr nur in bloßer Gestalt von Tatsachen, Fakten und Zeugenaussagen nahegebracht werden, es muss auch emotional in Form einer interessant erzählten Geschichte nachvollziehbar werden. Eine Bestätigung im Sinne von Jerzy Kosinskis „autofiction"?

> The extreme discrepancy between the facts as I knew them and the exiles' and diplomats' hazy, unrealistic view of the world bothered me intensively. I began to reexamine my past and decided to turn from my studies of social sciences to fiction. Unlike poli-

---

[9] „[...] Und Wiesel hat sich aufgegeilt, denn auf diesem Strumpfband hattest Du die Aufschrift ‚Holocaust'. Und du hast ihn überzeugt, dass das genau deine Geschichte ist. [...] Er hat seine miese Rezension zerrissen und eine neue, enthusiastische geschrieben. [...] Und was passierte? So eine Lappalie, dass das Buch sofort zu einem Meisterwerk wurde. Und dann folgten ihm alle Kritiker, du wurdest Beckett, Genet, Kafka und Dostojewski in einer Person" (Übersetzung HCT).

tics, which offered only extravagant promises of a utopian future, I knew fiction could present lives as they are truly lived. (Kosinski 1995, xi)

Literaturverzeichnis

Abrams, Garry 1984: Jerzy Kosinski Leaves 'em Amused, Bemused and Confused. In: Los Angeles Times, Sec. 5:1 (14th November 1984), S. 12.
Baumann, A.E.M 2014: Jerzy Kosinski's *The Painted Bird*. http://hatterscabinet.com/pages/kospaint.html (10.2.2016).
Begley, Louis 1991: Wartime Lies. New York (dt. 1994: Lügen in Zeiten des Krieges. Frankfurt am Main).
Behring, Eva 2004: Paradigmenwechsel in der Schreibstrategie – Elemente einer Ästhetik des Exils? In: dies. – Alfrun Kliems – Hans-Christian Trepte (Hrsg.): Grundbegriffe und Autoren osteuropäischer Exilliteraturen 1945 – 1989. Ein Beitrag zur Systematisierung und Typologisierung. Stuttgart, S. 439-529.
Behring, Eva – *Brandt*, Juliane – *Dózsai*, Mónika – *Kliems*, Alfrun 2004: Kulturelle Identität. Zwischen Selbstbehauptung und Akkulturation. In: Eva Behring – Alfrun Kliems – Hans-Christian Trepte (Hrsg.): Grundbegriffe und Autoren osteuropäischer Exilliteraturen 1945 – 1989. Ein Beitrag zur Systematisierung und Typologisierung. Stuttgart, S. 286-348.
Blanchot, Maurice – *Derrida*, Jacques 2000: Demeure. Fiction and Testimony. The Instant of Death. Stanford.
Colonna, Vincente 1989: L'autofiction (essai sur la fictionalisation de soi en Littérature). In: Linguistics, École des Hautes Études en Sciences Sociales. tel-00006609.pdf.
ders. 2004: Autofiction et autres mythomanies littéraires. Paris.
Czermińska, Małgorzata 2000: Autobiograficzny trójkąt. Świadectwo, Wyznanie i Wyzwanie. Kraków.
Doubrovsky, Serge 2008: Nah am Text. In: Kultur & Gespenster. Autofiktion 7, S. 123-133.
ders. 2014 [1977]: L'autofiction existait avant moi. Simplement je lui ai donné un nom. http://www.telerama.fr/livre/serge-doubrovsky-l-autofiction-existait-avant-moi-simplement-je-lui-ai-donne-un-nom,116115.php (10.2.2016).
ders. – *Lecarme*, Jacques – *Lejeune*, Philippe (ed.) 1993: Autofiction et Cie. Cahiers RITM. Paris.
Douglas, Laurence 1995: Wartime Lies. Securing The Holocaust in Law And Literature. In: Yale Journal of Law & the Humanities 7,2, Art. 4, S. 367-396.
Głowacki, Janusz 2010: Good night Dżerzi. Warszawa.
Grynberg, Henryk 1979: The Holocaust in Polish Literature. In: Notre Dame English Journal 2 (April 1979), S. 115-140.
Kliems, Alfrun – *Trepte*, Hans-Christian 2004: Der Sprachwechsel. Existentielle Grunderfahrungen des Scheiterns und des Gelingens. In: Eva Behring – Alfrun Kliems – Hans-Christian Trepte (Hrsg.): Grundbegriffe und Autoren osteuropäischer Exilliteraturen 1945 – 1989. Ein Beitrag zur Systematisierung und Typologisierung. Stuttgart, S. 349-392.
Kosinski, Jerzy 1960 [publ. unter d. Pseudonym Joseph Novak]: The Future Is Ours, Comrade. Conversations with the Russians. New York (dt. 1961: Uns gehört die Zukunft, Genossen. Gespräche mit russischen Menschen. Bern).

ders. 1962 [publ. unter d. Pseudonym Joseph Novak]: No Third Path. New York (dt. 1964: Homo Sowjeticus. Der Mensch unter Hammer und Sichel. Bern – Stuttgart – Wien).
ders. 1965: The Painted Bird. Boston (dt. 1965: Der bemalte Vogel. Zürich).
ders. 1976: Afterward. In: The Painted Bird. Second Edition. New York, pp. ix-xxvi.
ders. 1986: Death in Cannes. In: Esquire Magazine. Documentary Section 3 (March 1986), S. 82-89.
ders. 1988 und 1991: The Hermit of 69th Street. The Working Papers of Norbert Kosky. New York.
ders. 1995: Passing By. Selected Essays 1962 – 1991. New York.
Kremer, S. Lilian 2003: Holocaust Literature. An Encyclopedia of Writers and their Works. Vol. I. New York – London.
Landesman, Rocco 1972: The Art of Fiction. In: The Paris Review 46, S. 8.
Lavers, Norman 1982: Jerzy Kosinski. Boston.
Lejeune, Philippe 1994: Der autobiographische Pakt. Aus d. Franz. v. Wolfram Bayer u. Dieter Hornig. Frankfurt am Main.
Lubas-Bartoszyńska, Regina 2005: Kłopoty z autofikcja – Mimowolne autofikcje Romy Ligockiej. In Ruch Literacki, z. 6, S. 633-641.
Michineau, Stéphanie 2010: Autofiction. Entre transgression et innovation. Ecritures Evolutives. In: Presses universitaires de Toulouse: Le Mirail, (6) juin 2010, S. 17-23.
Myers, David G. 1996: A Life Beyond Repair. In: First Things. October 1996, S. 58-64.
Siedlecka, Joanna 2011: Czarny ptasior. Warszawa.
Sloan, James Parker 1996: Jerzy Kosinski. A Biography. New York.
Stokes, Geoffrey – *Fremont-Smith*, Eliot 1982: Tainted Words. In: The Village, Nr. 1 (22nd June 1982), S. 41-43.
Tal, Kali 1996: Worlds of Hurt. Reading the Literature of Trauma. Cambridge.
Teicholz, Tom 1993: Conversations with Jerzy Kosinski. Jackson.
Tepa Lupack, Barbara 2012: Oral Pleasure. Kosinski as Storyteller. New York.
Trepte, Hans-Christian 2015: Einige Bemerkungen zur Problematik Holocaust und Comic im polnischen Kontext. In: Jiří Holý (ed.): The Aspects of Genres in the Holocaust Literatures in Central Europe. Praha, S. 143-155.
Ubertowska, Aleksandra 2014: Holokaust. Auto(tanato)grafie. Warszawa.
Vande Wyngaerde, Annelies 2006/07: Holocaust Literature. Reality and Fiction in Jerzy Kosinski's *The Painted Bird* and Raymond Federman's *The Voice in the Closet*. lib.ugent.be/.../RUG01_001228060_2010_0001_AC.pdf (10.2.2015).
Vice, Sue 2000: Holocaust Fiction. London – New York.
Wagner-Engelhaaf, Martina 2013: Auto(r)fiktion. Literarische Verfahren zur Selbstkonstruktion. Bielefeld.
Wiesel, Elie 1965: Rev. of *The Painted Bird* by Jerzy Kosinski. In: New York Times Book Review 31, S. 46-48.

Jerzy Kosinski's „Autofiction" – a Possible Strategy to Write about the Holocaust?

The American writer of Polish-Jewish descent Jerzy Kosinski was thought to be one of the world's great writers and intellectuals. He was acclaimed as an extraordinary, heroic survivor and witness of the Holocaust. Following different scandals Kosinski was denounced as a literary fraud. The long controversy and dispute on truth and fiction was closely related to his bestseller, *The Painted Bird* (1965). Was it a Holocaust document, as stated by Elie Wiesel, or was it a mixture of personal biography and literary fiction or even a testimony of a (Jewish) liar and Holocaust survivor? After many attacks on him Kosinski stated, that his novel would be „autofiction", a vision of himself as a child. In his last novel, *The Hermit of 69th Street*, Kosinski tried to explain himself and his work, giving also a definition of his writing strategy. In contemporary literature such an autofictional approach is an often used method to express the experience of holocaust survivors of the second and third generation, to explain the horror of war and genocide especially to the younger generation of readers.

Arnošt Lustig's *Colette, dívka z Antverp* – Between Historical Facts and Fiction

Jiří Holý, Praha

1.

This article will present some critical reflections on Arnošt Lustig's novel *Colette, dívka z Antverp* (*Colette, a Girl from Antwerp*). The first version was published in 1992, the rewritten and extended second version in 2001, and the third in 2005. The novel is a part of the so called Jewish Trilogy (*Colette, Tanga* and *Lea*). Colette is a Belgian Jewish woman who is arrested and taken to Auschwitz, where she falls in love with Vili Feld, a Czech Jew. But she is also abused by a sadistic German guard named Weissacker. The ending of the story is left open, but it is clear that Colette would not survive.[1]

> Zůstane po ní méně než ozvěna původního výkřiku, šepotu o lásce, přátelství a solidaritě, o odvaze, strachu a cti. […] Colette. Popel. Colette Cohenová. Číslo C 324459-69 vytetované na jejím levém předloktí. Ani to už ne. (Lustig 2014 , 196f.)[2]

The first version was presented only as *Colette, dívka z Antverp* (*Colette, a Girl from Antwerp*). The second as well as the third versions were subtitled *The Jewish Trilogy II*. The author connected this work with two other pieces of prose depicting beautiful young women, which were victims of the Nazis and the Holocaust. The character Vili Feld appears in all of them. The second edition of the third version of Colette from 2013, released simultaneously with the film version directed by Milan Cieslar, was subtitled *Strhující román o lásce silnější než smrt* (*A Riveting Novel about a Love Stronger than Death*).

Arnošt Lustig survived the Holocaust. When he was sixteen, he was imprisoned in Terezín, then for a short time in Auschwitz (where *Colette* is set), and later in Buchenwald. Thus for him, literature about the Shoah became the topic of his entire life. His first works are among his best: the short stories *Noc a*

---

[1] This article was supported by the research grant FF UK PRVOUK P13.
[2] „An echo of her original scream remains behind her. The whisper about love, friendship and solidarity, about courage, fear and honor. […] Colette. Ashes. Colette Cohen. Not even number C 324459-69 that was tattooed on her left forearm. Not even that". (All translations from Czech by J.H.)

naděje (1958; *Night and Hope*; translated into English in 1962) and *Démanty noci* (1958; translated into English as *Diamonds in the Night* in 1962, a new translation as *Diamonds of the Night* in 1977). Lustig's characters are not heroic figures, mainly in his first short stories. They are often outsiders, children, or old men and women. Despite the difficulties which these people must repeatedly undergo, donning an outer shell just to survive, the majority of them try to maintain basic moral values.

Arnošt Lustig's later books however, accentuate the more abrasive side of life in the camps (violence, brutality, homosexual prostitution, lack of unity among the prisoners, etc.). He often records the stories of young Jewish girls and women. Their beauty and youth form a moving contrast to the horrors of the Shoah. He first applied this approach in *Dita Saxová* (1962; translated into English in 1966) and *Modlitba pro Kateřinu Horovitzovou* (1965; *A Prayer for Kateřina Horovitzová*; translated into English in 1973), and also to *Nemilovaná* (1979; *The Unloved*; translated into English in 1985), the story of a young Jewish prostitute in Terezín, written as a fictional diary, capturing the period from August to December 1943 with both naïveté and abrasive matter-of-factness.

2.

The extermination camp in Auschwitz-Birkenau is described in many scenes in *Colette*. Most of them are violent and cruel. They provide a strong contrast to Colette's beauty and her love for Vili. Some critics stressed the author's personal experience of Nazi concentration camps as a guarantee of the novel's authenticity and credibility.[3] Nevertheless, some implausible and untruthful situations and speeches can be found in the novel, when compared with known historical facts. Several examples are given below.

In the first chapter Colette learns about the decisions of the office of the commandant Rudolf Höss. It is in October 1944. Around the same time Colette says to Vili that prisoners are repairing Höss's villa in Auschwitz (ibid., 75). But Rudolf Höss was the commandant of Auschwitz from May 1940 to November 1943. In October 1944 the commandant was Josef Kramer. However, Höss be-

---

[3] So Alena Badinová: http://www.klubknihomolu.cz/62233/colette-%E2%80%93-laska-za-ostnatym-dratem/ (3.2.2016); Jarmila Stráníková: http://www.kukatko.cz/colette/ (3.2.2016).

came a symbol of Auschwitz. After the war, he was captured by British troops and appeared at the Tribunal of Nuremberg as a witness. He spoke openly about the gas chambers and the process of extermination in Auschwitz. Later he was handed over to Polish authorities. He was accused of mass murder, and sentenced to death and hanged in Auschwitz in April 1947. While awaiting execution, he wrote his autobiography, where he describes in detail his activities, the camp and system of extermination in Auschwitz and other camps (*Kommandant in Auschwitz*, in German 1958). Among other things, his life inspired the famous novel *Death Is My Trade* (in French *La mort est mon métier*, 1952) by Robert Merle.

In the same chapter at the beginning of the novel, the narrator recounts Colette's arrival to the camp. It is January 1944. The transport from Belgium to Auschwitz was terrible. The German guard Rottenführer Kollwitz unloads the frozen children's corpses onto trucks from the transport. „V lednu přijel její transport z Antverp. V karanténě umrzlo dva tisíce dětí. […] Rottenführer vystřeloval ještě přede dvěma roky na Antverpy a Londýn rakety V-1 a V-2" (ibid., 7).[4] Belgium, including Antwerp, was occupied by the Germans in May 1940 and liberated in September 1944. Therefore, to fire rockets at Antwerp in 1941 or 1942 would have meant to shoot at Germany's own soldiers. V-1 rockets were being launched against targets in London at that time. But V-2 rockets were also launched against London and later against a liberated Antwerp beginning in September 1944.

Vili and Colette speak together French with some German words. The narrator writes several times that Colette's native language is French (ibid., 9, 45, 52: „potřebovala šeptat slova ve svém jazyku, do kterého se narodila"; „milostný šepot francouzských slov").[5] However, Antwerp is not a part of French-speaking, but of Flemish-speaking Belgium. Therefore, Colette's native language should be Flemish. But, like in the previously mentioned case, the author works with familiar and conventional symbols. French women and French lan-

---

[4] „Colette's transport arrived from Antwerp in January. Two thousand children froze to death in quarantine. […] Two years ago, Rottenführer Kollwitz fired V-1 and V-2 rockets at Antwerp and London".

[5] „she needed to whisper words in the language in which she was born", „love whispers in French".

guage tend to be connected with erotica and sex. Therefore Colette's mother tongue in the novel is French.

In the second chapter, the narrator describes Colette's visit to Vili Feld's block. She spends the night with him in his separated room. When Colette leaves „věděla jako V.F., že než před úsvitem projde do Odvšivovací stanice, bude tu o deset tisíc neznámých méně, stejně jako včera a jako zítra, už od roku jedenačtyřicet" (ibid., 49).[6] In fact, only in the summer of 1944, during the Hungarian transports, such a large number of victims was gassed (about 9,000 per day). Mass killing in the gas chambers was not possible until 1943, after the completion of the whole complex of gas chambers and crematoria in Auschwitz-Birkenau. If ten thousand people had died daily from 1941 until 1944 in Auschwitz, the total number of victims would have had to be more than ten million. In fact, it was approximately one million. Moreover, the narrator repeats these false data at the end of the novel. He tells one and half million people were killed only during Colette's stay in Auschwitz-Birkenau (ibid., 194).[7]

The main antagonist in the novel, Nazi warden Weissacker has a younger brother. He is a Luftwaffe pilot and is killed during *Operation Sea Lion*, the Invasion of Great Britain (ibid., 63). In reality, *Operation Sea Lion* was only a German plan to invade Britain. The German Luftwaffe didn't destroy the British Royal Air Force (RAF) or establish superiority during the Battle of Britain. In September 1940 *Sea Lion* was postponed indefinitely and was never carried out.

Weissacker joined the Nazi Wehrmacht during the campaign to Poland in September 1939, „začali *Blitzkrieg*, který už trvá šest let" (ibid., 67).[8] Six years from September 1939 should be September 1945, but the plot of the novel takes place in 1944.

---

[6] When Colette is leaving and „is passing in front of the Delousing Station before dawn she knows as well as V.F. that there would be ten thousand fewer unknown people here, just like yesterday, and like tomorrow, ever since the year 1941".

[7] „Po devět měsíců viděla pomíjivost a bezcennost života z první ruky. Během její existence v Auschwitz-Birkenau zaplynovali, ubili a vyhladověli Němci přes půldruhého milionu lidí".

[8] „started the *Blitzkrieg* that has lasted for six years".

3.

Naturally, each novel with historical themes, including *Colette* can build imaginative scenes and situations. Nevertheless these inaccuracies of time and factual data cause Lustig's fictional world to lose some of its claimed authenticity. Scholars of fiction theory argue that any literary textual world is fictional. Although these images are related to the actual world in which we live, they have their own specific laws. According to Lubomír Doležel

> by composing a written or oral text, the author creates a fictional world that was not available prior to this act [of writing, J.H.]. Textual poiesis, like all human activity, occurs in the actual world; however, it contructs fictional realms whose properties, structures, and modes of existence are, in principle, independent of the properties, structures, and existential mode of actuality. (Doležel 1998, 23)

In this sense, Arnošt Lustig would have a right to write anything within his fictional world. But Lustig's work was presented as a true depiction of Auschwitz, not as an autonomous literary construction. Therefore it refers also to the *mimesis* as well as to the actual world. It depends on the reader's approach. If we read *Colette* as fiction treating it „*as if"/„als ob"* it is true even when we know that it is not true, we can accept all these historical inaccuracies mentioned as a part of an imaginary fictional world. But the Holocaust was an event that became a generally recognized embodiment of evil, inhumanity and immorality. Most readers perceive it as something still alive and factual. Arnošt Lustig as a Holocaust survivor acts as a guarantor of the truthfulness and accuracy of his works. That's why we treat the situations and characters in *Colette* as true and credible.

4.

Nevertheless, the credibility of the presented figures in *Colette* disappears very often. In the second chapter, the narrator remarks that Colette „[...] znala muže ze Sonderkommanda, kteří pracovali v krematoriu, pekaře z pekáren, ševce z ševcáren, vykladače vagonů, zřízence z rampy" (Lustig 2014, 65).[9] Colette worked in the so-called Canada square, where belongings of those arriving were

---

[9] „[…] knew men from the Sonderkommando who worked in the crematoria, bakers from bakeries, cobblers from shoemaker's workshops, wagon unloaders and assistants from the ramp".

sorted, and valuables like money, gold and gems collected. She was an ordinary inmate, not a capo and could not have had such contacts. In particular, men from the Sonderkommando were strictly isolated from other prisoners. It was completely improbable for her to know all these people. Nevertheless, these contacts allow the narrator to inform readers about various events in Auschwitz. Similarly, Colette reflects her situation in the fifth chapter:

> Podle Himmlerova tajného rozkazu se mělo přestat plynovat. Budou chtít vyhodit plynové komory do povětří? Zatím se plynovalo dál jako předtím. Nezdálo se, že by esesačky byly v říjnu méně zpupné než v září. (ibid., 147)[10]

How could Colette gain access to this secret information? Even most of the Nazi guards didn't know about it.

Vili Feld, too, is similarly omniscient. „Vili věděl, že je tu padělatelská dílna, kde nacisti vyrábějí anglické a americké peníze..." (ibid., 73).[11] Here, the narrator is referring to the closely guarded secret *Operation Bernhard* whose aim was to destabilize the British economy by counterfeiting British banknotes and dropping them over Britain from planes. Only a few notable Nazis knew about it. It took around forty years, before publications and films have been released on this subject (Adolf Burger, *The Devil's Workshop*, initially in Czech in 1983; an Austrian Oscar-winning film *The Counterfeiters*, directed by Stefan Ruzowitzky, 2007). It is worth noting that the main forgery workshop was in Sachsenhausen, not in Auschwitz.

The character of Vili Feld appeared in several of Lustig's works since the 1950s. He is the main figure in the novella *Můj známý Vili Feld* (1961; *My Friend Vili Feld*), which was originally published as a short story in *Ulice ztracených bratří* (1959; *Street of Lost Brothers*). Here Vili Feld is presented ambiguously. On the one hand, he is a pragmatist and boaster who always knows what to do in occupied Prague, in Terezín and in Auschwitz. On the other hand, he is an unhappy loser and emigrant whom the narrator meets after years in Rome. Vili Feld was to become the main character in Lustig's announced novel

---

[10] „According to Himmler's secret order, gassing should be stopped. Will they want to blow up the gas chambers? Meanwhile the gas chambers continued working the same as before. In October, SS-women did not seem less arrogant than in September".

[11] „Vili knew that there was a forgery workshop where Nazis made English and American money...".

Král promluvil, neřekl nic (*The King Spoke, Said Nothing*). This long-awaited work, however, was never released, and Vili appeared in several shorter stories and novellas. Nevertheless, Vili in *Colette* loses his ambiguity, he only plays the role of Colette's lover and observer.

The main negative figure Weissacker also has information on many things and events beyond the possible knowledge of a German Unterscharführer (this rank corresponds to corporal). „Myslel na tajná konta, švýcarské účty na heslo. Velké bohatství propadlo mlčenlivým švýcarským peněžním ústavům" (ibid., 79f.).[12] Weissacker is a primitive sadist, who kills prisoners and rapes women prisoners. It seems highly improbable that this simple-minded character would be intelligent enough to follow this line of thinking. Weissacker is also involved in the *Lebensborn* (fount of life) programme (ibid., 108) based on Nazi racial ideology. According to this, selected German soldiers and racially pure women would beget flawless Aryan children in extramarital relations. Moreover, Weissacker is present during Himmler's visit to Auschwitz. „Překvapilo ho, že nejvyšší říšský vedoucí u okénka z tlustého skla do plynové komory málem omdlel. Museli mu rychle přistavit židli" (ibid., 109).[13] Heinrich Himmler really attended Auschwitz in 1942 and apparently personally witnessed the gassing of the Jews in the gas chamber of Bunker 2. Rudolf Höss describes this visit in detail in his memoirs. Himmler, however, only met with senior officers. It is inconceivable that an Unterscharführer from the so-called Canada square would be present at Himmler's inspection of the gas chamber. Apart from this, the narrator remarks in elsewhere that Weissacker has been in Auschwitz since January, 1943 (ibid., 27f.).

5.

By using this information and these statements, the author constructs a kind of Auschwitz-Birkenau encyclopedia, a shareable common knowledge of facts, events and persons. The result of this is a loss of authenticity and credibility of

---

[12] „He was thinking about secret accounts, Swiss password protected accounts. Big money forfeited to discreet Swiss financial institutions".
[13] „He was surprised that the Reichsführer nearly fainted when he looked through the little window with thick glass into the gas chamber. Quickly, they had to bring him chair".

presented figures and situations on the one hand. But on the other hand, a lot of data of this ‚encyclopedia', as I have demonstrated, is not accurate. While critics and readers perceive the novel as authentic, it still oscillates between authenticity and fiction, with elements of romance as well as the brutality of a prison story (the prisoner caught while fleeing is skinned alive; the commandant in Auschwitz organizes a concert with the performance of a famous Jewish singer, who is immediately sent to the gas chamber after the performance).

Lustig's narrative uses many conventional images. Already on the first page, the initial comparison of Colette with birds occurs.

> Měla v očích rozpětí křídel ptáků v letu. Dráhu odněkud někam. Co připomínají ptáci, kteří letí místo na jih na sever. Zmátlo ji otáčení Země. Po celých devět měsíců, co ji znalo pár lidí v Auschwitz-Birkenau, se podobala ptáku, jemuž selhala magnetická střelka. (ibid., 5)[14]

And then it repeats many times: „Připomínala mu tažné ptáky, jimž pod křídly hoří oheň" (ibid., 11)[15]; „Colette byla pták, který letí nad vodami mezi břehy [...] pták, který se nemůže vyhnout dravcům" (ibid., 26)[16]; „Připadala si jako pták chycený do obrovské klece" (ibid., 34)[17] etc. This comparison is well-known from prison stories (e.g. F.M. Dostoevskij's *The House of the Dead*) and has become trivial. The picture of a flying bird is mentioned forty times in the dialogues, or in the narrator's commentary.

Another repeated phrase can be found for the first time on page two of the novel. It belongs to a large part of the text which is based on dialogues between Vili and Colette. They do not tell each other everything they know and what they are reflecting on. The narrator comments on their words, often in parentheses: „(Vyšší a nižší poschodí pravdy, vyšší a nižší poschodí lži)" (ibid., 6).[18]

---

[14] „Wing-span of flying birds was in her eyes. The course from somewhere to somewhere. What birds bring to mind which are flying to the north instead of the south. The rotation of the Earth confused her. She resembled the bird whose magnetic needle failed for the entire nine months that she was known to several people in Auschwitz-Birkenau".
[15] „She reminded him of migratory birds with fire under their wings".
[16] „Colette was a bird that flies over the waters between the shores [...] a bird that cannot avoid predators".
[17] „She felt like a bird caught in a huge cage".
[18] „(Upper and lower floors of the truth, upper and lower floors of the untruth)".

He repeats the phrases about floors of truth and untruth about thirty times. The narrator uses both these and analogous rhetoric devices (also images of ashes, chimneys, etc.) almost on every page.

Other usual stereotypes and well-worn clichés can also be found in the dialogues between Vili and Colette.

„Jsem?"
„Jsi," odpověděl jí V.F.
„Z masa a krve?"
„Z masa a krve." (ibid., 76f.).[19]
„Proč bůh stvořil tebe a mne?" (ibid., 151).[20]

The narrator comments on these clichés: „Slova měla deset dalších významů" (ibid., 9)[21], even later „Každá zmínka o čistotě měla sto významů" (ibid., 150).[22] Such dialogues and remarks should provide an impression of considerable depth. However, they are trivial.

Well-worn terms like Auschwitz as a „death factory" are used here very often. Sometimes the narrator paraphrases other authors without citing them (Tadeusz Borowski: ibid., 94; Primo Levi: ibid., 96). In one case, Lustig refers to his own work, *A Prayer for Kateřina Horovitzová*. This story was inspired by actual events which took place in Auschwitz in 1943 – the murder of a group of rich Jews whom the Nazis had promised safe passage across the border for a high price. One woman among them rebelled: she grabbed the gun of SS man Schillinger and shot him. In Lustig's story her name was Kateřina Horovitzová. Now, in *Colette*, Colette tells Vili about this woman and her brave act, unique in Auschwitz. But Colette adds, she was a Gestapo's informer and she lived with other Jewish prominent persons in Hotel Polski in Warsaw. „Jí slíbili, že za služby gestapu bude smět odjet do Švýcarska..." (ibid., 39).[23] Nevertheless, she was sent to the gas chamber.

---

[19] ,,Am I?' ,You are,' answered V.F. ,From flesh and blood?' ,From flesh and blood.'".
[20] „Why did God create you and me?".
[21] „These words have ten different meanings".
[22] „Any reference to ,purity' has a hundred different meanings".
[23] „They promised her that she will be allowed to leave for Switzerland, as remuneration for her services…".

But while *A Prayer for Kateřina Horovitzová* depicts this figure through a comparison with the Biblical character Judith, in *Colette* she is a nameless prostitute and a collaborator of the Gestapo.

In actual fact, this woman's name was Franziska Mann, stage name Lola Horovitz (Amann/Aust 2013). She was born in 1917, was a dancer and began her career in Warsaw before the war. She was among the best dancers of her generation in Poland. She was imprisoned in the Warsaw Ghetto, and later, like other prominent Jews, interned in Hotel Polski and in Bergen-Belsen. Rumours that she was a Nazi informer have never been confirmed. Her killing of SS man Schillinger in Auschwitz was described by the only surviving eyewitness of this scene, the Slovak Jew Filip Müller, a member of the Sonderkommando (Müller 1979; in English *Eyewitness Auschwitz – Three Years in the Gas Chambers*, 1979). Although Lustig could not know Müller's report in the sixties, when *A Prayer for Kateřina Horovitzová* was written and edited, his description of this event is much more authentic and impressive than later in *Colette*.

6.

This article wanted to present some reflections on Arnošt Lustig's novel *Colette, dívka z Antwerp*. It was published for the first time in 1992, followed by a new version in 2001 and again in 2005. The story is a part of the so called Jewish Trilogy (*Colette, Tanga* and *Lea*) depicting three beautiful young women as victims of the Nazis and the Holocaust. Colette is a Belgian Jewish woman who is arrested and taken to Auschwitz. Here she falls in love with Vili Feld, a Czech Jew. But she is also abused by a sadistic German guard named Weissacker.

Arnošt Lustig survived the Holocaust and was imprisoned in Auschwitz, as well, for a short time. The extermination camp in Auschwitz-Birkenau is described in many scenes which are mostly violent and cruel. Some critics have stressed the author's personal experience of concentration camps as a guarantee of the novel's authenticity and credibility. Nevertheless, there can be found some implausible and untruthful situations and speeches in the novel, in comparison with known historical facts. The credibility of the presented figures vanishes very often. The author constructs a kind of Auschwitz-Birkenau's common shared encyclopedia; the result of this is a loss of authenticity. Lustig's story uses conventional images and familiar symbols. One example is a flying bird which is in contrast with the inmates. It is mentioned forty times in the dialogues or narrator's commentaries. While critics have said the novel is authentic, it still oscillates between fact and fiction, with elements of romance as well as the brutality of a prison story.

Bibliography

Amann, Thomas – *Aust*, Stefan 2013: Hitlers Menschenhändler. Das Schicksal der „Austauschjuden". Berlin.
Badinová, Alena 2013: Láska za ostnatým drátem. http://www.klubknihomolu.cz/62233/colette-%E2%80%93-laska-za-ostnatym-dratem/ (3.2.2016).
Doležel, Lubomír 1998: Heterocosmica – Fiction and Possible Worlds. Baltimore.
Höss, Rudolf 1958: Kommandant in Auschwitz. Stuttgart.
Lustig, Arnošt 2014 : Colette. Dívka z Antverp. Praha.
Müller, Filip 1979: Sonderbehandlung. Drei Jahre in den Krematorien und Gaskammern von Ausschwitz. München.
Straníková, Jarmila 2014: Colette – kniha, u které se pláče. http://www.kukatko.cz/colette/ (3.2.2016).

Arnošt Lustigs *Colette, dívka z Antverp* – Zwischen Authentizität und Fiktion

Arnošt Lustigs Roman *Colette, dívka z Antverp* (*Colette, das Mädchen aus Antwerpen*) wurde erstmals 1992 herausgegeben, die zweite Fassung folgte 2001 und die dritte 2005. Der Roman ist Teil der sog. Jüdischen Trilogie. Darin sind drei Geschichten von jungen Frauen vereinigt (*Colette, Tanga* und *Lea*), die Opfer der nazistischen Gewaltherrschaft wurden. Die Schönheit und Wehrlosigkeit dieser Frauen bilden einen deutlichen Kontrast zur Brutalität der Massengräuel des Zweiten Weltkriegs und des Holocaust. Alle drei Geschichten verbindet auch die Gestalt des tschechisch-jüdischen Häftlings Vili Feld, der auch in zahlreichen weiteren Werken Lustigs in Erscheinung tritt.

Arnošt Lustig, ein Überlebender des Holocaust, war auch kurze Zeit in Auschwitz-Birkenau, dem Schauplatz des Romans, interniert. Das Vernichtungslager wird dem Leser in vielen grausamen Details und drastischen Szenen geschildert. Einige Kritiker verstanden dies als Authentizität, für die der Verfasser selbst als Augenzeuge garantiere. Allerdings lassen sich im Text so manche Ungenauigkeiten wie auch offensichtliche Abweichungen von den historischen Fakten ausmachen. Damit verliert der Roman an Glaubwürdigkeit und Authentizität. Darüber hinaus arbeitet der Autor mit übertrieben oft benutzten, häufig abgedroschenen Symbolen, wie z.B. mit dem vierzigmal (!) wiederholten Bild eines verletzten und gefährdeten Vogels, das Colettes Situation andeuten soll. Gleiches gilt für die Dialoge zwischen Vili und Colette, die voller Phrasen und Klischees sind. Der Roman kann also kaum als ein hervorragendes literarisches Werk eingeschätzt werden.

The Film *Colette* –
Risks of a ‚Modern' Approach to the Depiction of the Holocaust

Šárka Sladovníková, Praha

Over thirty films about the Holocaust have been made in Czechoslovakia and later in the Czech Republic since 1948. Naturally, the visual depiction of this topic has changed dramatically through the decades. Evolution of the depiction is strikingly visible in portrayal of violence and eroticism. Films made in 1960s are more psychological and violence and eroticism are portrayed more discreetly. Films made after 2000 contain an increasing amount of violence and explicit eroticism. The film *Colette* is one such example of this new approach to the depiction of this topic.

The film *Colette* was made in 2013 by Milan Cieslar.[1] This film, based on the eponymous novella written by Arnošt Lustig (1992), narrates a love story with the death factory of Auschwitz as a backdrop. In the framing story that takes place in the 1970s, Vili meets Yvette, the mother of his future daughter-in-law. During dinner both talk about their experience of surviving Auschwitz. After dinner, inspired by the recollections of the past, Vili stays up to write the novella Colette. Although the manuscript is visibly thick, Vili manages to finish it by dawn. In the morning Yvette comes and the framing storyline closes. As the audience already suspects, it turns out that Yvette[2] is actually the love of his life, Colette, a girl that he had met in the extermination camp. The main story line of the film is set in Auschwitz between the July 1943 and January 1945 and tells the love story of Vili and Colette (see Morávková 2010).

The arrival of Colette in Auschwitz-Birkenau can serve as a synecdoche for thousands of other transports. Vili meets Colette during the selection and advises her to leave her family and to lie about her profession. Subsequently, the rest of her family is gassed; she is the only one to survive. We then see the everyday

---

[1] *Colette* was made as a Czech-Slovak-Dutch co-production with many foreign actors, the film was shot in English. For the Czech audience, the film was dubbed into Czech during post-production.

[2] Yvette is the name of Colette's sister who died in Auschwitz. Colette adopted her sister's name after the Second World War.

reality of the camp through the eyes of a man and a woman. Firstly, the film shows the workday of a woman in the quarry, later in the Canada labour squad, where women were forced to look for hidden valuables and jewelry in the clothes belonging to people who have just arrived on a transport. The film also depicts the topic of forced ‚night shifts' because Colette has to serve as a sexual slave to the ‚Hauptsturmführer' of the camp, Weissacker. On the other hand, the film narrates the story of Vili's life in the camp. Vili starts to work in the Canada squad before Colette. Therefore, he is at the train station when Colette and her family arrive in Auschwitz. Vili serves as a ‚Läufer'. He delivers blankets full of clothes from the transports to the women in the Canada squad. Occasionally, he delivers letters and other things. When he is caught delivering French soap and delicacies to the lover of his kapo, he is punished with twenty-five lashes from a wooden staff. On the brink of death, he is operated on under the difficult conditions of the camp. His friends protect him until he fully recovers. Colette steals diamonds she finds hidden in the clothes, and buys a better care for Vili. After Vili recovers miraculously, he starts to work as a scribe. Afterwards, Colette and Vili manage to meet alone and they make love to each other. Vili wants to escape from Auschwitz and he includes Colette in his escape plan. Unfortunately, Colette is unable to come to the meeting place because she is caught by Weissacker. Vili decides not to leave without her, and he relinquishes their places to his two friends who hide in the escape van under a pile of wood. Nevertheless, both of his friends are caught and shot. Near the end of the war, Colette finds out that she is pregnant and she manages to be transported to Sachsenhausen. Vili is liberated while on the death march, when the march is stopped by Russian Cossacks, the prisoners then beat Weissacker to death.

Naturalistic Depiction of an Extermination Camp

The aim of the filmmakers was to create a complex naturalistic picture of an extermination camp. Therefore, there are piles of human corpses and clothes on the ground between the barracks. We can see flames coming out of the chimneys, corpses burned in the furnaces of the ‚Sonderkommando', and ashes from the burned corpses flying through the air. In contrast to the harsh picture of the camp life the sound of Strauss's playful waltz can often be heard, either being played on the gramophone in Weissacker's house, or by a prison band.

Although the film makers claim that their film corresponds with historical reality, some scenes are not credible. For instance: at the end of the film there is a scene of the death march, where the prisoners are liberated by Soviet Cossacks. The armed Cossacks watch passively, as Weissacker shoots a couple of the prisoners who are trying to escape. It is not plausible that Soviet soldiers would let Germans shoot prisoners at the end of the war. Moreover, while prisoners are beating Weissacker to death, one Cossack nods gravely to their revenge. In addition, the Cossacks look like characters from an operetta. The character of one of Vili's friends is also questionable. The big corpulent prisoner (albeit a kapo) does not look like a man who has just left Auschwitz. Moreover, he wears a heavy gold chain.[3] The presence of the ramp in Auschwitz is also historically inaccurate. Although this ramp was built in Auschwitz in the middle of 1944, it is mentioned at the beginning of the film which is set in 1943. Furthermore, the height difference between two actors who play young and old Vili Feld seems amateurish.

As is common in contemporary films about the Holocaust, directors assume an uninformed audience. Therefore, they try to overinform the audience by putting too much information into the plot of the film or in the set piece. For example, when Vili and Colette kiss for the first time, film makers found it important to tell the viewer how dangerous it was. Therefore, after the kiss another scene follows, where Vili and his kapo pass the gallows. A man is hanging by his arms on the gallows. The kapo tells Vili that this would happen to anybody who would be caught with a woman.

Concentration camps were previously depicted in Czechoslovak films such as *I Survived My Death* (*Přežil jsem svou smrt*) made in 1960 by Vojtěch Jasný (see Dvořák 1961) and *Surprised by the Night* (*Zastihla mě noc*) made by Juraj Herz in 1985. Jasný's film depicts the story of a boxer named Tonda who is interned in Mauthausen concentration camp because he had a street fight with a

---

[3] Although it is possible that workers in the Canada squad and members of the ‚Sonderkommando' managed to hide some valuables, the chain of gold worn by the liberated prisoner is unplausibly heavy.

member of the Gestapo. This film depicts life in a concentration camp through a man's eyes. The film portrays violence; Nazis and Capos beat the prisoners mercilessly. The film also depicts hard work in the quarry and the topic of resistance.

Surprised by the Night depicts life in the Ravensbrück concentration camp through a woman's eyes. The film depicts the life story of a communist journalist named Jožka Jabůrková (1896 – 1942). As the director Juraj Herz personally experienced internment in the concentration camp himself, he tried to tell the story, not only of Jožka Jabůrková, but also of the writer Milena Jesenská (1896 – 1944).[4] Female Nazis are very cruel and brutal in this film. One of the Nazis beats one prisoner to death with a stick and a riding crop. Children are taken away from the women's barracks and all of them are killed. The film also portrays the topic of medical experiments on female prisoners. Nudity is explicitly portrayed in the scene where newly arrived women shower, have their hair cut and are examined by a doctor. As both of these films were made during the Communist rule in Czechoslovakia, both suppress the topic of the Jews while glorifying the Soviets.

Colette was partly made with the help of computer graphics, which is rare in Czech cinematography. Computer graphics helped make the extermination camp look more realistic and added the needed special effects and film extras. This way of making films can possibly mark a new direction in Holocaust cinematography in the Czech Republic.

Depiction of Violence, Eroticism, and Nazis

As mentioned above, Czechoslovak and Czech filmography depicting the topic of the Holocaust has kept evolving since 1948 (see Koura 2007). Changes are visible in the presentation of violence and eroticism. Concerning the representation of violence, obvious differences can be found between films made in the USA and in Europe. For instance, two American films, the *Holocaust* series

---

[4] In many aspects, both ladies shared a similar history. Both of them were deported to Ravensbrück, where they died. Before the war, Milena Jesenská joined an underground resistance movement and helped many Jewish and political refugees emigrate.

made in 1978 by Marvin J. Chomsky or *Sophie's choice* made in 1982 by Alan J. Pakula, both portray a picture of almost kind Nazis. When Sophie arrives at Auschwitz, nobody screams at the Jews, prisoners are peacefully unloading luggage from the trains, and children are sitting on the suitcases. Almost an idyll, one would say. Similarly, when in the series *Holocaust*, Nazis beat the Jews, they hardly touch them, compared to European films. On the other hand, *Schindler's List* is different and contains a huge amount of violence. In *Colette*, Nazis beat prisoners with a stick and the injuries are shown on the camera. Also short, only two-second long shots appear in the film depicting brutal scenes, such as a cart pulled by prisoners and driven by a Nazi who is whipping them to make them pull faster. Elsewhere are short shots of piles of dead bodies, etc. Humiliation of prisoners is portrayed more harshly than in previous films. For example, in *Nackt unter Wölfen* (*Naked Among Wolves*) made in 1963 by Frank Beyer, the commanding officers humiliate prisoners by repeatedly ordering them to take their caps off their heads and put them back on. The Nazis in *Colette* have a different approach. When they want to humiliate prisoners, they repeatedly order them to get down on the ground covered with sewage, and get back up. While ordering them to do so, they laugh at the prisoners. Eroticism and nudity are very common motifs in *Colette*. There is a scene of men showering and another of women, both show full nudity (except for the main characters). The film contains three scenes of sexual intercourse between Weissacker and female prisoners and one scene, where Vili and Colette make love to each other. Such an approach to expressive nudity and eroticism was also used in *Schindler's List*. In Czechoslovak and Czech context, the evolution of depicting eroticism is visible, for example in three eponymous film adaptations of Jan Otčenášek's novella *Romeo, Juliet and Darkness* (*Romeo, Julie a tma*). The first and second adaptations, made at the end of the 1950s by Eva Sadková and Jiří Weiss (see Zvoníček 1960 and Mareš 2013), discreetly depict the tragic love story of Pavel and Esther. Almost forty years later, in 1997, director Karel Smyczek chose a completely different approach for the depiction of the topic. Between Pavel and Esther love is physical and explicit, the film contains a scene of sexual intercourse. Such depiction would be unacceptable at the end of the 1950s.

The Nazis are portrayed in several ways. In one scene Jewish women shower and two Nazis observe them lecherously while smoking cigarettes. Weissacker is a brutal beast who shoots Jews for his own amusement and makes female prisoners his sexual slaves. Yet, he is also able to do something good. Firstly, he saves Colette from hard work in the quarry, secondly he saves her from being sterilized, albeit on purpose because he wants to make her a sexual slave; he saves her life by getting her out of the quarry. Weissacker saves Colette once more, although he doesn't know it. When Vili and Colette want to escape from Auschwitz, Weissacker prevents Colette from getting to the meeting place on time. Subsequently, both escapees are shot by the Nazi driver who robs them and kills them. If Colette and Vili had managed to hide in the car, both would have been dead. It is also interesting that Weissacker knows the prisoners in the Canada squad by name: „So what, Chaim? Haven't given up, yet? You're idiot. And you, Jacek? Still breathing. Breathe, you still have a while, yet". Although he is humiliating his workers, they are not an anonymous crowd to him. In several scenes Weissacker drinks alcohol while sitting in his office or going through the camp. These scenes imply that he is an unhappy man. Because of these attributes, his character is not a prototypical negative one, as Nazis are often portrayed in films about the Holocaust, but an ambivalent one. In fact, there are very few ambivalent Nazi characters in Czechoslovak and Czech filmography, for example the character of petty officer Binde in *Transport from Paradise* (*Transport z ráje*) made by Zbyněk Brynych in 1962 or Rolf Harting in the film *I, Justice* (*Já, spravedlnost*) made by Zbyněk Brynych in 1967. Also, another Nazi in *Colette* is portrayed in an interesting way. In the scene of the selection where Vili saves Colette's life, an SS man talks to her mother, gives her compliments about her perfect German, quotes the Bible in Latin and gently takes her hand to help her as he is sending her to the ‚wrong' side to the gas chamber.[5] The character of Bedřich Brenske in the TV film *A Prayer for Catherine Horovitz* shows a similar type of a genteel, yet beastly Nazi. The film was made in 1965 by Antonín Moskalyk and was based on the eponymous novella by Arnošt Lustig *Modlitba pro Kateřinu Horovitzovou*. In *Colette*, Nazism is also ridiculed

---

[5] This scene possibly refers to Dr. Josef Mengele.

in the scene, where Weissacker enjoys oral sex from Colette while he is standing by the window next to a portrait of Adolf Hitler.

Hollywood Techniques in the Film

In order to raise tension and add drama in *Colette*, the film makers repeatedly used the common Hollywood technique of ‚rescued at the last moment'. On the death march, when Weissacker is shooting prisoners, he aims his gun at Vili. He pulls the trigger but nothing happens, he has run out of bullets. When Colette wants to escape from the camp on a transport going to Sachsenhausen, Weissacker rushes to the train station to get her back. Nevertheless, the train has already departed and he gets furious while watching the rear of the last wagon. In the middle of the film, when women are getting sterilized, Weissacker saves Colette from being sterilized at the very last moment.

As with many other contemporary films covering the topic of the Holocaust, *Colette* also emphasizes emotional effect on the audience. Unfortunately, some of these phrases are clichés, for example, when ashes from burned bodies are called ‚Jewish angels'. In the first part of the framing story, Vili asks Yvette if she has also survived the death camp. Then her daughter asks Yvette why they moved to the USA from Israel. Yvette explains:

> We lived in a small town. I stuck out like a sore thumb. They all knew I have been in Auschwitz. [...] I survived at the expense of those who did not. It is unforgivable. I've never forgiven myself.[6]

Or, elsewhere, when Vili starts to write his novella Colette, he writes:

> Man is both a lie and truth. Good and evil. He has the highest and lowest levels of truth and the highest and lowest levels of lies which help us to survive. Words float towards me. Life and death. Like birds and their shadow which always flies with them. No one knew about us. We were lost to the world just as the world was lost to us. We were lost in a hell called Auschwitz. That day we were selected for a new horror. Birkenau, a factory for death, a workshop for evil. God created man and man created a concentration camp.

---

[6] Such an attitude to the survivors is clearly a cliché, as there were many different approaches to the survivors. According to memoirs, some survivors who emigrated to Israel, suffered from the incomprehension and lack of empathy by Israelis. For example, Israelis did not understand how it was possible that six millions Jews did not fight back, when Israel was able to defend itself in the wars against the Arabs with very little soldiers.

These words clearly refer to the novella written in the film. These sentences are phrases. Yet, it is not the style of writing that makes the words a cliché, it is the content of the words. In the main story, after Colette's arrival, her head is shaved, she is disinfected and a number is tattooed on her forearm. When being tattooed, she asks the man who is tattooing her, about the purpose of the number. He replies: „Phone numbers to heaven".

Holocaust films also present a handful of demonstrative Jewish traditions and religious rituals, such as Jewish celebrations of feasts or weddings, the singing of Hebrew and Yiddish songs, praying in the synagogue etc. Usually they serve as a reference to a happy pre-war life, for example in *All My Loved Ones* (*Všichni moji blízcí*) made by Matej Mináč in 1999 or in *The Last Cyclist* (*Poslední cyklista*) directed by Jiří Svoboda in 2014. In *Colette*, in the framing storyline, Colette's daughter marries Vili's son in a synagogue. Since there was an orthodox Jewish community in New York in the 1970s, this scene is plausible.

The (Non)Uniqueness of *Colette*

The film *Colette* is not innovative in the depiction of the Holocaust, it uses stereotypical images and techniques that were used in previously made films. For example, *Colette* resembles the well-known film *Schindler's List* made by Steven Spielberg in 1993. Also Spielberg incorporated several historical inaccuracies into his film in order to raise both dramatic and sentimental effect of the film. In *Colette*, the character of the brutal SS man Weissacker was clearly inspired by Spielberg's commanding officer of Płaszow Amon Göth. Similarly to Weissacker, Göth is sexually attracted to his female servant Helena; and he humiliates her and beats her. He also lives in a house close to the camp which enables him to shoot prisoners from his villa. Moreover, his gun fails when he wants to shoot a prisoner.[7] The motif of sexual abuse of female prisoners is also

---

[7] It is possible that Spielberg copied one scene from *Surprised by the Night* (*Zastihla mě noc*). At a specific moment during the film women are forced to go to a large bathroom. The women are terrified that they are in a gas chamber, and they scream. Nevertheless, the shower heads release water. However, it is also possible that Herz got an inspiration for this scene from some other film made before *Surprised by the Night*.

present in older films, for example in *The Pawnbroker* by Sidney Lumet made in 1964. In *Colette*, Vili is accused of being part of a resistance movement, and he is tortured. Such motifs were also used for example in *Nackt unter Wölfen*. Smoking chimneys are a stereotypical image used in films about the Auschwitz camp since *The Last Stop/Ostatni etap* by Wanda Jakubowska in 1948. Another conventional image, a shot of barbed wire, is used at least since *Nuit et Brouillard* (*Night and Fog*) made by Alain Resnais in 1955 (see Baron 2006). The love story between two prisoners was visualized for example in *Pasażerka* (*The Passenger*), a film made by Andrzej Munk and Witold Lesiewicz in 1963. Film makers also use child characters very often, both dead and alive, alone or with their families. These innocent creatures are supposed to create a striking contrast to the atrocities of the Holocaust. Fortunately, *Colette* doesn't contain this kitsch. Although Colette has a baby at the end of the war, the little one is not used as a contrast to the horrors of the Holocaust but as reconciliation with the past and with her own self. At the end of the framing story, Colette claims that „Colette Cohen" died when her daughter was born. Then she changed her name to Yvette and married an old man.

As it is common in the films of this kind, *Colette* also deals with the topic of the trauma from survival. At the beginning, in the framing story, Colette says that she left Israel because her neighbours could not forgive her for surviving the Holocaust. In the main plot, one woman is outraged at Colette and says that other woman Wanda from the Canada had to be gassed to make space for Colette in the labour squad. At the beginning of the film a very interesting and not often depicted topic of a deliberately changed story of the survival emerges. While sitting at the dinner, Yvette tells a story from Auschwitz. She says that an SS man tried to touch her, she pushed him away and he never demanded anything else from her. She then concludes that some other women were not that lucky. When Vili leaves the home of his future daughter-in-law, he says to his son that Yvette did not tell the truth:

„You know what they did with women like Hannah's mother in the camp?" „No, I don't." „They used them as sex slaves." „Because she was beautiful?" „Yes. If she had really done what she said at dinner, she would have been killed".

Naturally, some survivors changed the story of their survival, either because they were not proud of what they had had to do in order to survive, or they simply blocked their memories. Unfortunately, film makers did not develop this motif any further.

Conclusion

Colette shows the current Czech trend in the visual depiction of an extermination camp and the Holocaust. The film presents a naturalistic picture of an extermination camp, and stresses violence and nudity. The film itself is not innovative in the style of its depiction. In fact, almost everything in the film has been depicted before in world cinematography. Yet, it is the first of its kind in the Czech Republic and there are not many possibilities of how to describe the extermination camp in an innovative way. The topic of the Holocaust is still very popular with film makers in the Czech Republic and a new film comes out every year. In my opinion new films have to face new dangers. The span of time between history and the present is growing. In order to overcome this, film makers include more historic information in their films. In this way, they have the power to manipulate the facts. The contemporary mass media present violence on a daily basis and the audience becomes increasingly used to it, as their resistance threshold is raised. As a consequence, new films might need to be even more explicit and naturalistic. The question is if such future films will not manipulate the audience and change the perception of history and our cultural memory (cf. Insdorf 2003, Baron 2005, Ebbrecht 2011).

Bibliography

Baron, Anne-Marie 2006: The Shoah on Screen. Representing Crimes Against Humanity. Vol. 1. Straßburg.
Baron, Lawrence 2005: Projecting the Holocaust into the Present. Oxford.
Dvořák, Ivan 1961: Přežil jsem svou smrt. Kritika. In: Film a doba 7, pp. 58-60.
Ebbrecht, Tobias 2011: Geschichtsbilder im medialen Gedächtnis. Filmische Narrationen des Holocaust. Bielefeld.
Insdorf, Annette 2003: Indelible Shadows. Film and the Holocaust. Cambridge.
Koura, Petr 2007: Obraz holokaustu v českém hraném filmu. In: Jiří Holý (red.): Holokaust – šoa – zagłada v české, slovenské a polské literatuře. Praha, pp. 227-236.

Lustig, Arnošt 1992: *Colette. Dívka z Antverp*. Praha.
Mareš, Petr 2013: Vedlejší postavy, vedlejší motivy. K filmovým adaptacím dvou románů Jana Otčenáška. In: Česká literatura 61, pp. 218-240.
Morávková, Jitka 2010: Holokaust v české kinematografii. In: Svět filmu, č. 10, pp. 12-13.
Zvoníček, Stanislav 1960: K filmu Romeo, Julie a tma. In: Film a doba 6, pp. 420-423.

Der Film *Colette* –
Risiken einer ‚modernen' Annäherung an die Darstellung des Holocaust

Seit dem Zweiten Weltkrieg wurden in der Tschechoslowakei und später in der Tschechischen Republik mehr als dreißig Filme zur Thematik des Holocaust gedreht. Es gibt ziemlich große Unterschiede zwischen den Filmen aus den sechziger Jahren und jenen, die nach 1989 gedreht wurden. Die älteren Werke sind eher psychologisch aufgefasst, die Filme nach der Wende und vor allem nach 2000 dagegen sehr naturalistisch, sie sind voller Gewalt und expliziter Erotik. Der Beitrag befasst sich mit dem Film *Colette* (2013, Regie Milan Cieslar), gedreht nach der gleichnamigen Novelle von Arnošt Lustig. Der Kern der Handlung spielt zwischen Juli 1943 und Januar 1945 im Konzentrationslager Auschwitz, die Rahmenhandlung etwa dreißig Jahre später in New York. *Colette* stellt einen neuen Ansatz in der Behandlung der Holocaustthematik dar, der dem aktuellen Trend der visualisierten Darstellung der Vernichtungslager sowie des Holocaust entspricht. In diesem Werk wird ein derbes, schockierendes Bild von Auschwitz-Birkenau präsentiert, Gewalt und Nacktheit werden in vielen Szenen stark akzentuiert. Obwohl diese Art der Handlungswiedergabe keine Innovation bringt und beinahe alle hier inszenierten Situationen aus der Holocaust-Kinematographie bereits bekannt sind, ist *Colette* dennoch der erste Film dieser Art in der Tschechischen Republik. Die Darstellung des Holocaust in *Colette* deutet zukünftige Bearbeitungsmöglichkeiten dieser Thematik an, einschließlich aller damit verbundenen Risiken.

Zeitbrücken. Erinnerungen an den Holocaust in Ivan Klímas Erzählband *Moje nebezpečné výlety*

Anna Artwińska, Hamburg

> „Um nichts in der Welt hätte ich ihm gestanden […], daß ich mich selbst in sonnigeren Momenten, wenn ich eine Zukunft außerhalb des Ghettos für möglich hielt, in der Rolle eines Zeugen sah: als Dichter, Schauspieler oder Maler" (Klíma 1997, 9f.).

Ivan Klímas Erzählsammlung *Moje nebezpečné výlety* (*Meine gefährlichen Ausflüge*) ist ein literarisches Zeugnis des Holocaust, das dieses Ereignis aus einer zeitlich längeren Distanz erinnert und vergegenwärtigt. Der Band erschien 2004 in Prag, fast siebzig Jahre nachdem der Autor (Jg. 1931) aus dem Ghetto bzw. Konzentrationslager Theresienstadt[1] befreit wurde, und besteht aus mehreren Erzählungen, die punktuell die Erlebnisse aus der Zeit der Gefangenschaft sowie aus der Zeit ‚davor' und ‚danach' rekonstruieren und erzählen.[2] Bis auf den Text *Miriam,* der im Jahr 1979 geschrieben und 1981 im Samisdat publiziert wurde, entstanden die restlichen Erzählungen in den Jahren 2003 und 2004 und sind in dieser Sammlung zum ersten Mal erschienen. Obwohl sich Klíma auch in seinen anderen Werken mit der Erinnerung an den Holocaust beschäftigte, können sie nur bis zu einem gewissen Grad mit dem Erzählband aus dem Jahr 2004 verglichen werden.[3] Der besondere Status von *Moje nebezpečné výlety* besteht nicht so sehr in dem Thema selbst, sondern in dem ‚Wie' der Darstellung – in Klímas ästhetischem Umgang mit der Erfahrung der Katastrophe. „Mit Vergegenwärti-

---

[1] Für die Bezeichnung von Theresienstadt benutzt Klíma synonymisch die Begriffe „Lager" und „Ghetto". Diese Praxis wird in meinem Text übernommen. Über Theresienstadt vgl. Benz 2013.

[2] Der Teil der Erzählungen, der sich auf die Zeit in der sozialistischen Tschechoslowakei bezieht, wird im folgenden Aufsatz nicht diskutiert.

[3] Erinnerungen an den Holocaust sind u.a. die Erzählungen *Moje první lásky* (*Meine ersten Lieben*) aus dem Jahr 1981 und ein Teil des fiktionalen Romans *Soudce z milosti* (*Richter in eigener Sache*) aus dem Jahr 1986. Ein wichtiges und interessantes Zeugnis bilden zudem die autobiographischen Texte Klímas, wie z.B. das Gespräch mit Martin Doerry *Die Menschen verstummten* (Klíma 2008) und ein Teil seiner Memoiren *Moje šílené století* (Klíma 2009a; *Mein verrücktes Jahrhundert*).

gung", schreibt Ludger Schwarte, „wird meist ein Vorgang benannt, bei dem etwas zeitlich oder räumlich Entferntes oder Abwesendes in die Gegenwart geholt wird" (Schwarte 2013, 133).[4] Ivan Klíma ruft das „zeitlich Entfernte" in Erinnerung und stellt es in die Schreibgegenwart, um durch die Rekonstruktion „eine Sinnproduktion im Horizont nachzeichnender Erinnerung" (Wansing 2001, 480) zu erzeugen. Es ist die Vielschichtigkeit der zeitlichen Strukturen und die Verschränkung von verschiedenen Zeitebenen, die sein Werk interessant machen. Die Katastrophe des Holocaust ist in den Erzählungen kein punktuelles Ereignis, sondern wird als Prozess konzipiert und in die postkatastrophische Situation hinein verlängert. Klíma beschreibt seine Zeit im Lager und zugleich die Reperkussionen und Nachwirkungen: Das katastrophische Erleben verschränkt er mit der postkatastrophischen Erinnerung. Den tschechischen Autor interessieren dabei unerwartete Wendungen, überraschende Begebenheiten und die „gegenläufige[n] Gedächtnisse" (Diner 2007) der Opfer und der Täter, die die Komplexität und verschiedenen Dimensionen der Katastrophe zeigen. Indem er die tschechische Kollaboration anspricht, stellt er gleichzeitig die Frage nach der tschechischen Mitschuld am Holocaust und schreibt sich in diejenigen Diskurse ein, die die starre Dichotomie zwischen Täter und Opfer bzw. die tradierten Interpretationsmuster des Zweiten Weltkriegs revidieren (vgl. Hallama 2015, 211). Bei der Rückholung der Vergangenheit kommen dabei Interpretationskonflikte und Gedächtnislücken zum Vorschein, so dass „[…] všechno můze být jiné, než jak se to jeví na povrchu" (Klíma 2004, 21).[5]

In Klímas Texten kommen verschiedene Zeitformen und Zeitschichten vor – kulturelle Versetzungen und „Flexionen" (Heeg/Denzel 2011, 7), die Wolfgang Schwarz als ein allgemeines Merkmal der tschechischen Holocaustliteratur nach dem Jahr 2000 bezeichnet (Schwarz 2014, 158). Diese Literatur bewegt sich in einem Überschneidungsbereich zwischen *facta* und *ficta* und experimentiert mit den ästhetischen Formen und Verfahren, die die Grenzen des Sagbaren über den Holocaust neu definieren und verschieben. Ivan Klímas Erzählband *Moje nebez-*

---

[4] Schwarte signalisiert auch die Probleme des Konzeptes der Vergegenwärtigung, indem er auf einen unsicheren Status von Gegenwart hinweist (ebd., 133ff.).
[5] „[…] alles ganz anders sein kann, als es auf der Oberfläche zu sein scheint". Ich danke Prof. Dr. Anja Tippner und Prof. Dr. Reinhard Ibler für die Hilfe bei der Übersetzung von Klímas Texten ins Deutsche.

pečné výlety ist ein interessantes Beispiel solcher Versetzungen. In der Rekonstruktion des Vergangenen geht es dem Autor nicht primär um die ‚wahrheitsgetreue' Abbildung des Lebens in Theresienstadt. Er stellt nicht den Anspruch, „durch Zeugenschaft einem Wahrheitsanspruch gemäß rekonstruieren zu können" (Wansing 2001, 480), sondern nimmt auf die stattgefundenen Geschehnisse einen interpretativen Bezug. Im Fokus seines Interesses liegen zwischenmenschliche Interaktionen und das zwischenmenschliche Agieren im Zeichen einer Extremsituation und deren zeitlicher Wandel. Ein relevanter Handlungsrahmen ist in den Erzählungen oft die Familie, die nicht nur als ein Zufluchtsort, sondern auch als ein Ort transgenerationeller Konflikte zwischen dem Ich-Erzähler und seinen Eltern fungiert. Klíma interessieren die Beziehungen zwischen den Familienmitgliedern, aber auch zwischen den Nachbarn, Schulfreunden, Stadtbewohnern, Gefangenen und Überlebenden: Sie sind die Akteure, deren Handeln er beobachtet und beschreibt. Die Geschehnisse werden dabei teilweise aus der Perspektive eines Kindes, teilweise aus dem Blickwinkel eines Erwachsenen geschildert, so dass es dem Leser möglich ist, unterschiedliche Einblicke in die erzählten Geschichten zu gewinnen. Auch diese Fokalisierung steht im Dienste der zeitlichen Komplexität und ermöglicht, Entwicklungen, Brüche, Linien und/oder die Kontinuitäten im Leben des Erzählers und seiner Mitmenschen darzustellen.

Der Band *Moje nebezpečné výlety* ist eine literarische Vergegenwärtigung des Holocaust, aber kein autobiographischer Text. Obwohl der Autor zur so genannten Erlebnisgeneration gehört, überschreitet er in seinen Erzählungen die Grenzen zwischen Faktualem und Fiktionalem und vermischt seine Erinnerungen mit den Narrativen des tschechischen kulturellen Gedächtnisses.[6] Es handelt sich hier nicht um ein prothetisches, „geliehenes" Gedächtnis (*prosthetic memory*) im Sinne von Alison Landsberg (2004) – denn der Ausgangspunkt der Sammlung sind eigene Erlebnisse – sondern um ein Gedächtnis, das persönliche Erfahrungen und kulturelle Muster der Erinnerung miteinander verschränkt. Es steht außer Zweifel, dass die Figur des Erzählers an den realen Autor erinnert

---

[6] Im Kontext der autobiographischen Bezüge im Roman *Soudce z milosti* signalisierte Klíma exemplarisch das Problem der Fiktionalisierung der Erinnerungen: „Ich bin mir nicht sicher, ob dieses Detail nicht erfunden ist. Ich habe damals so viele tote Menschen gesehen, dass man sich einfach daran gewöhnte" (Klíma 2008, 121).

und aus seiner *vita* schöpft, dennoch bleibt ihr Status fiktional. Der tschechische Literaturkritiker Aleš Haman spricht in diesem Zusammenhang von der Rückkehr des Autors zu den autobiographisch fundierten Themen und Problemen (Haman 2004, 30). Dadurch, dass die Figur des Erzählers erfunden ist, ist sie nicht an die Pflichten eines autobiographischen Paktes gebunden und kann – um mit Hayden White zu sprechen – auch „dichten" (White 1991). Durch die „Dichtung" steigert sich der Grad der Literarizität und es werden neue ästhetische Zugänge zum Holocaust geschaffen.

Schwebende Katastrophe

Die Handlung vieler Erzählungen in *Moje nebezpečné výlety* spielt in der Zeit vor dem Transport des Erzählers ins Ghetto und nach seiner Rückkehr nach Hause. In bestimmter Hinsicht gilt hier das, was Reinhard Ibler in Bezug auf die narrativen Strategien in Holocaust-Texten des tschechischen Schriftstellers Josef Škvorecký herausgearbeitet hat:

> Obwohl keine der Erzählungen im Holocaust selbst angesiedelt ist, schwebt die Katastrophe dennoch über allem (als drohendes Unheil vor bzw. traumatisierende Erfahrung nach dem Krieg) und wird semantisch gesehen zum einigendem Prinzip, das die einzelnen Erzählungen des Zyklus zusammenhält. (Ibler 2015, 127)

Auch in denjenigen Erzählungen Klímas, deren Handlung nicht im Konzentrationslager angesiedelt ist, lässt sich eine Figuration des Katastrophischen feststellen. Dies ist möglich, weil das heutige Wissen über das Verbrechen des Nationalsozialismus erlaubt, viele textuelle Merkmale entsprechend zu deuten bzw. zu dechiffrieren. „Die Erinnerung ist […] eine Rekonstruktion der Vergangenheit mit Hilfe von der Gegenwart entliehenen Gegebenheiten und wird im Übrigen durch andere, zu früheren Zeiten unternommene Rekonstruktion vorbereitet", schrieb Maurice Halbwachs in seinem epochalen Werk *Das kollektive Gedächtnis* (Halbwachs 1967, 55). Die Tatsache, dass Klíma seine Erinnerungen erst vor ein paar Jahren niedergeschrieben hat, führt dazu, dass sie durch die gegenwärtige Perspektive („mit Hilfe von der Gegenwart entliehenen Gegebenheiten") beeinflusst werden bzw. beeinflusst werden können. Auch der Zugang des Lesers zu dem Text ist durch die postkatastrophische Konstellation bestimmt. So kann man z.B. durch semantische Merkmale einerseits und durch Lektüre-

Konventionen anderseits in vielen Erzählungen den prospektiven Opferstatus der Protagonisten erkennen, obwohl sie sich (noch) in ihrem gewöhnlichen Alltag, und nicht in dem Ausnahmezustand des Lagers, befinden. Die postkatastrophische Lektüre aktiviert das kulturelle Gedächtnis über die Shoah und verbindet die unterschiedlichen Zeitstrukturen. In den Erzählungen, die über die Zeit nach der Rückkehr aus dem Konzentrationslager berichten, lässt sich wiederum das traumatische Nachleben der Katastrophe ablesen. Sie hat keine kathartische Wirkung und hört nicht einfach auf, sondern stellt eine Herausforderung auch für die Zeit danach dar. Aus der gegenwärtigen Sicht ist es beispielsweise möglich, die von Klíma beschriebenen Objekte, Gegenstände und Reste als materielle Spuren der traumatischen Vergangenheit zu lesen und zu deuten.[7]

Für den homodiegetischen Erzähler ist die Zeit ‚davor' mit der Entdeckung seiner jüdischen Identität – und infolgedessen mit der Angst vor den Transporten – verbunden. „V domě žily také tři židovské rodiny, mezi něž, jak jsem se ke svému úžasu dozvěděl, počítali i tu naši" (Klíma 2004, 6), stellt er schon im ersten Text des Bandes fest.[8] Die jüdische Identität wird dem Protagonisten, der in einer völlig assimilierten Familie aufwächst, *per dictum* zugeschrieben und danach durch das Tragen eines gelben Sterns markiert. Die Bezeichnung ‚Jude', die in der Zeit ‚davor' sowohl von den deutschen Nachbarn als auch von den tschechischen Kollaborateuren immer häufiger als Ausgrenzungsmerkmal verwendet wird, führt zu einer kulturellen Neuverortung der bislang als tschechisch geltenden Familie. In der Wahrnehmung des kindlichen Erzählers ist der Unterschied zwischen Identifizierung und Identifikation noch nicht kognitiv fassbar, aber mit Sicherheit spürbar. Aus diesem Grund reagiert er ablehnend auf die ihm zugefügten identifikatorischen Zuschreibungen. Dennoch wird das ‚Anderssein' des Erzählers und seiner Familie von außen nicht ausschließlich negativ bewertet. Die Reaktionen der Umgebung zeigen, dass es sich hier vor allem um die Markierung einer Differenz und nicht um deren Bewertung handelt. Der pol-

---

[7] In der Erzählzeit erfüllen Dinge vor allem eine praktische Funktion: So sind fremde Möbelstücke z.B. einfach nur Möbelstücke, die es leichter machen, sich im Leben wieder einzurichten. Erst im Laufe der Zeit wird – das wissen wir – den Dingen ein zweites Leben und ein neuer Status als Spuren des Vergangenen verliehen. Vgl. hierzu Tippner 2015.
[8] „In unserem Haus lebten auch drei jüdische Familien, zu denen, wie ich zu meinem Erstaunen erfuhr, auch wir gezählt wurden".

nisch-jüdische Philosoph Zygmunt Bauman hat für diese Art der Einstellung zum Judentum den Begriff Allosemitismus eingeführt und gezeigt, dass es bei diesem Phänomen nicht zwingend um den Hass gegen die Juden, sondern um die Hervorhebung der Fremdheit geht, die sowohl aus anti- als auch als philosemitischen Gründen erfolgen kann (vgl. Bauman 1995, 43ff.; vgl. auch Thurn 2015). „Myslela jsem, že Židi mají jiného [Pánaboha]", sagte seine Nachbarin Vlasta zu dem Erzähler, um dann hinzuzufügen: „To musíte cítit jako velkou nespravedlnost, co se s vámi děje" (Klíma 2004, 17f.).[9] In der Zeit vor dem Transport nach Theresienstadt weckt die jüdische Identität des Erzählers das (nicht zwingend negative) Interesse seiner Mitmenschen – die Verbindung zwischen dem gelben Stern und dem Tod in einer Gaskammer ist hier nicht ultimativ gegeben. Ein Jude zu sein bedeutet (noch) vor allem, ein ‚Anderer' zu sein. Das zukünftige, katastrophische Schicksal ist allerdings bereits absehbar.

Die Abwehrhaltung des Erzählers gegen den Status eines Juden resultiert teilweise aus dem Protest und der Angst vor der Ausgrenzung, teilweise ist sie ein Ergebnis der Erziehung durch seine Eltern, die sich im Gestus der Emanzipation vom Judentum realisiert. Die Mutter des Erzählers ermahnt ihn häufig noch im Lager, nicht „mit den Zionisten" zu spielen; außerdem wählt sein Vater die Identität eines internationalen Kommunisten. Das Schicksal des Ich-Erzählers und seiner Familie steht somit symptomatisch für eine ganze Generation ostmitteleuropäischer Juden, die im Zuge der rassistischen Gesetze ihre Akkulturation aufgeben mussten. Die ungewollte Zuschreibung der jüdischen Identität führt im Text dazu, dass in den potenziellen Opfern Hass und Affekte sowie Abwehrreaktionen entstehen. Interessant ist, dass die Opfer bei Klíma nicht *per se* gut sind und nicht über, häufig Juden zugeschriebene, moralisch ‚höhere' Standards verfügen. Das „Gutheitskorsett" (Weigel 1996, 188) wird somit im Text auf die Seite gelegt bzw. gar nicht erst angezogen. In der Erzählung *Marcela* werden die Rachegefühle und die Mobilisierung durch Affekte direkt artikuliert:

> Přesto mi právě ten nepochopitelný posměšný výkřik od někoho, kdo se ke mně ještě před několika dny choval přátelsky, to první ponížení, utkvěly v paměti a staly se

---

[9] „Ich dachte, die Juden haben einen anderen [Herrgott]."; „Das muss sich für euch wie eine riesige Ungerechtigkeit anfühlen, was jetzt mit euch geschieht".

jakoby ztělesněním všeho, co mě potkávalo. Nikdy jsem nebyl mstivý a měl jsem přirozený odpor k nenávisti, ale tu copatou plavovlásku jsem nenáviděl, její obraz se po celý zbytek války uchoval v mé paměti, a já si představoval den pomsty (Klíma 2004, 25).

Und dennoch war es gerade dieser unbegreifliche spöttische Ausruf von jemandem, der sich mir gegenüber noch einige Tage zuvor freundschaftlich verhalten hatte, diese erste Erniedrigung, die mir im Gedächtnis haften blieben und gewissermaßen zur Verkörperung all dessen wurden, was mir widerfuhr. Ich war nie rachsüchtig und hatte einen angeborenen Widerwillen gegen Hass, aber diese Blondine mit ihren Zöpfen hasste ich, ihr Bild blieb mir den ganzen restlichen Krieg über im Gedächtnis haften, und ich malte mir den Tag aus, an dem ich Rache nehmen würde.

Die erwünschte und projizierte Rache wird dennoch nicht persönlich ausgeübt – die Erzählung endet mit der Vertreibung der Deutschen aus der Stadt. Das Mädchen, das den Erzähler als „Jude" beschimpfte, muss ebenfalls ihren bisherigen Wohnort verlassen, und obwohl sie ihm zum Abschied ihre „baldige Rückkehr" versichert, ist klar, dass sie nie zurückkommen wird. Solche unerwarteten Veränderungen in menschlichen Hierarchien und Beziehungen, wenn sich der Status von Opfern und Tätern verändert, schildert Klíma sachlich und mit leichter Ironie. Die plötzlichen Wendungen und überraschenden Entwicklungen scheinen aus seiner Sicht ein immanenter Bestandteil des Lebens zu sein, über den man sich lediglich wundern kann. Das Leben besteht aus Kommen und Gehen; die Rolle des Opfers liegt in unmittelbarer Nähe zu der des Täters. Es gehört zu den häufig verwendeten Verfahren in *Moje nebezpečné výlety*, die Handlung der Erzählungen durch einen Wendepunkt zu strukturieren. In vielen Erzählungen kommt es auf der Handlungsebene zu plötzlichen Veränderungen, es ergibt sich etwas Neues, oder eine vorher nicht absehbare Dynamik tritt in Kraft. In der Erzählung *Slečna Vlasta* (*Fräulein Vlasta*) wird z.B. durch dieses Verfahren (hier: die unerwartete Reise Vlastas) das Ende einer Bekanntschaft angekündigt, das zugleich metonymisch für die sich nähernde Katastrophe steht:

Ale víckrát jsme už na hřbitov stejně nešli. Ona někam odjela, a když se vrátila, už jsem musel nosit hvězdu a pak nás odvezli do *ghetta*, odkud jsme už neměli nikdy živí vyjít. Když jsme se po válce vrátili, sotva jsem ji zahlédl. Nosila smutek, protože jí za revoluce zastřelili tatínka, prý *kolaboranta* a *udavače* (Klíma 2004, 19).

Aber wir gingen ohnehin nicht mehr zusammen auf den Friedhof. Sie war irgendwohin verreist, und als sie zurückkam, musste ich schon den Stern tragen, und dann brachte man uns ins *Ghetto*, das wir eigentlich nicht mehr lebend verlassen sollten. Als wir nach dem Krieg zurückkamen, habe ich sie kaum bemerkt.. Sie trug Trauer, weil ihr Vater während des Aufstandes erschossen worden war, angeblich weil er ein *Kollaborateur* und *Denunziant* war.

Klímas Erinnerungen an die Zeit im Lager fokussieren drei Themenkomplexe: Die Versuche, den Alltag möglichst ‚normal' zu gestalten; die Reflexionen über die unendlich lange Zeit, die überbrückt werden muss; und die Todesangst, die die Transporte „nach Osten" auslösen. Auch hier gilt das Prinzip der plötzlichen Veränderung als ein strukturelles Merkmal der erzählten Geschichte. Unerwartet geht der Unterricht in der Erzählung *Benjamin* zu Ende; plötzlich stirbt Frau Heda, die noch einen Tag zuvor die Zukunft aus den Karten vorhergesagt hatte (*Paní Heda*); in *Hodiny básnictiví* (*Stunden der Dichtung*) kommt es zu einer raschen Vergrößerung der Zahl der Transporte. Das Leben in Theresienstadt folgt keinem Plan, es ist unberechenbar und unzuverlässig – es gilt, sich anzupassen und zu versuchen, trotz der ständigen Veränderungen den Mut nicht zu verlieren und um das Überleben zu kämpfen. Dennoch ist das Überleben kein heroischer Akt – Klíma ist nicht an dem Wiederholen einer aufbauenden Narration über Kampf und Widerstand interessiert –, es ist eher ein Akt, zu dem man sich immer aufs Neue überwinden muss. In *Moje nebezpečné výlety* ist die Katastrophe, ähnlich wie auch in der Theorie zur Holocaustliteratur und extremer Erfahrung, als eine Notsituation konzeptualisiert, die sich nur dank der Perspektive einer Zeit *danach* ertragen lässt.

Klímas Theresienstadt ist ein Ort, der tiefere Einblicke in die Tragödie des Holocaust ermöglicht. Seine Erinnerungen bestätigen Dan Diners These, ein Ghetto als „ein Schwellenort im Übergang von einer Welt der Normalität in das Weltende der Vernichtung" sei ein Ort der „den Todgeweihten geliehenen Zeit", einer Zwischenzeit, die „einen Blick auf das Geschehen, der sich auf den anderen Stufen des Weges in die Vernichtung so nicht einzustellen vermag", erlaubt (Diner 2007, 25f.). Der Erzähler in *Moje nebezpečné výlety* erkennt und versteht den Ernst der Lage, in der er sich befindet, auch wenn es sich teilweise um ein kindliches Erkennen und Verstehen handelt. Er registriert die Diskontinuitäten des Lebens im Lager und weiß, dass er Opfer und Zeuge eines Zivilisationsbruches ist. Dieser Bruch wird durch den Tod und das Verschwinden der Menschen, die in regelmäßigen Abständen in die Gaskammer verbracht werden, signalisiert. Die Erzählung *Benjamin* schildert die Geschichte einer angehenden

Freundschaft zwischen dem Ich-Erzähler und einem Jungen namens Benjamin, dem Sohn eines Ältestenrates im Ghetto. Die Freundschaft wird aus der Perspektive des Erzählers dargestellt und endet mit seinem zeitlich versetzten Kommentar, der sich auf die früheren Spekulationen der Freunde über die Zukunft bezieht: „Já přežil, zatímco jeho odvezli několik týdnů nato *na východ*. Prý neskončil v plynu, zastřelili ho" (Klíma 2004, 59).[10] Durch den Metastandpunkt nimmt der Erzähler hier Bezug auf die Tatsache, dass während des Krieges jeden Tag Menschen in die Gaskammer geschickt wurden, und wird zu einem Zeugen dieser Katastrophe. Bereits im Ghetto wusste der Erzähler, dass die Transporte „nach Osten" eine Reise in den Tod bedeuten; die Frequenz solcher Reisen hat das Wissen immer aufs Neue vor Augen geführt und befestigt. Deswegen war er, wie in der Erzählung *Paní Heda* zu lesen ist, jedes Mal froh, wenn eine solche gefährliche Reise ohne ihn stattgefunden hat.[11]

Täterschaft verstehen

Die Rückkehr aus dem Lager und das Leben danach gehören zu den Motiven, die sich durch viele Erzählungen des Bandes wie ein roter Faden ziehen. Das Thema des Neuanfangs und der Wiederherstellung der Normalität nimmt Ivan Klíma zum Anlass, um sich mit der Problematik der Täterschaft und der Verantwortung für das Verbrechen der Judenmorde auseinanderzusetzen. In seinen Erzählungen sucht er, wie František Cinger bemerkt, „vinu i nevinu, spravedlnost i bezmocnost prožívané křivdy" (Cinger 2004).[12] Einer der zentralen Punkte, die ihn in diesem Zusammenhang beschäftigen, ist die Frage danach, warum so viele Menschen sich am Holocaust beteiligt haben und welche Menschen das waren.[13] Sein Interesse gilt gleichermaßen den Tätern aus der ersten

---

[10] „Ich habe überlebt, während man ihn einige Wochen darauf *nach Osten* transportiert hat. Angeblich endete er nicht im Gas, er wurde erschossen."

[11] Das Motiv des Transports wird in dieser Erzählung mit dem Motiv des Kartenspielens verbunden: „Také jsem věděl, že pikové eso s křížovým znamená dlouhou cestu a začínal jsem chápat, proč bylo dobré, že mi nevyšla" (Klíma 2004, 42; „Ich begriff, dass Pik-As mit Kreuz eine lange Reise bedeutet und ich begann zu verstehen, warum es gut war, dass ich diese Karte nicht bekam").

[12] „Schuld und Unschuld, Gerechtigkeit und die Machtlosigkeit erlebten Unrechts".

[13] Am Rande sei angemerkt, dass Klíma diese Frage auch in seinen anderen Schriften verfolgt. Im Essay *Ideologičtí vrazi* (*Ideological Murderers*) schreibt er über die Memoiren von

und der zweiten Reihe (wie z.B. Rudi Heindl aus Theresienstadt) wie den „ganz gewöhnlichen" Tätern von nebenan (vgl. hierzu Paul 2002). Die Letzteren verkörpern im Text die ehemaligen tschechischen Kollaborateure und die deutsche Bevölkerung, die nach dem Krieg immer noch auf den Straßen zu treffen sind. In der neuen Situation sind sie diejenigen, die ihr Zuhause verlassen und sich vor Selbstjustiz fürchten müssen. Nur mit Koffer und auf der Flucht verlieren sie ihre frühere Macht, obwohl die Tatsache, dass sie weggehen müssen, den Opfern ihre Traumata nicht wegnehmen kann. Klíma registriert die Veränderung in der Gesellschaftsstruktur und beschreibt, wie z.b. die Häuser der Täter nun von den Opfern bewohnt werden oder wie die ehemaligen Täter nun die Opfer um Hilfe und Unterstützung bitten, wie die Familie Topol in der Erzählung *Luisa*. Anders als in der Literatur, die unmittelbar nach dem Krieg geschrieben wurde, sind die Täter hier keine Monster, sie werden weder dämonisiert noch entkonkretisiert. Nichtsdestotrotz ist der Erzähler häufig in seiner Vorstellung eines ‚Idealtäters' gefangen und gleitet deswegen in der Beschreibung der Täterschaft in ein tragisch-pathetisches Narrativ ab. Dieses Narrativ wird in der Erzählung *Paní Truda* (*Frau Truda*) interessant eingesetzt – mit ästhetischem Rückgriff auf das Konzept der Ekphrasis.

Die Handlung der Erzählung *Paní Truda* ist in der Nachkriegszeit angesiedelt. Da überall Wohnraumknappheit herrscht, verbringt der Erzähler einige Tage bei seiner deutschen Nachbarin Truda. Als er kurz in der Wohnung allein bleibt,

---

Rudolf Höß („Žádnou knihu jsem nečetl tolikrát" – „I've never read a book so many times"), die er für ein beispielloses Täternarrativ hält und für einen von wenigen Texten, die die Skala der ideologischen Verblendung zeigen. Klíma reflektiert dabei die zentralen Probleme der Täterforschung und weist, ähnlich wie viele Wissenschaftler, darauf hin, dass es sich bei den Täterprofilen um Menschen handelt, die sich häufig an dem Verbrechen freiwillig beteiligen wollten: „Tohoto vraždění se zúčastňovaly tisíce mužů a žen, úředníků, dozorců, chladnokrevných zabijáků, sadistů i poslušných vykonavatelů, kteří rozhodně nebyli ve stavu vojáků zapitých krví, měli dny, týdny a měsíce k tomu, aby mohli zvážit vše, co konají. Vykonávali přesně, snaživě rozkazy, ať byly jakékoliv, ať se třeba dotýkaly jejich citů nebo byly dokonce v rozporu s jakýmisi zbytky jejich morálky a svědomí" (Klíma 2009a, 63) – „Thousands of men and women, officials, guards, cold-blooded killers, sadist, and obedient administrators participated in this slaughter, and they were clearly not in the condition of a soldier drunk with blood. They had days, weeks, and months to consider what they were doing. They painstakingly – and soberly – carried out orders, whatever they were, whether they impinged on their emotions or perhaps were in conflict with whatever remnant of morality and conscience they had" (Klíma 2009b, 419).

entdeckt er eine Sammlung von Fotografien. Einige davon zeigen „einen hübschen Jungen", Klaus, den Sohn seiner Gastgeberin, der als deutscher Soldat in den Krieg gezogen ist. Auf einer der Fotografien posiert Klaus auf einer Hafenmole in Odessa und wirft der Kamera einen entspannten Blick zu. Diese Aufnahme, die an ein Urlaubsfoto und nicht an ein Kriegsdokument erinnert, verändert die Wahrnehmung des Erzählers, der Bilder der Gewalt und nicht private Aufnahmen erwartete: „[...] hledal jsem snímek, kde by byl Klaus někoho vraždil, věšel anebo aspoň bil, ale žádnou takovou fotografii jsem nenašel" (Klíma 2004, 115).[14] Die zufällig gefundene Fotografie übt auf ihn eine Wirkung aus, die wir nach Roland Barthes *punctum* nennen können. Anders als das *studium*, das eher die allgemeine Rezeption einer Fotografie ohne besondere emotionale Beteiligung bezeichnet, kommt es beim *punctum* auf das emotionale Engagement des Rezipienten an. Diese Wirkungsweise zielt darauf ab, den Betrachter anzusprechen, ihn zu berühren: „[...] *punctum*, das bedeutet auch: Stich, kleines Loch, kleiner Fleck, kleiner Schnitt [...] Das *punctum* einer Photographie, das ist jenes Zufällige an ihr, das mich *besticht* (mich aber auch verwundet, trifft)" (Barthes 1989, 35). Die Tatsache, dass auf der Fotografie ein Täter außerhalb der Täterrolle zu sehen ist, wirkt auf den Erzähler befremdlich. Auf einer Metaebene stellt sich hier aber immer die gleiche Frage: Wer sind die Täter, die Millionen von Juden vergast haben?

Eine weitere Konzeptualisierung der Täterschaft findet in der Erzählung *Mengele* statt. Hier berichtet der Erzähler über ein – fiktives, dennoch nicht fingiertes – Treffen mit Josef Mengele, dem Arzt aus dem KZ Auschwitz, der durch seine grausamen Experimente an Zwillingen in die Geschichte des Nationalsozialismus eingegangen ist. Das Treffen findet einige Jahre nach dem Krieg statt und wird sehr theatralisch inszeniert. Der Erzähler und Mengele treffen sich dank der Vermittlung der deutschen Ärztin Hilde an einem abgeschiedenen Ort in der Schweiz. Der Erzähler wird zu dem Treffen mit einem Auto gefahren und muss während der Fahrt eine Augenbinde tragen.[15] Mengele wird als ein „Mann

---

[14] „[...]Ich suchte nach einem Bild, auf dem Klaus jemanden ermordete, erhängte oder wenigstens schlug, aber ich habe keine solche Fotografie gefunden".
[15] Ein möglicher Referenzrahmen für diese Erzählung ist der Kitsch-Diskurs. Zur bewertenden, anti-deskriptiven Anwendung der Kategorie des Holocaust-Kitsches vgl. Kertész 1998 und Kuon 2015.

ohne Eigenschaften" beschrieben: nicht schön, nicht interessant und auch nicht abstoßend (vgl. Klíma 2004, 137). Das Opfer und der Täter teilen sich während des Gesprächs einen engen Raum, der wie eine Theaterbühne nur mit einem Tisch und zwei Stühlen ausgestattet ist. Über die Funktion von solchen *face-to-face*-Konversationen schreibt Anja Tippner:

> Wir kennen verschiedene Formen der Verschriftlichung von nationalsozialistischer Täterschaft: In den Akten der Strafverfolgung, den Berichten der Opfer und eher selten auch in autobiographischen Texten oder Bio-Interviews. [...] Gegenüber konventionellen Täterbiographien haben biographische Gespräche oder Interviews den Vorteil, dass sie scheinbar unser Bedürfnis nach Authentizität, nach dem O-Ton, nach einer face-to-face-Situation und einer Unmittelbarkeit, die das geschriebene Wort vermeintlich nicht bietet, befriedigen. [...] Doch soll man das Gespräch mit einem Täter überhaupt suchen? Soll man wirklich in seine Welt eindringen? Und welchen Preis muss man dafür zahlen? (Tippner 2013, 45f.).

Klímas Bedürfnis, „in die Welt des Täters einzudringen", resultiert aus dem Wunsch, durch ein persönliches Gespräch ein Täterprofil und mit ihm relevante Erkenntnisse zu gewinnen, auch im Rahmen einer inszenierten Begegnung. Eine *face-to-face*-Situation soll ermöglichen, die Täterschaft Mengeles verstehen zu können, insbesondere das, „[...] co cítí člověk, který vynáší tisíc rozsudků denně nad lidmi, které ani nezná" (Klíma 2004, 138).[16]

Das Gespräch mit Mengele ist von Anfang an als eine Art Verhör aufgebaut, auch wenn die Voraussetzung der klassischen Verhörsituation, „eine unauflösliche Beziehung zwischen Kommunikation und Gewalt" (Niehaus 2003, 11), nicht erfüllt ist. Das Ziel des Erzählers ist es, durch gezielte Fragen ein Geständnis zu bekommen, denn nur wenn es ein Geständnis gibt, kann das Bedürfnis nach Strafe erfüllt werden (vgl. Brooks 2000, 61). Der ehemalige Häftling möchte Mengele zwingen, über seine Tätigkeit auf der Rampe in Auschwitz zu sprechen und über deren Konsequenzen zu reflektieren. Mengele möchte sich jedoch auf ein solches Verhör nicht einlassen, und statt ein Geständnis abzulegen, versucht er die Opferrolle für sich zu vereinnahmen[17], weshalb das Gespräch scheitern muss. In seiner Konzeptualisierungen der Täterschaft stuft

---

[16] „[...] was ein Mensch fühlt, der jeden Tag tausend Urteile über Menschen fällt, die er nicht einmal kennt".

[17] Der Soziologe Harald Welzer hat überzeugend gezeigt, dass die „Wechselrahmung", d.h. die Inanspruchnahme von Opferrollen durch den Täter, eine gängige Praxis in biographischen Gesprächen ist (vgl. Welzer/Moller/Tschuggnall 2002, 82).

Klíma Mengele in einem Überschneidungsbereich von vielen Täterprofilen ein: Er scheint ihm ein ideologischer Fanatiker, ein Befehlstäter sowie ein pragmatischer Karrierist gleichzeitig zu sein. Er glaube an Hitler und habe sich in den Dienst des medizinischen Fortschritts gestellt, die Kosten (vergaste Kinder) waren ihm dabei unwichtig – so das Fazit dieses Austauschs.

In Anbetracht dessen, dass es sich hier um eine fiktive Gesprächssituation handelt, ist es interessant, dass Klíma die Figur Mengeles in solch einem Maße klischeehaft konzipiert hat. Mengeles Erklärungen und Antworten bedienen sich tradierter Vorstellungen über die Denkweise eines Täters. Der Mephisto aus Auschwitz bekommt nicht die Chance, eine eigene Argumentationslogik zu entwickeln oder das Gespräch zu vertiefen. Durch eine solche Figuration scheint Ivan Klíma indirekt signalisieren zu wollen, dass es sich doch nicht lohnt, einem Täter eine eigene Stimme und eine eigene Persönlichkeit zu verleihen. Um diese Position zu verstärken, lässt er Mengele abschließend einen Satz sagen, der dem Erzähler die Schuld für das Scheitern des Gesprächs zuweist: „Vidím, že se chystáte napsat to, co píšou všichni. Jste plní nenávisti, která vám nedovolí vidět věci tak, jak se staly" (Klíma 2004, 144).[18] Die Pluralität möglicher Deutungen für das *face-to face* Treffen mit einem Täter ist somit ausgeschlossen.

Fazit

Jede Vergangenheit ist uns nur durch mediale Vermittlung zugänglich, oder, wie es Didi-Huberman formuliert hat, „sie existiert oder sie besteht nur noch aus den Bildern, die wir uns von ihr machen" (Didi-Huberman 2000, 47). Ivan Klímas Erzählsammlung entwirft Bilder, die uns an traumatische Orte und Schauplätze der Vergangenheit zurückversetzen. Dennoch geht die Bedeutung seiner Texte über das Dokumentarische hinaus – die nationalsozialistische Vernichtungspolitik ist kein zentrales Sujet des besprochenen Erzählbandes. Klímas Ziel ist nicht die literarische Darstellung des historischen Ereignisses selbst, sondern seine Neukontextualisierung. Das Nachleben der Shoah zeigt sich in Klímas Interpretationen als ein langwieriger und komplizierter Prozess, in dem es zu Verschie-

---

[18] „Ich sehe, dass Sie das schreiben wollen, was alle schreiben. Sie sind voll von Hass, und dieser erlaubt es Ihnen nicht, die Dinge so zu sehen, wie sie geschahen".

bungen in der Triade Täter – Opfer – Zuschauer kommt und wo die Vergangenheit mit der Gegenwart verschränkt wird. Das Wissen über die Katastrophe stellt am Anfang des 21. Jahrhunderts also nicht mehr eine Herausforderung dar; zentraler scheint die Frage zu sein, wie man das Wissen immer wieder aufs Neue aktivieren und ästhetisch interessant erzählen kann. Die Tragödie der Judenvernichtung wird in Klímas Texten indirekt, durch Ellipsen und Metaphern („Transport *nach Osten*", „Koffer packen") beschrieben und in einen Kontext der zwischenmenschlichen Interaktionen gestellt. Das Ghetto Theresienstadt wird in seiner tragischen Dimension als Ort der Vernichtung, aber zugleich auch als ein Raum des menschlichen Handelns vergegenwärtigt. Konsequenterweise zeigt der Autor die Veränderungen, die die Shoah, sowohl bei den Opfern wie auch bei den Tätern, hinterlassen hat. Die Freundschaft und Liebe, Rache und Hass, Vergebung und Aussöhnung sind für Ivan Klíma wichtige Koordinaten, mit denen man eine Erzählung über die traumatische Vergangenheit gestalten kann. Ein Merkmal dieser Vergangenheit besteht darin, dass sie die Gegenwart und die Zukunft bestimmt und dazu führt, dass die Zeit nach der Katastrophe zu einer untergeordneten Zeit wird, einer Zeit, die sich stark an das Vergangene anlehnt. Die durch Veränderungen und Diskontinuitäten gekennzeichneten Texte des Erzählbandes *Moje nebezpečné výlety* leisten einen Beitrag zum tschechischen kollektiven Gedächtnis und entwerfen Bilder einer verschobenen und multiplen Zeitlichkeit.

Literaturverzeichnis

Barthes, Roland 1989: Die helle Kammer. Bemerkung zur Photographie. Aus dem Franz. übers. v. Dietrich Leube. Frankfurt am Main.
Bauman, Zygmunt 1995: Große Gärten, kleine Gärten. Allosemitismus: Vormodern, Modern, Postmodern. In: Michael Werz (Hrsg.): Antisemitismus und Gesellschaft. Zur Diskussion um Auschwitz, Kulturindustrie und Gewalt. Frankfurt am Main, S. 44-61.
Benz, Wolfgang 2013: Theresienstadt. Eine Geschichte von Täuschung und Vernichtung. München.
Brooks, Peter 2000: Troubling Confessions. Speaking Guilt in Law and Literature. Chicago.
Cinger, František 2004: Literární procházky vlastním životem. In: Právo 14, 289, S. 11.
Didi-Huberman, Georges 2000: Vor einem Bild. Aus dem Franz. übers. v. Reinhold Werner. München.
Diner, Dan 2007: Gegenläufige Gedächtnisse. Über Geltung und Wirkung des Holocaust. Göttingen.

Halbwachs, Maurice 1967: Das kollektive Gedächtnis. Aus d. Franz. übers. v. Holde Lhoest-Offermann. Stuttgart.

Hallama, Peter 2015: Nationale Helden und jüdische Opfer. Tschechische Repräsentationen des Holocaust. Göttingen.

Haman, Aleš 2004: Klímův návrat k autobiografickým povídkám. In: Lidové noviny 17,260, S. 30.

Heeg, Günther – *Denzel* Markus A. (Hrsg.) 2011: Globalizing Areas, kulturelle Flexionen und die Herausforderung der Geisteswissenschaften. Stuttgart.

Ibler, Reinhard 2015: Ist Ladislav Fuks' *Leichenverbrenner* ein Werk der Holocaustliteratur? In: The Aspects of Genres in the Holocaust Literatures in Central Europe. Ed. by Jiří Holý. Praha, S. 127-142.

Kertész, Imre 1998: Wem gehört Auschwitz? In: Die Zeit v. 19.11.1998 (Nr. 48), S. 55-56.

Klíma, Ivan 1997: Miriam. In: ders.: Meine ersten Lieben. Aus d. Tschech. übers. v. Anja Tippner. München, S. 7-24.

ders. 2004: Moje nebezpečné výlety. Praha.

ders. Ivan 2008: Die Menschen verstummten. In: Nirgendwo und überall zu Haus. Gespräche mit Überlebenden des Holocaust. Hrsg. v. Martin Doerry. München, S. 116-126.

ders. 2009a: Moje šílené století. Praha.

ders. 2009b: My Crazy Century. Translated from the Czech by Craig Cravens. London.

Kuon, Peter 2015: Holocaust-Kitsch? Zur Polemik um Jonathan Littells Bestseller *Les Bienveillantes* in Frankreich, Deutschland und in den USA. In: Kitsch und Nation. Zur kulturellen Modellierung eines polemischen Begriffs. Hrsg. v. Kathrin Ackermann u. Christopher F. Laferl. Bielefeld, S. 99-119.

Landsberg, Alison 2004: Prosthetic Memory: The Transformation of American Remembrance in the Age of Mass Culture. New York.

Niehaus, Michael 2003: Das Verhör. Geschichte – Theorie – Fiktion. München.

Paul, Gerhard 2002: Von Psychopathen, Technokraten des Terrors und ‚ganz gewöhnlichen' Deutschen. Die Täter der Shoah im Spiegel der Forschung. In: ders. (Hrsg.): Die Täter der Shoah. Fanatische Nationalsozialisten oder ganz normale Deutsche? Göttingen, S. 13-93.

Schwarte, Ludger 2013: Die Architektur der Zeit. In: Johannes Myssok – Ludger Schwarte (Hrsg.): Zeitstrukturen. Techniken der Vergegenwärtigung in Wissenschaft und Kunst. Berlin, S. 133-147.

Schwarz, Wolfgang F. 2014: Holocaust und KZ im Fokus tschechischer Literatur nach 2000. Zu Arnošt Goldflams *Doma u Hitlerů* und Radka Denemarkovás *Peníze od Hitlera.* In: Der Holocaust in den mitteleuropäischen Literaturen und Kulturen seit 1989. Hrsg v. Reinhard Ibler. Stuttgart, S. 157-171.

Thurn, Nike 2015: Allosemitismus als ‚Anderung' der Juden. In: dies.: ‚Falsche Juden'. Performative Identitäten in der deutschsprachigen Literatur von Lessing bis Walser. Göttingen, S. 38-54.

Tippner, Anja 2013: Moczarskis Gespräche mit dem Henker. Zur Verschränkung von Opfern und Täterdiskursen. In: Silke Segler-Meßner – Claudia Nickel (Hrsg.): Von Tätern und Opfern. Zur medialen Darstellung von politisch und ethnisch motivierter Gewalt im 20./21. Jahrhundert. Frankfurt am Main, S. 41-61.

dies. 2015: Postkatastroficzne relikty i relikwie: los obrazów po Szoa. In: Po Zagładzie. Narracje postkatastroficzne. Red. Anna Artwińska, Przemysław Czapliński, Alina Molisak, Anja Tippner. (= Poznańskie Studia Polonistyczne 25,45), S. 237-257.

Wansing, Rudolf 2001: Rekonstruktion. In: Gedächtnis und Erinnerung. Ein interdisziplinäres Lexikon. Hrsg. v. Nicolas Pethes u. Jens Ruchatz. Hamburg, S. 480.

Weigel, Sigrid 1996: Shylocks Wiederkehr. Die Verwandlung von Schuld in Schulden oder: Zum symbolischen Tausch der Wiedergutmachung. In: dies. – Birgit R. Erdle (Hrsg.): Fünfzig Jahre danach. Zur Nachgeschichte des Nationalsozialismus. Zürich, S. 165 -192.

Welzer, Harald – *Moller,* Sabine – *Tschuggnall,* Karoline 2002: Wechselrahmen. Leidens- und Heldengeschichten als Tradierungstypen. In: dies. (Hrsg.): „Opa war kein Nazi".. Nationalsozialismus und Holocaust im Familiengedächtnis.. Frankfurt am Main, S. 81-105.

White, Hayden 1991: Auch Klio dichtet oder Die Fiktion des Faktischen. Aus dem Amerik. übers. v. Brigitte Brinkmann-Siepmann u. Thomas Siepmann. Stuttgart.

Time Spanning Bridges.
Remembrance of Holocaust in Ivan Klíma's Short Story Collection
Moje nebezpečné výlety (My Dangerous Excursions)

This article focuses on Ivan Klíma's short story collection *Moje nebezpečné výlety,* published in 2004 in Prague. Although in most of them the author (born in 1931) draws upon his own experiences at Theresienstadt ghetto, these texts are not of autobiographical nature. Instead, they may be classified as a literary, fictional testimony of the Holocaust. Their characteristic feature – and this is the main thesis of the article – is the multilayered temporality: the narrator of the short stories combines various time levels and moves seamlessly from the traumas of the past to the present, exploring the consequences and the ‚long duration' of the catastrophe. Holocaust is depicted here not as a state, but as a process, which bears impact on contemporary constellations, too. In this article, I analyse the strategies and methods of reminiscence and of updating the past as applied by Klíma, as well as the main theme and motifs of the stories. What comes to the fore is the tendency to present Holocaust through the lens of metonymy: the narrator does not strive to give a realistic account of the past events or to ‚bear witness' to them, but rather to capture the insidious, ominous workings of the traumatic events, whose negative echoes impede catharsis. Many of these stories revolve around the topic of perpetration and perpetrators – the narrator, on the one hand, lets on how difficult it is to present the literary perspective of the perpetrator and, on the other hand, points out the impossibility of reconciliation of the remembrance of perpetrators with the remembrance of victims. *Moje nebezpečné výlety,* in this sense, is an interesting post-catastrophic narrative, reflecting how the catastrophe of the Holocaust is updated and represented in modern Czech literature.

Zum Motiv des Holocaust in der Vertreibungsliteratur

Marta Škubalová, Praha

0. Vorbemerkung

Für die Literatur über die Zwangsaussiedlung der Deutschen etablierte sich der Begriff ‚Vertreibungsliteratur'. Seit dem Zweiten Weltkrieg wurde eine große Zahl von (überwiegend, aber nicht ausschließlich belletristischen) Texten publiziert, die sich dem Thema der Zwangsaussiedlung widmen.[1] Es wäre ein Irrtum zu glauben, dass es sich nur um solche Texte handelt, die von beteiligten Akteuren geschrieben wurden. Vor allem seit dem Jahre 2000 beschäftigen sich mit diesem Thema auch junge Autoren, die den Diskurs der Vertreibungsliteratur in die tschechische Gesellschaft einbrachten.

Das Ziel des vorliegenden Artikels ist es zu zeigen, wie das Holocaustmotiv als Nebenmotiv in einem anderen Diskurs verwendet werden kann, und zwar innerhalb der Literatur über die Zwangsaussiedlung der Deutschen aus Mittel- und Osteuropa nach dem Zweiten Weltkrieg. Im Vergleich zum Holocaustmotiv stellt das Thema der Zwangsaussiedlung einerseits die Frage nach Tätern und Opfern auf den Kopf, anderseits kann man gewisse Berührungspunkte finden. Zu diesen gehören vor allem Darstellungen traumatischer Ereignisse wie z.B. der Heimatverlust und der Tod nahestehender Familienmitglieder.

Der wichtigste Punkt scheint hier die Problematik der Schuld zu sein. In den Erzählungen, in denen die Motive des Holocaust und der Zwangsaussiedlung zusammen vorkommen, taucht die Frage danach auf, wie Schuld verglichen werden kann. Generell werden die Deutschen in erster Linie als diejenigen dargestellt, die für die Judenverfolgung verantwortlich waren. Ähnlich werden die Tschechen im Hinblick auf die Zwangsaussiedlung ganz allgemein als die Täter wahrgenommen. Es stellt sich die Frage, ob die Verbindung dieser Themen innerhalb von Prosatexten neue Facetten der Problematik bieten kann, und, wenn ja, dann welche.

Für den vorliegenden Artikel wurden drei Texte ausgewählt, die sowohl die Zwangsaussiedlung als auch den Holocaust thematisieren, wobei die Au-

---

[1] Es gibt eine Bibliographie der Vertreibungsliteratur, die mehr als 2000 Eintragungen beinhaltet: vgl. Dornemann 2005.

tor(inn)en unterschiedlicher Herkunft sind und auch die Sprache der Texte differiert: es geht um zwei deutschsprachige und ein tschechisches Werk. Wichtigstes Auswahlkriterium waren die Diskrepanzen in der Behandlung des Holocaust im Vertreibungsdiskurs. Konkret handelt es sich um Olga Barényis *Prager Totentanz*, Radka Denemarkovás *Peníze od Hitlera* und Josef Mühlbergers *Der Galgen am Weinberg*.

1. Zur Terminologie

Für die Zwangsaussiedlung der Deutschen als historisches Ereignis gibt es eine Reihe unterschiedlicher Bezeichnungen. Die Verwendung dieser Begriffe verweist nicht nur auf die Position des jeweiligen Sprechers, sondern ist meist auch mit bestimmten Konnotationen verbunden.

Im tschechischen Umfeld überwiegt der Terminus ‚odsun', was sich am besten mit dem deutschen Ausdruck ‚Abschiebung' wiedergeben lässt.[2] Dieser Begriff bringt nach Eva Hahnová zum Ausdruck, dass die deutsche Bevölkerung aus der Position der Sieger verdrängt, d.h. ‚abgeschoben' wurde. Für Hahnová beinhaltet der Begriff keine ethischen oder juristischen Konnotationen (vgl. Hahnová 1999, 158). Im (deutschen) *Lexikon der Vertreibung* heißt es dagegen, dass im Tschechischen der Terminus ‚odsun' „[…] tendenziell relativierende, z. T. verharmlosende Interpretationen" beinhalte. „[…] Ähnliches gilt teilweise für die Bez. *Transfer* im Englischen" (Brandes u.a. 2010, 695). Ganz offensichtlich hängt die Wahrnehmung des Begriffs ‚odsun' von der Perspektive des Sprechers ab. Meiner Meinung nach wird dieses Wort auf tschechischer Seite zwar als neutral wahrgenommen, dennoch ist es auch mit gewissen rechtlichen Positionen verbunden.[3] Innerhalb der tschechischen Gesellschaft wird ‚Abschiebung' aber irrtümlicherweise als Synonym zum Begriff ‚Vertreibung' benutzt. Mit ‚Abschiebung' sollte eigentlich nur der Zeitraum gekennzeichnet werden, der im Herbst 1945 begann. Denn in diesem Herbst beruhigte sich die Rachsucht der

---

[2] Im Deutschen wird diese Terminologie kaum verwendet, selbst im Deutschen Universalwörterbuch (vgl. Duden 2006) ist der Begriff ‚Abschiebung' in dieser Bedeutung nicht zu finden.

[3] Der Terminus ‚odsun' wurde sogar Teil des tschechischen bzw. tschechoslowakischen Rechtssystems (vgl. Jech 2003, 90).

befreiten Tschechen schon in gewissem Maße und die Lebensbedingungen der Deutschen verbesserten sich.

Im Unterschied dazu sollte man korrekterweise als die ‚Vertreibung' nur den Zeitraum zwischen 8. Mai und 2. August des Jahres 1945 bezeichnen (vgl. Pešek 2004, 29), in dem die Mehrzahl der Deutschen ums Leben kam. Das auf deutscher Seite bevorzugte Wort ‚Vertreibung' beinhaltet aber eine klar negative Bewertung im Sinne einer Vertreibung z.b. von Schädlingen (vgl. Hahnová 1999, 158). Es ist eine Tatsache, dass der Begriff ‚Vertreibung' von deutschsprachigen Sprechern für die Bezeichnung der Geschehnisse in den Nachkriegsmonaten häufig genauso unkritisch benutzt wird wie von den Tschechen das Wort ‚Abschiebung'. Der Differenz zwischen der spontanen Vertreibung und der späteren, stärker organisierten Zwangsaussiedlung der Deutschen kann man durch die Benutzung beider Termini ‚Vertreibung' (‚vyhnání') und ‚Abschiebung' (‚odsun') gerecht werden.

In der Fachliteratur finden noch weitere Termini Verwendung, so etwa ‚Umsiedlung' (‚přesídlení'). Dieser suggeriert, es habe sich um eine Art organisierten, zumindest teilweise freiwilligen Umzug gehandelt – was freilich nicht der Fall war, durften die Deutschen doch kaum mehr als das Lebensnotwendigste mit sich nehmen.[4] Für angemessener halte ich den Begriff ‚Aussiedlung' (‚vysídlení'). Er betont wesentlich stärker den negativen Aspekt, weist „Aus-siedeln" doch auf die Folgen hin: den Verlust des Siedlungsortes, der Heimat. Andere Bezeichnungen wie z.B. ‚Auswanderung' (‚vystěhování') oder ‚Ausweisung' (‚vykázání') werden in diesem Zusammenhang seltener benutzt.

Der nächste Terminus, ‚Transfer', wurde aus dem Englischen übernommen. Zu seinen Vorteilen gehört nicht nur, dass er weitgehend frei von negativen Konnotationen ist, sondern dass er auch in breitem Maßstab Anwendung finden kann. Im Prinzip bildet er eine Art Oberbegriff für alle bisher erörterten Begriffe. „Transfer" ließe sich sogar auch auf die spätere Ausreise der Deutschen beziehen. Gemeint sind hierbei diejenigen Fälle, in denen Menschen, die nach 1947 in der Tschechoslowakei bleiben konnten, sich aus verschiedenen Grün-

---

[4] Zu den Ausnahmen gehörten die nachweislichen Antifaschisten. Sie konnten entweder regulär übersiedeln oder aber in der Republik bleiben.

den⁵ dafür entschieden, die Republik freiwillig zu verlassen (vgl. Arburg/ Staněk 2010, 298f.).

Schließlich sei noch der Ausdruck ‚Zwangsaussiedlung' erwähnt (vgl. Wiedemann 2007, 11). Es scheint mir, dass er am besten zu dem behandelten Geschehen passt. Deshalb habe ich mich dafür entschieden, diesen Terminus zu benutzen, wenn der Stoff es nicht erfordert, die Unterschiede zwischen den einzelnen Phasen der Zwangsaussiedlung konkret zu benennen. Ich stimme zwar mit den Herausgebern der Edition *Vysídlení Němců a proměny českého pohraničí 1945 – 1951* (*Die Aussiedlung der Deutschen und die Veränderungen der tschechischen Grenzgebiete 1945 – 1951*) überein, dass alle anderen Bezeichnungen dazu tendieren, die dargestellte Problematik jeweils zu vereinfachen. Es wäre aber höchst umständlich, immer penibel zu differenzieren zwischen „international nicht abgesprochener (nicht genehmigter) Zwangsaussiedlung/Abschiebung" und „international abgesprochener (genehmigter) Zwangsaussiedlung/Abschiebung" (vgl. Arburg/Staněk 2010, 300).⁶

2. *Prager Totentanz* (1958)

Olga Barényis deutschsprachiger Roman *Prager Totentanz*⁷ spielt in der Zeit des Prager Aufstands am Ende des Zweiten Weltkriegs. In raschem Tempo wechseln die Bilder einer stürmenden tschechischen Bevölkerung, die in den letzten Kriegstagen und kurz danach angefangen hat, sich an den Deutschen zu rächen. Protagonist ist der Tscheche Martin Novák, eine Art Salonkommunist, der an den Vorbereitungen des Aufstands beteiligt war. Nach dem Ausbruch der Erhebung des tschechischen Widerstands ändert er aber seine Meinung und ist darum bemüht, nicht nur sich selbst, sondern vor allem auch andere Leute vor Gefahren zu schützen.

---

⁵ Hier sind z.B. die Sehnsucht nach Kontakten mit der Familie und mit Freunden oder der Druck der gesellschaftlichen Verhältnisse gemeint.

⁶ Im Original: „mezinárodně nedohodnuté (neschválené) nucené vysidlování /odsun" und „mezinárodně dohodnuté (schválené) nucené vysidlování/odsun".

⁷ Olga Barényi gab bis zum Ende des Zweiten Weltkriegs alle ihre Werke auf Tschechisch heraus. Erst nach Kriegsende schrieb sie ausschließlich auf Deutsch, als sie wegen ihres deutschen Mannes nach dem Krieg die Tschechoslowakei verlassen musste. In Bezug auf ihre Herkunft wird sie entweder als „deutsch-ungarische Schriftstellerin, die tschechisch schrieb" oder als „Prager deutsche Schriftstellerin" bezeichnet (vgl. Šišler 1993).

Charakteristisch für diesen Roman ist, dass die Frage nach der Schuld nicht problematisiert wird. Mit Ausnahme des Protagonisten werden alle Tschechen gleichsam als Bestien dargestellt, die den deutschen Frauen und Kindern Unrecht antun. Dem entspricht auch die Erzählperspektive der Geschichte. Man kann von einer heterodiegetischen Erzählweise bei variabler interner Fokalisierung sprechen: Der Leser folgt einzelnen Figuren, erhält aber keine – weder objektive noch subjektive – Bewertung der Situation. Für die Figuren spricht nur ihr Handeln. Im Rahmen der Erzählung müssen nicht alle Umstände konkret und detailliert dargestellt werden. So werden etwa Konzentrationslager und der Holocaust nur am Rande erwähnt.

Als bestes Beispiel dafür kann die Geschichte von Elfriede Blümelein dienen. Als Jüdin wurde diese Frau während des Krieges im Ghetto Theresienstadt interniert. Sie überlebt und kehrt in den letzten Kriegstagen nach Prag zurück, und zwar in der Hoffnung, an ihr altes Leben anknüpfen zu können. In ein, zwei Bildern wird aber sichtbar, wie die Juden in dieser Zeit behandelt wurden.

„Ich bin eine Jüdin, ich war im Ghetto. Ich suche mein Recht, ich habe..."
„Lerne zuerst richtig Tschechisch sprechen," und einer von den Ledermänteln – es sind jetzt viele von ihnen da, zehn oder fünfzehn – stößt sie mit der Maschinenpistole weg.
„Richtig so!" kreischt eine Frauenstimme. „Die Juden wollen sich schon wieder wichtigmachen! Dabei waren sie alle immer Deutsche, diese Dreckschweine!" (Barényi 1958, 72)

Vom Roten Kreuz wird sie als eine Deutsche angesehen und folglich vertrieben, von ihrem ehemaligen Liebhaber um ihr Vermögen gebracht und betrogen. Man sollte wohl eher von ‚verraten' sprechen. Sie wird zu den Aufständischen gebracht, um den Reichtum eines charakterlosen Mannes zu schützen. Was sie im Ghetto erlebte, interessiert niemanden; auch der Leser soll eigentlich auf Distanz gehalten werden. Die vertuschte, nur am Rande erwähnte Realität des Ghettos (die an Unterernährung und Typhus sterbenden Menschen, um ein Beispiel zu nennen) soll nicht die Aufmerksamkeit des Lesers ablenken. Das Schicksal der Juden wird nur nebenbei erwähnt. Im Zentrum des Geschehens steht doch die deutsche (Prager) Bevölkerung, die unter den Tschechen leidet.

Wozu aber dienen dann die seltenen Hinweise auf den Holocaust? Ich sehe die Bedeutung vor allem darin, die Grausamkeit der Tschechen in einem noch stärkeren Lichte erscheinen zu lassen. Denn die Rolle der eindeutigen Täter spielen in diesem Roman *nur* die Tschechen. Es ist Zeichen ihrer Bosheit, dass sie auch die armen Juden, die den Holocaust überlebt haben, verfolgen. Freilich wird die Frage nicht gestellt, wer mit dem Krieg angefangen hat und wer – vor allem – für das Schicksal der Juden verantwortlich. Die Deutschen werden hier völlig einseitig nur als typische Opfer dargestellt.

3. *Peníze od Hitlera* (2006)

Radka Denemarkovás Buch *Peníze od Hitlera*[8] (in der deutschen Übersetzung wurde es 2009 unter dem Titel *Ein herrlicher Flecken Erde* herausgegeben) erzählt von einem Mädchen aus einer deutsch-tschechisch-jüdischen Familie. Nach Kriegsende kehrt sie als Überlebende aus Theresienstadt nach Hause in ihr tschechisches Dorf zurück und erfährt, dass in ihrem Elternhaus schon jemand anderes lebt. Im Prinzip ist die Entwicklung der Geschichte derjenigen Elfriede Blümeleins nicht unähnlich. Gita Lauschmanová wird misshandelt, verprügelt und als eine Deutsche aus ihrer Heimat vertrieben.

Der Unterschied besteht in zwei Aspekten. Erstens erstreckt sich die Geschichte von *Peníze od Hitlera* über einen den längeren Zeitraum. Der Leser folgt Gitas Leben in zahlreichen Retrospektiven. Erinnerungen an das KZ ziehen sich durch die ganze Erzählung, die im Jahr 1945 einsetzt und bis zur Gegenwart reicht. Jedoch liegt der Schwerpunkt der Erzählung nicht im Motiv des Holocaust, sondern in demjenigen der Zwangsaussiedlung, weshalb man über Gitas Theresienstadt-Erfahrungen auch nur wenige Informationen erhält. Einmal erinnerte sie sich daran, wie ihre Schwester ihr das Leben gerettet hat, als sie während eines Häftlingsappells vor ihr stand und so Gitas Operationsnarbe verdeckte. An einer anderen Stelle erwähnt Gita, dass ihre Schwester an Unterernährung starb. Andere Aspekte des Lagerlebens und der Judenvernichtung werden nicht erwähnt. Am stärksten kommt das Holocaustmotiv dort zur Geltung, wo sich Gita mit den Umständen in einem Inter-

---

[8] Der Roman, dem 2007 der Preis Magnesia Litera zuerkannt wurde, gehört zu den bekanntesten tschechischen Texten der Gegenwart im Rahmen der sog. Vertreibungsliteratur.

nierungslager für die Deutschen konfrontiert sieht, da hier Erinnerungen an das Lager wach werden.

> Sie mögen es genau und ordentlich. Das kenne ich von *dort*. Alles ordentlich verpackt, sortiert, mit Etiketten versehen. Damit der Tod den Überblick behält und nicht raten muss. Merkwürdig ist nur, dass der frisch entstandene Haufen gleich wieder zerbröselt, luftiger und kleiner wird. [...]
> Und genau das erschreckt mich, zwingt mich den Kopf zu heben. Diesen hinterhältigen Trick kenne ich noch nicht. Etwas Neues. Auf den Ellbogen robbe ich zum Pritschenrand, mein Kopf ragt hinaus wie versteinert. (Denemarková 2009, 73)[9]

Einige Tschechen misshandelten und beraubten die Deutschen, andere hingegen benahmen sich menschlich und dem Recht entsprechend, was für Gita neu war. Die Tschechen werden hier nicht als homogene Masse von Bestien dargestellt. Es gibt auch viele, die sich korrekt verhalten. Als Beispiel sei der Kommandant des Internierungslagers erwähnt, der befiehlt, den Deutschen den geraubten Schmuck und das geraubte Geld zurückzugeben. Auch diese Erfahrung kann als großer Unterschied zu Barényis Geschichte wahrgenommen werden.

Zweitens unterscheiden sich die beiden Werke auch hinsichtlich der Erzählperspektive. Im Unterschied zu Barényis Roman ist diese in *Peníze od Hitlera* homodiegetisch, und zwar stark (wenn auch nicht absolut) auf Gita fokalisiert. Die ganze Geschichte wird dadurch beeinflusst, dass keine der Informationen für objektiv und wahr gelten können. Sogar die zentrale Behauptung, dass Gitas Vater ein guter Mensch, ein deutscher Jude war, wird auf den letzten Seiten des Romans in Zweifel gestellt. Kurz vor ihrem Tod realisiert Gita in einer ihrer Vorkriegserinnerungen, dass ihr Vater doch zu den Nazis gehörte.

An dieser Stelle möchte ich einen gewissen Vorbehalt gegen Gitas Geschichte und zugleich auch gegen die Verwendung des Holocaustmotivs zum Ausdruck bringen. Das Thema der Geschichte bleibt eindeutig die Zwangsaussiedlung, die Heimkehr und das Versagen der Kommunikation (vgl. hierzu auch Škubalová 2016). Die Protagonistin – die zudem einer gemischten

---

[9] Im Original: „Mají rádi přesnost a řád. Znám to *odtamtud*. Všechno pečlivě zabavené, roztříděné, rozškatulkované. Aby smrt měla přehled a netápala. Podivné je, že čerstvě vzniklá hromada se vzápětí zase rozdrobuje, tenčí, ubývá. [...]
A právě to mě vyděsí, pozdvihne. Tenhle úskok já neznám. Novinka. Přisunu se na loktech k okraji pryčny, hlava zkamení v převisu" (Denemarková 2006, 62).

deutsch-tschechischen Ehe entstammte – musste als Halbjüdin die grausamen Erfahrungen des Lagerlebens machen. Später in der Erzählung verliert sie ihr Baby und muss den Tod des Jungen miterleben. Die Grausamkeit von Gitas Lebenserfahrungen wird erzählerisch immer wieder verstärkt, was m.E. mit dem Ziel geschieht, beim Leser Emotionen hervorzurufen. Sogar die Frage nach der Identität von Gitas Vaters wird im letzten Moment, auf den letzten Seiten des Textes, durch eine Erinnerung daran in Frage gestellt, dass er ein Nazi-Symbol trug. Die Problematik einer Geschichte über die Zwangsaussiedlung wäre m.E. auch ohne diese zusätzlichen Facetten kompliziert genug. Im vorliegenden Zusammenhang dienen die Verweise auf den Holocaust als etwas, was schockieren, was den Eindruck und vor allem die Emotionen steigern soll.

4. *Der Galgen am Weinberg* (1951)

Der Protagonist des letzten ausgewählten Textes, Josef Mühlbergers[10] Novelle *Der Galgen am Weinberg*, stammt aus Schwaben. Mit Beginn des Zweiten Weltkriegs meldet er sich auf eine günstige Stellung im Ausland. Er wollte seine Heimat verlassen und in den okkupierten Ländern arbeiten, wo er darum bemüht war, kein Unrecht zu begehen. Nach seinen Worten verstand er sich als einfacher Zivilist, der mit der mächtigen Kriegsmaschinerie nichts zu tun hatte. Er verbringt sämtliche Kriegsjahre in Prag, und nach dem Ende des Zweiten Weltkriegs ist er in der Tat davon überrascht, dass die tschechische Bevölkerung beginnt, sich an den Deutschen zu rächen. Mit anderen deutschen Männern wird er im Gefängnis in Pankrác inhaftiert und dann in einem Sportstadion interniert. Noch vor dem Rücktransport in seine Heimatstadt erlebt er die Hölle des ehemaligen jüdischen Ghettos in Theresienstadt, wo sein Sohn ermordet wird.

Über die Figur des Sohns wird somit das Motiv des Holocaust aufgerufen. Obwohl der Sohn in dieser Erzählung fast überhaupt nicht handelt – er ist nur Objekt in der Geschichte – wird er zum Symbol der Schuldlosigkeit, welche die Kindheit mit sich bringt. Und er stirbt: Ein Kind muss sterben, weil bei

---

[10] Seine Bekanntheit erlangte Mühlberger vor allem als Literaturwissenschaftler, insbesondere als Autor der *Geschichte der deutschen Literatur in Böhmen 1900-1939* (1981).

ihm ein verbotenes Buch gefunden wurde. Es stirbt im Ghetto, wo jetzt die Deutschen an Stelle der Juden konzentriert werden, wo die Deutschen ähnliches Unrecht wie die Juden erleben müssen. Ich widme diesem Buch etwas mehr Aufmerksamkeit, weil ich den Text für den besten der drei hier untersuchten halte und weil das Motiv des Holocaust hier am ehesten in einem konstruktiven Sinne verwendet wurde.

In diesem Text lässt sich eine homodiegetische, lediglich auf den Erzähler fokalisierte Erzählperspektive erkennen. Der Erzähler führt eine Konversation mit anderen Personen, die mit ihm in einem Gasthaus am Tisch sitzen. Die Form des Gesprächs, insbesondere die direkte Hinwendung zu den anwesenden Personen, ermöglicht es, dass auch der Leser sich in gewisser Weise in die Konversation eingeschlossen fühlt. Nach Elke Mehnert sollte das wiederholte Ansprechen der Anwesenden durch den Erzähler den Leser daran erinnern, dass es sich in dieser Erzählung um einen ungewöhnlichen Monolog handelt, der nicht nur an die unmittelbaren Zuhörer, sondern vor allem auch an den Leser gerichtet ist (vgl. Mehnert 2004, 155).

Das Bild des Protagonisten weist Spuren einer subjektivierenden Manipulation auf. Wie aus der Handlung folgt, ist der Erzähler darum bemüht, sich selbst als einen Menschen zu präsentieren, der abseits des Kriegsgeschehens stand und der sich deshalb nach Kriegsende in keiner Gefahr wähnte:

> Doch zur Sache! Ich blieb in Prag, bis der Spuk zu Ende ging. Das Grauen begann sich zu lichten; so meinte, so hoffte ich. Es hatte uns dieses Ende schon einige Male vorgetäuscht, aber jetzt war es wirklich da. Ich hatte es mir nicht überstürzt eilig gemacht, aus Prag herauszukommen. Warum auch? Ich fürchtete nichts. (Mühlberger 1951, 12f.)

Gleichzeitig vermittelt der Erzähler seine Situation nach dem Krieg, nach den für ihn so tragischen Ereignissen. Er durfte an eine günstige Wiedereinstellung nicht denken, gerade weil er seit 1938 in Prag gewesen war. Schließlich waren doch nur die zuverlässigsten, linientreuen Beamten ins Ausland gekommen.

Für die Interpretation des Werks ist aber etwas anderes wichtig. Durch den ganzen Text zieht sich wie ein roter Faden die Geschichte von Kain und Abel aus dem Alten Testament. Aber wer ist wer? Nur die Juden werden als absolute Opfer dargestellt, Tschechen und Deutschen hingegen wechseln die Positionen: Zuerst gibt ein Aufseher dem Sohn ein zusätzliches Stück Brot, dann wird der Sohn von einem anderen Aufseher getötet. „Jeder Mensch kann beides sein: Kain oder Abel – in der Binnenerzählung: Brandmarkender oder Gebrandmarkter, Täter oder Opfer" (Mehnert 2004, 155). Oder anders gesagt: Die Mordgeschichte um Kain und Abel kettet beide Völker eng aneinander. Sie hatten beide die gemeinsame Urmutter Eva.

Der thematische Schwerpunkt bei Mühlberger liegt in der Darstellung der Theresienstadt-Periode. Der Mann und sein Sohn wurden gemeinsam mit anderen Deutschen gezwungen, die Juden aus den Massengräbern zu holen und dann jede Leiche in einem Einzelgrab zu bestatten. Obwohl sich die Tschechen hier nach Michaela Peroutková nur an den Deutschen rächen wollten und es nicht um Mitleid mit den Juden ging (vgl. Peroutková 2008, 58), kommt meiner Meinung klar zum Ausdruck, dass es sich in den Augen des Erzählers um eine ganz humane, menschliche Idee handelt. Man könnte in der Ausführung dieser Rache auch Spuren des alttestamentarischen „Auge um Auge, Zahn um Zahn" finden: Die Achtung vor den Opfern gebietet es, dass sie in einem eigenen Grab bestattet werden, und wer anders als die Täter sollte die Bestattung durchführen? Gleichzeitig wird in der Erzählung knapp geschildert, wie die internierten Deutschen, so wie zuvor die Juden, an Wassermangel, an Unterernährung und allgemein schlechter Behandlung starben. Die Situation ändert sich in fast ironischer Weise: Wo die Massengräber mit den Juden lagen, entstehen jetzt die neuen Gemeinschaftsgräber für die Deutschen. Bemerkenswert ist die Einschätzung dieser Situation durch den Erzähler:

> „Nicht Deutsche, nicht Tschechen haben das getan, wodurch uns die Welt zu einer Pestgrube wurde, sondern Menschen, in denen etwas den Menschen aufgefressen hat."
> Lassen Sie sich also gesagt sein, das waren nicht die Tschechen, wie es damals nicht wir Deutsche gewesen sind. Denn das alles geht weiter, davon bin ich überzeugt. Es werden einmal Tschechen die Leichen der Deutschen aus den Massengräbern herausholen, wie wir jetzt mit den Leichen der Juden tun mußten." (Mühlberger 1951, 28)

Der zweite Absatz des Zitats ist für eine weitere Interpretation höchst interessant. Man könnte es so begreifen, dass der Erzähler sich doch eine Rache an dem tschechischen Volk wünschte. Es werde die Zeit kommen, in der sich die Tschechen in einer ähnlich schrecklichen Situation befinden werden – auch sie werden ihre Schuld sühnen müssen. Wahrscheinlich ist dieser Passus aber eher so gemeint, dass die Zeit kommen wird, in der die Tschechen ihre eigenen Missetaten durchschauen und auf diese Weise ihre Schuld sühnen werden.

5. Schlussbemerkung

Die vorliegende Analyse versuchte an drei unterschiedlichen Beispielen zu zeigen, wie sich das Holocaustmotiv mit der Vertreibungsthematik verknüpfen lässt und welche Funktionen es dort einnehmen kann. Im Vordergrund stand dabei die Frage, ob diese Verbindung neue Gesichtspunkte in die Rezeption der Werke einbringen kann. Es sollte deutlich geworden sein, dass insbesondere die Problematik der Schuld hier zusätzliche Dimensionen erfährt, wobei namentlich die narrative Struktur des betreffenden Werks zu beachten ist. Je nach Intention des Erzählers vermag das Holocaustmotiv die gewählte Perspektive der Schuld zu verstärken oder zu relativieren. Wie gezeigt wurde, bietet sich eine breite Skala an Rezeptionsmöglichkeiten, die von der Betonung der von Tschechen nach dem Zweiten Weltkrieg begangenen Grausamkeiten bis hin zur Hoffnung auf die Versöhnung der Menschen unabhängig von Rasse, Nationalität oder Sprache reicht.

Literaturverzeichnis

Arburg, Adrian von – *Staněk*, Tomáš (red.) 2010: Vysídlení Němců a proměny českého pohraničí 1945 – 1951. Díl I: Češi a Němci do roku 1945. Úvod k edici. Středokluky.
Barényi, Olga 1958: Prager Totentanz. München.
Brandes, Detlef – *Sundhaussen*, Holm – *Troebst*, Stefan (Hrsg.) 2010: Lexikon der Vertreibung. Deportation, Zwangsaussiedlung und ethnische Säuberung im Europa der 20. Jahrhunderts. Wien – Köln – Weimar.
Denemarková, Radka 2006: Peníze pro Hitlera. Letní mozaika. Brno.
dies. 2009: Ein herrlicher Flecken Erde. Roman. Aus d. Tschech. v. Eva Profousová. München.
Dornemann, Axel 2005: Flucht und Vertreibung in Prosaliteratur und Erlebnisbericht seit 1945. Eine annotierte Bibliographie. Stuttgart.
Duden, Deutsches Universalwörterbuch 2006. Mannheim – Leipzig – Wien – Zürich.
Hahnová, Eva 1999: Sudetoněmecký problém. Obtížné loučení s minulostí. Ústí nad Labem.
Jech, Karel 1993: Němci a Maďaři v dekretech prezidenta republiky. Studie a dokumenty 1940 – 1945. Brno.
Mehnert, Elke 2004: Böhmen im Herzen. Flucht und Vertreibung in Texten sudetendeutscher Autoren. In: Transfer. Vertreibung. Aussiedlung im Kontext der tschechischen Literatur. Hrsg. v. Gertraude Zand u. Jiří Holý. Brno, S. 149-157.
Mühlberger, Josef 1951: Der Galgen im Weinberg. Eine Erzählung aus unseren Tagen. Esslingen.
ders. 1981: Geschichte der deutschen Literatur in Böhmen. 1900 – 1939. München.

Peroutková, Michaela 2008: Vyhnání. Jeho obraz v české a německé literatuře a ve vzpomínkách. Praha.
Pešek, Jiří 2004: Vertreibung und Transfer 1938 – 1949 im Spiegel der tschechischen Geschichtswissenschaft seit 1989. In: Transfer. Vertreibung. Aussiedlung im Kontext der tschechischen Literatur. Hrsg. v. Gertraude Zand u. Jiří Holý. Brno, S. 29-42.
Šišler, Petr (= pš) 1993: Olga Barényi. In: Lexikon české literatury 2,II. Red. Vladimír Forst. Praha, S. 1263-1264.
Škubalová, Marta 2016: Literární aspekty vícejazyčnosti v dílech o odsunu. In: Vícejazyčnost. Český, polský a německý jazyk, literatura, kultura v komparaci. X. mezinárodní studentská konference. Praha [im Druck].
Wiedemann, Andreas 2007: „Komm mit uns das Grenzland aufbauen!". Ansiedlung und neue Strukturen in den ehemaligen Sudetengebieten 1945 – 1952. Essen.

On the Holocaust Motif in Expulsion Literature

The present article is concerned with how the concept of guilt is used in literary works dealing with themes of two historical events connected with the Second World War, namely with the Holocaust and the transfer of Germans from Czechoslovakia. The main analysis focuses on the work of authors writing about the post-war transfer and at the same time dealing with the Holocaust. Bearing in mind these characteristics, following texts have been chosen for the analysis: *Prager Totentanz* by Olga Barényi, *Peníze od Hitlera* by Radka Denemarková and *Galgen am Weinberg* by Josef Mühlberger. The concept of guilt is treated differently in these texts. A recurring motif is the life story of people, who have survived a concentration camp, but having returned home they are treated by Czechs in the same way as Germans are. Furthermore, both the characters and the narrator struggle with the concept of collective guilt. It seems that the way the aforementioned themes are treated and interconnected corresponds to the narrator's point of view of the matter of guilt.

Personenverzeichnis / Index of Names

Abrams, Garry 217, 227
Achleitner, Friedrich 163, 165, 168
Ackermann, Kathrin 269
Adamczak, Katarzyna 8, 23-41
Adorno, Theodor W. 7, 14, 19, 22, 47, 130, 143f., 155, 173, 217
Agamben, Giorgio 186, 198
Aksamit, Bożena 51, 54
Amann, Thomas 240f.
Améry, Jean 166, 168
Andrzejewski, Jerzy 18
Ankersmit, Frank 103, 105, 112
Apollinaire, Guillaume 147
Arburg, Adrian von 274, 281
Arendt, Hannah 18, 111, 113
Artwińska, Anna 9, 29, 39, 255-270
Ashbery, John 172, 175, 183, 197f.
Asholt, Wolfgang 37, 39
Aškenazy, Ludvík 204
Assmann, Aleida 46, 54
Assmann, Jan 33f., 39
Atkinson, John William 144
Attridge, Derek 198
Aust, Stefan 240f.

Babel', Isaak 77
Bach, Johann Sebastian 125
Badinová, Alena 232, 241
Bäcker, Heimrad 9, 161-169
Balák, Luboš 106, 113
Balík, Štěpán 9, 129-144
Baranowski, Julian 161, 168
Barényi, Olga 272, 274-277, 281f.
Baron, Anne-Marie 251f.
Baron, Lawrence 252
Barthes, Roland 265, 268
Bator, Joanna 226
Bauer, Katharina 10
Bauman, Zygmunt 105, 111f., 260, 268
Baumann, A.E.M. 221f., 227
Bayer, Wolfram 228
Beckett, Samuel 226
Bednář, Kamil 129-132, 142-144

Begley Louis (Ludwik Begleiter) 224, 227
Behring, Eva 218, 220, 227
Bělohradská, Hana 204
Benigni, Roberto 40
Benjamin, Walter 26-28, 33, 39, 175, 198
Benz, Wolfgang 126, 203, 214, 255, 268
Bereś, Stanisław 199
Berger, Julius 120, 127
Bernard, Luc 50
Beyer, Frank 247
Biebl, Konstantin 129, 135f., 138, 143f.
Bielik-Robson, Agata 198
Bieńczyk, Marek 31
Binsch, Anika 120, 126f.
Blanchot, Maurice 186, 198, 217f., 227
Blatný, Ivan 130
Błoński, Jan 34, 36, 39, 129, 143, 155, 157
Bloom, Harold 174, 181, 185, 198
Böhme, Hartmut 40
Bojarska, Katarzyna 54
Bolecki, Włodzimierz 40, 158
Boltansky, Christian 105
Bolton, Jonathan 204, 214
Bondyová, Edita 204, 210
Bondyová, Hana 205, 210
Bondyová, Věra 205, 210
Bor (Bondy), Josef 9, 203-215
Bor, Vladimír 107
Borchardt, Elisabeth 215
Borowski, Tadeusz 13, 15-18, 21f., 34, 57, 76, 156f., 239
Borwicz, Michał M. 148, 157
Bosley, Keith 157
Boštík, Václav 79, 88
Braese, Stephan 89, 100
Brahm, Alcanter de 109
Brand, William 148
Brandes, Detlef 272, 281
Brandt, Juliane 218, 227
Branislav, František 129f., 138f., 143f.
Bratny, Roman 14, 22
Braun, Eva 108-111

Brenton, Howard 109
Breysach, Barbara 36, 39, 118f.
Brinkmann-Siepmann, Brigitte 270
Brodzka-Wald, Alina 40
Brooks, Peter 266, 268
Browning, Christopher 76
Brumlik, Micha 30, 39
Brummack, Jürgen 92, 100
Bruno, Giordana 129
Brycht, Andrzej 146, 157
Brynych, Zbyněk 248
Bullock, Marcus 198
Burger, Adolf 236
Burkot, Stanisław 19, 22
Bursa, Andrzej 146, 157
Buryła, Sławomir 30, 34, 39

Camus, Albert 108
Čapek, Karel 65, 76
Caputo, John D. 179, 198
Carroll, David 24, 39
Caruth, Cathy 53f.
Čechov, Anton 77
Celan, Paul 117f., 126f., 155, 173, 177, 184, 198
Černý, Václav 130
Červinka, Josef 87
Chang, Briankle G. 187, 198
Chęciński, Michał Mosze 109f., 112
Chmielewski, Henry Jerzy 48, 54
Chomsky, Marvin J. 247
Christ, Michaela 61, 76
Cieslar, Milan 231, 243, 253
Cinger, František 263, 268
Cisło, Maciej 172, 198
Clarke, Melvyn 81
Colón, Ernie 49, 54
Colonna, Vincente 225, 227
Corsini, Raymond J. 143
Cravens, Craig 269
Czaplejewicz, Eugeniusz 150, 157
Czapliński, Przemysław 28, 31, 34-36, 39, 269
Czechowicz, Józef 147
Czermińska, Małgorzata 224, 227
Czerniawski, Adam 158f.

Daniel, Jiří 130
Daumier, Honoré 112
Dębicz, Maria 150, 152, 157
Dehnel, Jacek 21f.
Denemarková, Radka 269, 272, 276-278, 281f.
Denzel, Markus A. 256, 269
Derrida, Jacques 24, 103, 171, 173, 175-177, 179f., 183, 185f., 198, 200, 217f., 227
Descartes, René 220
Didi-Huberman, Georges 267f.
Diner, Dan 37-39, 256, 262
Dobeš, Karel 206, 215
Dobrovský, Pavel 47, 54
Doerry, Martin 255, 269
Doležel, Lubomír 235, 241
Dornemann, Axel 271, 281
Dostoevskij, Fedor 226, 238
Doubrovsky, Serge 225, 227
Douglas, Laurence 224, 227
Dózsai, Mónika 218, 227
Drábková, Květa 80
Drewnowski, Tadeusz 147, 156f.
Duniec, Krystyna 15, 22
Dvořák, Ivan 245, 252

Ebbrecht, Tobias 252
Eichmann, Adolf 113, 210, 212, 214
Eimermacher, Karl 77
Eisner, Pavel 60, 206
Eke, Norbert Otto 33, 39
Emerson, Ralph Waldo 174
Emmerich, Wolfgang 94, 100
Erdle, Birgit R. 270
Ette, Ottmar 39

Fantová, Jana 49, 54
Federman, Raymond 228
Feuchert, Sascha 9, 58, 76, 161-169
Ficowski, Jerzy 149, 157
Firbank, Ronald 172
Firlej, Agata 8, 103-113
Fischer, Torben 39
Fischer-Lichte, Erika 41
Forman, Miloš 221

Forst, Vladimír 208, 215, 282
Foucault, Michel 186
Frank, Anne 49
Frankl, Michal 79
Frantová, Milada 60
Frei, Norbert 41, 76
Freisler, Roland 167
Fremont-Smith, Eliot 222, 228
Friedländer, Saul 41
Fritsch, Werner 39
Fritz, Regina 127
Fučík, Julius 136
Fuks, Ladislav 204, 269
Fuksa, Karl 106
Fulda, Daniel 65, 78

Gagnebin, Jeanne Marie 27, 39
Gancarczyk, Anna 146, 157
Gavran, Miro 108, 113
Gazda, Grzegorz 76
Genet, Jean 226
Genette, Gérard 225
Gerould, Daniel 158
Gerz, Jochen 105
Gillon, Adam 158
Głowacki, Janusz 225-227
Głowiński, Michał 109, 112
Goebbels, Magda 109
Goethe, Johann Wolfgang von 122, 125f.
Gogol', Nikolaj 64, 68, 76
Goldflam, Arnošt 8, 103, 106-113, 269
Goldschmidt, Georges-Arthur 37, 39
Golebiowski, Anja 8, 13-22
Gombrowicz, Witold 13, 20, 22
Graf, Karin 166, 168
Grebeníčková, Růžena 63, 66, 76, 83, 88
Greenberg, Martin S. 129, 143
Gronczewski, Andrzej 150, 157
Gross, Jan Tomasz 37, 39
Grotowski, Jerzy 26, 29, 38, 40
Grübel, Rainer 77
Grupińska, Anka 45, 54, 103, 112
Grynberg, Henryk 34, 40, 217, 227
Grynberg, Mikołaj 44-46, 54, 112
Gutorow, Jacek 174, 198

Hahnová, Eva 272f., 281
Halas, František 129f., 133-135, 143f.
Halbwachs, Maurice 258, 269
Hallama, Peter 256, 269
Haman, Aleš 258, 269
Hammermeister, Philip 39
Hamšík, Dušan 111, 113
Handke, Peter 37
Hansen-Löve, Aage A. 71, 77
Hantz, Stanisław 166, 168
Harris, William 178, 198
Harting, Rolf 248
Heeg, Günther 256, 269
Heftrich, Urs 60, 76
Hegel, Georg Wilhelm Friedrich 125
Heidegger, Martin 155, 179, 186, 198
Hejl, Vilém 43, 54
Heller-Roazen, Daniel 198
Heraklit von Ephesos 178, 198
Herrmanová, Eva 212, 215
Hertling, Viktoria 100
Herz, Juraj 245f., 250
Herzfeld, Manfred 117-127
Hesse, Hermann 137
Hetman, Grzegorz 180, 198
Heydrich, Reinhard 50, 82-84
Hiemer, Elisa-Maria 10
Hilberg, Raul 104f., 112
Hilgard, Ernest 144
Hillach, Ansgar 27, 40
Himmler, Heinrich 106, 113, 236f.
Hiršal, Josef 129, 132f., 142-144
Hirsch, Marianne 44, 54, 113
Hitler, Adolf 8, 83, 93, 100, 103, 106-113, 157, 167, 249, 267, 272, 276f.
Hlaváčová, Jana 87
Höber, Ulla 77
Hölderlin, Friedrich 125
Höß, Rudolf 232f., 237, 241, 264
Hoffmann, Eva 44
Hoheisel, Horst 105
Holý, Jiří 7, 9, 69, 76, 88, 130, 143, 199, 203, 207, 215, 228, 231-241, 252, 269, 281f.
Hornig, Dieter 228
Howard, Tony 159

Hříbková, Hana 8, 60, 69, 76, 79-88
Hrubín, František 130, 136-138, 143f.
Huelle, Paweł 31
Hulc, Vladimír 112
Hušek, Hugo 107

Ibler, Reinhard 7-10, 57, 76, 203-215, 256, 258, 269
Iltis, Rudolf 86, 88
Insdorf, Annette 252
Irigaray, Luce 186

Jabůrková, Jožka 246
Jacobs, Michael 148
Jacobson, Sid 49, 54
Jakowska, Krystyna 57, 76
Jakubowska, Wanda 251
Jameson, Fredric 25
Janečková, Ester 87
Jankowicz, Grzegorz 199
Jaroš, Rudolf 107
Jarosiński, Zbigniew 14, 22
Jasný, Vojtěch 245
Jech, Karel 272, 281
Jennings, Michael W. 198
Jesenská, Milena 60, 246
John, Jiří 79

Kästner, Erich 92, 100
Kafka, František 204
Kafka, Franz 69, 105, 107, 155, 185, 226
Kaiser, Joachim 38, 40f.
Kaiserová, Kristina 65, 76
Kamuf, Peggy 198
Kansteiner, Wulf 41, 76
Kant, Immanuel 125
Kantor, Tadeusz 26, 29, 38, 40
Karas, Joža 212, 215
Kasper, Judith 39
Katz, Shalom 87
Kaźmierczak, Marek 48, 54
Keff, Bożena 32, 38, 40, 226
Kermisz, Józef 147, 157
Kertész, Imre 35, 40, 265, 269
Kitzinger, Charlotte 8, 89-101, 119
Kłak, Tadeusz 155, 157

Klejnocki, Jarosław 172, 198
Kliems, Alfrun 218-220, 224, 227
Klíma, Ivan 9, 255-270
Koepke, Wulf 100
Kofránková, Hana 87
Kogon, Eugen 93, 100
Kohlschmidt, Werner 100
Kokoszka, Iwona 48, 54
Kołakowski, Leszek 108
Kolář, Jiří 130, 139-144
Korman, Jane 50f.
Korzeniowski, Bartosz 54
Koselleck, Reinhart 46
Kosicka, Jadwiga 159
Kosinski, Jerzy 9, 217-229
Kossak-Szczucka, Zofia 15-17, 19, 22
Kostka, Petr 87
Kott, Jan 17
Koubová, Věra 86, 88
Koura, Petr 246, 252
Kovács, Éva 127
Kowalska, Urszula 8, 43-55
Koźniewski, Kazimierz 145, 157
Kragen, Wanda 145, 157
Krakowska, Joanna 15, 22
Krall, Hanna 44, 76, 103f., 112
Kramer, Josef 232
Kramer, Sven 39
Kratochvil, Alexander 43
Kraus, Karl 89, 100
Kraus, Ota 136f., 141, 143f., 203
Krausová, Irena 133f.
Krawczyk, Alicja 159
Krawczyńska, Dorota 34, 39f.
Kremer, S. Lilian 221, 225, 228
Kren, George M. 75, 77
Kreuder, Friedemann 41
Kropáček, Pavel 107
Kruszewska, Felicja 159
Krynski, Magnus J. 158
Krysiak, Sebastian 35, 40
Krzyzanowski, Ludwik 158
Kudliński, Tadeusz 145, 157
Kühn, Volker 91, 100
Kühnl, Olaf 22
Kula, Agata 186f., 198

Kulesza, Dariusz 16, 22
Kuon, Peter 265, 269
Kurek, Jalu 145f., 157
Kuwałek, Robert 148, 157
Kvíz, Rudolf 87
Kwaśniewska, Monika 28, 40
Kwieciński, Bartosz 47, 54
Kydryński, Juliusz 145, 158

Lachmann, Peter 22
Lacoue-Labarthe, Philippe 198
Laferl, Christopher F. 269
Lam, Andrzej 147, 154, 158
Lampart, Fabian 14, 22
Landesman, Rocco 220, 228
Landsberg, Alison 257, 269
Lang, Berel 103, 112
Lange, Valerie 10
Langer, Lawrence L. 23, 40
Lavers, Norman 221, 228
Leavey, John P. 198
Lecarme, Jacques 227
Lehmann, Hans-Thies 25, 40
Leibfried, Erwin 164, 168
Lejeune, Philippe 217, 227f.
Lenin, Vladimir Il'ič 136
Leociak, Jacek 34, 39f.
Lesiewicz, Witold 251
Lessing, Gotthold Ephraim 269
Leszczyńska, Jadwiga 166
Leube, Dietrich 268
Levi, Primo 103, 239
Leyko, Małgorzata 76
Lhoest-Offermann, Holde 269
Ligocka, Roma 228
Lindner, Burkhardt 39
Littell, Jonathan 269
Loewy, Hanno 39, 169
Loewy, Miriam 121, 127
Lubas-Bartoszyńska, Regina 226, 228
Ludvíková, Miroslava 54
Lüthi, Max 67, 77
Lumet, Sidney 251
Lustig, Arnošt 9, 204, 231-241, 243, 248, 253

Maciejewski, Maciej 180, 199
Maciejewski, Mariusz 199
Madejski, Jerzy 40
Maguire, Robert A. 158
Majchrowski, Zbigniew 150, 158
Majeran, Tomasz 199
Maliszewski, Karol 180, 199
Malvezzi, Piero 165, 169
Mann, Franziska (Lola Horovitz) 240
Mann, Thomas 169
Marcuse, Bruno 117f., 120f., 126f.
Mareš, Petr 247, 253
Markowski, Michał Paweł 199
Martinovský, Ivan 65, 76
Masłowska, Dorota 44
Mehnert, Elke 279f., 281
Mehring, Walter 94f., 100
Menasse, Robert 39
Mengele, Josef 83, 85, 111, 248, 265-267
Mercks, Kees 60, 77
Merle, Robert 233
Meyer-Fraatz, Andrea 57, 76f.
Michael, Peter 169
Michineau, Stéphanie 224, 228
Mickiewicz, Adam 155, 174
Miłosz, Czesław 18, 20-22, 26, 129, 147
Mináč, Matej 250
Mizerkiewicz, Tomasz 199
Mocková, Zuzana 52, 54
Mohr, Wolfgang 100
Moldenhauer, Eva 40
Molisak, Alina 39, 269
Moller, Sabine 266, 270
Moltmann, Bernhard 39
Momro, Jakub 172, 199
Morávková, Jitka 243, 253
Morawiec, Arkadiusz 9, 145-159
Mościcki, Paweł 198
Moskalyk, Antonín 248
Mozart, Wolfgang Amadeus 125
Mühlberger, Josef 272, 278-282
Müller, Filip 240f.
Müller-Ott, Dorothea 166, 169
Munk, Andrzej 251
Mussolini, Benito 108
Muth, Ursula 169

Myers, David G. 219, 228
Myssok, Johannes 269

Nałkowska, Zofia 18, 34, 57, 77, 139
Nancy, Jean-Luc 198
Nickel, Christa 269
Niehaus, Michael 266, 269
Nietzsche, Friedrich 155
Niziołek, Grzegorz 28f., 36, 40, 103
Nofikow, Ewa 173, 181, 199
Nolen-Hoeksema, Susan 129, 144
Norwid, Cyprian 155
Novák, Jan 106f.
Novak, Joseph s. Kosinski, Jerzy

Oakeshott, Michael 24
Ohme, Andreas 8, 57-78
Ojrzyńska, Katarzyna 157
Okulska, Inez 172, 182, 199
Oltermann, Philip 111f.
Opelík, Jiří 58, 63, 69, 74, 77, 207, 215
Opitz, Michael 40
Orliński, Marcin 173, 199
Orten, Jiří 130, 133
Osborne, John 146, 158
Ostachowicz, Igor 21, 44, 226
Otčenášek, Jan 247, 253
Otto, Wojciech 50, 54
Ozick, Cynthia 103

Pakula, Alan J. 247
Paloff, Benjamin 174f., 199
Pałyga, Artur 23, 28, 31-33, 35, 37-41
Pankowski, Marian 146, 158
Paul, Gerhard 264, 269
Paulin, Tom 158
Pavelka, Zdenko 112
Pavlata, Michal 87
Penkala, Vít 134, 144
Pensky, Max 199
Peroutková, Michaela 280, 282
Pešek, Jiří 273, 282
Petersdorff, Friedrich von 10
Pethes, Nicolas 270
Petříček, Miroslav 143
Pflug, Isabel 41

Piejko, Magdalena 30, 40
Pietrych, Piotr 155, 158
Pirelli, Giovanni 165, 169
Piscator, Erwin 90
Piwowarski, Krystian 21
Plebanek, Barbara 159
Podolska, Joanna 168
Polentz, Wolfgang von 33
Polouček, Jan 49, 54
Pořízková, Lenka 107, 112
Pound, Ezra 172
Prenowitz, Eric 198
Próchniak, Paweł 174, 199
Profousová, Eva 281
Propp, Vladimir 67, 77
Proust, Marcel 36
Przyboś, Julian 146, 155, 158
Putrament, Jerzy 145, 158
Pytlík, Radko 107, 113
Pyzik, Agata 173, 199

Radziszewska, Krystyna 168
Radzymińska, Józefa 146, 158
Rand, Richard 198
Rappoport, Leon 75, 77
Rásky, Béla 127
Reder, Rudolf 148f., 151-155, 158f.
Resnais, Alain 251
Řezníček, Pavel 106
Riecke, Jörg 164, 168
Rohde, Reinhard 121, 127
Rokem, Freddie 28, 40
Romanowiczowa, Zofia 146, 158
Romanska, Magda 26, 29, 38, 40
Rosenfeld, Alvin H. 23, 40, 103
Rosenfeld, Oskar 76, 161-166, 169
Rost, Nella 148, 157
Rousseau, Jean-Jacques 183
Różewicz, Tadeusz 9, 103, 145-159, 172, 217
Ruchatz, Jens 270
Rudnicki, Adolf 13, 19f., 22
Rudnicki, Piotr 28, 31, 40
Rudzka, Zyta 23, 28-31, 35, 37f., 40f.
Ruta-Rutkowska, Krystyna 28, 40
Rutkiewicz, Paweł 76

Ruzowitzky, Stefan 236
Rybak, Magdalena 199

Sachs, Nelly 117, 126f.
Sadková, Eva 247
Safdie, Moshe 103
Salamon, Avri 86
Saltzman, Lisa 47, 54
Sandauer, Artur 18f., 22
Sandberg, Herbert 90, 99f.
Saryusz-Wolska, Magdalena 54
Scarry, Elaine 103, 113
Schächter, Rafael 211-215
Scherpe, Klaus R. 24, 38, 40f.
Schillinger, Horst 239f.
Schindel, Robert 39
Schindler, Oskar 247, 250
Schlegel, Friedrich 108
Schmid, Wolf 64, 68, 70f., 77
Schmidt, Siegfried J. 162, 169
Schmidt, Thomas 76f.
Schmitz, Walter 215
Schnog, Karl 8, 89-101, 119
Schön (Kulka), Erich 136f., 141, 143f., 203
Schreiner, Stefan 204, 215
Schuenke, Christel 41
Schulhoff, Ervín 87
Schwarte, Ludger 256, 269
Schwarz, Wolfgang F. 256, 269
Segler-Meßner, Silke 269
Seifert, Jaroslav 143f.
Semprún, Jorge 23, 40
Seydl, Zdeněk 86
Siber, Karl Heinz 77
Sicher, Efraim 214
Sidney, Philip 174
Siedlecka, Joanna 221, 228
Siepmann, Thomas 270
Singer, Oskar 76
Šípová, Alexandra 131
Šišler, Petr 274, 282
Šisler, Vít 46, 50, 54
Skibska, Anna Maria 9, 171-200
Šklovskij, Viktor 182
Skrendo, Andrzej 155f., 159

Škubalová, Marta 9, 271-282
Škvorecký, Josef 76, 258
Sladovníková, Šárka 8f., 243-253
Slánský, Rudolf 79, 205
Sławiński, Janusz 158
Śliwiński, Piotr 172, 199
Sloan, James Parker 221, 223f., 228
Słobodzianek, Tadeusz 36
Smyczek, Karel 247
Snyder, Timothy 57, 75, 77
Somr, Josef 87
Sosnowski, Andrzej 9, 171-200
Soukup, Jiří 43
Soukup, Pavel 87
Speer, Albert 111
Spiegelman, Art 48
Spielberg, Steven 44, 250
Srp, Karel 79, 88
Staff, Leopold 147
Stalin, Iosif 107, 110
Staněk, Tomáš 274, 281
Štědroň, Miloš 106
Štědroňová, Eva 63, 77
Stein, Michael 79, 88
Stokes, Geoffrey 222, 228
Stolz-Hladká, Zuzana 64, 77
Straníková, Jarmila 232, 241
Strathausen, Carsten 194, 199
Strauss, Johann 245
Strupková, Elena 87
Sundhausen, Holm 281
Svoboda, Jiří 250
Szczypiorski, Andrzej 21
Szewc, Piotr 31
Szmaglewska, Seweryna 34
Szpociński, Andrzej 46, 54
Szrojt, Eugeniusz 148, 159
Szuster, Marcin 198
Szych, Magdalena 10

Tabori, George 109
Tal, Kali 218, 228
Tarantino, Quentin 44
Taylor, Charles 104
Teicholz, Tom 219f., 228
Teigová, Helena 139

Tepa Lupack, Barbara 222f., 228
Thunecke, Jörg 100
Thurn, Nike 260, 269
Tippner, Anja 256, 259, 266, 269
Tomaševskij, Boris 61, 77
Tomaszewski, Feliks 146, 150, 159
Topol, Jáchym 44, 53-55
Traxler, Petr 87
Trepte, Hans-Christian 9, 217-229
Troebst, Stefan 281
Tschuggnall, Karoline 266, 270
Tucholsky, Kurt 96, 100
Tulli, Magdalena 34, 41
Turczyńska, Agata 172, 199
Tuwim, Julian 32f., 40

Ubertowska, Aleksandra 155, 159, 217, 228
Udolph, Ludger 211, 215

VandenBos, Gary R. 129, 144
Vande Wyngaerde, Annelies 221, 228
Verdi, Giuseppe 211-215
Vermes, Timur 108f., 111, 113
Vice, Sue 222, 228
Vidlařová, Eva Trúda 106
Vogler, Henryk 146, 152f., 159
Volavková, Hana 79, 88
Voskovec, Jiří 108

Wagner, Richard 108
Wagner-Engelhaaf, Martina 225, 228
Walicki, Jacek 168
Walser, Martin 269
Wandycz, Krystyna 157
Wansing, Rudolf 256f., 270
Weber, Christiane Charlotte 8, 117-127
Wedel, Erwin 203
Weigel, Sigrid 260, 270
Weil, Jiří 8, 57-88, 203
Weiler, Christel 35, 41
Weinberg, Mieczysław 39
Weisenborn, Günther 90
Weiss, Jiří 247
Welsch, Wolfgang 186, 194, 199
Welzer, Harald 266, 270

Wendt, Christel 77
Werich, Jan 108
Werner, Ulrich 77
Werz, Michael 268
White, Edmund 172
White, Hayden 23-27, 41, 103, 113, 258, 270
Wiedemann, Andreas 274, 282
Wiegandt, Ewa 34, 41
Wiesel, Elie 222, 225f., 228f.
Wirthensohn, Andreas 77
Wittgenstein, Ludwig 155, 186
Wizisla, Erdmut 40
Wodecka, Dorota 104, 113
Wojna, Ryszard 146, 159
Wołowiec, Grzegorz 34, 40
Wolter, Kurt 93, 100
Wulf, Józef 157
Wyka, Kazimierz 151, 159

Young, James E. 23, 41

Żabicki, Zbigniew 17, 22
Zagajewski, Adam 146, 159
Zamjatin, Evgenij 77
Zand, Gertraude 281f.
Žantovský, Jiří 134, 144
Zimmerman, Moshe 51
Ziomek, Jerzy 158
Zucker, Aleš 44
Zvoníček, Stanislav 247, 253
Zych, Adam 166, 169

Literatur und Kultur im mittleren und östlichen Europa

herausgegeben von Reinhard Ibler

ISSN 2195-1497

1   *Elisa-Maria Hiemer*
       Generationenkonflikt und Gedächtnistradierung
       Die Aufarbeitung des Holocaust in der polnischen Erzählprosa des 21. Jahrhunderts
       ISBN 978-3-8382-0394-2

2   *Adam Jarosz*
       Przybyszewski und Japan
       Bezüge und Annäherungen
       Mit einem Vorwort von Hanna Ratuszna und Quellentexten in Erstübertragung
       ISBN 978-3-8382-0436-9

3   *Adam Jarosz*
       Das Todesmotiv im Drama von Stanisław Przybyszewski
       ISBN 978-3-8382-0496-3

4   *Valentina Kaptayn*
       Zwischen Tabu und Trauma
       Kateřina Tučkovás Roman *Vyhnání Gerty Schnirch* im Kontext der tschechischen Literatur über die Vertreibung der Deutschen
       ISBN 978-3-8382-0482-6

5   *Reinhard Ibler (Hg.)*
       Der Holocaust in den mitteleuropäischen Literaturen und Kulturen seit 1989
       The Holocaust in the Central European Literatures and Cultures since 1989
       ISBN 978-3-8382-0512-0

6   *Iris Bauer*
       Schreiben über den Holocaust
       Zur literarischen Kommunikation in Marian Pankowskis Erzählung *Nie ma Żydówki*
       ISBN 978-3-8382-0587-8

7   *Olga Zitová*
    Thomas Mann und Ivan Olbracht
    Der Einfluss von Manns Mythoskonzeption auf die karpatoukrainische Prosa des tschechischen Schriftstellers
    ISBN 978-3-8382-0633-2

8   *Trixi Jansen*
    Der Tod und das Mädchen
    Eine Analyse des Paradigmas aus Tod und Weiblichkeit in ausgewählten Erzählungen I.S. Turgenev
    ISBN 978-3-8382-0627-1

9   *Olena Sivuda*
    "Aber plötzlich war mir, als drohe das Haus über mir zusammenzubrechen."
    Komparative Analyse des Heimkehrermotivs in der deutschen und russischen Prosa nach dem Zweiten Weltkrieg
    ISBN 978-3-8382-0779-7

10 *Victoria Oldenburger*
    Keine Menschen, sondern ganz besondere Wesen ...
    Die Frau als Objekt unkonventioneller Faszination in Ivan A. Bunins Erzählband *Temnye allei* (1937–1949)
    ISBN 978-3-8382-0777-3

11 *Andrea Meyer-Fraatz, Thomas Schmidt (Hg.)*
    „Ich kann es nicht fassen, dass dies Menschen möglich ist"
    Zur Rolle des Emotionalen in der polnischen Literatur über den Holocaust
    ISBN 978-3-8382-0859-6

12 *Julia Friedmann*
    Von der Gorbimanie zur Putinphobie?
    Ursachen und Folgen medialer Politisierung
    ISBN 978-3-8382-0936-4

13 *Reinhard Ibler (Hg.)*
Der Holocaust in den mitteleuropäischen Literaturen und Kulturen:
Probleme der Politisierung und Ästhetisierung
The Holocaust in the Central European Literatures and Cultures:
Problems of Poetization and Aestheticization
ISBN 978-3-8382-0952-4

Sie haben die Wahl:

Bestellen Sie die Schriftenreihe
Literatur und Kultur im mittleren und östlichen Europa
einzeln oder im **Abonnement**

per E-Mail: vertrieb@ibidem-verlag.de | per Fax (0511/262 2201)
als Brief (***ibidem**-*Verlag | Leuschnerstr. 40 | 30457 Hannover)

Bestellformular

☐ Ich abonniere die Schriftenreihe *Literatur und Kultur im mittleren und östlichen Europa* ab Band #____

☐ Ich bestelle die folgenden Bände der Schriftenreihe *Literatur und Kultur im mittleren und östlichen Europa*
#____; ____; ____; ____; ____; ____; ____; ____; ____

Lieferanschrift:

Vorname, Name ....

Anschrift ....

E-Mail... | Tel.: ....

Datum .... | Unterschrift ....

Ihre Abonnement-Vorteile im Überblick:

- Sie erhalten jedes Buch der Schriftenreihe pünktlich zum Erscheinungstermin – immer aktuell, ohne weitere Bestellung durch Sie.
- Das Abonnement ist jederzeit kündbar.
- Die Lieferung ist innerhalb Deutschlands versandkostenfrei.
- Bei Nichtgefallen können Sie jedes Buch innerhalb von 14 Tagen an uns zurücksenden.

ibidem-Verlag
Melchiorstr. 15
D-70439 Stuttgart
info@ibidem-verlag.de

www.ibidem-verlag.de
www.ibidem.eu
www.edition-noema.de
www.autorenbetreuung.de